DR. ORONHYATEKHA

DR. ORONHYATEKHA

Security, Justice, and Equality

KEITH JAMIESON
MICHELLE A. HAMILTON

DUNDURN
TORONTO

Printer: Webcom

Library and Archives Canada Cataloguing in Publication

Jamieson, Keith, author
        Dr. Oronhyatekha : security, justice, and equality
/ Keith Jamieson and Michelle A. Hamilton.

Includes bibliographical references and index.

Issued in print and electronic formats.

ISBN 978-1-4597-0663-7 (paperback).--ISBN 978-1-4597-0664-4 (pdf).--ISBN 978-1-4597-0665-1 (epub)

1. Oronhyatekha, 1841-1907. 2. Indian physicians--Canada--Biography. 3. Mohawk Indians--Canada--Biography.
I. Hamilton, Michelle A., 1972-, author II. Title. III. Title: Doctor Oronhyatekha.
E99.M8J36 2016   971.004'9755420092   C2016-904840-3
                                                C2016-904841-1

1   2   3   4   5   20   19   18   17   16

  Canada

We acknowledge the support of the **Canada Council for the Arts** and the **Ontario Arts Council** for our publishing program. We also acknowledge the financial support of the **Government of Ontario**, through the **Ontario Book Publishing Tax Credit** and the **Ontario Media Development Corporation**, and the **Government of Canada**.

VISIT US AT

Dundurn
3 Church Street, Suite 500
Toronto, Ontario, Canada
M5E 1M2

To the memory of my father, Robert L. Jamieson (1917–1966), whom I miss very much, and to my mother, Phyllis, who continues to support and encourage me.

Most importantly, I want to express my appreciation to my wife, Cathy, and my son Nathan and daughter Rebecca for tolerating endless hours, days, months, and years of Dr. "O" stories.

CONTENTS

PREFACE

BY KEITH JAMIESON

I became actively engaged in the Oronhyatekha story in about 1996 while I was working on other projects at the Royal Ontario Museum. During this time Dr. Trudy Nicks, one of the curators for the North American collections, started discussing with me the Oronhyatekha collection, which is a significant part of the holdings of the ROM. She told me that she and Tom Hill, the museum director of the Woodland Cultural Centre (WCC) on Six Nations of the Grand River, had discussed creating an exhibit of this collection.

I know Tom, and I had worked with WCC on many other projects through the museum. In fact, I have worked there since its opening as a cultural centre in the early 1970s. I let Tom know about my discussions with Trudy and indicated my interest in pursuing the project. The WCC took the lead in this initiative and the exhibit opened at the Woodland museum on July 29, 2001, and later at the ROM in March of 2002. I express my deepest gratitude to both Tom and Trudy personally and thank the staff and many people at the ROM who willingly offered their expertise and assistance to this effort. To the Woodland Centre staff I owe my appreciation for providing me with a home away from home and their support and friendship for so many years.

During those six years, I spent most of my time between the communities of Six Nations and Tyendinaga, interviewing and discussing the project with many, many people who wanted to share their stories about Oronhyatekha. Many were relatives and many knew of him through these stories. At Tyendinaga were two elderly women who proved to be invaluable in accepting me into this community: the late Ella Clause, who grew up with my father, ushered and directed me in my stays at Tyendinaga, and Edith Green, who went out of her way to make sure I felt secure and welcome and very comfortable. To them, I owe a great debt of gratitude.

As I continued my work, I visited the headquarters of the Foresters on several occasions, and there as well I was given access to documents and records of the order as could be accommodated by Sharon Sinclair, who accompanied me and acted as my interpreter to help me gain access where perhaps none would otherwise be granted.

I had also begun working on a catalogue to accompany the exhibit. This was completed in 2001, but because budgetary restrictions faced by Woodland prevented its publication and printing, owing in large measure to the number of images of the more than 240 objects featured, it allowed me the opportunity to create the storyline that is the basis of this book.

I continued to write the book on my own time and this book is the culmination of that work now, twenty years later. During this time, I had occasion to work with two more individuals who would substantially contribute to what we have now. First, I would like to thank Sheryl Smith of Parks Canada. She saw the Oronhyatekha story as a way to make the case to have Oronhyatekha named as a Person of National Historic Significance. Through her efforts and work this, in fact, has been done.

And, finally, to Michelle Hamilton. I met Michelle many years ago, or so it seems, when she was working on her book. When I approached her about working on this manuscript, she seemed surprised. I had a sense then that she was the best person for this and I could trust in her exceptional research and writing skills, which she has proven in this book. She brought excitement when more new information about Oronhyatekha surfaced, and resolved issues, deploying strategies and expertise to continually enhance the story. I owe her a debt of gratitude and appreciation for her contributions.

ACKNOWLEDGEMENTS

BY MICHELLE A. HAMILTON

I initially encountered the legend of Dr. Oronhyatekha, or "Dr. O" as he is more fondly known, almost twenty years ago while serving a Master's internship in public history at the Woodland Cultural Centre (WCC) at the Six Nations of the Grand River. At this time, the WCC and the Royal Ontario Museum (ROM) in Toronto had begun to plan an exhibit to reconstitute Dr. Oronhyatekha's artifact collection, which had been transferred to the ROM in the early twentieth century. Later, the research for my first book about the nineteenth-century collection and display of First Nations' archaeological and ethnographic artifacts included Dr. Oronhyatekha's museum at the Temple Building of the Independent Order of Foresters. Upon Keith's invitation to assist with this biography, I found the opportunity to explore Dr. Oronhyatekha's many other accomplishments impossible to resist.

I would like to thank the staff at Weldon Library and the Archives and Research Collections Centre, Western University; the London Room of the London (Ontario) Public Library; the Diocese of Huron Archives, Huron University College, London, Ontario; the Canadian Museum of History (Ottawa); Kenyon College (Ohio); Library and Archives Canada (Ottawa); the Bodleian Library and the Museum of the History of Science, Oxford University; the Mary Evans Picture Library (London, England); the Chancellor Robert R. Livingston Masonic Library of Grand Lodge (New York City); the Toronto Reference Library; the Archives of Ontario (Toronto); the University of Toronto Archives; the National Anthropological Archives of the Smithsonian Institution (Maryland); the Royal College of Physicians and Surgeons (Toronto); the Stratford-Perth Archives (Stratford, Ontario); the Queen's Own Regiment Museum at Casa Loma (Toronto); the Deseronto Archives; the Lennox and Addington Archives (Napanee); the Vaughan Memorial Library at Acadia University; the Brantford Historical Society; and the Woodland Cultural Centre, all of whom assisted in piecing together Dr. Oronhyatekha's multifaceted life.

Dr. Trudy Nicks, ROM, provided her wealth of knowledge about and enthusiasm for Dr. Oronhyatekha and his museum collection. Likewise Kate Rounthwaite, SVP, General Counsel, Chief Compliance Officer, and Executive Secretary of the Foresters, shared her passion for the company's history. She, Shelley Wilson, and Desirée Davis allowed me access to the wealth of materials still held by Foresters House. I am particularly grateful for the use of their copies of the *Independent Forester* magazine — the only complete set in Canada. Michele Horton gave me insight into Dr. O's personality through her family stories, and Amorin Mello and Nancy Stewart provided their family history about and pictures of Dr. Kenwendeshon, who was related to and practised with Dr. O. Alan MacEachern pointed the way towards meteorological data, and J. Andrew Ross advised on the history of insurance. Guy Vanderhaeghe graciously discussed his reasons for including Dr. Oronhyatekha in his 2003 novel, *The Last Crossing*, and Dr. Victoria Freeman her motivations for creating her spoken word performance about Dr. Oronhyatekha's life. Manolo Lugo generously allowed use of his photo of Freeman's performance. John Lutman and Paul Maka provided designation information for Dr. Oronhyatekha's residences in London and Toronto respectively. Forrest Pass gave access to relevant collections at the Canadian Museum of History. Kaitlin Wainwright of Heritage Toronto, and Erin Semande and Beth-Anne Mendes of the Ontario Heritage Trust supplied information about the plaques installed by their organizations. Doug Rivet expertly made our map, and Adrian Petry took the rest of the contemporary photos in the epilogue. Lois Fenton, Jenn Nelson, Priya Vaughan, Alex Souchen, Frank J. Smith, and Juliette DeVries all assisted with research. Donald B. Smith shared sources collected through decades of his own research and generously volunteered to read a rough draft of our manuscript; a more capable and insightful assessor I cannot imagine. Jamie Mather assisted with the index. Thanks also to Kirk Howard, Beth Bruder, Allison Hirst, Kathryn Lane, Cheryl Hawley, Laura Boyle, Jaclyn Hodsdon, and the rest of the team at Dundurn Press, who have been extraordinarily patient during the completion of this book.

I am more than grateful to my good friend and colleague Mike Dove who took over my teaching and administrative duties at Western while I was researching and writing this book. It is rare to find someone in whose hands you can leave everything with complete trust.

The biggest thanks I owe to Keith Jamieson for inviting me on this journey and allowing me the opportunity to "live" with Dr. O.

A NOTE ON TERMINOLOGY

There are a multitude of names to describe the indigenous peoples of North America. We have chosen to use the term Mohawk as it is the most widely known and used term for those more traditionally called Kanyen'kehà:ka. In Ontario, three Mohawk communities live within the Six Nations of the Grand River, Tyendinaga, and Akwesasne territories. The Mohawk are one of the Five (later Six) Nations, often termed as a whole, the Iroquois. When referring to this larger body, we have used the name Haudenosaunee or the People of the Longhouse.

As writer Tom King has humorously pointed out, there is no good collective term for the diverse peoples of Canada, but we use *native* and *First Nations* interchangeably to mean such, with the exception of the Inuit and the Métis who have their own problematic history of labels.* We use the word *Indian* to refer only to the nineteenth- and twentieth-century stereotype of native people held by wider Canadian society, or as a legal term, which has a specific definition under the federal Indian Act. To find an encapsulating term for the non-indigenous living in Canada is also challenging. We have often used the terms *white, non-native, Victorian,* and occasionally *settler society,* the latter which underscores its recent establishment in the country, to refer to Canadians and Canadian society.

---

* Thomas King, *The Inconvenient Indian: A Curious Account of Native People in North America* (Canada: Doubleday, 2012), xii–xiv.

ABBREVIATIONS

AO   Archives of Ontario (Toronto, Ontario)
COF   Canadian Order of Foresters
CCMR *Canadian Craftsman and Masonic Record*
DIA   Department of Indian Affairs
GSCA   Greenslade Special Collections and Archives (Kenyon College, Gambier, Ohio)
IF   *Independent Forester and Forester's Herald/Independent Forester*
IGT   *International Good Templar*
IOF   Independent Order of Foresters
IOGT   Independent Order of Good Templars
LAC   Library and Archives Canada (Ottawa, Ontario)
MT   *Monetary Times: Trade Review and Insurance Chronicle*
NEC   New England Company
ROM   Royal Ontario Museum
SC   Statistics Canada
WCC   Woodland Cultural Centre

Martin/Oronhyatekha Family Tree

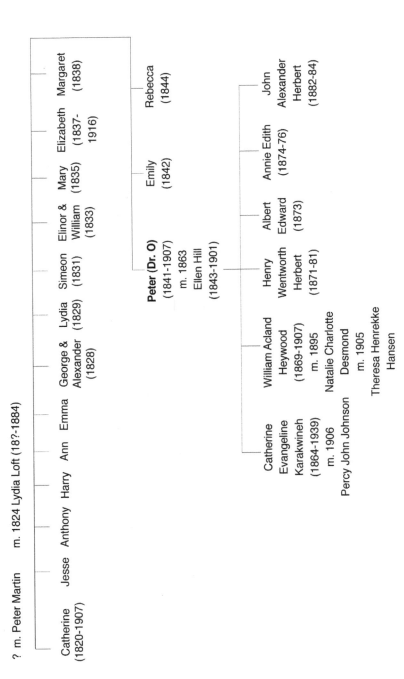

? m. Peter Martin   m. 1824 Lydia Loft (182-1884)

Catherine (1820-1907)   Jesse   Anthony   Harry   Ann   Emma   George & Alexander (1828)   Lydia (1829)   Simeon (1831)   Elinor & William (1833)   Mary (1835)   Elizabeth (1837-1916)   Margaret (1838)

Peter (Dr. O) (1841-1907) m. 1863 Ellen Hill (1843-1901)

Emily (1842)   Rebecca (1844)

Catherine Evangeline Karakwineh (1864-1939) m. 1906 Percy John Johnson

William Acland Heywood (1869-1907) m. 1895 Natalie Charlotte Desmond m. 1905 Theresa Henrekke Hansen

Henry Wentworth Herbert (1871-81)   Albert Edward (1873)   Annie Edith (1874-76)   John Alexander Herbert (1882-84)

Names without dates are due to the loss of those birth records

Dr. Oronhyatekha's Ontario

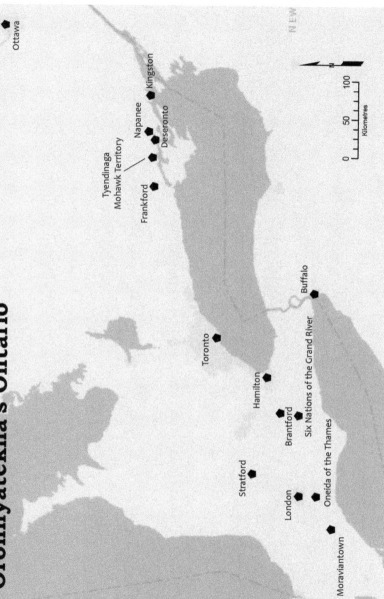

Ottawa

Kingston

Napanee

Deseronto

Tyendinaga
Mohawk Territory

Frankford

Buffalo

Toronto

Hamilton

Brantford

Six Nations of the Grand River

Stratford

London

Oneida of the Thames

Moraviantown

N EW

0   50   100
Kilometres

INTRODUCTION

SORROWING THOUSANDS

At eleven o'clock on the morning of Wednesday, March 6, 1907, a Canadian Pacific Railway train drew slowly into Toronto's Union Station. Met by hundreds of sombre Foresters, members of City Council, mounted police, and mourning Toronto residents, the train carried the body of the man known around the Western world as Dr. Oronhyatekha, the supreme chief ranger of the Independent Order of Foresters (IOF), a fraternally organized life insurance company.

Accompanied by a formal procession and music performed by the regimental band of the 48th Highlanders of Canada, a hearse drawn by four black velvet-draped horses brought Dr. Oronhyatekha to Massey Music Hall where he lay in state for the rest of the day. On the way, the procession passed the Temple, the IOF headquarters, which Dr. Oronhyatekha had built, its flags flying at half-mast and its rooms draped in black. The IOF shortly ordered that all court charters be hung with emblems of mourning for the next three months.

Over the afternoon, nearly ten thousand people paid their respects to Dr. Oronhyatekha at Massey Hall. Typical of Victorian era coffins, his had a glass top so that mourners could gaze upon the face of the man they had lost. At 7:30, another three to four thousand people, including Foresters from across North America, gathered for the evening funeral service

Dr. Oronhyatekha's funeral procession in the streets of Toronto.

conducted by the Reverend Frederick Wilkinson, the Anglican rector of St. Peter's Church, Dr. Oronhyatekha's place of worship in Toronto.

Characteristic of Dr. Oronhyatekha's IOF gatherings, the funeral was elaborate. On the platform at the front of Massey Hall sat the mayor of Toronto and high-ranking IOF dignitaries from across North America. Draped in black and purple, the stage was banked with masses of colourful, fragrant flowers sent by his family, friends, and loyal IOF members. Organist E.R. Bowles of the Canadian Academy of Music, a soloist, and a quartet of male singers provided the music for the service.

Dr. William J. McCaughan, the IOF Supreme Orator from Chicago, delivered the eulogy. McCaughan emphasized Dr. Oronhyatekha's tireless efforts on behalf of the Foresters, his benevolence, and the force of his personality. "We part with one tonight," said Dr. McCaughan, "who has touched every Forester, and in touching him has done something in shaping that Forester's character.

"The chief's influence," McCaughan continued, "was not confined to the great organization … but had reached out and touched others, and inspired other activities outside of the … Foresters. The words of the deceased would be treasured, and they would inspire to noble deeds." According to the Toronto *Globe*, so stirring was McCaughan's eulogy that the mourners forgot the gravity of the occasion and applauded in response.[1]

The four Royal Foresters who had guarded his casket during the service stood vigil long into the night. The next morning, a specially commissioned Grand Trunk train returned Dr. Oronhyatekha home to the Tyendinaga Mohawk territory where his wife, Ellen, had been buried six years earlier. A special rail car carried the floral tributes, so many that several carriages had to transport them from Massey Hall to the railway station.

The train stopped at Napanee, where Dr. Oronhyatekha had once practised medicine, so that citizens could say goodbye, and then continued on to Tyendinaga. There, eight pall-bearers took the coffin to Dr. Oronhyatekha's splendid home, The Pines, to lie in state. He was kept company by the Mohawk choristers who had often performed at IOF celebrations, and the orphans of the nearby home established by Dr. Oronhyatekha. On Friday morning, a service was conducted at The Pines, and another at Christ Church, the family's place of worship. The procession to the cemetery included members of the Deseronto Council and

Floral tributes to Dr. Oronhyatekha taken in a rail car from Toronto to Tyendinaga.

Floral tributes at Dr. Oronhyatekha's memorial at Plymouth Church, San Francisco.

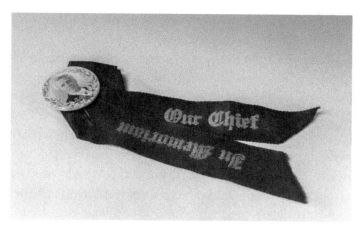

The IOF honoured Dr. Oronhyatekha with this memorial ribbon.

The Oronhyatekha family gravesite at Tyendinaga.

the Citizen's Band. At the family plot, the Foresters conducted their own funeral ritual, and vowed to maintain Dr. Oronhyatekha's legacy.

Those who eulogized him in the days to come emphasized his intellect and resourcefulness, but most important, his generosity, his concern for his fellow man, and his true belief in fraternity. Today, in the Christ Church cemetery, Dr. Oronhyatekha and his family are memorialized by a tall white marble obelisk topped with a cross. In Victorian culture the obelisk symbolized immortality and white marble was the fashionable stone of choice. Rumoured that medical students sought to procure and study Dr. Oronhyatekha's skull, likely as part of the Victorian belief that skull shape and size determined evolutionary status and intellect, his grave was also sealed with a two-foot layer of cement as a deterrent to grave robbers.[2] Two plaques, one erected in 1957 by the Archaeological and Historic Sites Board (now the Ontario Historical Trust) and another in 2005 by the National Historic Sites and Monuments Board, stand near his grave and testify to his important legacies.

Dr. Oronhyatekha sitting in his library. Originally published in May 1902 in the *Independent Forester* magazine, its caption said this was the best photo of Dr. Oronhyatekha because "[a]round the mouth ... a smile is beginning to play, and his eyes have already lighted up with that merry twinkle which always appears when he hurls a piercing shaft of wit at an opponent or humorously hits a friend."

ORONHYATEKHA'S ACHIEVEMENTS

North American newspapers noted Dr. Oronhyatekha's death and funeral widely, as did medical publications such as the *British Medical Journal* and the *Canadian Practitioner and Review*, along with others such as the premier journal of its discipline, the *American Anthropologist*. The fraternal magazine the *International Good Templar* superlatively deemed him the "most unique character in the history of the world." Perhaps more apt was his obituary in the journal of the National Fraternal Congress, which stated, "He did nothing by halves."[3]

Baptized Peter Martin in the Mohawk territory of the Six Nations of the Grand River in 1841, Oronhyatekha (Burning Sky) rose to prominence in medicine, sports, politics, business, fraternalism, and social reform.[4] At the turn of the twentieth century, he was a well-known personality in North America, England, and Australia, as well as some European countries, and had achieved a wide range of accomplishments. He was one of the first native medical doctors to achieve accreditation and to practise in Canada, and the first native to attend Oxford University, a bastion of upper class Englishness. The Six Nations of the Grand River chose him to represent their community to the Prince of Wales during his 1860 tour of Canada, and Dr. Oronhyatekha later helped plan the activities of the royal visit to Toronto in 1901. An excellent marksman, he competed at the first Wimbledon rifle match in England in 1871. He became Chairman of the Grand General Indian Council of Ontario in 1872, and a consul-general for the African state of Liberia in 1901.[5] He served on various company boards, including the Farmer's Co-operative Harvesting Machine Company in Winnipeg and the Gold Hills Exploration and Development Company in Toronto.[6] With two other men, he even invented a banding system for twisting or spinning frames, presumably for making yarn, string, rope, or other fibre products.[7] He was well known by the national and international press, and was invited to speak at various gatherings, such as the centenary celebration at Niagara-on-the-Lake of the granting of constitutional government to Upper Canada in 1792, the 100th anniversary of the United Empire Loyalists in 1884 at Deseronto, and the 1891 annual meeting of the National Educational Association of the United States, where his speech on the importance of native education received a standing ovation.[8]

Deeply committed to the temperance cause, Oronhyatekha joined the Six Nations Temperance Society, the U.S. National Temperance Society, and the Canada Temperance Union, and while living in Stratford, served on the Diocese of Huron's temperance committee.[9] He moved through the ranks of the International Order of Good Templars, one of the largest and "most militant" temperance organizations, whose members elected him to the highest post of Right Worthy Grand Templar in 1891. He also held high ranking posts with numerous Masonic organizations.[10] A member of the Orange Order, he served as District Master for South Hastings in 1869, County and District Master for Middlesex East in the 1880s, and as the Canadian representative for the triennial meeting of the Imperial Grand Orange Council of the World in Glasgow, Scotland, in 1873. He became president of both the Canadian Fraternal Association and the National Fraternal Congress in the United States.

He was the first non-white member of the Independent Order of Foresters, a fraternally organized life insurance company — having successfully challenged its constitutionally set racial criteria for membership — and ultimately became its supreme chief ranger. Under its auspices, he built the IOF Temple, the tallest skyscraper in the British Empire in its time, established an orphanage, and accumulated the largest museum collection under the direction of a native person in Canada. While historians have debated the long-term financial soundness of the IOF's actuarial practices, Dr. Oronhyatekha did transform the order from a small and divided organization into a populous and international one. Business allowed him, along with his wife and children, to travel the world, trips only wealthy Canadians could have afforded at that time. As he expanded the IOF to the United Kingdom, Europe, Australia, India, and Egypt, he met many political and business leaders, making connections that would have been the envy of any Canadian. He counted among his friends Sir John A. Macdonald, the first Prime Minister of Canada and a long-time Minister of Indian Affairs, numerous Conservative party cabinet ministers and politicians, American President Teddy Roosevelt, Daniel Wilson, a renowned anthropologist at Toronto University, and Sir Henry Wentworth Acland, British physician to the Prince of Wales. At a time when native communities struggled under the assimilative restrictions of the Canadian Indian Act and the settler society's racial assumptions about First Nations, these achievements and networks were remarkable, and served as an inspiration to his fellow Mohawks, as they do today.

The backdrop of these events was an expanding Canada and a tumultuous time in native-government relations. During Dr. Oronhyatekha's lifetime, the 1841 Act of Union joined the two provinces of Upper and Lower Canada into one. In addition, he witnessed the loss of a significant amount of land from his home — the Grand River territory — as well as the beginnings of the Indian residential school system and the restrictive Indian Act, the Fenian Raids (1866), Canadian Confederation (1867) and the resulting geographical expansion of the country and treaty-making with native groups in the west, the Riel Uprising in 1885, the Boer War in South Africa (1899–1902), and, in 1906, a Royal Commission that changed the life insurance industry in Canada.

DR. ORONHYATEKHA REMEMBERED

When asked why he chose to be called Oronhyatekha, rather than his baptismal name, Peter Martin, he reputedly replied that while there were thousands of Peter Martins in the world, there was only one Oronhyatekha. In the nineteenth and early twentieth century, Dr. Oronhyatekha was known around the world. But outside of Haudenosaunee (or Six Nations) communities and IOF institutional memory, his accomplishments had mostly faded from mainstream memory before the 1990s, when joint exhibit research between the Royal Ontario Museum and the Woodland Cultural Centre revived awareness.

During his lifetime and shortly after his death, Dr. Oronhyatekha's biography appeared widely in newspapers, magazines, and in memoirs of those who had met him. Unable to deny his numerous accomplishments, those seeking to reconcile them with his supposedly inferior native heritage explained him as a remarkable exception to his race. Despite his evident pride in his Mohawk heritage, Canadians who believed in typical nineteenth-century native stereotypes interpreted his success as a result of assimilation; his attendance at residential school and other white educational institutions, his medical degree, residence in urban Toronto, his leadership of a Western-style business, and even his professional attire could be seen in opposition to his native birth. Whatever "Indian-ness" remained was simply exotic, quaint, or entertaining. Canadians who accepted him as the head of the IOF did not necessarily believe in equality of natives in general and likely believed that the government policies of assimilation were well-intentioned and beneficial; in fact, how could they be otherwise, when Dr. Oronhyatekha had so clearly benefited from them? On the other hand, his opponents slurred his Mohawk heritage as a way to undermine his credibility and authority and dismiss his achievements. He was not to be celebrated or remembered; as a successful "Indian," he made some uneasy, even fearful. He did not fit the comfortable stereotypes of either a passive assimilated Indian or an untamed wild Indian of the west, but rather challenged the settler society that believed in them.

By the 1980s, historians were more likely to see Dr. Oronhyatekha as an accomplished man who used, merged, and valued aspects from his native background *and* the surrounding non-native society to build a world that fit him best. Native individuals were no longer seen as either part of a dichotomous native *or* white world, a traditional society *or* a modern one; instead it was accepted that identity is fluid and that individuals can both preserve values stemming from one's past and adapt new ones.

The first lengthier biographical treatment to appear after his death is Edward J. Dunn's chapter in his 1924 book *Builders of Fraternalism in America*. In describing Dr. Oronhyatekha, Dunn relied on well-worn stereotypes. He called him "clean and comely, strong and lithe of limb, well mannered, well educated and well spoken," but also a "young man of bronze." Like many other biographers, though in fact it was incorrect, Dunn pointed out that Dr. Oronhyatekha was a "full blooded" Mohawk. To oppose government legislation, he "got out his fraternal tomahawk and scalping knife and went upon the war-path," Dunn wrote. Even his skills at rifle-shooting were a "legacy from his ancestors," and his delight in "pomp and show" a "trait inherited from his ancestors." Dunn found Dr. Oronhyatekha's assertions of native equality to be "pardonable" but "foolish when measured by the facts." After a brief recital of his early life, Dunn, with his focus on fraternalism, emphasized Dr. Oronhyatekha's IOF career, most particularly with its struggle against commercial insurance companies and the controversial difference between the two systems of determining insurance rates.[11]

Maclean's magazine featured Dr. Oronhyatekha and the IOF in a 1951 article. Like others, the author commented on his striking height and appearance, partly in racial terms; he had a "round, copper-red face topped by wavy, un-Indianlike hair." The continued success of the Foresters was "almost enough to raise a warwhoop" from the statue of Dr. Oronhyatekha still standing in the lobby of the IOF building.[12]

In 1960, Ethel Brant Monture chose to feature Dr. Oronhyatekha in her trio of biographical portraits, along with other notable leaders Crowfoot and Joseph Brant. Compared to other biographical treatments, Monture explores Dr. Oronhyatekha's early life and personal side in greater detail, and includes oral knowledge not found elsewhere. A Six Nations historian, Monture aimed to educate all Canadians about the accomplishments of native peoples and in doing so, challenge the stereotype of native inferiority commonly held by settler society. She also believed it important that native history should be written by a native person. The publishing house of Clarke, Irwin invited her to contribute to its Canadian Portraits series, which targeted junior high level students. Her aim is clear from the first page of his biography: "[T]hough his life is not part of the official history of Canada, his influence was far-reaching — into the lives of hundreds of thousands of Canadians of all races." She saw aspects of his life such as his skill in diagnostic medicine and his membership in fraternal societies not as a racially determined trait, as Dunn might, but as a choice to continue traditional elements of Mohawk society in new ways.[13]

A 1971 article in *Tawow*, a magazine written by native authors to promote native culture, also emphasized his cross-cultural reach: "Oronhyatekha went beyond Indian leadership and became a leader of men, white, red, black, and yellow."[14]

Due to the primacy of sources related to fraternalism and the length of Dr. Oronhyatekha's career with the IOF, most historians focus on these aspects of his life.[15]

The Foresters' institutional histories pay homage to Dr. Oronhyatekha as an important early leader who greatly expanded the IOF and established the foundations of its success and philanthropy. Its 1967 organizational history acknowledges but does not elaborate on his Mohawk heritage. The IOF's 1997 publication to celebrate its 25th anniversary, however, emphasized his "dual culture," and his ability to live in, and choose elements of, both Mohawk and Victorian worlds.[16]

Dr. Oronhyatekha's time at the Toronto School of Medicine and in early politics does appear, however, in Allan Sherwin's recent biography of Dr. Peter E. Jones, a native doctor from the New Credit territory who moved in the same circles.[17] In the late 1990s, as the ROM and the WCC began to prepare for the *Mohawk Ideals, Victorian Values* exhibit, research began to centre on Dr. Oronhyatekha's museum collection. As curators Trudy Nicks and Keith Jamieson have shown, Dr. Oronhyatekha's eclectic collection of objects demonstrates his successful negotiation and merging of Mohawk and Victorian worlds. Further, Nicks argues that these objects and accompanying catalogue have preserved oral histories not recorded elsewhere.[18]

SECURITY, JUSTICE, AND EQUALITY

Oronhyatekha lived in between two worlds; that is, the largely non-native Victorian culture outside of native territories, and Haudenosaunee society. As a legally registered "Indian," his entire life — his education, multiple careers, band membership, place of residence, and political activities — was shaped by nineteenth-century evolutionary beliefs about native peoples and monitored by the Department of Indian Affairs (DIA). Even his will had to be approved by the DIA. He was also greatly influenced by, and proud of, his Mohawk heritage and language. His 1885 statement at an American temperance conference was typical: "I am an Indian, and of all the blessings I enjoy upon this earth, the fact that I am an Indian is the one I appreciate the most."[19] Consequently, he believed he should use his prominence to better the conditions of his people.

The medical journal *The Lancet* began its obituary for Dr. Oronhyatekha with a stanza excerpted from Henry Wadsworth Longfellow's epic poem *The Song of Hiawatha*.

> He prayed:
> Not for greater skill in hunting,
> Not for greater craft in fishing,
> Not for triumphs in the battle,
> And renown among the warriors,
> But for profit of the people.[20]

Who penned this obituary is unknown, but the choice of quote neatly captures one of Dr. Oronhyatekha's guiding principles. He spent his life attempting to fulfill the obligations and responsibilities to which he and other Haudenosaunee were born. Unlike Western society, which believes each child is born with rights, the Haudenosaunee believe that each person is born with a number of responsibilities, to themselves, to their families and nation, to the Confederacy that represents of all the Haudenosaunee (Mohawk, Seneca, Cayuga, Oneida, Onondaga, and Tuscarora), and to the natural and spiritual worlds around them. It is when these responsibilities are ignored or unfulfilled that the Haudenosaunee lose their rights. In his early life, Oronhyatekha repeatedly expressed his desire to be successful and a person of influence in order that he could help his people. Often when he faced a setback in his education, he became despondent and feared he would never be of any use to his community. Ultimately, after qualifying as a doctor and later becoming head of the Independent Order of Foresters, he went to great lengths to meet these obligations. The IOF's slogan "liberty, benevolence and concord" resonated with the Mohawk guiding values of governance — security, justice, and equality. His early career choices of missionary and then physician were partly predicated on his aim to help his people.

As chairman of the Grand General Indian Council of Ontario, he attempted to alleviate the increasing restrictions of the Indian Act on native communities. He joined numerous fraternal societies whose foundations rested on helping their fellow man. One of these, the International Order of Good Templars, preached abstinence from alcohol; Dr. Oronhyatekha believed prohibition of the sale of alcohol to native communities particularly important based on the exploitive practices of fur traders in the recent past. As supreme chief ranger of the IOF, he built an orphanage at Tyendinaga to house needy children. He also lobbied to expand IOF membership to include more than just white males. A man who had been judged harshly, he held no prejudices against women, francophones, and Roman Catholics, groups commonly considered inferior at that time.

Security, justice, and equality can be understood on another level. Growing up in a dislocated and divided community struggling to cope with shifting and discriminatory government policies and a broader society blind or even hostile to native issues, Oronhyatekha saw no security, justice, or equality on the Grand River territory. This insecurity, paired with his natural ambition, drove him to be accomplished in many fields, and perhaps even to flaunt his success in the faces of those who questioned his personal abilities or the general ability of native individuals to succeed. Until the mid-1880s, he hoped to be a leader for change at the Grand River and later at Tyendinaga. Further, acting as a "cultural broker" of sorts, Oronhyatekha was often called upon to explain elements of each society to the other.[21] But finding only controversy, he increasingly focused more on building his own world, a place in between Mohawk and Victorian society, and one that he controlled. In the end, he literally created a place apart — Foresters' Island — as his own domain.

Foresters' Island, 1896.

HISTORICAL SOURCES

Many published biographies repeat the same — sometimes legendary, sometimes apocryphal — facts, particularly about Dr. Oronhyatekha's early life, which is partly shrouded in darkness. There are also varying versions of the major events of his life, and it has been challenging to sort through these, especially when we discovered that some of the most well-known statements have proven not *quite* accurate.

Not surprisingly, most documentation covers the period 1878–1907, the time span of his official career with the IOF. The 1906 Royal Commission on Life Insurance generated its own records, including Dr. Oronhyatekha's testimony. Entering his name into historical newspaper databases for North America, the United Kingdom, and Australia generates hundreds of articles that tell the story of his travels around the world to expand the IOF, and in some cases the resistance he met. The IOF magazine, the *Independent Forester*, edited by Dr. Oronhyatekha, provides institutional insight, though, of course, a rosy one. Articles in this magazine demonstrate the growth of the IOF, as it built its Toronto headquarters, the Temple, and Foresters' Island, a resort for the organization and location of its orphanage. The current Foresters insurance company holds a full run of this magazine, as well as photographs and ephemera. The provincial government's insurance reports, the *Canadian Forester*, the publication of an IOF rival, and documents left by other prominent Foresters and those involved in the Union Trust, the investment arm of the IOF, provide other perspectives.

Unfortunately, Dr. Oronhyatekha left little behind of his own writings, particularly personal ones. All that is left are a handful of letters written to Dr. Henry Acland, his mentor at Oxford University, two articles on linguistics published in the *Canadian Journal*, the organ of the Canadian Institute in Toronto, and his tediously comprehensive and sometimes defensive tome, the *History of the Independent Order of Foresters*, published in 1894 and again in 1895. It is some 870 pages in length and includes reprinted sources such as annual reports of the IOF Supreme Court, actuary tables, death rates, constitutional changes, and correspondence. Many of these records reveal a man who invited controversy. His museum collection, numbering into the thousands of artifacts, is another source, but one harder to read. Much of the information gained reveals his professional, but not personal, life; his early family, and his wife, Ellen, and their six children are only glimpsed briefly. His charm and eloquence do seep through, as does his imposing larger than life presence; his grand-niece remembered being scared of his stern-looking portrait that hung in the front hall of her grandmother's home, so much so that she refused to enter the house that way. His legendary sense of humour, his sharp and sometimes barbed wit, and a fondness for practical jokes has also been preserved; there is, for just one example, the story of James

Casey, a fellow Mason, who one day opened the front door of his Toronto home to find a baby elephant left on his front step by Dr. Oronhyatekha.[22]

Many prominent people whose lives crossed Dr. Oronhyatekha's — Reverend Abraham Nelles, Indian agent Jasper T. Gilkison, A.J. Beresford Beresford Hope of Oxford, Daniel Wilson of Toronto University, and politician and business colleague George Foster — left behind only fragmentary, if any, papers. For Oronhyatekha's early life, there are the papers of Sir Henry Acland, the Royal Physician to the Prince of Wales who met Oronhyatekha at the age of nineteen during the 1860 royal visit to Canada, and the memoirs by A.B. Rockwell, his former roommate at Kenyon College in Ohio. The Kenyon College Archives hold brief, but rich, documents from his time, including administrative records about his studies, grades, room assignments, and his social activities, such as his membership in the Alpha Delta Phi fraternity and the literary and debate club, the Philomathesian Society. In addition to Acland's papers, Oronhyatekha's time at Oxford University appears in the memoirs and letters of Max Müller, another noted faculty member. The early records of the Toronto School of Medicine have only partially survived. The decisions to fund his studies at these institutions appear briefly in the records of the New England Company, the missionary society that operated within the Six Nations of the Grand River territory.

There are no records of Dr. Oronhyatekha's varied medical practice, but his entry into the political realm of the 1870s can be seen through letters and petitions sent to politicians like John A. Macdonald and to government agencies such as the Department of Indian Affairs. The New England Company reports also record some of his activities during this period. Institutional publications of the numerous fraternal organizations he joined demonstrate his rising importance in these groups. There is less evidence remaining about his roles in Freemasonry and Orangeism than there is about his efforts in the National Fraternal Congress, the Canadian Fraternal Association, and the International Order of Good Templars.

Dr. Oronhyatekha's life and career are remembered today through a diversity of sources such as travel literature, fiction, spoken word performances, in his object collection now held by the Royal Ontario Museum and the archives of the IOF, the remaining buildings he constructed, and of course, in the history and memories of the Tyendinaga and Six Nations of the Grand River communities.

THE LIFE OF ORONHYATEKHA

Our re-telling of Oronhyatekha's life story in the following chapters high-lights his negotiation of two worlds, native and Victorian, both the notable achievements and difficulties that arose, and his attempts to become a man of influence who sought to uphold his responsibilities to his own people and to wider society. Chapter 1 introduces the political, social, and historical context of the Six Nations of the Grand River community into which Oronhyatekha was born in 1841. Against this background, we trace his early family and cultural life, education at the Mohawk Institute in Brantford and at Wesleyan Academy and Kenyon College in the United States, his teaching career, and the beginnings of his ambitions first to be a missionary, and later a physician.

Chapter 2 begins with one of the most pivotal events in Oronhyatekha's life — his representation of the Grand River community during the royal visit of Edward, Prince of Wales, in 1860, and in so doing, his intro-duction to Sir Henry Acland, who recommended he study medicine at Oxford University. This chapter also explains the volatile political atmos-phere at Grand River, including the debate over maintaining its trad-itional Confederacy Council, and the mismanagement of the council's investment in the Grand River Navigation Company by the Department of Indian Affairs. As a representative of the council, Oronhyatekha was implicated in these contentious issues, which may have partly provided the impetus for his move to England.

Though he would not stay in England long, his attendance at Oxford began his medical career. This trip also exposed him to some of the greatest world museums and sparked his interest in collecting. His role as anthropological informant to noted Oxford linguist Max Müller fur-ther bolstered this interest. Upon his return from England, Oronhyatekha chose to live at Tyendinaga, where he met his future wife, Ellen Hill. Chapter 3 tells the story of his brief stay at Oxford, his decision to enter the Toronto School of Medicine, his relationship with Sir Daniel Wilson, one of Canada's most important nineteenth-century anthropologists, and the beginnings of Oronhyatekha's fraternalism through his membership in the Good Templars and the Orange and Masonic orders.

Chapter 4 explores the newly graduated Dr. Oronhyatekha's med-ical practices at Frankford, Stratford, Tyendinaga, Buffalo, the Oneida of the Thames reserve, and London, as Canada's second native doctor. In between, he campaigned for Sir John A. Macdonald and the Conservative party, and headed the Grand General Indian Council of Ontario, a political organization that attempted to influence policies of the DIA. Throughout the 1860s and 1870s, Dr. Oronhyatekha sought out opportunities for personal and professional influence and leadership, and for those that could improve the lives of his people. Having been embroiled in community and national politics, he increasingly turned to investing this energy in fraternalism in the 1880s.

Chapter 5 focuses on Dr. Oronhyatekha's attempt to merge traditional Haudenosaunee values with the beliefs of fraternal organizations, mainly the IOF. We trace his membership from being the first non-white member to supreme chief ranger, and his subsequent transformation of the organization. Dr. Oronhyatekha's "monuments"— the IOF Temple Building in Toronto, the orphanage, Foresters' Island, and his museum collection, now housed by the ROM — are explored in Chapter 6. The following chapter relates the story of the 1906 Royal Commission on Life Insurance, which investigated the financial practices of the Canadian insurance industry. While the IOF was exonerated of fraud, the commission did find some of its business practices in need of reform, as it did with almost of all of the companies investigated.

The final chapter presents Dr. Oronhyatekha's ongoing legacy, including numerous historical designations and commemorations, his inspiration to popular culture, the surviving built heritage associated with him, the exhibit *Mohawk Ideals and Victorian Values*, and his importance to and remembrance within the Haudenosaunee communities at Tyendinaga and the Grand River.

CHAPTER 1
AMBITIONS

A DISLOCATED COMMUNITY

The Haudenosaunee had called the Grand River valley home since 1784. At the end of the American Revolution, they had lost much of their ancestral homelands in what became New York State, many having allied with the British Crown against the colonial revolt of 1776. In recognition of that alliance, the Crown procured the valley in Upper Canada for the exclusive use of the Haudenosaunee (Mohawk, Onondaga, Cayuga, Seneca, Oneida, and Tuscarora) that chose to move to this expansive territory of some one million acres. Negotiated between the Haudenosaunee and the governor of Quebec, Sir Frederick Haldimand, the Haldimand Deed stipulated that this fertile valley would be set aside for them forever. This tract stretched six miles on each side of the Grand River, from its mouth on Lake Erie to its source near what is now Dundalk. The Haudenosaunee quickly established villages in the southerly half of the tract. They began to farm, hunt, and fish consistent with their historical traditions.

Still a formidable British military ally, they were called upon twice more to rekindle their alliance, actively engaging the advancing Americans in the War of 1812, and to a lesser extent during the Upper Canadian Rebellion of 1837. But in 1841, the bitterly cold east winds of February brought changes that still dramatically affect the Six Nations. On February 10, 1841, the Act of Union united the British colonies of Upper and Lower Canada into one administrative unit, the Province of Canada, renaming them Canada West and East in the process. The act also loosened the apron strings between the new provinces and the court of Queen Victoria and the British Parliament, allowing increased self-government in local matters such as the administration of Indian Affairs. Although formal control of Indian Affairs passed to the Province of Canada in 1860, in the 1840s the governor general became responsible for administering the Indian Department.

For almost two hundred years, the Haudenosaunee had operated as allies to the British Crown, joined together by the metaphorical covenant chain, a series of diplomatic treaties between the two parties. The chain also embodies the meanings of the earlier Two Row Wampum, which features five stripes of alternating white and purple beads. The two purple stripes represent the British and the Haudenosaunee; parallel but never touching, it symbolizes that neither would interfere with the other, thus implying the autonomous sovereignty of both nations. The three white stripes represent peace, friendship, and respect. These meanings were codified in Haudenosaunee law by the exchange of wampum belts. The exchange of presents during and after diplomatic treaties also symbolized loyalty and friendship. In 1710, for example, Queen Anne reaffirmed their relationship when she invited four Mohawk emissaries on a diplomatic visit to Britain. Afterwards, she erected an Anglican church in New York State, and sent a silver communion set, a Bible, and a reed organ as gifts. Another chief visited King George II in 1740. In 1768, Joseph Brant visited the court of King George III, and after his death, his son John maintained the diplomatic relationship with the court until his own death in 1834.

After 1841, the long-term impact of the transition of power from Britain to Canada proved devastating for the Six Nations of the Grand River community. The honoured relationship they enjoyed with the Crown was reinterpreted by the Province of Canada as one that relegated the Haudenosaunee as wards of the government, and their sovereign lands as reserves to which they would be restricted. Over the next twelve years, the Six Nations of the Grand River were herded onto a parcel of 50,000 acres (a mere 5 percent of their original holdings), faced skirmishes with settlers streaming into their valley, and, forced to relocate, armed interventions with squatters.

Born on August 10, 1841, Oronhyatekha, a Mohawk of the Wolf clan, experienced these portentous changes from birth. He inherited at once a proud and honourable past and a future fraught with strife, overt racism, and uncertainty.

AN INFLUENTIAL FAMILY

The members of Oronhyatekha's nuclear family are not entirely clear. His nephew, also named Peter Martin, wrote in his diary that there were ten children in the family — six boys and four girls — but when adding up the various references to Oronhyatekha's siblings across numerous sources, the names total seventeen: Jesse, Anthony, Ann, Emma, Harry, Catherine (1820–1907), twins George and Alexander (b.1828), Lydia (b.1829), Simeon (b.1831), Elinor (b.1833), William (b.1833), Mary (b.1835), Elizabeth (1837–1916), Margaret (b.1838), Emily (b.1842), and Rebecca (b.1844). We know Oronhyatekha was the sixth son of the family, as he recorded this in his Oxford University matriculation record. Many

Elizabeth Martin Powless or Dayo-Ra-Co-Sa (Sun in Water).

Margaret Martin Flanders.

Jesse Martin and his great-niece.

Lydia Martin Atkins and her children, Lizzie, George, Charles, William, Thomas, and Robert.

William Martin or Ke-Yon-Ron-Tea (Flying Arrow).

Lydia Loft, Oronhyatekha's mother. She was in her late thirties or early forties when she gave birth to him.

of his older brothers and sisters had left home and established their own families when he was an infant. Oronhyatekha and his younger siblings were raised together.[1] His father, Peter Martin, a veteran of the War of 1812, had apparently abandoned his family when Oronhyatekha was quite young.[2] As a consequence, he and his sisters carried a greater share of the work of the homestead with their aging mother, Lydia.

Lydia Loft (18?–1884) was a Mohawk of the Bay of Quinte, or Tyendinaga Territory, near Belleville, Ontario. After the American Revolution, a contingent of Mohawk people under the leadership of warrior captain John Deseronto chose to settle in this location. While seemingly isolated from each other by distance, the Tyendinaga and Grand River communities maintained frequent contact. Lydia and Peter Martin married about 1824 and at that time she moved from Tyendinaga to the Grand River.[3]

Oronhyatekha was born into a prestigious and influential family. Lydia's maternal grandmother was the sister of John Deseronto. On his father's side, Oronhyatekha's aunt Helen was a clan mother, a powerful position in the Haudenosaunee Confederacy, and Helen's husband, John Smoke Johnson, was a well-respected pine tree chief. One of their children, George Henry Martin Johnson, held a position as interpreter and chief. Born twenty years after Oronhyatekha, George's second cousin (John and Helen's granddaughter) became the famed poetess and performer E. Pauline Johnson.

Perhaps it was George Martin, a Haudenosaunee Confederacy council sachem, veteran of the American Revolution, war chief, and Oronhyatekha's paternal grandfather, who influenced him the most. George Martin had married Catherine Rolleston, a Dutch girl from Philadelphia who had been captured at the age of thirteen by Mohawk warriors during border conflicts and consequently adopted by the Confederacy Chief Teyonhahkewea and raised as Mohawk.[4]

The Martins played an important role in the establishment of the Mohawk community at the Grand River. It is purported that George Martin had accompanied war chief Captain Joseph Brant on the initial trip to the Grand River valley and assisted in the selection of the Haldimand Tract. It is also said that George and Catherine retrieved from their village in New York State the Queen Anne silver and Bible. This silver communion service had been buried during the Revolution for safekeeping, and the Martins smuggled it across the border disguised as a bundle of rags. A potent symbol of the British recognition of Haudenosaunee loyalty, the Tyendinaga and Grand River communities divided the service.

Having established the Martin settlement, or Martin's Corner, at the Grand River, George Martin continued to be a staunch ally of the British Crown and became an interpreter for, and confidant of, William Clause, the deputy superintendent general of Indian Affairs. During the first year of the War of 1812, it was partly due to Martin's influence that Haudenosaunee warriors fought with Major-General Isaac Brock at Amherstburg. In 1813, Martin acted as interpreter at the battles of Beaver Dams in Upper Canada and Fort Niagara in New York State, both British victories over the Americans. His family homestead, located on the high bluffs overlooking Mohawk Village (now Brantford), was the site for the distribution of gifts given to the Haudenosaunee as Crown recognition for their loyalty and loss during these wars. Martin further demonstrated his loyalist zeal when, in 1814, he used his influence with William Clause to threaten to deny gifts to families who had refused to support the Crown during the war. Not all Haudenosaunee wanted to fight in the War of 1812, especially since it meant being on the opposite side of their kin who had stayed in the United States after the American Revolution.

Martin was a devout Anglican who maintained a watchful eye on the incursions of missionaries into the valley, and he frequently reported on these efforts. Tasked in 1815 to prevent non-native squatters on the Grand River territory, he found this duty increasingly difficult as settlers jealously eyed the rich land, and government officials were lacklustre, if not negligent, in their protection of the area. Martin's loyalty to the British would continue to be tested during the next several decades.

In the 1830s, a questionable land transfer still in dispute today gave title to white residents who lived on Mohawk land in the young town of Brantford, and handed over a further plot to the burgeoning village. These transfers reduced the territory of the Mohawk Village under control of the Haudenosaunee. More were to come. As Brantford and the surrounding area boomed, increasing numbers of white squatters illegally built houses and cleared farmland on Haudenosaunee territory. In response, some individuals conducted land sales, unapproved by either the provincial government or the Haudenosaunee Council. In hopes of resolving the resulting confusion, many of these transactions, though illegal, were belatedly ratified in 1835. However, this patchwork of transfers worried both the Haudenosaunee and those in charge of Indian Affairs in Upper Canada, since they increasingly left the Haudenosaunee villages isolated and vulnerable to further land loss. Samuel Peters Jarvis, superintendent of Indian Affairs of Upper Canada, recommended that the separate Haudenosaunee settlements be consolidated within a smaller, more compact area, and that the rest of their land be sold — a highly contested proposal.

In November 1840, the Upper Canadian government passed an order-in-council that legislated just this. In the end, approximately 50,000 acres — a fraction of the original grant — were allocated to the Haudenosaunee, today mostly composing the townships of Tuscarora, Onondaga, and Oneida. While some, like John Smoke Johnson, George Martin's son-in-law and Oronhyatekha's uncle, agreed with the plan, others like George Martin himself strongly opposed it; the conflict over consolidation divided the community, even families, for decades. Most of the families of the Martin settlement wished to remain in their village, which now fell outside of the 50,000 acres. The older generations remembered their dislocation after the American Revolution, and in fact were still homesick and had hoped to return home if the British had won the War of 1812 against the Americans.

While the order-in-council was confirmed in 1847, the relocation of people took another six years, and was partly achieved through violence. One of the most devastating events at the Martin settlement occurred in 1847, when Oronhyatekha was six. The settlement was peopled by several families, and while no record exists of who they were, they were likely family and close friends and a few settlers who had leased land.[5] Reverend Abraham Nelles, the Anglican missionary of the New England Company, reported to his superiors that late one evening a mob from Brantford descended on the settlement and forcibly removed the occupants from their homes. Oral history recounts that the mob roused families from their homes, loaded them into carriages, and buggy-whipped them out, torching their homes and barns, burning them to the ground. Nelles complained in his report of the treatment that the Haudenosaunee suffered at the hands of the local townspeople and government officials, and sought the intervention of British authorities, but with little result.

The incident sternly reminded the Martin family and the Haudenosaunee more generally that they could not count on protection from the Crown, even in their own territory. This conflict would repeat itself several times downriver from Brantford. Despite the fact that the consolidation of the Haudenosaunee land was partly done to prevent trespassers, squatters still had to be removed from the newly constituted reserve, which often incited more violence. The Haudenosaunee Confederacy sought the assistance of Colonel David Thorburn, appointed in 1844 as visiting superintendent within the Indian Department, to police removals, and while the Haudenosaunee compensated squatters for their improvements to the land and buildings, the squatters often returned to destroy and burn whatever was left on the property.

Originally, each of the six Haudenosaunee nations had established separate villages in the Grand River valley, their traditional settlement pattern in what became New York State. Relocation after 1841 resulted in a new pattern, this one based on religious affiliation, and it redefined the community as a whole. Many had adopted the numerous branches of Christianity, while others advocated a return to traditional spirituality, and a third group followed the teachings of Handsome Lake, a prophet who merged Christianity and Haudenosaunee beliefs into a new religion. Those of Christian faiths tended to settle in the western end of the reserve near the original Mohawk Village while those following traditional beliefs relocated downriver to the eastern end of the reserve. This division became more pronounced and troublesome for the community in later years. As well, the relocation of families so much closer in proximity than they had been in the past caused a change in the Haudenosaunee Confederacy Council. In the past, individual nations made their own decisions unless an issue concerned the entire confederacy, in which case all representatives of the council met. In 1847, the Confederacy Council began to meet as a whole more regularly and discouraged independent meetings of each nation, decisions that some strongly opposed. Some nations continued to make decisions independently anyway. Indian Affairs officials, missionaries, and individual settlers exploited these divisions and conflicts to achieve their own ends.

For George Martin, the events following 1841 through to his death in 1853 at the age of eighty-six must have been devastating. His allies whom he thought unassailable had betrayed his people, and his faith in the honour and integrity of the Crown faced immense scrutiny by the community. In his waning years, Martin became a very vocal critic of those in and outside the community who sought further surrender of lands in the Grand River valley. The relocation of families to the fifty-thousand-acre tract was not considered complete until his death in 1853, when the Martin settlement, some eight thousand acres, was parcelled out and leased to settlers to the area.[6]

A childhood amidst community strife, political conflict, and the challenges of a shrinking land base and its attendant violence and dislocation shaped young Oronhyatekha. Although he maintained belief in the sovereign status of the Haudenosaunee throughout his life, Oronhyatekha also witnessed firsthand the betrayal of his grandfather's trust in the British. As a teenager, he sought approval from missionaries and Indian Affairs officials, but found only hypocrisy and disillusionment. As a young man he tried to represent the Grand River community but became mired in controversy. At the same time, born into a family legacy of leadership and exposed to George Martin's statesmanship, he sought a way to better the situation of his people. Questioning his upbringing, the ways in which his community had dealt with social change, and the path of assimilation proposed by Indian Affairs officials, Oronhyatekha was unsure how to proceed. From this position of uncertainty and insecurity, he charted an unlikely course.

ORONHYATEKHA'S EDUCATION

Oronhyatekha was raised in the language and values of the Mohawk Nation. From a very early age, he was taught the importance of land and the relationship that the Haudenosaunee shared with all living things. Although the Haudenosaunee had interacted with European colonists for centuries, they had retained many of their own institutions, rituals, and oral traditions.

While the Mohawk Village had been all but abandoned, many families, including the Martins, still attended the nearby Anglican Church of St. Paul, more commonly known as the Mohawk Chapel. Mohawks also valued a Western-style formal education, and he attended the Martin's Corner School, one of three schools erected and operated by the New England Company (NEC), the missionary arm of the Anglican Church. The NEC often reported that the Martin school was the best attended of the three, and described it as providing an "English education sufficient to enable them to transact any business they may have with their white neighbours." Five-year-old Oronhyatekha appears as a student in the NEC's 1846 report, along with twenty-five others, including his eleven-year-old sister Elizabeth and eight children from the extended Martin family.[7]

Although Mohawk was the first language in his home, George Martin also spoke English. Oronhyatekha may have learned the basics as a child, but he formally learned to speak and write English through the Irish National Readers, a newly implemented innovation at that time. Egerton Ryerson, the assistant superintendent of education, had been appointed in 1844 to reform education in Upper Canada. Studying the textbooks commonly used in schools, he found them to be largely written and published in the United States and to contain anti-British sentiments. As a result, he recommended that the national series of texts used in Ireland be brought over to Canada. They first appeared in classrooms in 1846, likely the year Oronhyatekha began school.

Martin's Corner School.

Besides reflecting a pro-British sentiment, there were a number of other reasons why Ryerson approved of the Irish readers. While they were non-denominational, readings and lessons still promoted Christianity and morality, and clergymen were portrayed in high regard, certainly features of which the missionaries would have approved. Ryerson believed moral teachings to be crucial for young minds, particularly those individuals he deemed to be of lesser intellect — lower classes and non-British groups such as First Nations — since they were purportedly ruled by their emotions, not their minds. These groups needed to learn control and discipline, emphasized not only by moral lessons, but by the rote memorization style of teaching and classroom discipline generally.

Like most students, Oronhyatekha was able to read by the time he reached the end of the second lesson book. The first book introduced the alphabet, the sounds of each letter, and numbers up to nine. The very first lesson featured simple words such as *cat* and *rat*. Students stood in a semicircle in front of the teacher, who pointed to each word written on the board, and repeated the words in succession. Then each child was asked to read a sentence from the text that used each of the words to be learned that day, such as "The cat has a rat." Even these simple sentences, such as "I hate to do ill; I was not made to be bad" or "A good boy will not tell a lie," contained moral lessons. The board was then wiped clean or turned around and the teacher asked students to spell each word from memory. Next, students read a short story or moral lesson from the textbook, which incorporated the words they had just learned. At home that night, students were expected to continue memorizing the pronunciation and spelling of words in preparation for a test the next morning.

The second and third lesson books exposed students to basic grammar and words with more than one syllable. Again, readings were biblical in nature, such as the story of Cain and Abel, which demonstrated the use of words such as *envy*, *hatred*, and *punish*, among others. Other lessons featured geography, history, classics, and natural history content as a way to learn vocabulary.[8]

After five years at the Martin school, in 1851, at the age of ten, Oronhyatekha entered the Mohawk Institution, another Anglican school run by the New England Company at Grand River.

THE MOHAWK INSTITUTION

At the request of Captain John Brant, the NEC established the Mohawk Institution in 1828 on farmlands of the Mohawk Village, a short distance from the Mohawk Chapel. It was built using the funds of the Six Nations, because they, particularly the Mohawks, believed that a good education in English language and traditions was essential for their survival and success.

Missionaries found their earlier educational efforts at day schools minimally successful; they expressed futility in their reports to the London head office that once the children had been educated, they would often return to their traditional ways. The Mohawk Institution would be different. At first a Mechanics' Institute teaching young boys useful trades such as blacksmithing, tailoring, carpentry, and wagon-making, it soon became a boarding school four years after it was established. As a residential school, children lived in dorms and were separated from their homes and family and totally immersed in their studies and, to a great extent, in the English culture. Like other residential schools across Canada, the Institute's twin goals aimed to "civilize" and Christianize native children. Attempts to assimilate native adults had met with a mixed response, and so missionaries began to focus on children, hoping to produce a new generation that would live according to the prescriptive morals and values of white society. The NEC defined success as the conversion, assimilation, and "civilization" of native people, as this, they believed, was the only way they could continue to live and ultimately prosper as the European colonists had. As long as they clung to their "old" ways, it was believed they would perish as a people.

The NEC missionaries were the Reverends Abraham Nelles and James Elliot. Nelles in particular became an important individual in Oronhyatekha's life, first as an adviser and mentor and later as an enemy. Growing up near Grimsby, Ontario, Nelles knew about the Grand River community as a boy. His grandfather and father had served in the British Indian Department and after the American Revolution had immigrated to Upper Canada. Joseph Brant granted the Nelles family land within the Haldimand Tract. After attending university in Toronto, in 1828 Nelles returned to the Grand River as a missionary. Nelles and Elliot had been appointed to minister at the Mohawk Chapel, and Nelles also acted as the headmaster of the Mohawk Institute until his retirement in 1872. The Confederacy Council also entrusted Nelles and Elliot to communicate with the British Crown through the NEC's headquarters in London and the Church of England, after the death of John Brant in 1832.

Although not all Haudenosaunee approved of this type of education for their children, it proved to be successful, and by the time Oronhyatekha enrolled at the Mohawk Institution in 1851, he was one of thirty-three children — twenty-two boys and eleven girls, according to the 1852 census.[9] Waiting lists began to grow. At the time, the Haudenosaunee nations did not fully know or appreciate the assimilationist goals of the institute's staff. What had been intended as a valuable investment by the Haudenosaunee for the education and training of their children proved to be an opportunity for the missionaries to convert and assimilate a "dying" people. They were at cross purposes from the outset, and this ill-fated social experiment has resulted in a modern-day crisis for both the students and their families.

Classroom lessons reinforced the assimilative values of the New England Company. Like at the Martin settlement school, these values included learning to read and write English, often using the Bible as their text. Teachers conducted lessons in English, but it was not until after Oronhyatekha had graduated that students were forbidden to speak to one another in Mohawk or other native languages. In fact, Nelles himself could read Mohawk. Oronhyatekha's studies also included arithmetic, geography, history, and from the range of trades, shoemaking. Although most Haudenosaunee had long lived as settled farmers, missionaries believed that their old way of life, stereotyped as nomadic hunting and fishing, was inferior to the white ways of self-sufficient sedentary farming. Stereotypes also suggested that if not taught otherwise, natives were lazy and would avoid work. The teaching of trades such as blacksmithing or wagon-making at residential schools thus provided skills useful in the modern economic world, reinforced assimilation, and ideally produced independent individuals who would no longer need government and missionary supervision once they had been totally acculturated. Manual labour, rather than advanced intellectual studies, was also thought appropriate for First Nations, who were not expected to be leaders in society.

Religion, of course, was central to the Mohawk Institute's purpose. The NEC's ultimate goal was to produce native ministers who could then spread out and perpetuate the Christianization of native communities. Each school day opened and ended with scripture readings, catechism, and prayers. Attendance at Sunday services was mandatory.

The Mohawk Institute followed the provincial curriculum and so used the Irish readers to which Oronhyatekha had been introduced at the Martin school. These textbooks reinforced the missionaries' opinions. The *Fourth Book of Lessons* stated that native peoples were inferior to Europeans. In general, the natives of North America were "ignorant savages" who easily succumbed to Europeans' superior warfare tactics, a statement that directly contradicted the Mohawk tradition that the English sought them as powerful allies in war. After suggesting that there was a variety of native groups, the text then described them as a generalized whole; they were usually at war, subsisted by hunting and fishing, dressed in animal skins, loved gaming, smoking, and dancing, had no formal religious worship, and treated their women as heavy labourers. While some had become settled Christians, the nomadic life of most natives prevented their civilization, the book concluded.[10]

Missionaries also believed native people needed to be taught discipline, and the repetitive school schedule was one way of enforcing it. School began at 9:00 a.m. and ended at 4:00 p.m. each day, except Saturday, when students only studied for the morning. Students enjoyed a few weeks of vacation at Christmas and one month during the summer, usually July, although the missionaries worried that exposure to their families would cause the children to revert to their traditional ways of life.

Missing their families and homes during the school year, students at residential schools often ran away. Although the New England Company records do not show any truancy, Oronhyatekha ran away at least three times. He returned each time, sometimes willingly, sometimes forcibly. Each time, he received a whipping and was made to promise not to do it again.

For three years, Oronhyatekha pursued general studies, but in his fourth year he spent a half day in school and the other half day learning the shoemaker's trade in the institute's shop. At the end of that year, he was told that he had learned all the trades taught, he later wrote, and thus left for good.

Equipped by the institute with some tools of his trade, he apprenticed for a local shoemaker. Unpaid for some of his work, Oronhyatekha quit and drifted for a time, unsure of what to do. As he later recounted, "My friends were all bad," and he learned to drink and swear; if fate hadn't intervened, he would have become a good example of the utter uselessness of educating native people.[11]

A PHRENOLOGICAL FATE

When Oronhyatekha left the institute in 1854, he had grown tall and lean. He was well on his way to achieving his imposing adult height of six foot, three inches. His Dutch heritage was evident in his appearance, which set him apart from many of the other youth. His hair was dark brown and wavy and his eyes hazel. At that time, a boy the age of fourteen and skilled in a trade was ready for economic independence, but he did not know what he wanted to do with his life.

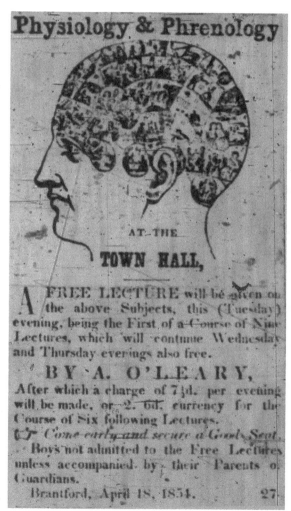

Advertisement for A. O'Leary's performance.

A few weeks after Oronhyatekha left his shoemaker apprenticeship, a chance meeting with a phrenologist travelling through Upper Canada redirected him. Phrenology was the science of reading the bumps and indentations on a person's head, and according to which the arrangement, sequence, and position of them supposedly indicated the measure of one's intellect, character, and personality. One of Oronhyatekha's physical attributes upon which many remarked throughout his life was his noticeably large head. Perhaps this drew the phrenologist's attention and enticed him to read the bumps on Oronhyatekha's head.

The phrenologist may have been A. O'Leary, a Boston practitioner and colleague of Orson Squires Fowler, one of the most famous phrenologists of the late nineteenth century. While O'Leary had a "studio" in Boston, like many phrenologists of his time he toured throughout North America, speaking at lecture halls and giving personal readings. In April of 1854, O'Leary gave a series of nine lectures on "Physiology and Phrenology" at the Brantford Town Hall.[12]

The phrenologist visited Oronhyatekha at his home twice. Almost identical to Fowler's guide, O'Leary's "delineation of character" relied upon assessment of thirty-seven traits and twenty-one degrees of development of each. The character traits included such elements as mirthfulness, benevolence, memory of names, vitality, mental and emotional temperament, self-esteem, and hope. The development of each of these thirty-seven traits could be assessed by examining the size and shape of the corresponding area of the skull.[13] After examination, phrenologists usually indicated the types of profession or trade for which the individual was best suited. After having examined his head, the phrenologist pronounced Oronhyatekha suitable for further education.[14]

Oronhyatekha later wrote that after the phrenologist's reading of his head, he had no ambition for further education and so ignored his advice. Instead, he returned to his apprenticeship with another shoemaker. Paid partly in board and lodging, Oronhyatekha left the reserve. But the phrenologist returned for a second visit, this time offering to take Oronhyatekha along on his tour, if for no further reason than he could see New York and other great cities.[15] Oronhyatekha accepted this offer, even though his family feared he would be sold into slavery by the Americans, as it was thought that this happened with native people as it did with African Americans. But Oronhyatekha believed in the phrenologist's offered friendship and left with him.

On the train to New York City, he passed through the ancestral homelands of the Haudenosaunee in upper New York State. His grandfather had told him of his leaving Canajoharie, his birthplace and one of the two principle "castles" as they were referred to by the Mohawks. Many of the Haudenosaunee at Grand River still spoke of their homeland with a kind of reverence tinged with homesickness.

Oronhyatekha and O'Leary visited New York for just a few hours before moving on to New Haven, Connecticut, staying with a friend of the phrenologist for a few days. Though the original offer had seemed attractive because it allowed Oronhyatekha to see large cities, they next travelled to the country, to stay at the phrenologist's father's farm. There Oronhyatekha worked for the next five months. It is unknown whether the farm was near Wesleyan Academy or if the phrenologist or his father had ties to that institution, but at the end of the five months, Oronhyatekha left with his pay and letters of introduction to teachers and other individuals at Wesleyan Academy in Wilbraham, Massachusetts.[16]

By now he had become convinced that further education beyond that available to him locally was necessary to be successful. He also knew that education conveyed a measure of power, particularly the ability to read and write English fluently, something that many of his community could not do. Oronhyatekha sought community approval for his decision to attend Wesleyan. He knew that the Confederacy Council offered financial support to those recommended by Reverend Abraham Nelles. Community history tells that Oronhyatekha successfully pleaded his case, persuading his family and securing Nelles's approval, but the council would not offer him financial support. The Confederacy Council had begun to perceive higher levels of education for what they were — a method through which their people might fully assimilate and disappear into English society. The council restricted access to higher education to those who could resist these pressures and return to the Grand River and contribute to the community. It may have also felt that Oronhyatekha was better off at home, supporting his mother and sisters.

WESLEYAN ACADEMY

The Methodist church originally established Wesleyan Academy in New Hampshire in 1817, but the institution moved to its permanent home in Wilbraham, Massachusetts, in 1824. The facilities were therefore fairly new during Oronhyatekha's time. In 1851, Fisk Hall, which contained club rooms, art rooms for ladies, and a large assembly space, was erected, and in 1854 Binney Hall replaced the old laboratory. It housed lecture and recitation rooms, a new laboratory, a museum, and space for women's literary societies.

Oronhyatekha likely enrolled for the winter term of 1854, which began in early December, joining approximately three hundred other students. William Bridge, a fellow class member, later wrote of Oronhyatekha's first day at Wesleyan. According to this account, an elderly gentleman from Canada brought the young Oronhyatekha into a morning recitation led by Professor Henry Warren, who taught ancient languages. Warren introduced him to the class and in particular encouraged Bridge to befriend him and to show him "how to live as an American should." This last instruction seems more assimilatory than culturally directed; Bridge wrote that at this time Oronhyatekha lived like "a true Indian in all his habits," even pulling off all his blankets from the bed and sleeping on the floor, since he "hated" beds. This seems highly unlikely since the Mohawks of the Grand River had long lived in European-style homes, and the Mohawk Institute had beds for their students.[17]

Although Oronhyatekha was only fourteen, he was well-prepared for his stay away from his home, having gained independence and self-reliance while attending the Mohawk Institute during the previous four years. At Wesleyan, however, he was required to pay tuition. The cost depended on the course of study each student undertook. In 1836, one term of English studies cost three dollars, chemistry and foreign language classes one dollar each, natural philosophy seventy-five cents, and for botany and each higher class in math, fifty cents. As there were four terms a year, these costs could add up quickly for a student living on one's own means, like Oronhyatekha. In addition to tuition, students needed to pay their board, which in 1836 cost one dollar and fifty cents per week. Board did not include laundry or fuel for heating and lighting one's room, however.[18]

For three terms, Oronhyatekha received free tuition in exchange for working as a bell-ringer, presumably at the college. He also worked before and after school at various jobs including shoemaking, mending, gardening, teaching Sunday school, and chopping firewood. He would later recall, in a much repeated quip, that while he was paid only forty cents a cord, "It kept me in bread even if I had not butter."[19] Similarly, he was quoted as saying he lived on "bread, salt and water for breakfast, salt, water and bread for dinner, and water, salt and bread for supper."[20] One year, he received eight shillings "from home." As well, he would later write cryptically that he received money from his friend "IPH," in a letter postmarked New Haven — possibly the individual with whom he and the phrenologist had stayed upon their arrival in the United States. At one point, he wrote to the New England Company asking for ten dollars to buy clothing, a request seemingly denied since one of his teachers, Oliver Massey, gave him some clothes. While he worked hard to pay for his education, it made him a studious pupil, because he was always glad to sit down to study after his chores.[21]

While it is unknown what courses he took, classes in English, mathematics, Latin and Greek, music, natural philosophy, botany, and chemistry were all available to the students. The academy had a six-year curriculum plan. First-year students began with simple reading, writing, arithmetic, and English grammar. Teachers added geography and astronomy to the lessons of the second-year students. In third year, Latin, Greek, and French were taught, and in the next year, mathematics and the beginnings of natural philosophy. Fifth-year students learned Hebrew and more Greek, focusing on the Bible as a text. Finally, sixth-year students studied divinity, logic, rhetoric, and moral philosophy. It is unknown at which level Oronhyatekha entered.

Student behaviour in class was governed by a set of rules, not unlike those of most schools of the time. Students were expected to remain silent unless called upon by the teacher, to be punctual at taking their seats as soon as the morning bell rang and stay until dismissed, and to refrain from any scuffling, wrestling, or any other sport. Night curfew was set at 9:00 p.m. Being a religious academy, of course all students were compelled to attend services on Sunday and to spend the rest of the day in "a serious and becoming manner." Wesleyan rules barred the use of profanity, vandalism, walking through farmers' fields, the purchase of liquor, and "every species of immoral conduct." Students violating the rules were fined or even expelled, depending on the seriousness of the offence.[22]

Wesleyan was a boarding school, and students either lived with families in the town of Wilbraham or on the academy grounds. Beginning in 1856, on-campus residences included the old president's home and a boarding house that accommodated 150 students. At least for part of his time, Oronhyatekha boarded locally, for he later wrote that one spring he assisted with gardening in exchange for his board and lodging at a farm. If he resided for the rest of his time at the campus boarding house, he may have lost all of his possessions when it was consumed by fire. Mid-morning on January 4, 1856, a drafty stove in one of the student's rooms shot out flames to the pile of firewood stacked behind it. The fire quickly spread up to the roof, and within the hour the boarding house was a pile of ashes. Entirely constructed of wood and with no local fire department, the building was impossible to save.

During the fire, most students were attending their recitations and were unharmed. In the confusion, a few attempted to throw as many possessions as possible out open windows to land in the yard below, but most objects were too broken to be of any use. Most students escaped with only the clothes on their backs, and had to either return home or lodge with families in town.[23]

In August of 1856, Oronhyatekha's friends wrote to him to ask him to return home, but he had no extra money to make the trip. Earlier, he had written to the NEC agent seeking a position as a schoolteacher, but with no result. But when his Sunday school students discovered he wished to return home, they took up a collection of money and books. Once back at Grand River, he repeated his request to be given a teaching position with the New England Company. But it was not until Oronhyatekha had taught for several months for the Baptist missionary board that Abraham Nelles relented and hired him. Nelles apparently accused him of ingratitude for teaching for a rival religious board after the NEC had supported him. Oronhyatekha decided to resign from the Baptist board, although the NEC position paid only half of his previous salary.[24]

While teaching, Oronhyatekha pondered his future and how he could be of the most service to his people. While at Wilbraham he had dreamed of attending Harvard University.[25] His mother wished him to become a minister.[26] He remembered Reverend Robert Lugger, the New England Company agent before Nelles. Lugger had been both a missionary and a physician, a combination that seemed to inspire Oronhyatekha. He confided his career goals to the Reverend Erastus A. Strong, the agent of the Missionary and Education Committees of the Diocese of Ohio, who visited Oronhyatekha and Nelles to discuss his future. Although this seems not to have been the course of action Nelles wished — to the point that the NEC declined to fund Oronhyatekha — Strong convinced Oronhyatekha to attend Kenyon College in Gambier, Ohio.[27] Strong, an 1850 Master's of Arts graduate from Kenyon, had long made it his personal mission to increase the number of Kenyon students who came from outside of Ohio. As well, in the past Kenyon had hosted a number of Mohawk students from northern Ohio, so Oronhyatekha's enrollment was not a precedent.[28] Strong also convinced the Anglican Bishop of Huron to approve of the plan and so the NEC in the end did grant Oronhyatekha $150 annually for three years.[29]

This time, however, pursuing higher education left Oronhyatekha vulnerable. Beginning in the 1830s, Canada East and West passed legislation that had seriously detrimental effects on native peoples.[30] Enfranchisement as stipulated in An Act to Encourage the Gradual Civilization of the Indian Tribes (1857) set out the terms and conditions by which native people could escape the "protection" of Indian Affairs and enable them to become full Canadian citizens. Any adult male judged by a board of examiners to be free of debt, educated, and having a moral character could be enfranchised. Enfranchisement meant native individuals would no longer be considered wards of the state. They could vote, and after three years they would be given fifty acres of land to own individually and to do with as they pleased. But it also meant their land would no longer be part of their home reserve and that they had renounced their native status. As a result, they would not receive yearly annuities as mandated by treaties, or be able to participate in community decisions.[31]

At first voluntary, enfranchisement became compulsory in law in 1876. If a native person attained a higher level of education than that provided by a residential school, they could be forcibly enfranchised by their Indian agent, and once enfranchised, a native person's spouse and children could no longer claim native status either. In practice, forcible enfranchisement was never implemented until after the First World War, but native communities feared it for decades before implementation. Suggesting that the two were incompatible, the law essentially forced individuals to choose between becoming educated or remaining a legally recognized Indian with special status. So while Oronhyatekha desired an education, such a path could threaten his community ties to the Grand River and his native status, of which he was very proud. And he must have known how his home community reacted.

At Six Nations of the Grand River, three Mohawk individuals applied for enfranchisement in 1858. Two were brothers who had never lived there and likely concealed their heritage over the years, but the third was born and raised in the community. The Crown rejected the first two applicants as unfit, but the third, Elias Hill, was accepted. Coincidentally, Hill had also trained to be a shoemaker at the Mohawk Institute. Hill's property was deemed as having been surrendered and the title listed in the land registry of Canada West. He, along with his family, was de-listed from the Indian census register. While Hill was not physically removed from the community, the Confederacy Council's rejection of enfranchisement was swift and extremely negative. The chiefs saw it as a deliberate government effort to alienate land and a direct affront to their sovereignty and authority to determine the citizenship of their people and disposition of the lands they held.[32]

Oronhyatekha, or at least his family, must have understood the potential cost of his goal to gain a higher level of education. They were very reluctant to support his effort to attend college for fear that he would be lost to them, but he remained determined to pursue further education.

KENYON COLLEGE

Like Wesleyan, Kenyon College had been established to train theological students, although for the Episcopal Church rather than the Methodist one as at Wesleyan. It also offered a four-year undergraduate arts course. For students not yet old enough or prepared enough to enter as college students, Kenyon ran a preparatory grammar school called Milnor Hall. It was here that Oronhyatekha first enrolled in 1857, along with seventy-six fellow classmates.[33]

MILNOR HALL;
THE JUNIOR PREPARATORY SCHOOL, OF KENYON COLLEGE.

Oronhyatekha attended Milnor Hall before enrolling at Kenyon College.

At Milnor Hall, instructors valued close contact with students as a way to ensure the development of a proper Christian moral character in these younger boys. Unlike the college, the hall was run like a family home, with a matron and a nurse who cared for students and performed household duties, like the washing and mending of clothes. Students also ate with the principal, instructors, and their families.

To cultivate group morale and prevent class distinctions among students, all Milnor pupils wore uniforms consisting of a coat, pants, and vest. In the 1870s, these were described as being made from West Point Cadet grey cloth with fine black stripes and brass buttons. Presumably, the military style reflected the expected discipline of the boys.

Milnor Hall was overcrowded and so a handful of students boarded in the village adjacent to the school. Oronhyatekha, along with Alphonso David Rockwell and Austin Stowe Humphrey, both of whom were from Connecticut, lived with Reverend Strong.[34] Rockwell, who in later years earned the dubious distinction of co-inventing the electric chair, wrote about his experiences at Kenyon College and of his roommate Oronhyatekha in his published memoirs. Their house was only a quarter of a mile from Kenyon campus, and Rockwell remembered that he and Oronhyatekha could reach the college chapel during the five minutes that its bell rang, as it called students to prayer.

According to Rockwell, Oronhyatekha was fond of practical jokes, although one in particular backfired on him. Late one night, Oronhyatekha decided to sneak into Humphrey's room and pretend he was going to attack him. He grabbed his tomahawk, which Oronhyatekha claimed belonged to Joseph Brant, and painted his face to look like a "wild Indian." He snuck into the room, flailing the tomahawk over the head of his would-be victim. Unbeknownst to Oronhyatekha, however, visitors from Boston had been invited to stay for the night and had been assigned to this room. Once he realized his gaffe, Oronhyatekha dashed out of the room, leaving behind a terrorized woman, although her husband slept on soundly. Rockwell knew of the change in room assignments but hadn't mentioned it, for which Oronhyatekha "vented a large amount of abuse" on him.[35] Perhaps he considered it suitable revenge for all of Oronhyatekha's jokes.

Later biographies state that in his first year Oronhyatekha took two years of schooling in one.[36] It is not known what he studied, but Milnor students could choose between a classical course of study with Greek and Latin literature and languages and Greek and Roman history, or an English and science path that included classes in math, business, physiology, and geography. French and German languages were available at an extra cost. The latter course of study was intended for those students who would not attend college, so Oronhyatekha likely pursued the classics training.

While Oronhyatekha's classes were held at Milnor Hall, the grammar school students attended daily church services in the basement of Rosse Hall on the college campus with the undergraduates, and used the college gymnasium as well. If desired, students could also attend lectures and recitations at the college in topics not offered at Milnor. Located a half mile from the college, Milnor was separate, yet close enough to share facilities.[37]

After completing grammar school in June 1858, Oronhyatekha entered Kenyon College proper that fall. Kenyon's academic year had three terms: fall (September–December), winter (January–March) and spring (April–June). Oronhyatekha enrolled in classes in English, history, Latin, Greek, math, and rhetoric. The daily schedule was a full one. Students rose with the college bell at 6:20, allowing them ten minutes to arrive at the basement chapel in Rosse Hall for morning prayers. Breakfast followed at 7:00 and recitations at 8:00. Students lunched between noon and 2:00 p.m., when classes resumed until supper at 5:00 p.m. At 6:30,

Oronhyatekha roomed here, at Kenyon hall, in his freshman year.

evening prayers commenced, and afterwards students were expected to study until 9:00 p.m. Between 9:00 and 10:00 p.m., a tutor or professor visited each room to ensure that students were present.

Not surprisingly, religion played a large role in the students' daily activities. In addition to morning and evening services, students attended two on Sundays, a social prayer meeting each Tuesday, a lecture on Thursday nights, and a prayer meeting on Fridays.[38] Students absent from services and classes or missing from their rooms at night were awarded demerit points. With the exception of Oronhyatekha's last term, when he seemed to be absent from church a fair amount, he garnered few of these points.[39]

Rockwell envied Oronhyatekha because he rarely had to study. Though surely Rockwell exaggerated, he said that because Oronhyatekha possessed a phenomenal memory, he could study from a crib sheet for five minutes and pass his examinations as well as anyone else. While Oronhyatekha later wrote that his studies were hindered by his anxiety over finances, this certainly did not affect his grades. The Kenyon College archives hold partially complete grade books for the time that Oronhyatekha attended the college, and these reveal that he held perfect or near-perfect marks in each. He was also said to have been very successful in the written and oral examinations that ended each term.[40]

However, Oronhyatekha did struggle to meet the costs of his education. Milnor Hall charged eight dollars tuition and five dollars for board and incidentals per term. Uniforms were approximately twenty dollars. Kenyon was considerably more expensive than Wesleyan. Tuition in Oronhyatekha's last year cost thirty-two dollars, room rent twelve dollars, incidentals six dollars, heating fuel six to seven dollars, washing ten dollars, and gas for lighting four to eight dollars. A one-dollar damage deposit had to be paid at the beginning of each year. Costs to buy textbooks and stationery and to furnish rooms were extra. In fact, students even had to provide their own mattresses. As a freshman, Oronhyatekha roomed in Kenyon Hall, but in his sophomore year, he returned to board in the village with the Reverend Dr. Smith of the Theological Seminary, perhaps because it was cheaper. That he found it difficult to meet his expenses may also be supported by the fact that he was absent in the fall term of 1859.[41]

Reverend Strong had applied on his behalf to the New England Company, and as a result, the missionaries awarded him a grant for three years. While helpful, his expenses exceeded the grant, especially because it was costly to go home each summer. Oronhyatekha continued to look for other ways to make money. One of his professors hired him to do such tasks as gardening and chopping firewood. Oronhyatekha later wrote that his tuition was reduced because he was a student for the ministry, but records show that he was not a student at Bexley Hall, the theological school at Kenyon.[42] Later biographies mention that Oronhyatekha staged plays and shows for the college faculty and students, supporting himself at Kenyon with the proceeds.[43] Certainly his siblings were actors, including his sister Maggie, who achieved a fair amount of fame as "Princess Viroqua," a travelling healer and performer.[44] As well, in the fall of 1860, he rented the town hall at Napanee, near Tyendinaga, for an "exhibition" of some sort, the proceeds of which were to assist with his education expenses.[45]

Although few of his classmates became his intimate friends, Oronhyatekha certainly had a wide social life at Kenyon. He joined the Alpha Delta Phi fraternity, the Kenyon Sporting Club, and the Wicket Club. He is said to have joined the newly established (1858) Kokosing

Princess Viroqua, Emma Martin or Neoskelata (Prairie Rose), and Emma's daughter.

Tribe. Named after the nearby river, this group seems to have been a fraternity with "Indian" overtones, possibly associated with the Improved Order of Red Men. Its nonsensical motto, *N'dahoalaneen Aninshilhilleisak*, apparently meant "I love chickens" in the Delaware language, and was divided into the levels "Old Men," Old Warriors," and "Braves." Because all members received an "Indian" name, it is hard to prove that Oronhyatekha did indeed join this group.[46] Oronhyatekha was also a member of the Philomathesian Society, a literary club that met weekly to debate such weighty questions as the legalization of prostitution, the colonization of convicts, protective tariffs, and the possibility of reaching the North Pole.[47] Meetings were held in the society's club room in Ascension Hall, which also housed a library of several thousand books and newspapers for its members' reading pleasure.

Oronhyatekha also served on the invitation committee for the "Burial of Homer," an annual tradition in which the freshman class celebrated the end of their first year by burning their textbooks, similar to that of the Burial of Euclid at Yale. Cast as "funeral obsequies," the ceremony included a torchlight procession to Rosse Hall by those dubbed His Satanic Majesty, the Great High Priest, Priest's Escort, Senate, Orator, Poet, and other assorted satiric titles. Over a blazing keg of tar, which provided light, the ceremony included a "dead march," songs, a funeral oration, music, and poems such as:

> *Come gather all ye tearful Sophs,*
> *And stand around the ring;*
> *Old Homer's dead, and to his shade,*
> *A requiem we'll sing;*
> *Then join the mournful chorus all*
> *Ye friends of Homer true;*
> *Defunct, he can no longer bore*
> *The Class of 62.*

The funeral ended with the burning of books on a pyre and the burial of the ashes. A banquet followed, to mark the end of the freshman year, and the students' graduation to being sophomores.[48]

While later biographies state that Oronhyatekha graduated from Kenyon College in 1860, having completed a four-year program in three years, records do not bear out this claim. After his first year at the preparatory grammar school, Milnor Hall, he entered Kenyon College proper in the fall term of 1858 as a freshman. As tradition required, he signed the Matriculation Book in the spring of 1859, indicating he would graduate in 1862, after his senior year. In the school year of 1859–60, Oronhyatekha completed his sophomore class work. That at least some of his classmates expected him to return in the fall of 1860 for his junior year may be borne out by the records of the Philomathesian Society, which marked him as absent for their first few meetings that fall. Oronhyatekha did not return to Kenyon for his senior year either. He is listed in alumni records as a "non-graduate."[49]

In his last year at the school, an incident between faculty and students resulted in some of the students being suspended and expelled. In a series of letters with his future mentor, Sir Henry Acland, Oronhyatekha explained this incident, but parts of the relevant letters are missing. The remaining pages show that during his sophomore year his class rebelled against the college authorities. Of the thirty-three students, thirty were suspended, including himself, and told to leave the college. Oronhyatekha, not having the money to do so, stayed, as did most others. After three days of suspension, most students agreed to submit, and electing Oronhyatekha as their speaker, visited the college president. The student newspaper, the *Kenyon Reveille*, wrote obscurely in June 1860 that "the causes and incidents are too well known to need repetition."

A full explanation of this "rebellion" appeared in the *Kenyon Collegian*, the senior class publication. On the evening of Monday, January 30, students, professors, and town residents attended a musical concert led by a Miss Lerned of the Granville Female Seminary, an institution approximately fifty kilometres south of Gambier. The concert had been sponsored by Kenyon's Nu Pi Kappa Society. Normally, students spent their evenings prepping for their morning recitations, but because of the time spent at the concert and the need to clean up the next morning, the freshmen and sophomores voted to miss their 8:00 a.m. class. Deeming this a violation of college law, President Lorin Andrews announced at evening prayer that students must sign a pledge to make up their recitation on the following day, and to never again "evade, disobey, or resist" any college regulations. The students agreed that their actions had been hasty, promised to make up their class, but many refused to sign the pledge. Faced with expulsion, however, by the end of the week on Friday, most students, including Oronhyatekha, submitted and signed the pledge.

Oronhyatekha finished out the term in June, ready for summer vacation, but having only ten pounds left in his grant from the New England Company, decided to procure a letter of honourable dismissal and letters of reference from President Andrews and mathematics instructor and dean Benjamin Lang, in order to find a teaching position. Oronhyatekha hoped to return to Kenyon College in the future, after he had saved enough money.[50]

Twenty years later, at a class of 1862 reunion, the alumni remembered their expulsion through a song composed by Edward Bates as a student:

Oh, we deemed it perfectly right, sir,
On a certain Monday night, sir,
For the Sophies to unite, sir,
From class to stay away...

Prexy was awfully mad, sir.
His face looked tearfully sad, sir;
He said 'twas terribly bad, sir.
From class to stay away...

In solemnity they met, sir,
And concluded they would let, sir;
The Sophomores regret, sir,
That from class they stayed away...

Some wrote out explanations.
Others interpretations,
To break up our combinations,
From class to stay away...

But our honor we could not kill, sir.
By signing the President's bill, sir;
Our trunks we'd rather fill, sir.
And homeward wend our way...

They were under a fatal delusion.
When they thought without confusion.
To enforce their resolution.
"Sign, or go away!"

The pledge we cannot obey, sir;
It don't mean what they say, sir;
They explained it all away, sir,
For fear we would not stay...

The pledge has winged its flight, sir —
Has departed out of sight, sir:
Once more we may unite, sir,
From class to stay away.

Despite the minor nature of the "rebellion" of 1860, and the light-hearted way alumni remembered the event, it and Oronhyatekha's involvement would come back to haunt him in later academic efforts, contribute to ruining his relationship with Reverend Nelles, and hamper his chances at Oxford University.[51] He would spend the next twelve years attempting to clear his name.

CHAPTER 2
THE ROYAL VISIT

RETURN FROM THE U.S.

Upon leaving Kenyon College, Oronhyatekha visited his family at the Grand River for a few days and then travelled to the Tyendinaga Mohawk community. After four weeks, his people at home, in his own words, sent for him to organize affairs for the visit of the Prince of Wales, later Edward VII, who would arrive in Canada West in late August 1860.[1] Oronhyatekha exaggerated his role — rather than organizing the event, he was chosen to present a speech to the prince on behalf of the Haudenosaunee Confederacy Council — but like his chance meeting with the phrenologist in 1854, the royal visit became a pivotal event in his life.

When Oronhyatekha returned to the Grand River, he found the community rife with tension, as members dealt with the loss of land and the re-establishment of their farms, increasingly restrictive government legislation, differing religious beliefs and missionary attempts to convert them, and debates over natural resources and political reform. The intense pressures from outside had become internalized, and the actions of the Confederacy Council chiefs came under microscopic scrutiny by many in the community. Their decisions were openly questioned, to the point where accusations were made of incompetence, even deceit.[2]

These tensions had been brought to a simmer in 1859 with the controversial appointment of a specific chief. Traditionally, there were fifty chiefly titles and when a chief died or was deposed, another individual would be chosen. Clan mother Helen "Nellie" Martin Johnson, the daughter of George Martin and Oronhyatekha's paternal aunt, had appointed her son, George Henry Martin Johnson, as a Mohawk chief. He had been chosen over a rival, Isaac Powless, and as Powless's childhood friend, Oronhyatekha must have felt conflicted during the controversy that followed.

It was not unusual for a clan mother to name a son as a Confederacy Council Chief, but the community contested Johnson's appointment on three fronts. The least of the three infractions was that he had married against the wishes of the clan mother, who was also his own mother Nellie. It was the clan mother's duty to arrange and approve marriages within her clan, particularly for those members who could potentially become a chief. In George Johnson's case, he also had married a non-native woman, Emily Susanna Howells, who had recently arrived in the community. Howells had come to visit her sister and brother-in-law, the Reverend Adam Elliott, a missionary working for the New England Company (NEC). At the time, this marriage broke traditional laws, and further, their children would never be able to hold a chiefly title. As a matrilineal culture, Haudenosaunee children traced their clan through their mother, and since Emily was white, her children would be clan-less.

The second issue of contention was that George Johnson's father, John Smoke Johnson, was a pine tree chief, an appointment that carried influence and a strong advisory capacity but was decided by council chiefs, not clan mothers. It was unusual to have a father and son serve on the same council, and as Isaac Powless protested, the appointment had been heavily influenced by NEC missionaries Abraham Nelles and Adam Elliott, the latter now related to Johnson by marriage.

Finally, the Confederacy Council also rejected George Johnson's appointment based on the fact that he was a paid government official. He was the Indian Department interpreter, or as some would accuse, an informant. Like the Martin family, the Johnsons were known to be strong and vocal British loyalists, and many now viewed this particular attribute with suspicion, even disdain. Many in the community now believed that the British Crown's actions over the previous twenty years had inflicted significant hardships on the Haudenosaunee.

The Confederacy Council could reject a nominee for a chief's title and ask the clan mother to reconsider, but Nellie Johnson refused to do so, instead choosing to confront the council and threaten to extinguish the chiefly title forever. This was a serious action, because it would permanently reduce the number of Mohawk representatives in council. She reasoned that the chiefs had made their decision based on what her son *might* do, rather than what he had done, or could do for the community.

Based on the vehemence of Nellie Johnson's argument, the Confederacy Council accepted the appointment, and further, named George Johnson to the very powerful position of council interpreter. This position was a crucial one as chiefs not fluent in English or all six of the Haudenosaunee languages needed to be able to trust the verbal and written record of council discussions and recommendations made by the interpreter. Perhaps the council chiefs saw it as a strategic move to keep him, the trusted Indian Department interpreter, close at hand and under their influence. As well, a compromise was struck so that Johnson's vote as chief would not count as long as he remained a government employee.[3]

The Confederacy Council's reversal infuriated Isaac Powless, and he embarked on a campaign to discredit it, advocating an elected rather than a hereditary and appointed council. But the decision had been made and the council had other issues with which to be concerned, the most immediate being the impending royal visit by the young Prince of Wales, Albert Edward, Queen Victoria's son and heir to the British throne.

ROYAL PLANS

In the summer of 1860, the Confederacy Council called for submissions of potential speeches from the community in anticipation of the first nineteenth-century royal visit to Canada. While Prince Edward's main purpose was to represent the Queen at the official dedication of the new Victoria Bridge, which spanned the St. Lawrence River at Montreal, he also planned to tour much of the colonies.

The Indian Department believed that the Grand River community should make a presentation to welcome the prince. It was a fortuitous opportunity for the Confederacy Council as it would serve several purposes. First and foremost, it would divert attention from the recent internal struggles within the community and focus instead on presenting a united front. It would also draw the attention of both native and non-native communities to their long-standing alliance with the Crown. The chiefs hoped they could convince the Canadian government to heed their assertions of nationhood and sovereignty. They would take this opportunity to remind the prince, and by extension all Canadians, of the many commitments made between them and the government, responsibilities and obligations they had assumed in taking over the administration of Indian affairs. The royal visit also offered an opportunity to re-establish a direct line of communication with the Crown in Britain, lost over the previous few decades.

Oronhyatekha, and two of the NEC missionaries, presumably Nelles and Elliott, first answered the call for submissions. Fearing that grievances might be raised, the Indian Department expressed concern that any speech to the prince should not allude to any government policies; "no business" was to be transacted, and the address was to be "confined to expressions of loyalty and welcome to the Prince." On August 20, the council approved a speech, ostensibly presented by John Smoke Johnson, Oronhyatekha's uncle and speaker of the council. It was signed by Johnson, his son George H.M. Johnson, and David Thorburn, the visiting superintendent of Indian Affairs for the community. However, three days later George Johnson wrote to Thorburn, stating that the chiefs had not yet decided on the content of the speech to be given because of the "absurd notions" of some individuals. George Loft from the Bay of Quinte reserve, a man Johnson dismissed as full of a "good deal of nonsense," had also written a speech. Unfortunately, George Johnson noted, Loft had influenced some of the chiefs. In his letter, Johnson also informed Thorburn of a suggestion offered by Isaac Powless — that if the council would not approve the speech, the Anglican Church could do so instead, thus bypassing the chiefs altogether. But he hoped that council would see reason and agree to the address already written and approved of by Thorburn.

Interestingly, this address was more pointed than the one ultimately presented by Oronhyatekha. It included grievances, particularly those regarding land issues. It noted that the Haudenosaunee had endured "deeply felt, severe pressure" from the number of immigrants to Upper Canada. Nevertheless, the petition stated that they remained loyal to Britain. The address reminded the prince that they had a long history of fighting for the Crown when it had needed their military assistance, even sacrificing their land in the United States for England. In conclusion, the address subverted the idea of "progress" — so prevalent in most royal speeches — that lauded the immigrants who had improved the land of Upper Canada through farming, establishing towns, and pursuing commerce; while the Haudenosaunee hoped the prince would enjoy the improvements "everywhere visible," they suggested that he would also enjoy "our ancient lakes and rivers and the wilds and solitudes." Reminding the prince of the original native ownership of the country, they hoped that they would "never be required to surrender" more of it.

However, this speech also contained slightly fawning sentiments that seem to be influenced or written by Abraham Nelles, or the New England Company as a whole. The address acknowledged the "immense debt of gratitude" to the NEC for its churches and schools, and lamented the fact that the queen could not visit the Mohawk Institute and the Mohawk Chapel. The oddest statement is that the Six Nations found it "quite natural ... to entertain feelings of loyalty to the Rulers of a Nation which [they] have always been accustomed *to look upon as superior.*"[4]

According to a community historian, the Confederacy Council instead selected Oronhyatekha's submission due to his accomplishments and ability to meet people, and invited him to deliver the speech himself.[5] Presumably, the council also preferred a member of the community, not a non-native missionary, to present it. The relationship between Oronhyatekha and Nelles, once his benefactor, turned to one of competition and would later prove adversarial.

Oronhyatekha, though only recently turned nineteen years old, may have sensed that presenting this speech was a significant opportunity to further his ambitions. If he was anything, Oronhyatekha was skilled at sensing opportunities and then deploying his other traits — his height and demeanor, his stage presence, eloquence, and flair for the dramatic — to gain the greatest advantage. To make the most of this royal opportunity, Oronhyatekha needed to look the part. He enlisted his sisters to craft a suit of clothing, and an impressive suit it would be.[6]

A NEW MENTOR

With his suit and speech prepared, in early September Oronhyatekha travelled to Toronto on his first official duty to solicit a meeting for his people.[7] It was during this visit that he met his soon-to-be mentor Henry Wentworth Acland, Regius Professor of Medicine at Oxford University and personal physician to the Prince of Wales. As Acland later recounted, their first meeting occurred inauspiciously in a "passage" in Toronto. Very much interested in the native peoples of Canada, Acland "accosted" Oronhyatekha and his native companion. According to Acland's account, his companion responded rudely, while Oronhyatekha answered, oddly, "I do not speak much." Acland asked Oronhyatekha to return to his hotel room in order that he could sketch him, as he had done with other native peoples during his trip. Described by Acland as "herculean," painted, and with a ring in his nose, Oronhyatekha must have stirred Acland's artistic muse. Although Oronhyatekha responded to this invitation by saying, "I do not much like it," Acland dismissed it and replied, "Oh! Never mind, I have drawn many: they never object, come to my room." According to Acland, Oronhyatekha followed him slowly, "but not sullenly."[8]

While sketching, Acland questioned Oronhyatekha about himself and the Haudenosaunee in Canada, a conversation recorded in some detail by Acland in his letters to his wife. One question in particular evoked a response clearly indicative of Oronhyatekha's sense of opportunity, or perhaps of Acland's misunderstanding of Oronhyatekha's appointment as a representative for the royal visit. Acland asked Oronhyatekha if he was a chief, and if chiefs were elected or hereditary. Oronhyatekha's response was obliging, replying, "Sometimes one, sometimes the other, sometimes both, as in my case," the latter statement being untrue. Acland also questioned Oronhyatekha about the Mohawk language, his dress, and the preservation of traditional customs.

Oronhyatekha strongly defended the right of the Haudenosaunee to maintain their way of life. When Acland asked about the ring in his nose, he said it was part of traditional dress. Acland replied it to be an unpleasant custom, and Oronhyatekha responded, "It is the custom, that is enough."

"But surely," Acland argued, "you do not mean to advocate every custom, you might now scalp me in no time." Oronhyatekha answered that he supported all customs that were harmless, while at the same time he hoped to help elevate his people both intellectually and morally.

Oronhyatekha also commented on the relationship between natives and the government. He stated that even the government officials appointed to assist native communities treated them as inferior, like children. As long as this was so, Oronhyatekha argued, it would be impossible for natives to be independent. Acland replied that this must be the fault of both the government officials and the native communities. Acland continued with the question, "What else depresses your race?" Acland's account records Oronhyatekha as saying, "The condition of our women. No cultivated Indian can find in his tribe a suitable wife, and no superior white woman will marry an Indian." This response seems unlikely, as Oronhyatekha's own paternal grandmother, Catherine Rolleston, and the wife of his cousin, George H.M. Johnson, were both non-native. Rolleston, and her daughter, Oronhyatekha's paternal aunt, Nellie Martin Johnson, were both highly respected by the Mohawk.

Acland suggested education as a remedy for this problem, yet observed that few individuals attended, or stayed any length of time, at school. Oronhyatekha agreed, but argued that the schools themselves were not advanced enough and that certainly non-native parents would never agree to such an education for their own children. At that point, Oronhyatekha told Acland that he himself had been to Kenyon College, surviving on charity and a shoemaker apprenticeship. He had hoped to be able to fund further education for his two younger sisters but had not been able to do so. Instead, he had returned to his community to teach the children what he himself had learned. Although Acland did not record his reaction to Oronhyatekha's attendance at Kenyon, this fact must have built some common ground between the two men since Acland's own father had helped finance the establishment of this college.[9]

Acland concluded their session by saying obliquely, "I think I can help you in more than one way. But, my friend, you had to leave by a train at four. It is now 3:30 … write to me your thoughts and your wishes. I will do anything for you, except give money, and that I cannot. Good-bye." Oronhyatekha replied, "Your red brother thanks you: you will hear."

It is difficult to know how accurately Acland represented his conversation with Oronhyatekha. But clearly the two men established a friendly and respectful rapport, one that would last the rest of their lives. They met again just a few days later.

Oronhyatekha presented his speech to the Prince of Wales, a man only three months younger than him, at Brantford, on September 14, 1860.

THE ROYAL VISIT

Originally, the Indian Department proposed that the Haudenosaunee and the nearby Mississauga New Credit communities participate in a much grander and lengthier ceremony with the Prince of Wales. At first, the Indian Department planned for representatives to travel to Queenston Heights, where the prince would also meet veterans of the War of 1812, review numerous militia companies, and unveil the newly rebuilt monument to Sir Isaac Brock, who had died nearby during the war. As British allies in this war, Haudenosaunee participation in this event was logical. As was common at the time, the prince would also award them silver medals with a likeness of the young Queen Victoria, another historically symbolic gift between the Crown and its native allies. In the end, local organization proved insufficient for such a grand display.

By early September, the Indian Department thought the Haudenosaunee should meet the prince in Hamilton on the 18th, but ultimately Richard Pennefather, the superintendent general of Indian Affairs, ordered that they should attend a ceremony in Brantford on the 14th. This decision was made only one week before the prince was scheduled to arrive in the city, and even city officials did not receive a final confirmation that the royal tour would stop at Brantford until a few days before the fourteenth. The Indian Department did not even compile the list of chiefs to receive medals until September 27, almost two weeks after the royal visit. Such last-minute and inefficient planning resulted in a much briefer and less elaborate ceremony than that at Sarnia between the prince and numerous Anishinabe (Ojibwa) groups. There, chiefs presented speeches, including those referring to the loss of their land, and received medals from the prince.[10]

The prince's train arrived in Brantford on the clear and cool afternoon of September 14, having first made whistle stops at Ingersoll,

Woodstock, and Paris. The prince disembarked from the train under a ceremonial arch of greenery to the sound of 20,000 people cheering and cannons mounted atop a nearby hill booming. Those selected to present addresses to the prince waited in a separate section next to the train platform. Under the reception canopy, Governor-General Sir Edmund Walker Head introduced to the prince several individuals, including the mayor of Brantford, the warden and judge of Brant County, the reeve of Simcoe, presidents of the St. Georges and St. Andrews benevolent societies, C.A. Jones from the Mississauga New Credit reserve, and finally, Oronhyatekha. The Haudenosaunee also presented the prince with gifts of clubs, tomahawks, and arrows.

Next, a procession of fraternal society members, firemen, city and municipal officials, clergymen, militiamen, and veterans of the War of 1812 accompanied the prince to the Kerby House Hotel. Marshalled by George H.M. Johnson and marching in the middle of the procession were the council chiefs, "Old Warriors," a band, and members of the community in "full Indian War Costumes." Presumably, Oronhyatekha marched with them. The procession passed under several more ceremonial arches, including one erected by the Haudenosaunee that was painted with a chief at the apex. On top, four men posed with bows and arrows, ready to salute the prince, another symbol of their military alliance. The procession stopped at Kerby House for lunch. After a grace intoned by the watchful Reverend Abraham Nelles, visitors feasted on a meal of the "choicest meats and fruits" before the prince re-boarded the train for Niagara.[11]

MISUNDERSTOOD MESSAGES

At his full adult height, Oronhyatekha stood 6'3", and adorned in his ceremonial suit and feather headdress, he appeared to be virtually seven feet tall. He presented a lean, impressive figure dripping with a history predicated on diplomatic alliance, military authority, and sovereignty. He was not a figure from a people defeated or subjugated by settler nations, but rather one of national pride and success.

Approved by the Confederacy Council at the end of August, Oronhyatekha's speech was replete with allusions to loyalty and the

Haudenosaunee historical alliance with the British Crown. It is worth reproducing in full.

Brother,

We the Chiefs, Sachems, and Warriors of the Six Nations of Canada, are glad of this opportunity to welcome to our native land, the Son of our Gracious Sovereign Queen Victoria, and to manifest our continued loyalty and devotion to the person and Crown of your Royal Mother. We return thanks to the Great Spirit that He has put it into your Royal Highness's mind to come to this country, and that He has preserved your Royal Highness safe, that we may meet together this day. He has ordained Princes and Rulers to govern His people; and it is by His will that our beloved Queen, your Royal Mother, is so pre-eminent in power and virtue.

Brother, — Although we have been separated from our Sovereign by the "Great Water," yet have we ever kept the chain of friendship bright, and it gives us joy to meet with the Heir Apparent to the Throne, that we may renew and strengthen that chain, which has existed between the Crown of England and the Six Nations for more than two hundred years. Our confidence in our Sovereign is as lasting as the stars in Heaven. We rejoice at the presence among us of your Royal Highness, who is destined to fill the place of your Royal Mother, and her illustrious predecessor, whom we also loved.

Brother, — We thank the Great Spirit, that we have had an opportunity of addressing your Royal Highness, and we pray that He who watches over all men may return your Royal Highness in health and safety to your Royal Mother, our beloved Queen Victoria.[12]

Oronhyatekha's speech welcomed the prince to "our native land," a gentle reminder that the Haudenosaunee were one of the original inhabitants of North America. Oronhyatekha also made clear the depth of their alliance, noting that it was at least two hundred years old, and also referred to the Haudenosaunee's love for the queen's predecessor, King William IV. The chain of friendship, commonly called the covenant chain, had been a well-used metaphor in the longstanding diplomacy between the Haudenosaunee and the British Crown since the 1600s. Figuratively made of silver, the chain anchored the English and the Haudenosaunee Confederacy together. The links between represented peace, friendship, and respect between the two nations.

Oronhyatekha emphasized that the Haudenosaunee had kept the chain "bright," that is, they had maintained their side of the agreement, rather than allowing it to tarnish or let it fall into disuse. To the Haudenosaunee, this royal visit, like previous diplomatic meetings, symbolically renewed and strengthened the chain. Further, at some point during the royal visit, the prince signed the Bible given to the Haudenosaunee by Queen Anne in 1712, a gesture that surely could have only been interpreted by the community as affirmation of their alliance with the Crown.[13]

The fact that the council chose Oronhyatekha to represent the Grand River community during the royal visit would be made much of throughout the rest of Oronhyatekha's life. For the Martin family, it restored their belief that they were themselves Mohawk elite; through Oronhyatekha's presentation they had restored their position in Mohawk society.

Unfortunately, the prince and the general public appeared oblivious to these allusions to loyalty and autonomy. Most public speeches to the prince followed a template of sorts, expressing welcome to the local area, pledges of loyalty and best wishes to the queen, appreciation for her beneficent government, and hopes for an enjoyable trip. In many ways, whether planned or not, Oronhyatekha's speech followed this protocol, making it easier to ignore the underlying political messages intended by the Haudenosaunee. In fact, the *Brant Expositor* recorded that *none* of the speeches at Brantford were actually given verbally; due to a lack of time, the speeches were simply presented on paper to the prince, as was customary at many stops on his tour. Written responses were prepared if the speeches had been submitted to the prince ahead of time, but again these were not read aloud, but simply exchanged. The whole interchange, the *Expositor* noted, took about five minutes. While the *Expositor* printed all other speeches for the community to read, the only copy of Oronhyatekha's speech provided to the paper was in a Haudenosaunee language, and thus was not included. Two days later, the prince wrote to his mother that "nothing of interest" had occurred on the trip to Brantford, "but we were obliged to stop ... as [it was] on our route." The Duke of Newcastle, who had been appointed by the queen to investigate the treatment of natives across Canada, was ill that day and didn't even leave the train.[14]

It also appears that the Indian Department deliberately hindered the Grand River community in presenting any grievances. According to Oronhyatekha, Pennefather denied the Haudenosaunee deputation admission to the prince in Toronto on the spurious grounds that such a visit had not been approved by council or the local Indian agent. Oronhyatekha later stated to Acland that both had indeed approved the visit. Instead, Oronhyatekha submitted an official petition (a lobbying document meant to influence or cause change) from the Grand River to Acland in Hamilton, hoping that he could bring attention to it. The memorial had at least two purposes — one, to shed light on the fact that much of their territory, granted due to their allegiance in past wars, had been lost, and without any treaty of surrender; and two, to request greater control over their affairs, specifically the management of their trust funds and debts. Oronhyatekha later sent this memorial to Acland in early 1861. The Duke of Newcastle, who did write a report on the native situation in Canada after his return to England, relied heavily on information gathered from Pennefather. Of course, Pennefather either dismissed any grievances or assured the queen that new procedures were in place to deal with legitimate ones. The Six Nations of the Grand River community received no benefit from the royal visit.[15]

Not surprisingly, the press portrayed First Nations stereotypically, either as exotic primitive peoples or as justificatory examples of the government assimilation program. The message of First Nations as important military allies to Britain may have been interpreted by the public as more negative evidence of the supposed savagery of natives. Tour promoters, of course, preferred images of natives as "traditional" as possible in order to attract audiences and consumers. Spectacle equalled profits. Missionaries, on the other hand, felt that the wearing of traditional dress undermined the success of their own efforts; they also believed it hampered native attempts to have their grievances about land and loss of civil rights addressed because they could more easily be dismissed as "savage." The Indian Department advocated that First Nations wear traditional clothing for the royal visit, a direct contradiction to their ongoing attempts towards assimilation. Cynics said that the department wanted to suggest that First Nations would never be entirely civilized; only civilized people could understand the value of, and improve upon land, and consequently, native land claims need not be taken too seriously.

It is difficult to know why First Nations chose to wear traditional dress. Many likely saw it as a continuation and assertion of the importance of tradition. Perhaps they thought such clothing would bring more attention to them and their desire for political redress, or quite simply it was customary to dress ceremonially for such an important visitor.[16] Dress should be seen as a kind of medium through which an individual expresses cultural and political identity.[17]

ORONHYATEKHA'S SUIT

No expense was spared to craft Oronhyatekha's ceremonial suit. Constructed of brown velvet and black broadcloth, his sisters intricately sewed red and white beads onto it. The tunic was styled to resemble an English waistcoat with a flared bottom, trimmed with woven patterns that reflected ancient symbols of Mohawk design. Silk ribbons of blue, white, and red edged many of the seams. His moccasins were buckskin dyed black and adorned with beads and satin echoing the designs emblazoned on his waist coat, leggings, and breech cloth.

His sisters also fashioned a bandolier bag and strap made of the same materials that when worn, appeared sash-like across his chest and formed a waist belt. Oronhyatekha tucked a combination peace pipe-tomahawk made of brass and dark-stained oak through his belt at his waist. Tomahawk pipes were ceremonial items that the British often gave as symbols of alliance. His headdress was made of the same cloth, ribbons, and beads as the suit, and a wreath of turkey feathers perhaps ten inches high stood straight up from the head band.

At the age of nineteen, Oronhyatekha wore this suit to meet the Prince of Wales in 1860. The feathers are missing from the headdress.

His suit reflected the ever evolving style of the Haudenosaunee, as they selectively chose and reinterpreted elements of European style to match their own tastes and traditions. Almost the full suit, the coat being the exception, is native in style. The use of brown velvet mimics the older custom of using tanned deerskin for clothing in its colour and texture. The beadwork is Haudenosaunee, although the floral motifs had been so admired by non-native women that they had been adopted for their own needlework. As well, the public would have recognized such motifs as they were commonly used on beaded tourist items sold by the Haudenosaunee at spots such as Niagara Falls. His leggings, however, have geometric designs that are older in origin and cosmological in significance. The series of curved lines depict the sky-world resting on the Earth, and at the bottom opening of the leggings, the projections on the domes signify the celestial tree of life. These point outward, representing life, rather than inward, which means sleep or death. On the bag his sisters stitched a beaded design of a tomahawk and a bow and arrow next to a British Crown, a clear symbol of Haudenosaunee-British alliance. The shininess of the glass beads carried on the idea that light-reflective materials represented spirituality and wisdom. Oronhyatekha did not wear the traditional headgear, the *gustoweh*, but rather a Plains-style feather bonnet that was a highly recognizable symbol of "Indian-ness" to white audiences.

Would the prince and the public have understood the selective adaptiveness and symbolism in Oronhyatekha's clothing? Probably not. To the public, such dress likely seemed "traditional" — that is exotic — and harkened back to native cultures before European contact. Whatever the meanings imbued in his suit, clearly Oronhyatekha treasured it, for he later took it to England to visit Acland, and it remained in his family until his daughter died in the early twentieth century. He also preserved similar suits from the royal visit in what would become the museum at the Foresters' Temple.[18]

A FATEFUL INVITATION

A lavish lunch at Kerby House followed the exchange of addresses and replies, and the niceties that often accompany events of this nature may have provided Oronhyatekha the opportunity to speak with the young prince and members of his entourage, including Acland. After a brief discussion, the latter invited Oronhyatekha to come to Niagara Falls, the next stop on the royal tour.

Later that day, Oronhyatekha wrote to Acland, expressing his hopes for further education and his desire to visit Britain and understand the English culture and people. Clearly, the idea of attending Oxford had already been raised, since Oronhyatekha asked how much it would cost. He stated that he intended to pay for his education himself, and noted that in a few days he would be moving to Cincinnati for a few months where he would have what he called a lucrative position. In the spring, Oronhyatekha hoped to have saved enough to enroll at Oxford. During their discussion in Toronto, Oronhyatekha had said that he disliked being considered a "beneficiary" but he was cognizant of not going to extremes and insisting on being too independent.[19]

Their conversation continued in person a few days later. Oronhyatekha visited Acland in Hamilton when the party stopped there, bringing with him the petition from the Grand River community.[20] He

visited Acland again a few evenings later in Niagara, according to a letter Acland wrote to his wife. Acland was having tea with a Cayuga chief
whom he had also sketched when Oronhyatekha arrived. Compared
to Oronhyatekha, Acland portrayed the Cayuga man as "a real child
of the Red Men — and nothing more." The Cayuga man was "illiter-
ate" and "wiry," while Oronhyatekha was "philosophic" and "stately."
Oronhyatekha and Acland talked away the entire evening, as Acland
asked questions about native customs and how the native situation in
Canada might be improved. Despite their growing respect for each
other, they fundamentally disagreed over the assimilation of native
peoples; Acland felt that the preservation of their traditions was unwise,
whereas Oronhyatekha strongly defended his people's ways.

Acland also recorded their conversation about Haudenosaunee
grievances and their relationship with the British Crown. Treaties,
Oronhyatekha said, included presents for as long as the sun and moon
shone, but that the queen no longer fulfilled these promises. The petition Oronhyatekha had given to Acland was intended to be presented
to the Duke of Newcastle, setting forth this and other grievances.
Unsympathetic, Acland dismissed these grievances as the "dissatisfaction
of the doomed — and the clamour of children." The memorial was futile,
he told Oronhyatekha. Earlier treaties with the Crown had been replaced
with subsequent legislation, negating presents. Canada's government now
largely operated separately from England, loosening the promises made
by the Crown. If the native peoples did not adopt the white man's ways,
without his vices, then they would fade away. They must settle and learn
to be farmers, become educated in the white man's system, and adopt the
white man's economy. The queen could not be faulted for consequences
that came from the laws of nature. And, Acland concluded, the changes to
land laws that the Haudenosaunee protested had partly resulted from the
dishonesty of some of their own people.

"'I know all these things,'" Oronhyatekha supposedly said, "as big
tears rolled from his large soft eyes — 'I can write only what the greater
number of the chiefs in council agree — and the greater number will not
see.'" Still, Acland was impressed enough to introduce Oronhyatekha to
Sir Edmund Walker Head, the governor general of Canada, who also
questioned Oronhyatekha about treaties.[21]

Acland and Oronhyatekha hoped to see each other again as the royal party continued its tour in the United States. As he had written earlier, Oronhyatekha left for Cincinnati that fall, and though Acland wrote him there from Pennsylvania, Oronhyatekha had already left the city. What became of his "lucrative position" is unknown, but Oronhyatekha travelled as far as St. Louis, returning to the Grand River after almost four months.[22] He did not see Acland again for over a year.

Later biographies state that the Prince of Wales invited Oronhyatekha to study at Oxford. However, it is clear that it was Acland who suggested Oronhyatekha consider coming to Oxford. The governor general had also attended Oxford, and perhaps the three men further discussed the idea during their introduction. Head may have also known Oronhyatekha's grandfather, George Martin, and wished to act on behalf of this strong Mohawk loyalist's grandson. In any case, Oronhyatekha took this discussion to be an invitation, and set attendance at Oxford as a personal goal.

A CLOUD OF SUSPICION

The hoopla that preceded the royal visit quickly subsided at the Grand River. The agitation following the appointment of George H.M. Johnson to the position of Confederacy Council interpreter rekindled, and now there was a new crisis with which to contend. In 1861, the Crown trustees who managed the Grand River land and trust funds informed the council that all of their investment in the Grand River Navigation Company — a substantial part of their trust — had been lost with the company's declaration of bankruptcy. It was a devastating blow for the community.[23]

The company had been established in 1832 to build a series of dams and locks to make the Grand River navigable for the shipment of goods like milled flour and lumber between Brantford and the mouth of the river on Lake Erie. Without the knowledge of the Haudenosaunee, officials had funnelled large sums of their trust funds to buy company stock and sold their lands to finance further investments. While the company significantly benefited the developing economies of the Grand River valley, it never made a profit and relied heavily on infusions of Haudenosaunee funds and land sales to keep it in operation. Whenever the Haudenosaunee heard of any plans of the company, usually from disgruntled employees and investors, they vigorously protested to the Indian Department, but to no avail.

The death knell for the company had come several years before, in 1854, with the opening of the new and much more efficient steam railway service between Brantford and Buffalo, New York. By the time the navigation company claimed bankruptcy, some estimates placed the Haudenosaunee liability at as much as 80 percent of the debt.

A sense of mistrust permeated the community through much of 1861. These were uncertain times, and the different attempts to regain control over the community's fate divided it. In response, the Confederacy Council began to appoint disgruntled community members to be pine tree chiefs as a way to mollify the tide of criticism and paranoia, and to stop them from advocating for an elected council. Further, the council was constantly at odds with the Indian Department officials, often holding meetings without them and then informing them of their decisions rather than allowing consultations.

Oronhyatekha was not immune to this state of affairs. After he returned from the United States in February 1861, he came under an ever-growing cloud of suspicion. As an official delegate of the Confederacy Council during the royal visit, he was accused by his cousin, George Johnson, of misappropriating funds dedicated for the celebrations. Oronhyatekha demanded an investigation, and eventually the council cleared him of any wrongdoing and declared that he had done his duties faithfully. He stayed at home for a few months, and then in July moved back to Tyendinaga to teach until December 1861. Learning that Oronhyatekha intended to travel to England in the new year, the Tyendinaga council attempted to entice him to stay, offering to pay his board and lodging, give him cleared farmland, build him a house upon it, and increase his annual salary another ten pounds for a total of forty pounds. But Oronhyatekha was intent upon his goal of further education and returned to Grand River in mid-January 1862 to say goodbye to his family.[24]

By this time, the internal affairs of the Grand River community had burst open, and the gaping wound provided an opportunity for those disillusioned with the chiefs' leadership. Isaac Powless and other young Christian Mohawks circulated a petition that sought the dissolution of the Confederacy Council in favour of an elected style of government. They

SS *City of New York.*

presented their petition, signed by 167 individuals, to both the Indian Department and the Confederacy Council. Although divided on how to proceed, the council immediately dismissed the petition; the Indian Department distanced itself from these internal politics, rejecting the petition on grounds that no provision in current legislation permitted any native community in Canada to establish an elected form of government. They also rejected the petition on the racist basis that the Haudenosaunee were not adequately prepared for this style of government.[25]

But the petition sent shock waves through the community. Those who had authored it sought refuge in sister communities, but advocates continued to agitate for change long into the future, father to son to grandson. The unrest vexed the Grand River community for over sixty years, until 1924, when the federal government abolished the Haudenosaunee Confederacy Council and forced compliance with the provisions of the 1876 Indian Act, which called for the establishment of elected local governments, although very few supported this.

These controversies may have provided a further impetus for Oronhyatekha to consider his own options. It is rumoured that Oronhyatekha signed the petition for an elected council; if this is true, it could have reinforced his decision to move to England. By February 1861, when he was charged with misappropriation of funds, he had already decided to attend Oxford and wrote to Acland asking about the cost. On January 30, 1862, he left for New York City, and the next month he set sail across the Atlantic.[26] He was probably the first native person to ever attend Oxford.

SETTING SAIL

When Oronhyatekha packed his possessions, he did so with the intent of never returning to the Grand River valley to live. Whether he told his family is unknown, and while he would return to visit the Grand River, he never lived there again.

Such a mission was risk-laden. He had staked his future on the British, a people who had come to be seen by many at the Grand River, including himself, as having abandoned them. He had left the community under a cloud of suspicion. The mission was made even more perilous by Oronhyatekha's own actions — he had failed to seek permission from either the Indian Department or the New England Company to leave. In fact, he saw the Reverend Abraham Nelles the same day he left Canada and deliberately chose not to tell him of his plans.[27] Perhaps it was a touch of arrogance, bolstered by his recently acquired British connections, that caused him to exclude Nelles. Like the Haudenosaunee, he was as sovereign and independent as he had stated in his speech to the young Prince of Wales. Unless he acted, these were just words on a piece of paper.

On the trip overseas, Oronhyatekha may have mused about earlier Haudenosaunee who had travelled to Britain to visit the queen and Crown officials to reaffirm their alliance. Oronhyatekha travelled in a much more modern steam-powered vessel, the SS *City of New York*. Leaving from New York City on Saturday, February 15, 1862, he arrived in Liverpool, England, about a week later. From there, he likely boarded the train to London and then on to Oxford. While he had not asked permission to leave the reserve, his passage was noted far and wide in the British, Scottish, and American newspapers, a precursor to his fame later in life.[28]

CHAPTER 3
ORONHYATEKHA, M.D.

OXFORD UNIVERSITY

Oronhyatekha later advertised himself as an Oxford-trained doctor, despite the fact that he only spent one month enrolled at the university. However, Oronhyatekha cherished his friendship with Sir Henry Acland and his time in England for the rest of his life, despite its fraught beginnings.

Oronhyatekha arrived in England in late February 1862. While he had travelled throughout eastern Canada and the United States, he must have been impressed by the stately manors that dotted the countryside on his train ride to Oxford. As the train approached each station stop, the sparsely populated villages of farming communities and rolling green pastures of sheep and cattle gave way to cramped towns shrouded and discoloured by a monotonous shade of dark grey-black. A fog of coal dust, smoke, and ash replaced the fog of the sea. Oronhyatekha must have recognized place, street, and even family names as these had been dutifully replicated by the settlers near his home in the Grand River valley. He may have been pleasantly surprised by the mildness of the weather compared to the severity of the February ice and snow that blanketed the valley he had left behind. The average daytime temperature in Oxford that month was just over seven degrees Celsius; back at home, meanwhile, the average daily high was close to minus four degrees, and it had snowed for seventeen days that month.[1]

After days at sea bracketed by train travel, Oronhyatekha disembarked in Oxford, a town of approximately thirty-five thousand people.[2] Exhausted and near penniless, he strode into the train station with all that he possessed packed into a suitcase. He had accomplished a dream.

UNCERTAIN BEGINNINGS

Thomas Plowman recorded Oronhyatekha's arrival in Oxford in his memoirs. An employee of Oxford's Bodleian Library, Plowman met Oronhyatekha there, but he had also learned about him from Acland's neighbour. One day, Plowman wrote, the bell at Acland's home rang, and the servant who answered was surprised to see a "coppery-complexioned gentleman, with deep-set black eyes and prominent cheek-bones. His costume denoted a desire to defer to European susceptibilities, with an inadequate knowledge of how to give effect to it, for, although he had dispensed with his war paint, he retained his moccasins and deer-hide." Of course, by 1862, most Haudenosaunee individuals wore European-style clothing; Plowman's interpretation says more about the stereotypes held by the English than it does about reality. Instead, community history says that Oronhyatekha wore the formal outfit made by his sisters to meet the Prince of Wales in 1860.

Oronhyatekha explained to the servant that he wanted to see Acland, but was informed that he was out, Plowman continued. Oronhyatekha would wait, he said. Upon Acland's arrival home, Oronhyatekha greeted him with "outstretched hands," exclaiming "I am come, I am come … You say come, and I come." He wished to be educated and then return to his people to instruct them in what he had learned. According to Plowman, one of Acland's first thoughts was to find clothing for Oronhyatekha more suitable to Oxford. Having done so, Acland began to introduce Oronhyatekha to Oxford life, including bringing him to the Bodleian, where Plowman met him. Here, Plowman remembered that Oronhyatekha "signed his name … in good, bold characters in the visitors' book."

Although the Grand River community had supplied him with some money, little of which was left after his travels overseas, supposedly Oronhyatekha believed that Oxford would provide all of his necessities. Again, this interpretation of a native unaccustomed to white ways is unlikely; Oronhyatekha knew full well from his three years at Kenyon College the expenses involved in higher education. Plowman concluded his story by summarizing Dr. Oronhyatekha's future successes; it "is pleasant to know," he wrote, "that the child of the prairie amply justified the interest taken in him."[3]

Indeed, Acland took Oronhyatekha under his wing. Of most immediate concern was the financing of his education and other expenses. Acland's daughter, Sarah, remembered that Oronhyatekha arrived at the family home with four shillings and two pence in his pocket — less than twenty pounds in today's terms. James Heywood, an official of the New England Company (NEC), gave him a great coat and a pair of gloves to wear in the chill weather, and Lady Acland purchased household goods such as knives and forks for him.[4] The NEC seemed to be the obvious choice to fund the rest of his needs.

Oronhyatekha had written to Acland in February 1861 reaffirming his desire to attend Oxford University. That same month, Acland and the governor general of Canada, Sir Edmund Walker Head, contacted James Heywood in order to start a discussion about funding. Heywood informed Acland that the NEC had previously funded native students and offered to consult the NEC governor, Edward Busk, about Oronhyatekha's case. He also asked where Oronhyatekha lived in Canada so that an NEC missionary could visit him. At that time, Heywood was clearly unaware that Oronhyatekha was well known to the NEC in Canada, more specifically to his local missionary Reverend Abraham Nelles, and that the NEC had funded part of his time at Kenyon.[5]

When Oronhyatekha arrived in England almost one year later, the matter of his funding was far from resolved. In late February 1862, Heywood met Oronhyatekha at the NEC office in London but awaited the arrival of the treasurer to discuss funding. Heywood noted that the winter term of the medical school ended in March and the new one began in May. In between, Heywood suggested that Oronhyatekha attend lectures at the University Hospital, as was allowed for students intending to enter a medical program.[6]

Reverend Nelles soon interfered. Apparently, Nelles had written an uncomplimentary letter about Oronhyatekha to Acland in October 1860, when the royal party was still touring North America, so when the NEC in England contacted Nelles about Oronhyatekha attending Oxford, not only was he surprised, he was incensed. Nelles wrote back, charging Oronhyatekha with a number of offences. He noted that Oronhyatekha had been accused of appropriating Confederacy Council funds, even though it had acquitted him the previous year. Nelles also stated that Oronhyatekha had seduced one or more young women and fathered a child during his time at Kenyon College. This charge has never been substantiated in any other document, but Nelles gave this as the reason he had stopped funding Oronhyatekha's American education while he was at Kenyon. It is no wonder then that Oronhyatekha never informed Nelles that he was leaving for England.

Oronhyatekha was clearly distressed by this turn of events, for he wrote two separate letters to Acland on February 26, responding to the charges. In the second letter, Oronhyatekha asked Acland not to contact Nelles, but to allow the NEC to hear his side of the story at a meeting arranged for the following week. This was not because he wished to hide information from Acland, but because he himself wished to explain. As well, he did not want Nelles to think that his word had influence with Acland and other people of his standing.

His biggest opponent at home, he wrote, was his cousin George H.M. Johnson, who had a close relationship with the NEC missionary Adam Elliott and who had married Elliott's sister-in-law. It had been Johnson who had accused Oronhyatekha of embezzling funds meant for the royal visit, and Johnson had also declared several times that Oronhyatekha would not be received in England without the support of Elliott and Nelles. Thus, Oronhyatekha argued, if Acland wrote to Nelles, he would only receive a biased interpretation. If he returned home, Oronhyatekha continued, they would think themselves proven right. He pleaded with Acland to spare him that humiliation, however, Oronhyatekha concluded his letter by stating that he was willing to abide by the NEC's decision.[7]

OXFORD LIFE

While the NEC debated the validity of Nelles's charges, Acland integrated Oronhyatekha into his family and Oxford life. In 1930, Acland's daughter remembered him, commenting that he was always "very silent & never spoke even to us children unless spoken to." Acland also likely paired Oronhyatekha with Thomas Outram Marshall, a young student from the East Indies who had matriculated the previous fall. Studying for the ministry at Oxford's New College, Marshall took charge of Oronhyatekha.[8] Acland also introduced Oronhyatekha to the aristocracy and academics in his inner circle of friends. Whether this extended to royalty is not known, though community history tells of the queen's standing invitation to Oronhyatekha to visit her.

In later years, Oronhyatekha fondly remembered not only James Heywood, but also three other men — Captain Montagu Burrows, Sir Alexander Beresford Beresford Hope, and Max Müller — all of whom he met through Acland.[9] Burrows tutored students at Oxford to assist them in passing their exams, and in 1862, the same year that Oronhyatekha came to Oxford, Burrows was appointed to the first ever Chichele Professorship of Modern History. Burrows would continue to write to Oronhyatekha after he returned to Canada.[10]

Sir Alexander Beresford Beresford Hope was an author and Conservative politician. Oronhyatekha humorously reminisced about meeting Hope: he was sitting quietly for some time in a large room at Hope's home when Hope, a small man, threw open an unnoticed side door, rushed in, and grasped Oronhyatekha's hands with his. In the midst of this hurried greeting, Beresford Hope's monocle fell out; it was then, Oronhyatekha remembered, that he discovered that it was possible to need corrective lenses for only one eye.

Acland and Hope debated Oronhyatekha's future education. Hope suggested that perhaps King's College or St. Augustine College at Canterbury, the latter institution he himself having helped establish, would be best and offered to contact the warden at the latter institution.[11] Hope also offered his opinion about Nelles's charges, stating that he agreed with Acland's beneficent view of Oronhyatekha. He believed that if Oronhyatekha was now intent on being useful to his own people that he should not be judged too harshly. If the charges *were* true, he thought Oronhyatekha should own up to them, but if they were not, then he believed him to be much maligned.[12]

Acland also introduced Oronhyatekha to the noted linguist and professor Friedrich Max Müller. Müller wrote of their first meeting: "I had a visit to-day from a Mohawk Indian; he has learnt Latin and Greek, he has come to Oxford to study here, but fancy! he has brought his feather garb with him, but according to the statutes of the University, I am afraid he may not wear it. I found the man very intelligent, and the savages more tolerant than many a civilized man." He planned to have Oronhyatekha teach him how to speak Mohawk so that he could compare all of the Haudenosaunee languages. He was just waiting for some books to arrive, he wrote to Acland, before he began this research. Oronhyatekha willingly responded to his queries about Haudenosaunee law, customs, and language, and helped him prepare a skeleton Mohawk grammar.[13]

There was great interest in England and the academy in the indigenous peoples of North America during this time, fuelled by studies by amateur anthropologists such as Lewis Henry Morgan, who wrote the epic 1851 book, *The League of the Iroquois*, and by natural scientists like Charles Darwin, whose 1859 *On the Origin of Species* ignited debates over the origin of man himself. The fields of archaeology and anthropology began to emerge as serious scientific disciplines, and universities began to include such subjects in their course offerings. At the same "Indian clubs," which offered their members a way to learn about and even play-act as natives, became popular in Europe and North America.

Müller took an interest in Oronhyatekha's education. He agreed with Acland that Oxford would provide him a liberal and scientific education, believing that Oronhyatekha would never be satisfied in life with only scientific research. Oronhyatekha, Muller suggested, needed to have a more humanistic profession such as teaching, healing, or preaching. Naturally, Müller also hoped he would take an interest in the history of the Mohawk language. Müller further advised Acland that he should support Oronhyatekha, despite Nelles's charges, unless it would cause a public scandal. No one, he wrote, went through life without making mistakes, concluding that Oronhyatekha might yet become a successful man.[14]

For his part, Oronhyatekha discovered the venerable institutions of British academia. Heywood took him to University College and the British Museum during the first few days after his arrival in England. Oronhyatekha gave a talk at the University Galleries (now the Ashmolean Museum), located next to the Bodleian Library at Oxford, although the audience is unknown. It seems likely he talked about the state of native peoples in Canada, for Heywood wrote to Acland, saying that he did not object to Oronhyatekha speaking to the public; in fact, he believed a strong advocate for Canadian natives would have the power to obtain justice for them. He suggested that perhaps a talk at Exeter Hall, a London building that hosted religious and philanthropic meetings, would be a good place for Oronhyatekha to speak.[15] As noted in Plowman's memoirs, Oronhyatekha also visited the Bodleian Library, which houses an ancient collection of documents and books dating back hundreds of years, including a Gutenberg Bible, the first book printed by movable type in Europe.

These visits instilled in Oronhyatekha an appreciation for museums and collecting, a leisure pastime of prominent members of British society. During his lifetime, Acland acted as a curator of the University Galleries and the Bodleian Library and helped establish the Oxford University Museum of Natural History, which opened in 1861. Both he and Müller later donated collections to Oxford's Pitt Rivers Museum of anthropology and archaeology, which opened in the 1880s.

Acland and Oronhyatekha remained friends for life. This photo was taken during a visit to England in June 1892.

Oronhyatekha also secured a *carte de visite*, a calling card that featured one's photograph, an upper class fad that gained popularity in the 1860s. Visitors left their cards at the homes they visited, and traded them for cards of famous people. *De rigueur* individuals also compiled and displayed photo albums of such cards in their parlours. Oronhyatekha obtained his from the studios of Hills and Saunders, one of the leading social photographers of the nineteenth century, which carried with it the seal "by Appointment to Her Majesty." For his picture, Oronhyatekha dressed in his royal visit suit and re-created the tattoo on his face, although he did not wear the silver nose ring.

Oronhyatekha's presence did not go unnoticed by the British press. A long article appeared in the *London Review* in mid-March. It is hard to decide whether the tone of the article mocks Oxford conservativeness, adheres to long-held stereotypical and racist views of native peoples, or perhaps both. Certainly, the author was not well educated about the Canadian landscape and the lifestyle of mid-century Haudenosaunee.

The article is worth quoting at length. Couched as an example of how Oxford was becoming increasingly liberal, Oronhyatekha was supposedly the "earliest pioneer" of grateful native students from Canada who would come to Oxford "like some Eastern pilgrim to the shrine of Mecca." The article explained Oronhyatekha's background, including how he met the Prince of Wales in 1860. The Haudenosaunee, the article suggested, were "still no doubt disporting themselves in unrestricted enjoyment amid their native haunts besides the Grand River." But not Oronhyatekha:

> To chase the elk, to scour the prairie, to rob the beaver of its skin, and the buffalo of its tongue — to smoke the pipe of peace, or wield the tomahawk of mutual encounter, might satisfy a lower ambition, but possessed no charms for the loftier intellect, and grander schemes, which already predestined Oronhyatekha to a career of learning and civilization. To rear a dusky brood, and wear out an unhonoured and illiterate existence in forest pursuits, formed no part of the daring schemes which already were maturing in his breast.

His meeting with the prince, a former Oxford student, the *Review* depicted as turning "a vague desire into a distinct revolution, and a fond imaginative dream into a realized possibility." Stereotypically, the publication continued, "Oronhyatekha probably stood aghast at revelations of so extraordinary a character, emanating from so distinguished a source." At this point, the *Review* imagined, Professor Acland "lay open new domains of thought to the wondering denizen of the woods."

The *Review*'s unflattering depiction of Oronhyatekha's naïve response to these two learned men conveniently ignored the fact that Oronhyatekha was well-travelled, and had already completed two years of college, learning Greek and Latin, classics, and history. "Oronhyatekha's red skin would be died [*sic*] with a richer hue than ever, as he found how he had all his life been breathing, eating and digesting, in the most grovelling ignorance of arterial machinery, nervous organization, and muscular energies," the *Review* stated. It continued,

> Now probably the microscope was brought out, and the horror-stricken savage introduced to the horned monsters and long-coiled serpents which carry on a fierce campaign in the confines of a drop of water ... Oronhyatekha, no doubt, with native promptitude, produced his tomahawk, and was with difficulty restrained from assaulting an enemy, of whose size and vigour his eyesight gave him such convincing evidence. As wonder after wonder disclosed itself, how magical a glow must have seemed to be shed over the city where such discoveries could be made ... How dull did the gayest phase of Mohawk existence seem when contrasted with the intellectual excitements of an Oxford career?

The article concluded by wondering about the potential difficulties Oronhyatekha might encounter in England, again showing a lack of knowledge about native peoples generally, and the Haudenosaunee in particular. What would he wear, for instance, the *Review* asked its readers. If Oxford insisted that he wear the traditional academic gown, it hoped that the university would allow the rest of his person to remain in his "primitive and natural simplicity." Of course, he would want to be painted and show his tattoos, like any other "well brought-up young Indian." If he had had killed enemies in battle, which the *Review* suggested was likely, he would want to wear his trophy scalps. Surely, even if this seemed offensive, the vice-chancellor of Oxford would make allowances for so "natural a desire." Oronhyatekha would also likely wish to smoke during lectures, for it was well known that native peoples smoked pipes while thinking.

The author also speculated that Oronhyatekha might have trouble with the religious nature of the university; certainly, if he should "insist upon having a few favourite 'squaws' quartered in wigwams about the college gardens, no objection could be raised." After all, upset domestic arrangements were "fatal to intellectual exertion," and Oronhyatekha "must not be coerced into an unnatural celibacy." Any number of wives "short of three" would be "illiberal," the author declared. For what "Mohawk of ordinary sensibility could endure expatriation and the abandonment of field exercises without every solace that the partners of his joys and sorrows may be able to afford him?" the *Review* asked. However, the *Review* was sure that as "time goes on he will find the yoke of civilization less oppressive, and … that learning and pleasure go often hand in hand."[16] Unfortunately, we cannot know whether Oronhyatekha read this article, and if so, what he must have thought of how he and his people had been depicted.

A DREAM DENIED

While Oronhyatekha explored Oxford life, the NEC debated funding his education. Whatever transpired at the March meeting at which the NEC heard Oronhyatekha's response to Nelles's charges, the company decided to ask for more information. In early March, the former governor general of Canada, Sir Edmund Head, suggested that Heywood should contact David Thorburn, the former Indian agent at the Grand River. Head himself wrote to Thorburn in mid-March asking if he had any knowledge of Nelles's charge that Oronhyatekha had seduced a woman.[17] Thorburn replied that he knew of no charges against him.[18]

By this time, Oronhyatekha seems to have realized that his hopes of attending Oxford might not come to pass. In his most heartfelt letter to

Acland yet, Oronhyatekha explained that he had given up the study of divinity for a number of reasons, including being suspected of immorality. Even if he was a minister, he wrote, people would still speak ill of him and not believe his sermons. He also did not believe that playing cards or dancing was evil, and that with his independent spirit, he feared he would never rest content under the power of a bishop. He was uninterested in law and did not feel himself to have a talent for it. That left medicine, Oronhyatekha reasoned. A physician was independent, worked hard for his money, and could be successful if attentive. A doctor was called upon by friends and those who trusted in him. Relieving pain and suffering would be satisfying and would reflect credit onto his people. If ever this situation with Nelles was resolved, he would prefer to take a B.A. course and keep up with medicine at the same time. Then he could attend London University College, or if not, go home to Canada and enroll in college there to finish his medical degree. Any time he spent at Oxford might perhaps be counted towards a degree by another institution.

In any case, Oronhyatekha wrote that he trusted Acland, and so would tell him everything whether bad or good, so that Acland could judge him for himself. Seemingly enclosed in this letter is a brief history of Oronhyatekha's life, from his birth at the Grand River, to the royal visit two years earlier. In it, Oronhyatekha explained how his entire class at Kenyon was expelled, but then readmitted within a few days. Oronhyatekha had left at the end of term some months later, but only because he was short on funds and not because of the expulsion. He also explained how he had been charged with misappropriation of funds after the royal visit. No mention of Nelles's allegations of seduction and fathering an illegitimate child was included in this life story. Oronhyatekha thanked Acland for all of his assistance and asked him not to bother the NEC for funding. He was grateful for all their help, but he had come to England to see him, and having done so, could now go home contented.[19]

Ten years later, Oronhyatekha wrote that he remembered the day that Acland heard about his supposed expulsion like it was yesterday. When Acland told him he should come clean to Max Müller, Oronhyatekha feared that Acland believed the charges. Oronhyatekha almost, he wrote, decided to say that indeed he had been expelled so he could go home, because he could not bear to be with Acland if he believed it to be true.[20]

It is not clear when Oronhyatekha's short-term expulsion from Kenyon College came to the attention of Acland and the NEC. Perhaps Oronhyatekha's confessional letter was in answer to these charges. In early April, Head and Acland asked Richard Pennefather, the superintendent general of Indian Affairs, if he had ever seen the letter of honourable dismissal that Oronhyatekha procured on leaving Kenyon. Head was dubious that their query would amount to much since he had been told there was no such letter in the department's records. At some time in the past, Nelles had written to Francis Wharton, a professor at Kenyon College, asking about Oronhyatekha's conduct. Nelles told the NEC that Wharton wrote that the faculty at Kenyon had refused to provide such a letter of honourable dismissal because of Oronhyatekha's character. Whatever the truth may have been, Wharton's alleged letter was apparently one of the factors in Oronhyatekha leaving Oxford. Yet Oronhyatekha's patrons had faith in him. Head confessed to Acland that he did not attach much value to Nelles's statements. Müller was also lenient, though Head suspected that Müller was selfishly influenced by his desire to keep Oronhyatekha close to learn the Mohawk language.[21]

The NEC agreed to address the matter at its annual meeting in early May. There will be great discussion, Heywood wrote to Acland, for he thought that Nelles had been trusted too much and without question.[22] Seemingly, the NEC agreed with Heywood, for on May 6, 1862, Oronhyatekha enrolled at St. Edmund or "Teddy" Hall. Oxford recorded each matriculant in the same way, in a format that expressed the heritage and status of the student's family, a typical emphasis in British culture. Oronhyatekha's entry reads: "Oronhyatekha, Peter, 6s. 'Indiani,' of Grand River, or Ouse, Six Nations District, Canada. ST. EDMUND HALL, matric. 6 May, 1862, aged 21." The indication "6s." designated him as the sixth son of his father, but notably, Oronhyatekha omitted any other details about his father, Peter Martin, a silence he kept for much of his life. Most entries provided the name, location, and occupation of the student's father. Instead, Oronhyatekha included his native heritage.[23]

To begin, the NEC arranged for a twenty pound grant, and even Heywood's aunt contributed five pounds to the fund for Oronhyatekha.[24] This would have been enough money to pay his tuition for one year, but not living expenses.[25] The spectre of his expulsion from Kenyon persisted.

Acland consulted Müller about the situation, who thought the kindest thing was to send Oronhyatekha home but to still seek out financial assistance for his medical studies. Müller was hopeful about his future. If Oronhyatekha has learned, he wrote, that society has laws just as the natural world did, and that one's knuckles will be rapped if these are challenged, then this was a valuable lesson. Müller wrote that in a decade from then, he would not be surprised to hear that Oronhyatekha was a useful member of society. No effort was useless, he said, and Acland's kindness to Oronhyatekha would bear fruit.[26]

One month to the day that Oronhyatekha enrolled at St. Edmunds, he seriously considered returning home. Writing to Acland, he reasserted that he had left Kenyon under good standing and vowed to prove it in the future. He philosophized that suffering for his mistakes now would perhaps make him more virtuous in the future. In ten years, Oronhyatekha hoped to be able to show Acland that his assistance had benefitted him. In the meantime, he did not want Acland to think that all Indians were bad because he had been. If all else failed, Oronhyatekha proposed to return home and settle on his land and in five years have enough saved to pay for school. Even demonstrating that native people could be successful farmers would be almost as good as proving that native people were intelligent enough to become physicians, lawyers, or clergymen. Perhaps he would be able to influence the next generation to be what he himself had strived to be. The steamer from Liverpool left the following Thursday, Oronhyatekha noted, and he asked for a loan to pay for his passage. Presumably, Oronhyatekha left for home the following week.[27]

Why was Nelles so adamant about Oronhyatekha's moral character, to the point that he destroyed his chances to study at Oxford, despite his patronage by Acland and the former governor general of Canada? After three months in England, perhaps just as he was debating leaving, Oronhyatekha wrote to Acland, explaining Nelles — he strongly believed that no Mohawk could succeed without his approval and guidance, and acting without it would anger Nelles. Oronhyatekha knew if he went to England and succeeded, not only would Nelles be angry, but it would undermine his power at the Grand River. He also thought Nelles a hypocrite. While an apprentice shoemaker, Nelles saw Oronhyatekha fall in with unsavoury companions and said nothing. But Nelles disliked it when Oronhyatekha

Oronhyatekha's *carte de visite.*

tried to better himself without his guidance. Several years later, Daniel Wilson of University College, Toronto, who taught Oronhyatekha history and English, confirmed this impression of Nelles. Wilson wrote to Acland that Oronhyatekha was firmer and more self-reliant than most natives, and he suspected that this made missionaries uncomfortable. The Indian Department, Wilson continued, was so controlling that it treated First Nations like children, and so if individuals like Oronhyatekha had a streak of independence, they were labelled as *troublesome* and *rebellious.*[28]

Why did Oronhyatekha return to Canada when he had the support of Acland, Head, and the NEC in England? His last letter to Acland suggests a faltering of confidence in achieving his goals. His attempts to gain

Nelles's approval through education — a pillar of the missionary's assimilative program — had failed, and instead he found himself personally
attacked. He had begun to question Nelles's integrity; as a missionary he
was spiritually bound to help his fellow man, not spread rumours and
undermine attempts to improve himself. Yet Oronhyatekha also knew
that Nelles had power and influence at the Grand River and that he could
destroy his reputation and undermine any success in Canada. He preferred to go home to clear his name.

During the previous few years, Oronhyatekha's relationship with
Nelles had transformed from supportive to adversarial. However, it had
been replaced by a much deeper friendship between Oronhyatekha and
Acland, which lasted the rest of their lives. They continued to exchange
letters and Oronhyatekha returned to visit his old friend whenever he was
in the United Kingdom. In later years, Dr. Oronhyatekha said Acland was
more like a father to him than a tutor. It was providence, he believed, that
Acland had accompanied the Prince of Wales overseas.[29]

RETURN TO TYENDINAGA

Not surprisingly, when Oronhyatekha landed in Canada in June 1862,
he did not return to Grand River but chose instead to go to Tyendinaga.
He had family there. His mother, Lydia, had been raised at Tyendinaga,
and one of his older brothers had built his home and family there.
Oronhyatekha had been welcomed in the past by the community as a
valuable teacher. At Tyendinaga he found some time and space to reflect
on his recent journey abroad and to plot his next course of action.

As it is now, Tyendinaga was a predominately Mohawk community.
The people who settled here traced their homelands to the area around
Fort Hunter in upper New York State. They had embraced Christianity
early on, with a very small number following the more traditional
Longhouse religion. While the Grand River community had a large population of Mohawk people, they were a minority relative to the aggregate
population of the Onondaga, Cayuga, Oneida, Seneca, and Tuscarora.

Politics at Tyendinaga differed from that at Grand River. Tyendinaga's
founder, Captain John Deseronto, proved to be an autocratic leader.

Little escaped his attention in the development of the community. With his death in 1811, the community struggled to manage its affairs and for several decades after Deseronto's death, changes in leadership frequently occurred. By the 1850s, Tyendinaga had adopted a structure in which male heads of families received titles and positions that allowed them to make consensus-based decisions for the community. Like the Six Nations at the Grand River, however, they maintained their allegiance with the British Crown.

For the next year and a half, Oronhyatekha taught school at Shannonville, a town established on land leased by the Tyendinaga community, and in between semesters worked with Dr. John W. Fergusson of Hamilton, a recent graduate (1855) from a medical school in Ohio.[30] Fergusson was a physician, surgeon, and the coroner for Wentworth County. Unusually for the time, Fergusson also practised homeopathy, licensed in 1860 by the Homeopathic Medical Board, and perhaps Oronhyatekha found him sympathetic to native medicine.[31] During this time Oronhyatekha continued to make plans to attend medical school, and to clear his name from Nelles's charges about his conduct while at Kenyon College.

It is clear that Oronhyatekha's British patrons Henry Acland and James Heywood never gave up their faith in him. In July 1862, the very month after Oronhyatekha left Oxford, Acland and Heywood decided that Sir John Langton, a provincial politician and former vice-chancellor of the University of Toronto, should serve as the trustee for Oronhyatekha's grant. Originally, it seems as if Acland and Heywood planned that Oronhyatekha would begin at the medical school in Toronto in October of that year, when the new semester started, but it would take much longer for the NEC and Langton to set up the education grant. In the meantime, Heywood asked Acland to write a letter vouching for Oronhyatekha's behaviour while at Oxford, likely to stave off any future charges.

In the following months, Oronhyatekha wrote to Acland of his thoughts. He had felt like giving up upon his return to Canada, and feared staying at home since there were many temptations. Perhaps he should leave until he had become an important person. At first he begged to return to England, but he also contacted Dr. John Rolph, the founder of the Toronto School of Medicine. If he could not return to England, he wrote, perhaps he could attend this institution.

As always, money was an issue. His family made only enough to live, so he could not ask them for help. The Haudenosaunee Council made decisions unanimously, and he believed that it would not approve an application for a grant. He had his teaching salary, and ninety-six acres of land, which by August 1862 he had put up for sale. If they were purchased, it would give him $2,000 for the support of his mother and sister, and a stipend for school. He planned to return to teaching in October for at least one year. Before then, however, he would work with Dr. Fergusson.

Oronhyatekha also wrote to Benjamin Lang, now the acting president of Kenyon College. Lang replied that no records had been kept of his, or of the entire sophomore class's expulsion. Lang, a professor in 1860, surely must have known of this expulsion at the time. Kenyon was not a large school, having only 121 students that year, and the faculty numbered less than ten individuals. The fact that he could not remember it only two years later suggests the minor nature of the occurrence. Oronhyatekha notified Acland of Lang's letter, and also stated that he had asked Nelles for an apology, who had only replied that he would await the development of events. In the future, Oronhyatekha intended to dig up his tomahawk against Nelles, who, he calculated, had cost him at least four years of his life.

Hoping he could attend the Toronto School of Medicine in the fall of 1862, John Rolph wrote to Oronhyatekha in early October. Rolph agreed to write to Acland sanctioning his course of study, but said Oronhyatekha should start for Toronto immediately. Rolph promised to find him lodgings in the city. But at that point Oronhyatekha had already committed to the school trustees at Shannonville, and his grant money had still not yet been arranged.

By early November, the NEC had agreed to fund his medical education at fifty pounds a year, but it had not yet heard from John Langton. The NEC also agreed to pay off Oronhyatekha's debts at Kenyon College, which it estimated to be the equivalent of fifteen pounds. The NEC, Heywood told Acland, had ultimately concluded that Nelles had been wrong in cutting off Oronhyatekha's grant while at Kenyon, especially since he had not even notified the NEC.

In the absence of any response from Langton, in January 1863 the NEC began looking for alternative individuals to administer its grant for Oronhyatekha. At this time, Oronhyatekha mused about his career path in his letters to Acland. Acland had once suggested that he work for the Geological Survey of Canada after obtaining his medical degree. This not only would bring him influence, he believed, but also put him into contact with native peoples other than his own nation. The respectability of such a position weighed heavily, as always, with Oronhyatekha; he was convinced that the amount he could benefit his own people would be proportional to his position in society. But his patrons did not seem to give these thoughts serious consideration and felt that a medical education would not be of much use to the survey. If he was to pursue such employment, he would have to take mineralogy and geology at university, not medicine, Acland wrote. Oronhyatekha knew his true interest was medicine.

Later that month, the NEC finally heard back from Langton, who agreed to act as the trustee of an education fund. At the NEC meeting, however, one of the members raised the issue that Nelles had not yet responded with the amount of debts left at Kenyon College, nor about their enquiries about Dr. Fergusson. The NEC decided to wait to hear from Nelles before finalizing their plans. Whether the NEC ever heard from Nelles is unknown, and Langton had not replied to the NEC's plans to send him the first fifty pounds for Oronhyatekha's first year even as late as July. October, the month that medical school started, was drawing closer, with still no funds in place.

Despite Benjamin Lang's assurances the previous fall, Oronhyatekha continued to investigate the charges against him while he waited for his grant to be arranged. To Acland he wrote philosophically that he had been taught that the Great Spirit did not bring trouble to someone who loved him, but that his father had said that one should do their best to defend their life. Perhaps referring to Nelles, Oronhyatekha stated he did not see why if "one should pluck my right eye I should not pluck out both of his eyes instead of allowing him to operate upon my left eye also." While religion lauded forgiveness, Oronhyatekha himself believed there were exceptions to the rule. He had consulted with Dr. Fergusson, who had advised him not to contact Francis Wharton, now Kenyon's president. Oronhyatekha disagreed, and wondered if he could demand a correction to Wharton's earlier statement to Nelles that Kenyon had not issued him an honourable letter of dismissal.

It is unclear if Oronhyatekha did write to Wharton and if he replied, but Lang did in the spring of 1863. Lang believed Oronhyatekha had taken too much trouble to disprove these malicious charges. Instead he should show by his conduct that they were untrue. Lang assured him that he believed in his honourable dismissal by President Lorin Andrews at the time, since there was no evidence to the contrary. Even if Oronhyatekha had violated the rules, Lang said, he was sure an honourable discharge would have been provided anyway. Unfortunately, it was now impossible to get a dismissal letter because the faculty had changed since 1860, and Andrews had died in the American Civil War.

Lang did attempt to clarify the chain of events, however. Apparently Nelles had written to Wharton asking about Oronhyatekha's conduct at Kenyon. Whatever Wharton said, Lang asserted, had not been meant to disrupt his studies at Oxford.

Ever eager to prove his innocence, Oronhyatekha forwarded Lang's letter to Acland, hoping that it would clear his name and prove that he had been honourably dismissed from Kenyon. Never, Oronhyatekha wrote, had he forgotten the anguish of sitting in Acland's dining room in 1862 and finding out his behaviour at Kenyon had been questioned. If Acland found Lang's letter sufficient evidence, Oronhyatekha could accept that all things happened for a reason. No one could accuse of him not trying hard to become useful to his people, though he wondered whether it was in God's plan. Though very difficult to read, Oronhyatekha's letter also seems to further implicate Nelles in ruining his chances at Oxford. While Nelles had implied to Oronhyatekha in 1862 that Wharton prompted the questioning of Oronhyatekha's character, Wharton now said that Nelles had contacted him. Concluding his letter, Oronhyatekha asked Acland to send him the *Oxford Journal* so that he could keep up-to-date with his activities, and, if she consented, a photo of Mrs. Acland. Despite his anxieties over Acland's opinion of him, Oronhyatekha clearly still felt a bond with him and his family.

ELLEN HILL

While he continued to brood on his past, Oronhyatekha also planned for his future career and family. While teaching at Shannonville, Oronhyatekha caught the attention of Ellen Hill (1843–1901) or Deyorouseh (Pretty One). From a prominent family at Tyendinaga, she was a direct descendent of Joseph Brant and John Deseronto. Before she married, Ellen lived at home with her widowed mother Catharine. In her late teens, she, her older brother William, and her older sisters Hannah and Elizabeth helped out on the family farm, while her younger sisters, Lydia, Susan, Mary, and Sarah, attended school. Their father, John W., died sometime between 1852 and 1861 as he is recorded by the 1852 census but not in 1861. Together, the family lived in a one-storey frame house.[32] The Hill family held considerable amounts of land, including a low-lying island known as Captain John's Island, in the bay opposite the bustling town of Mill Point, later known as Deseronto. Mill Point was a busy place owing to its sheltered location for shipping goods by lake barges and, with the recent arrival of the railway to the north, it developed mills for lumber and farm produce. The town also included a church, an Orange Lodge, a school house, and a community meeting hall.

Ellen and Oronhyatekha married in the late summer or fall of 1863, and began to build their home, a double log cabin, in Deseronto.[33] Oronhyatekha planned to support himself and Ellen with a small farm and a herd of beef cattle. The council had granted him land in September 1863, but the following February he wrote to the Indian Department asking when he could take possession of it. Clearly this issue lay unresolved as in the late fall of 1865, he wrote again to say that this land had been ploughed by another man, indicating that this individual intended to retain possession of it. He asked the Indian Department to resolve this matter since he wished to farm it himself that coming spring.[34] This delay in his farming plans must have been compounded by his enrollment in medical school in fall 1863, because he planned that the farm income would help support his family while he was at university.

Compared to Oronhyatekha, relatively little is known about Ellen. Community stories describe her as slight but feisty and forthright. She more than capably managed their farm at Tyendinaga in her husband's absence, sometimes with the assistance of her brother who lived nearby. In later years, she was described as an "educated women" with a "girlish enthusiasm," and a "ready sympathizer" and "capable helpmate" to her husband, although she preferred to retire from the publicity that surrounded him. Fellow Foresters described her as "gentle," "gracious," hospitable, caring, and a good friend. An active member of the church — the "right hand"

Ellen Hill.

of the rector at Deseronto — she was "[s]trong in her convictions" and "lived her religion."[35] During his four years at medical school in Toronto, Oronhyatekha made frequent trips to Tyendinaga to be with his wife.

TORONTO SCHOOL OF MEDICINE

In 1827, the Church of England founded King's College, later to be known as the University of Toronto. In the 1860s, it did not offer a medical degree, but rather examined and granted degrees to medical students who attended proprietary schools, such as John Rolph's Toronto School of Medicine (TSM). By the time that Oronhyatekha enrolled at the TSM in 1863, Rolph's instructors had defected from his leadership and re-established another school with the same name.[36]

It is unclear if Oronhyatekha applied to the TSM through the usual process or through the ongoing agreement between Toronto University and the Haudenosaunee. In the 1840s, King's College floundered under financial strain, control over its endowment, and criticism from non-Anglican religious officials. As a partial remedy, in 1842 an Order in Council directed the Indian Department to secure an endowment of land from the Haudenosaunee's Haldimand Tract in order to generate an income. The Haudenosaunee Confederacy Council agreed to an endowment of some 1,200 acres with the condition that its community members could attend the university at no cost.[37]

Whether this arrangement factored into Oronhyatekha's admission is not known, but Indian Department officials must have taken it into consideration had they denied him permission to attend the university. By this time, Oronhyatekha was a known irritant to both government officials and missionaries. His firm resolve had brought him into conflict with those who tried to exercise their authority over him, and they interpreted his determination as arrogance. Even if Oronhyatekha entered the Toronto School of Medicine through the agreement between the university and Haudenosaunee, and thus did not pay tuition, the New England Company still established a fund for him of fifty pounds a year, held in trust by Henry Holmes Croft, a professor of chemistry at the university.[38] Seemingly, the first of this money arrived in late 1863 because he is listed as a student at the TSM for the academic year of 1863–64. Oronhyatekha entered the Bachelor of Medicine (M.B.) program with a small group of about twenty-five other students in his year.[39] Surprisingly, he was not the only native student. Peter Edmund Jones, the son of the Methodist missionary, Peter Jones, had also enrolled at the medical school. It is unknown whether the two young men had known each other previously. Peter Edmund had not attended the Mohawk Institute; a sickly child, he had spent much of his time at home. He was from the New Credit reserve, which abuts the Grand River, and his father was a prominent member of the community, so it is possible they had met before.[40]

In the mid-nineteenth century, physicians considered a broad liberal education the proper foundation for a medical degree, rather than the focus on science that developed closer to the turn of the twentieth century. A liberal education was thought to develop the "character and culture" of a gentlemen, which all doctors should be.[41] So Oronhyatekha's first year at university consisted of courses in classics, English, natural history, mathematics, and history. At the end of his first year, in April 1864, he wrote his matriculation exams. Of the nine young men examined in the Third Class honours group, Oronhyatekha placed first in classics, English, and natural history, second in history, and third in math.[42]

A few months later, in August, the question of Oronhyatekha's supposed past immoral conduct arose again. On behalf of the Reverend G.A. Anderson of Deseronto, W.R. Bartlett, a superintendent in the Indian Department, contacted the Grand River Indian agent, Jasper Tough Gilkison, asking about Oronhyatekha's past conduct. "Charges were made against him regarding some affair with an Indian woman or women," Bartlett wrote, "which he denies." Referring to correspondence left by David Thorburn, the previous agent, Gilkison noted that Thorburn had replied that he knew of no charges stemming from earlier inquiries. More recently, however, Nelles had told Gilkison that though he had never been convicted, Oronhyatekha had "seduced a young Indian girl & had a child by her." "Judging from what I have heard," Gilkison continued, "I should say the Six Nations have no particular confidence in Martin, but of late years he has not been much with them."[43] While this letter may have raised some questions, it did not prevent Oronhyatekha from continuing medical school, as it had at Oxford, nor did it prevent the NEC from furnishing him with his yearly grant. In fact, this particular charge never seems to have been asserted by anyone ever again.

In his second and third year, Oronhyatekha spent most of his time at what became called Moss Hall, the building for medical education, which was located near the current provincial legislature off College Street. His classes now focused on science and medicine, and included anatomy, botany, physiology, surgery, medicine, chemistry, obstetrics, pharmacy, and medical jurisprudence.[44] These classes reflected the fact that most physicians were general practitioners at that time, rather than specialists, and thus needed to be familiar with basic surgery, midwifery, and diagnosing and treating all diseases. A typical day consisted of lectures in the early morning and late afternoon. In between, students took clinical instruction at the Toronto General Hospital, the Toronto Dispensary, and the Toronto Lying-In Hospital, observing surgeries and making rounds with licensed doctors.

As he had at Kenyon College, Oronhyatekha had an active social life during his studies. He would later confess that he was a "joiner."[45] The

University of Toronto Monthly magazine noted that he became distinguished in boxing and shooting during his time at school.[46] As a member of the University Rifles, a militia unit for students, he participated in its second annual shooting match, winning a silver cup and four dollars. He also competed in the third annual meeting of the Upper Canada Rifle Association in 1865, tying for third place in the fifth match and winning first place in the seventh match, a competition class for those who had been unsuccessful in previous classes. Together these three prizes totalled twenty-eight dollars, a large sum for the time, over half of the amount that the New England Company granted him per year for his education.[47] In the late 1850s, he had joined the Independent Order of Good Templars, a temperance organization, and presumably attended meetings in Toronto.[48] He also joined King Solomon's Lodge, a Scottish Rite Masonic lodge in Toronto.[49]

Though he never became a member, in 1865 he delivered to the Canadian Institute a paper on the Mohawk language with a brief history of the Haudenosaunee people, the Confederacy, and its military contributions to North America. One of the pre-eminent historical and scientific societies of Canada at that time, Canadian Institute members met regularly to hear papers on a variety of topics and to examine the contents of their nascent museum. Oronhyatekha's professors likely introduced him to the organization. Daniel Wilson, who taught Oronhyatekha history and English, and Henry Croft, who taught him chemistry and held his education fund in trust, belonged to the institute and edited its publication, the *Canadian Journal*. Like Müller before him, in Oronhyatekha Wilson found a knowledgeable anthropological informant. One of Canada's early anthropologists, Wilson, who had an archaeological and ethnological museum at University College and also served as the institute's curator, certainly would have been interested in Oronhyatekha. How much time they spent together is unknown although two decades later Wilson described Oronhyatekha as a friend and in future publications he accredited information on the Mohawk language to him.[50]

Oronhyatekha introduced his paper to institute members as part of his hope to be able to contribute information to anthropologists. He argued that proof of the origin of native peoples was more likely found in oral tradition than in proposed theories that compared similar customs of various peoples. This theory of diffusion proposed that all cultural traits arose from one centre and then spread to other societies. Nevertheless, Oronhyatekha asserted that the science of language was useful, and further that a comparison of the six languages of the Haudenosaunee demonstrated that they all had a common origin in the past.[51]

As if he was not busy enough with his studies, voluntary associations, and the farm at Tyendinaga, Oronhyatekha and Ellen started a family. Their daughter Catherine Evangeline Karakwineh (Moving Sun), known always as Bena, was born in 1864.[52]

Oronhyatekha wrote his final exams for the M.B. in 1866, achieving Third Class honours in all of his classes. Perhaps the demands of his family life greatly preoccupied him, for he achieved lower rankings than he had during his matriculation exams, finishing near the bottom in all classes except chemistry and medical jurisprudence, in which he placed in the middle of the pack. Nevertheless, the M.B. degree entitled him to his provincial licence to practise.[53]

Acland and Oronhyatekha continued to correspond with each other throughout his studies in Toronto. In the one letter that survives from this time period, Oronhyatekha thanked Acland in November 1864 for the gift of his recently published biography on Sir Benjamin Brodie, an English physician who specialized in orthopaedics. Not a day had gone by, Oronhyatekha wrote, that he had not thought of Acland and his wife. When he felt in poor spirits, he imagined the advice that Acland would offer, and when he was joyous, he thought how happy Acland would be for his success. As he often did in his letters to Acland, Oronhyatekha again asserted his intent to clear his name; he would never be satisfied otherwise.[54]

Now, in May 1866, Oronhyatekha wrote that it was his great pleasure to announce that he was now entitled to a licence to practise, and once again emphasized that he had never once forgotten the kindness shown to him by Acland, his wife, and his Oxford friends. He anticipated that he would soon hold a position that would force his opponents to respect him, even though the circumstances that had forced him to leave Oxford were still a canker in his heart. He would never rest until the truth came out.[55]

Ever ambitious and eager to prove himself, Oronhyatekha enrolled in the Doctor of Medicine or M.D. degree.[56] In the meantime, his education was interrupted by the Fenian Raids during the summer of 1866.

MILITIA SERVICE

Strained relations between Britain and the United States during the American Civil War had raised the possibility of war, with the colonies on the front line. Young men throughout the British Empire were encouraged to enlist in rifle associations in preparation. The U.S. Civil War ended in April 1865, but a new fear arose — an invasion of Canada by the Fenian Brotherhood. Fenians were Irishmen who agitated against the British rule of Ireland, and many having fought for the north in the Civil War, they were trained in battle. In fall 1865, the Fenians' Third Congress called for an invasion. They hoped to force Britain to free Ireland by holding Canada for ransom. Fenians also expected that the many Irish immigrants in Canada would rise up and join their cause. Rumours of anticipated Fenian attacks flew throughout spring 1866. In particular, the rumour that an invasion would occur on March 17 — St. Patrick's Day — resulted in the call-out of the Queen's Own Rifles of Toronto at the end of January. Starting on March 7, the militia drilled daily, but by the end of the month, with no evidence of an invasion, drilling was reduced to only two days a week.

Oronhyatekha had joined the University Rifles, Company 9 of the Queen's Own Rifles of Toronto (QOR), as a private by August 1865. That year, he obtained his first- and second-class certificates in military instruction from the service militia in Hastings County. A first class certificate recognized that a student was able to "drill and handle a *Battalion* in the field, and who shall have acquired a competent acquaintance with the internal economy of a Battalion." On March 8, 1866, one day after the Queen's Own mobilized for duty, Oronhyatekha re-enlisted as a corporal. The Fenian Raids were his opportunity to follow in the footsteps of his grandfather, father, and uncles, distinguished veterans in their own right.[57]

The Queen's Own had been formed in 1860 by an amalgamation of several rifle companies. The next year, chemistry professor Henry Croft, a man who dreamt of a glorious military career, assembled students in the convocation hall at the university and rallied them to form a volunteer rifle company. This became Company 9 of the Queen's Own, led by Croft and John Cherriman, a math professor. Croft, also the holder of Oronhyatekha's education trust, may have influenced him to join. Trinity College also formed a militia, Company 10 of the QOR.

THE BATTLE OF RIDGEWAY

In April 1866, Fenians gathered in eastern Maine ready to capture Campobello Island in New Brunswick but they only managed to steal a flag from the customs house before the militia and the British army forced a retreat. A more serious threat came the next month. On May 31, the mayor of Buffalo, New York, telegraphed the mayors of Hamilton and Toronto, alerting them to hundreds of assembled Fenians preparing to cross the Niagara River into Canada. Church and fire station bells began to sound across Toronto, calling the militiamen to mobilize at their drill shed by 5:00 a.m. The university agreed to waive any remaining exams for those enlisted. Many students had already finished, however, and left the city, so Company 9 and 10 were not at their full strength.

The Queen's Own, including some of the University and Trinity College Rifles, boarded the *City of Toronto* steamer ferry that morning, accompanied by a brass band playing "Tramp! Tramp! Tramp! The Boys Are Marching," an adaptation of a popular American Civil War song. The ferry headed for Port Dalhousie at the northern mouth of the Welland Canal, one of the Fenian targets. After a three-hour trip, the militiamen took the train to Fort Erie, across the river from Buffalo, arriving there in the afternoon of June 1. They billeted with local families overnight.

Meanwhile, a number of students had been told to stay behind in order to find the rest of their company members. Eventually another 125 men gathered and were transported to the Niagara region, arriving at dawn on June 2. Like most other companies. Company 9 was poorly equipped, with insufficient ammunition, no food, water, medical supplies, or even maps. They also had had little or no training with the Enfield rifles given them and some had never even fired live ammunition.

Marching from the Ridgeway village train station at 6:00 a.m. on a hot and sunny Saturday, the Queen's Own Rifles encountered the Fenians around 7:30 a.m. With Company 9 in the middle of the formation, the militia advanced up Ridge Road, skirmishing in the fields to the left and the forested ridge to their right. The Fenians had raised fences in the fields and so the Queen's Own had to climb over or under them while coming under fire. Unknowingly, they were moving towards the main body of the Fenians, who were drawing them in. Company 9 came upon the main group of Fenians alone.

Confusion ensued, and later the militiamen reported a number of slightly different versions of what happened next. Seemingly, some of Company 9 heard someone give the order to form a defensive square with their bayonets fixed, which was the usual move against cavalry. However, the Fenians had no cavalry. They were then ordered to reform their columns and retreat. In the confusion, Company 9 received the brunt of the attack and retreated in panic to Port Colborne.

The two-hour Battle of Ridgeway left nine dead, two of whom died a few days later of their wounds, and twenty wounded. The heaviest toll was from Company 9. Toronto witnessed the funerals the following Tuesday.[58]

Numerous accounts of Dr. Oronhyatekha's life state that he fought in the Fenian Raids, but no documents exist to confirm this. Only twenty-eight company men made it to the battle as many students had left Toronto for home during the exam period. Only the dead and wounded are recorded by name and Oronhyatekha was neither. His name does not appear in the newspaper report of veterans who marched in the twenty-fifth anniversary of the battle in 1891, when 30,000 people gathered at the Volunteers Monument in Queen's Park in Toronto.[59] Nor did he apply for the Fenian Raid medal when the Canadian government made it available several decades later.

ORONHYATEKHA, M.D.

On November 16, 1866, Oronhyatekha received his M.B. at the annual convocation ceremony.[60] Earlier that fall, he had returned to university to obtain his Doctor of Medicine degree, which required him to write a thesis on a topic of his choice. That semester, Daniel Wilson sought advice from Acland about Oronhyatekha's future. Wilson wrote that at university, Oronhyatekha was diligent, energetic, had "shown good capacity," and won the favour of both his tutors and his professors. Now Wilson attempted to have him appointed as physician at the Grand River, or in another capacity within the Indian Department. But officials once again raised the charges laid against Oronhyatekha while he was at Oxford. Supposedly, they said, these allegations had resulted in the Prince of Wales abandoning Oronhyatekha. Wilson hoped Acland could shed some light

Dr. Oronhyatekha's
graduation photograph.

on these accusations so that they could be refuted.[61] But Oronhyatekha
would have to wait another six years before his name was finally cleared.

Unfortunately, we do not know what topic Oronhyatekha chose
to pursue as his thesis — if for instance, it was on a traditional native
medicinal topic like that of his classmate Peter Jones — but we know
that he had completed it by early summer of 1867. He sat the licence
examination administered by the newly established provincial College
of Physicians and Surgeons; registered on May 22, 1867, he was granted
licence number 709. His time at university officially ended with his convocation in early July 1867.[62]

Until recently, Oronhyatekha has been considered to be the first native doctor in Canada and commemorated as such. A recent biography of Dr. Peter Edmund Jones, however, demonstrates that, in fact, after attending the TSM for two years, Jones transferred to Queen's University in Kingston and graduated with his M.D. in spring 1866. He received his licence to practise just six months before Oronhyatekha did, in November 1866.[63] Nevertheless, Oronhyatekha's attainment of two university degrees in the mid-nineteenth century, a time when racism and the restrictions of the Indian Act hindered many from higher education, is remarkable and should not be dismissed simply because he was not the first to do so. In the next two decades, he would go on to achieve even greater accomplishments.

CHAPTER 4

A SEARCH FOR INFLUENCE

MEDICAL PRACTICE

After his graduation in 1867, Dr. Oronhyatekha practised in a number of small towns before settling for over a decade in London, Ontario. Moving frequently, he sought out professional and personal opportunities of influence. Having succeeded in his first goal to become a physician and defying his opponents like Reverend Nelles in doing so, he next sought to use his position and networks to improve the condition of his people. The result was a remarkable diversity of activities, though they were not without controversy.

Not surprisingly, Dr. Oronhyatekha initially returned to the Tyendinaga area. He had not really lived at the Grand River reserve since leaving for college in the United States, and in 1873 he transferred his band membership to Tyendinaga. He established his first practice in Hastings County, in the town of Frankford, a small centre of about five hundred people. Located on the Trent River, Frankford had been born of the lumber and grist-mill trade. Just under forty kilometres from Tyendinaga, Dr. Oronhyatekha was much closer to home than he had been when living in Toronto. If he wanted to travel home, there was a daily stage to the Grand Trunk station at Trenton, and from there a train to Deseronto.

In Frankford, he opened his practice as a physician, surgeon, and "accoucheur," or obstetrician, his office located at the back of the drugstore he took over from merchant M.B. Roblin. Oronhyatekha and Co. sold books and "pure drugs, chemicals, medicines, oils, etc." He also served as a coroner for Hastings County.[1] Dr. Oronhyatekha also took it upon himself to mentor his brother-in-law George Hill, who had followed in his footsteps and was attending medical school at Albert College, Belleville, an institution affiliated with the University of Toronto. Like Dr. Oronhyatekha, the New England Company (NEC) funded George's education, no doubt at his suggestion. During the summer of 1870, George assisted Dr. Oronhyatekha in compounding medicines for his patients in Frankford.[2]

ORONHYATEKHA, M.D.

TORONTO UNIVERSITY,

Physician, Surgeon & Accoucheur.

THE Doctor also studied in Oxford University, England, under the care of Doctor Acland, Physician to H. R. H. the Prince of Wales.

OFFICE AT ORONHYATEKHA & CO.'S DRUG STORE.

ORONHYATEKHA & CO.,

DEALERS IN ALL KINDS OF

Pure Drugs, Chemicals, Medicines,

OILS, &c.,

AT VERY LOW PRICES FOR CASH.

Like his other advertisements, Oronhyatekha's ad in the *Directory for the County of Hastings,* 1869, emphasized his training under Acland at Oxford, and Acland's association with the Prince of Wales. In the 1870s, his business card also referred to his skills in traditional native herbal medicine.[3]

In the mid to late nineteenth century, the medical profession began to professionalize and standardize. In 1865, just before Oronhyatekha graduated with his M.B., the General Council of Medical Education and Registration was established; four years later it merged with other organizations to become the College of Physicians and Surgeons of Ontario, which licenses and regulates doctors. In 1867, doctors formed the Canadian Medical Association in order to represent the emerging professional discipline of medicine and to advocate for the public on health issues. Dr. Oronhyatekha was part of this movement. In 1868, he helped co-found the Medical Association of the County of Hastings, which aimed to "advance Medical Science and the interests of the Profession," and in the following two years the membership elected him secretary and treasurer at its annual meeting.[4]

In 1871, Dr. Oronhyatekha chose to move his family to Stratford and partner with recently graduated physician Thomas D'Arcy Lucus. Originally from Stratford, Lucus had returned to his hometown to establish his practice after attending McGill University. Here, Dr. Oronhyatekha became known as a specialist in nervous disorders and throat and lung diseases. By 1872, Dr. Oronhyatekha practised with Dr. James A. Robertson, or perhaps the three men practised together. A local history called Dr. Oronhyatekha one of the town's "finest and most popular doctors" and noted that he was known by the nickname "Old Iron Tea Kettle," an approximate version of his name created by his fellow students at the Toronto School of Medicine as an easier pronunciation.[5] Despite his popularity, Dr. Oronhyatekha stayed only a few years in Stratford, moving closer to Tyendinaga in 1873 and establishing a practice in Napanee.[6]

This move may have been precipitated by his appointments in 1872 as an agent to sort out unpaid land rents at Tyendinaga, and as consulting physician for the Mohawk community, both appointments made by the Department of Indian Affairs. Several years earlier, in 1866, around the same time that Daniel Wilson had recommended Oronhyatekha to the department for a position, some of the Tyendinaga community had petitioned to have him appointed commissioner for the reserve, but due to opposition by other community members, that appointment had been suspended. Two years later, a group of chiefs requested that the appointment be carried through, and John A. Macdonald, then prime minister of the newly formed Dominion of Canada, strongly advised that Dr. Oronhyatekha be appointed in some capacity. Seemingly, Dr. Oronhyatekha and his brother-in-law, also a council member, canvassed the reserve, drumming up support for the proposal. Once again a number of chiefs objected, this time based on the fact that he was not a member of the Tyendinaga band. Indian Affairs officials responded that they would not impose Dr. Oronhyatekha onto the community.

In the fall of 1869, the issue of his appointment was raised once again at a council meeting. Another petition with fourteen signatures had been presented to the government. Dr. Oronhyatekha's brother-in-law spoke on his behalf, so strenuously that the council minutes describe him as "abusive" and having "been excited from drink." Opponents to the petition described supporters of Dr. Oronhyatekha, a strict temperance advocate, as also having been intoxicated; so noisy were these individuals that many of the chiefs abruptly left the council house.

Following this incident, several chiefs sent a letter to Indian Affairs characterizing Dr. Oronhyatekha as being from "a troublesome family who have for years caused dissension in the Bands to which they have been attached." He had a "smooth tongue," but they found him "distasteful" and "devoid of all principle." Not yet cleared of Nelles's charges, once again these were used against him. He had tried to study at Oxford, the chiefs wrote, but had to come home to clear his name; since he never returned, they assumed he had not been able to do so — obvious evidence of guilt in their minds. Yet he advertised himself as an Oxford-trained physician, they accused. The faction that did support him, the chiefs stated, was a small family one and were "some of the most abandoned drunkards." In fact, the chiefs concluded, so many people were opposed to Dr. Oronhyatekha holding the position of commissioner that if he indeed was appointed, it would divide the community, perhaps even to the point of bloodshed.

Yet in December 1872, he was appointed land agent and physician to Tyendinaga, although not all chiefs had been present during the council deliberations. Seemingly, his appointment was greased by his friendship with John A. Macdonald, for whose Liberal-Conservative party Dr. Oronhyatekha had campaigned in the 1872 election. Local Stratford history says his eloquence won the area for the Liberal-Conservatives. Dr. Oronhyatekha himself quipped in later years that this experience meant he spent $2,500 and six days in "buying poultry, pigs, and other farm produce." This must have bolstered their friendship, and in many cases nineteenth-century appointments often operated on trading favours. In writing to Thomas W. Casey, a newspaperman and fellow member of the International Order of Good Templars, who had lobbied on Dr. Oronhyatekha's behalf to be appointed no less than the deputy superintendent general of Indian Affairs, Macdonald said he hoped to "find an early opportunity of employing the Doctor usefully in the public service." This letter was written in late September; his appointment as Tyendinaga physician followed quickly in December. Dr. Oronhyatekha was contracted to visit and treat the sick on the reserve. At Napanee, he opened his office in the Cartwright Block and built a new red brick home at the top of Roblin's Hill.

In the early spring of 1873, several chiefs petitioned Indian Affairs. Dr. Oronhyatekha was attempting to overrule the chiefs in council, they wrote. Further, they feared that either the man in charge of mailing their petition had been bought off by Dr. Oronhyatekha to not do so, or that

The Oronhyatekha home on Roblin's Hill.

Dr. Oronhyatekha had surreptitiously altered the petition to be positive. Two chiefs, Thomas Green and Joseph Penn, wondered if their names had been on the original petition to have Dr. Oronhyatekha serve at Tyendinaga, and if so, said they were forged.

By summer, some chiefs charged him with failing to attend the sick at Tyendinaga. Several times, they accused, he had simply not responded to those who had asked him to visit sick family members. A special council was called to discuss the issue in July, and although others testified to Dr. Oronhyatekha's attentiveness, the council unanimously passed a resolution asking Indian Affairs to remove him as its medical officer at the end of the year. Moving cautiously, Indian Affairs asked Dr. Oronhyatekha to address these charges and also instructed William Plummer, the visiting superintendent in Toronto, to investigate during his visit in October of that year.

After several weeks in England that summer, Dr. Oronhyatekha arrived home to find a letter from Indian Affairs asking for an explanation of the charges of non-attendance. In response, he said that one complaint should be disregarded because the patient was not native, and thus not part of his obligations. Another he stated was a mistake, as the individual in question had visited Dr. Oronhyatekha in his office and said he had been misrepresented. This man later wrote a letter to Indian Affairs stating that he had never complained. The final complaint was also unreasonable, Dr. Oronhyatekha argued. A Mrs. Loft had sent him a message one morning to attend a family member, but his office hours extended until noon for band members who needed prescriptions and consultations. Because the illness was not serious, he decided to stay at the office until noon to serve his other patients. At noon, the second message arrived from Mrs. Loft, at which time Dr. Oronhyatekha left. On his way to the Lofts, he met a third messenger.

Some of the Mohawk community felt that his location at Napanee was too far from the reserve for sufficient medical attention, but Dr. Oronhyatekha said that upon his appointment he had made it clear that he would move there. For financial reasons, he needed to establish a practice in addition to working for Indian Affairs, otherwise he never would have left his large practice in Stratford. In conclusion, he stated that he treated his native patients as well as his white ones, and if any distinction was made, it was in fact in favour of the Mohawk community.

Dr. Oronhyatekha also appeared at a fall council meeting to ask if indeed there were complaints, since he had previously never heard of any. Contradictory to its previous action, this council resolved to write a letter stating it had never heard of any complaints against Dr. Oronhyatekha. When Plummer visited Tyendinaga in the fall, he found a "strong feeling of opposition to him, and the majority of Chiefs, both of the old Council and the new wish[ed] to have him removed." If the council refused to vote for another requisition for his salary, then Plummer took it for granted that his services would cease even though he believed that Dr. Oronhyatekha had carried out his duties well. Dr. Oronhyatekha protested this assumption, stating that the Mohawks provided only part of his salary and since the federal government paid the rest that it could not dismiss him purely based on community complaints.

By spring 1874, Dr. Oronhyatekha still served as the Tyendinaga medical officer although one of the chiefs wrote that no one from the community had called upon his services for the past six months. In consequence, the chiefs wished Plummer to reinvestigate. Plummer called another special council, at which the earlier charges of non-attendance were raised again. Plummer, however, characterized them as of "a frivolous nature." Dr. Oronhyatekha was also accused of ignoring a badly injured man; he countered by saying that the man had been placed under the care of a doctor much closer to his home, and even when Dr. Oronhyatekha had twice visited him, the other doctor objected to his presence. It was not that Dr. Oronhyatekha refused to visit any patients, he argued, it was that they refused to send for him. Although Plummer did not find any wrongdoing, he noted that the community had "no confidence" in Dr. Oronhyatekha and thus the council refused to contribute to his pay any longer. For this reason, Plummer recommended that Indian Affairs cancel his contract.

Likely sensing the inevitable, Dr. Oronhyatekha resigned in October 1874. He, who had professed his desire to help his people since his early twenties, must have been saddened and frustrated by this turn of events. However, he did press for the outstanding amount from an increase in salary that had been promised him by Indian Affairs at the end of his first year. Indian Affairs, although they accepted Plummer's report that he had not committed any wrongdoing, refused him the raise since they believed that he had made no visits for about six months in 1874. Despite

Dr. Oronhyatekha providing proof that he had indeed treated a number of patients throughout that time period, Indian Affairs did not budge.

Dr. Oronhyatekha explained his understanding of the controversy. One real cause of complaints, he asserted, was jealousy. As well, he said, the chiefs had falsely told community members that he would be dismissed in January 1874 and so if they asked him to visit they would have to pay for medical treatment themselves. Naturally, Dr. Oronhyatekha concluded, the community did not request his services after that.

His appointment as land agent also caused conflict. Plots of land at Tyendinaga had been leased out to farmers, but whether individual owners or the band as a whole received the rents was a source of confusion. Dr. Oronhyatekha, attempting to sort out the complicated chain of land leases and transfers, had recommended that all farms on the reserve should be registered. That way all owners and any transfers would be recorded in order to minimize title disputes. Perhaps more controversially, he saw this system of registration as a way to familiarize Mohawks with how whites conducted business and thus prepare them "eventually to take their place as other citizens."[7]

His political troubles were soon augmented by financial ones. In addition to his annual government salary of $500 and his fees charged to non-native patients, Dr. Oronhyatekha supplemented his income with half interest in a general store at Deseronto. Most doctors had a comfortable, but not affluent income, since often patients did not pay their bills in full. According to Ellen, her husband was too kind to his store customers and overextended credit. He took out a loan with his horse and property as collateral, but, shortly bankrupt, Dr. Oronhyatekha decided to move once again.[8]

Dr. Oronhyatekha had extended credit to Mohawks based on future payments of land rents and yearly annuities from the government, although Indian Affairs generally frowned upon the practice. They feared that men might spend more than their income or that they might use the credit to purchase only liquor, both situations that would have left families in need. After he had already begun extending credit, Dr. Oronhyatekha wrote to Indian Affairs asking for permission to do so. His store did not sell liquor and he wrote that when men whom he knew to be "dissipated" asked for credit, he ensured that the food and other goods went to the family. Other credit he gave to those genuinely in need. Most of the time the amounts were paid back, he wrote, but by the fall of 1873 he was owed between

$3,500 and $4,000 in total. Further, that year he had gone to England for two months and paid his locum $200 — almost half of his own annual salary. Dr. Oronhyatekha also provided medicines for the sick out of his pay, leaving him in 1873 with only $100 for his annual income. It is not surprising, then, that Dr. Oronhyatekha claimed bankruptcy. Even in the late 1870s, he was still attempting to settle the back amounts owed to him and the loans he had incurred to cover these amounts.[9]

In late 1874, rumours swirled that Dr. Oronhyatekha was trying to remove Robert H. Dee and William McCargow, the physicians who served the Grand River territory, so that he could become the community's doctor. Even if Dr. Oronhyatekha had wished to return to his home community, when Indian Affairs investigated, they found no evidence that he had ever proposed such a plan.[10]

Rather, from Napanee, Dr. Oronhyatekha moved to Buffalo, New York. The NEC, still a strong supporter, wrote to express disappointment that he was leaving Tyendinaga, since his presence served to "elevate ... their social condition." Was there any medical appointment with a native community for which the NEC could recommend him?[11] Seemingly there was not, for in 1875 the Buffalo *Courier* announced that Dr. Oronhyatekha, "the noted Indian physician and surgeon," had joined with Dr. Lafayette McMichael to open a practice in the Niagara Square. The two advertised regularly in the local newspaper.[12] As before, Oronhyatekha played up his Oxford and royal associations, noting that he had studied under Henry Acland, the Regius Professor of Medicine and Physician to H.R.H. the Prince of Wales. He also called himself the first government physician for the Indians of Canada. McMichael more simply included his previous professorship at the University of Philadelphia. Almost two decades later, the *Buffalo Express* reported that Oronhyatekha left the city when he was appointed as "chief physician to his people in Canada by the Canadian government," which is most likely a reference to his new position as doctor to the Oneida of the Thames, a reserve just south of London.[13] Appointed in either 1875 or 1876, he also opened a downtown practice in London, advertising himself as a specialist in cancer treatment, and in diseases of the nerves, throat, and lungs.[14]

Unfortunately none of Dr. Oronhyatekha's medical records remain, but it is possible to extrapolate what it was like to practise medicine in the

Dr. Oronhyatekha's medical office was located at 390 Richmond Street, in downtown London.

latter half of the nineteenth century from the experiences of one of his contemporaries, Dr. James Langstaff of Richmond Hill.[15] At that time, most physicians were general practitioners, with specialists only arising in the late nineteenth century. Most doctors spent about 80 percent of their time diagnosing and treating general medical problems and compounding medicines, with the remainder of their time split between surgery and midwifery. The most common causes of adult deaths in the last half of the century included pneumonia, tuberculosis, unspecified fevers, and for women, complications from childbirth. Children were most likely to die due to diphtheria, scarlatina, fever, and dehydration caused by diarrhea.

The nineteenth century witnessed the development and use of now commonplace instruments such as the stethoscope, thermometer, microscope, and ophthalmoscope to assist in medical diagnoses, shifting the emphasis on the observation of external symptoms to the detection of internal abnormalities. Opium, laudanum, alcohol, and, to a lesser extent, morphine, were commonly prescribed, and cupping and bleeding continued as popular treatments for a wide range of diseases. Electrotherapy, the use of electricity to treat disease, emerged as a treatment after the 1860s. Doctors began to recognize the importance of nutrition in warding off and recovering from illnesses.

Surgery remained fairly non-invasive until nearer the turn of the century. Anaesthesia had been invented in the 1840s and the use of carbolic acid to sterilize surgical instruments and dressings in the late 1860s. The theory that germs caused disease, rather than noxious airs or "miasmas," gained acceptance in the 1880s, resulting in more systematic disinfection of doctors' hands and instruments. Still, physicians remained reluctant to perform major surgeries due to the likelihood of infection and death. As a result, most surgery consisted of minor procedures such as setting bones, pulling teeth, and lancing abscesses. As the nineteenth century progressed, birth became increasingly medicalized. Still, doctors did not engage in prenatal care, but rather simply attended the delivery of a child, sometimes in addition to a midwife.

VINDICATION

During the first decade of his medical career, Dr. Oronhyatekha continued to keep in touch with his mentor Henry Acland. He visited the Aclands in the summer of 1871, during his trip to England as a member of the Canadian shooting team that competed in the British National Rifle Association competition at Wimbledon.

Rifle-shooting rose in popularity in Canada in the late nineteenth century. Not a purely leisure sport, shooting competitions grew out of the volunteer militia movement. After the withdrawal of British troops from Canada, the threat of the American Civil War and later the Fenians led the government to encourage young men to join volunteer companies and practise their skills through target-shooting matches. As a further inducement, merchants, prominent upper class officials, and local and provincial governments funded cash prizes. At a national level, the Militia Act of 1868 created active and reserve forces for the newly formed country, and that same year the Minister of Militia called for the establishment of a Dominion Rifle Association to promote training in marksmanship. Thus, while rifle-shooting fostered male camaraderie and social prestige through competition, it should also be seen in the context of patriotic duty, and based on the British model, one that included loyalty to England.[16]

As a member of the Queen's Own Rifles at Toronto University, in 1865 Oronhyatekha had placed once in its own match and twice in the annual competition of the seventh military district (Hamilton). He also competed in the 1868 match of the Ottawa Metropolitan Rifle Association, the 1869 and 1870 matches of the Dominion Rifle Association, and the Hastings Rifle Association in 1871. A prizewinner at these matches, Dr. Oronhyatekha also scored as the "best shot" in the 49th battalion (Hastings County) during its annual training in 1870. He later competed at matches of the County of Perth Rifle Association in 1872 and the Lennox and Addington Association in 1874.[17] He was a clear choice for the 1871 Ontario Wimbledon team organized and funded by the provincial government. Representing the town of Belleville, he and nineteen others sailed in mid-June for England. Dr. Oronhyatekha must have found the trip, via the port of Liverpool, reminiscent of his first trip overseas to attend Oxford almost ten years earlier.

As a member of the Queen's Own Rifles and of the 49th battalion, Dr. Oronhyatekha competed with the Ontario team in the Wimbledon competition in 1871. He is depicted in the middle of the scene wearing a top hat.

The British National Rifle Association had been founded in 1859 as a way to train volunteer corps against a threatened French invasion. By 1871, the association had held ten annual meetings on the Wimbledon Common in London, awarding a number of prizes in various categories each year. That year, Dr. Oronhyatekha placed individually and as a member of the Canadian team in a number of competitions, including the Queen's Prize, the Alexandra Plate, and the Rajah of Kolapore's Cup, among others. Altogether, he brought home nine prizes.

Camped with his team on the common, Dr. Oronhyatekha mixed with members of other international teams. The Canadians also entertained Sir Peter Tait, who funded the Challenge Cup at Wimbledon, Liberal politician the Earl of Ducie, Lady Lisgar, wife of the governor general of Canada, and a group of children from a local orphanage. Unfortunately, he missed the royal visit of Prince Arthur, the brother of the Prince of Wales, who came to the Canadian camp in July. This must have disappointed Dr. Oronhyatekha, for in 1869 the Haudenosaunee Confederacy Council had made Prince Arthur their honorary fifty-first chief, and named him Kavakoudge (the sun flying from east to west under the guidance of the Great Spirit).

"Evening at Wimbledon Camp."

The British press mentioned the Canadian team a number of times. The *Newcastle Courant* reminded its readers that Dr. Oronhyatekha had come to Oxford to study after the royal tour of 1860. The *Birmingham Daily Post* described the team's storytelling abilities. One reporter asked Dr. Oronhyatekha how long Canadians lived. He responded with a story about a woman in his band who had been taken prisoner by the French in the Seven Years' War over one hundred years earlier. "One story led to another," the reporter continued, "until the ages of the Canadians ran up to a century and a half." Dr. Oronhyatekha's eloquence also caught the attention of the press. Just before departing for home, the Canadians hosted a farewell party. Among the other speeches, Dr. Oronhyatekha rose to express the affection with which Canadians held England as their mother country and asked the British press to make their feelings known.[18]

This photo in Acland's scrapbook is labelled "Willie Acland Heywood Oronhyatekha."

This photo of a young
Dr. Oronhyatekha, circa
1871, was mounted next
to his son's photo in
Acland's scrapbook.

After his visit to England, the relationship between the Acland and
Oronhyatekha families continued to grow. Dr. Oronhyatekha sent Acland
a photo of his "little Dr. Acland," that is, his son William Acland Heywood
(Deyoronyathe), who had been born in July 1869 and was named after
his father's British mentors.[19] He and Ellen had a second son in 1871,
whom they named Henry Wentworth Herbert (Shorihowaneh), also
after Acland. Noting that one of Acland's sons was interested in farming,
Oronhyatekha invited him to try his hand on his Stratford farm and orchard.

But most important, in July 1872, Oronhyatekha finally proved to
Acland that he had not left Kenyon College under a black cloud. He forwarded to Acland a letter from Eli Tappan, the president of Kenyon, vow-
ing that Oronhyatekha had left in good standing. Tappan had examined

Henry Wentworth Herbert
(Shorihowaneh) was born
in 1871.

the records and questioned faculty; he reported that there was no evidence to suggest that Oronhyatekha had been expelled. Rather, he had left at the end of a complete and successful sophomore year. Apparently Oronhyatekha had also wondered whether he could be awarded either a baccalaureate or an honorary degree, but Tappan responded that this was only possible for those who had been seniors. Oronhyatekha, reliving his difficult time in England, asked Acland whether he now believed that he had not been expelled. In any case, he was well out of reach of Nelles and the others who had tarnished his name over a decade earlier. Please, he concluded, share Tappan's letter with Müller and Heywood. Clearly, Oronhyatekha still worried about the opinions of those who had tried to help him all those years earlier.[20]

Although he had finally cleared his name from these charges that had dogged him for over a decade, Dr. Oronhyatekha became embroiled in the complicated local politics of Tyendinaga, the Grand River, and the Department of Indian Affairs.

POLITICAL STRUGGLES

Often touted as a chief of the Mohawks, Dr. Oronhyatekha never actually achieved this office, although his son Acland would briefly do so.[21] While he had availed himself of a Western-style education and lived most of his life away from the Grand River or Tyendinaga reserves, Dr. Oronhyatekha rejected the assimilationist goals of the Canadian government. One of his dreams, recorded by Alma Greene (Gah-wonh-nos-doh), a Mohawk clan mother, relates his justifiable fears of the government's treatment of his people and motivated him to become involved in local and national politics.

To the Haudenosaunee, dreams can be messages sent from the spiritual world as guidance or warnings. During one of his visits home, Oronhyatekha dreamed that he was standing by the Grand River. As he gazed upon six miles of wheat growing on each side, he felt pleased, knowing that this crop would feed his community. Then, in the distance, he saw a great machine so large it covered both sides of the river. As it advanced along the river, the wheat disappeared and the ground became barren. Despairing, he sat down, his face lowered in his hands. When he looked up again, he saw six miles of corn growing on either side of the Grand. The corn beckoned to him and the rows opened to form a path for him to walk down. As he entered the field, the corn prophesied terrible things to come. He saw a native mother vainly trying to keep her dying baby warm. A wolf cried and a voice announced that yet another Indian had died. Next, Oronhyatekha saw his people forced to leave their land at gunpoint and their homes set on fire. While covering his face for a second time, he felt someone tap him on the shoulder. Opening his eyes, he once again saw the Grand River, but this time it ran black with blood and a nearby willow tree attempted to cover it with its drooping branches.

Although she stated that Oronhyatekha's dream was "like a jigsaw of many pieces; each year a piece falls into place," Green did not further interpret Oronhyatekha's dream.[22] But surely the reference to the wheat and corn on either side of the river symbolized the original land grant of six miles on each side of the Grand given to them by Haldimand, just as the large machine that steadily stripped the land of its crops and impoverished the people must be the slow but advancing program of assimilation by the Canadian government. For Oronhyatekha, who as a child had experienced the violent dispersal and relocation of his family from Martin's Corner and had faced pressure to assimilate, such a dream was all too real. Such dramatic and horrible imagery could be used to incite action and cause change, otherwise the Haudenosaunee culture would die; Dr. Oronhyatekha believed he could be a leader for change and survival of his people.

Although he would never live at the Grand River again, Dr. Oronhyatekha continued to be interested in his home community. Funded by the New England Company, in the early 1870s he delivered a series of well-attended lectures on physiology and temperance to the community.[23] He also offered his opinion on the NEC mission schools, stating that school inspectors should be appointed to visit each school quarterly. This was the case with common schools, and Dr. Oronhyatekha believed NEC implementation of this system would increase efficiency. He also informed the NEC when he moved to Stratford because he would be close to the Grand River in case the NEC wished to entrust him with any projects. When he visited England that summer to compete in the Wimbledon championship, he planned to visit the NEC.[24]

It appears that the NEC followed up on his offer. In 1871, it began to investigate the possibility of opening a fourth mission at the Grand River, this one among the Cayuga community, falling under the charge of Reverend Robert J. Roberts. The NEC charged Roberts with finding a plot of land to erect a church, parsonage, and school house. Two men named Peter Smith and George Loft offered six acres of land for this purpose, and Dr. Oronhyatekha visited them to assess the suitability of the location. Rather than asking for a surrender of land to the NEC immediately, Dr. Oronhyatekha recommended that Roberts begin his work, with the idea that the land transfer could occur later. Dr. Oronhyatekha obtained a quit-claim for the land, which he said, was "as safe to the Company as if they had a deed from the Government." He even contacted builders to obtain several estimates on the buildings required.

He also warned the NEC that a number of traditionalists objected to the presence of Roberts and the new mission. Other NEC missionaries who personally disliked Roberts encouraged these protests and lobbied Jasper Gilkison, the Indian agent, and Reverend Abraham Nelles to write the NEC to have him removed. By spring 1872, these protests blocked NEC attempts to obtain legal title to the land for the Cayuga mission, which required a formal surrender by the chiefs in council. Yet the quit-claim was a legal document, and many of the other churches and schools at the Grand River had been built using similar arrangements, Oronhyatekha explained.

As a way to assure the NEC of the legality of the quit-claim, Dr. Oronhyatekha explained that he himself had obtained a transfer of land at Tyendinaga and had erected a barn and home worth $5,000 on it. Unfortunately, the Reverend G.A. Anderson had objected to his presence at Tyendinaga. But when threatened with eviction based on the fact that he was a member of the Grand River reserve, not of Tyendinaga, Dr. Oronhyatekha declared he would challenge it in court. Since then, he had been left alone. Indian Affairs officials like to stamp out independence, he wrote, and since he was "not particularly fond of this stamping out process," he had made himself "exceedingly obnoxious to some of these officials," particularly Gilkison. For this reason, Smith and Loft had specifically chosen Dr. Oronhyatekha to hold the quit-claim. However, he did twice visit the office of Indian Affairs in Ottawa to try to have the government approve a 999-year lease to the NEC for that property. He had encountered some resistance but in the end had received approval, partly calling upon John Langton, who had once considered being the trustee of his education account and was now the Deputy Minister of Finance. He hoped to forward the legal papers soon, he wrote to the NEC.[25]

Around this time, Dr. Oronhyatekha also became involved in larger issues regarding the administration of the Department of Indian Affairs. In 1870, the New England Company and the Superintendent General of Indian Affairs, Joseph Howe, asked him to attend a Grand River council meeting to explain the new legislation affecting native communities in Canada and to assess their reaction. In 1867, with Confederation, control over native issues had passed from the British Crown to the Canadian federal government. In 1868, the jurisdiction of Indian lands fell under the secretary of state, and the governor-in-council was authorized to make all regulations for the management of these lands.

John A. Macdonald's government implemented the Enfranchisement Act of 1869, which instituted a policy for individual ownership of property rather than the status quo of land being held in common by the band.[26] This law meant to encourage individuals to obtain what were called location tickets, which acted as proof of individual land ownership. Without a location ticket, no native person would be considered as legally owning any plot of land, and anyone without a ticket could be ejected from that land. However, location tickets restricted how land could be passed down. If a man died without children, the land would revert to the band as a whole. If a man had children, they could use the land under the location ticket for their lifetime but not pass it down to their children.

Underlying these changes was the government's goal of converting traditional communal ownership of land to the private property model valued by Western society. Implicit in the private property model was the idea that land owners maintained and farmed it more intensely than land held by a third party; this Eurocentric idea suggested that private property might make native people less lazy, a common nineteenth-century stereotype. Yet the government feared going too far down this path; paternalistically, it worried that if native people owned their land with *no* restrictions they might sell it off and be left homeless.

The 1869 act further promoted the idea of enfranchisement that had been previously implemented in 1857. Enfranchisement meant that a native man would no longer be a ward of the government — the equivalent status of a child — but become a full citizen with all of the rights and privileges that entailed, such as voting. An enfranchised man received an allotment of land split from one's home reserve. To become enfranchised meant being assimilated in the eyes of the government and thus necessitated giving up one's Indian status and the special rights it accorded, such as yearly annuity money, living on one's home reserve, and band membership. Women could lose Indian status through marriage to a non-native man under the 1869 act. Their children also lost their status. One could not be a Canadian citizen and an Indian at the same time. But, the government believed, who would want to remain an Indian rather than become a full Canadian citizen?

Although he later changed his mind, Dr. Oronhyatekha initially believed the Enfranchisement Act to be of great advantage to First Nations and felt that the "more intelligent" of the native community agreed.[27] While it is not known what Dr. Oronhyatekha said about the legislation to the Confederacy Council, both the chiefs and Agent Gilkison objected to his presence. If indeed he supported the legislation at council, his opinion would have been unpopular; the chiefs had protested enfranchisement since its inception in 1857.

Gilkison resented his interference, noting that he had already explained the legislative changes to the chiefs. The council agreed that it had heard Gilkison's report and consulted a Brantford lawyer for further information. Therefore it did not need Dr. Oronhyatekha to attend council and in fact refused him use of the council rooms at one point. Nor would council recognize Dr. Oronhyatekha in any official capacity.[28]

In the summer of 1871, Gilkison complained to the New England Company both about Dr. Oronhyatekha's scientific lectures and his perceived meddling in Gilkison's duties. He also explained that part of the Grand River community believed that the NEC had lobbied the Canadian government to make these legislative changes, which angered them. While the NEC representative thanked Gilkison for his honesty and apologized for any interference, he wrote that recent experience with complaints among its missionaries had taught the NEC to avoid any conflict that stemmed from "personal jealousies." But the NEC characterized Dr. Oronhyatekha's actions as an "indiscretion" at best, undermining the seriousness of Gilkison's complaints. As well, the NEC confirmed that it had not lobbied the government to change Indian laws but it had heard that the community believed the missionaries had done so, and thus asked Dr. Oronhyatekha to explain the situation. At the same time, he could encourage the community to view the new legislation in a positive light.

Gilkison remained dissatisfied. Writing back to the NEC, he stated that the council had unanimously passed a resolution that Dr. Oronhyatekha should not be considered a representative of the Grand River community. He lived too far away from the reserve, and the council had "no confidence in him." Nor did they wish to hear any lectures or receive visits from him as they would not be beneficial but "quite the contrary." Some of the chiefs, Gilkison said, wanted the NEC to be aware of its deliberations. Further, these chiefs told Gilkison about several letters the council had received from Tyendinaga. This community had heard that Dr. Oronhyatekha's brother, Jesse, was attempting to have him appointed to "some office or deputation" and that Dr. Oronhyatekha was planning on visiting the NEC in England as a representative of the Grand River reserve. The Tyendinaga community wanted to know if it was true, and their inquiries had stimulated the council resolution of which Gilkison spoke.

Again the NEC responded that it refused to take sides. In fact, while Dr. Oronhyatekha had indeed visited the NEC members in the summer of 1871 during the Wimbledon competition, he never had said he represented the Grand River community. At the same time, contradictory to the Tyendinaga letters to the Grand River council, seven Tyendinaga chiefs had indeed appointed Dr. Oronhyatekha to petition the NEC for funding for missionaries and teachers on their reserve. Since he was travelling to England that summer anyway, they had asked him to consult on their behalf.[29]

THE GRAND GENERAL INDIAN COUNCIL OF ONTARIO

Dr. Oronhyatekha also became involved in politics on a larger scale. By 1872, the Grand General Indian Council of Ontario elected him as its chairman. Formed in 1870 by the Haudenosaunee and Anishinabe (Ojibwa) communities in the province, the council's immediate purpose was to deal with the recent legislative changes.[30] Meeting in 1872 with groups from Quebec as well, the General Council prepared a petition. Writing from Napanee in June 1872, Dr. Oronhyatekha summarized the complaints to Joseph Howe, the superintendent general of Indian Affairs, as Howe had invited him to do earlier.

The first issue was the policy of location tickets. Dr. Oronhyatekha's report suggested that all native occupants of land should be confirmed as legal owners instead of receiving tickets. This is not surprising since the Haudenosaunee believed they owned their reserve land in fee simple, that is, they could sell or lease it, will it to family members, or as with all Canadians, do with it as they pleased. Dr. Oronhyatekha also suggested implementation of a policy of land title registration similar to that of whites. Again Dr. Oronhyatekha asserted that such a system would familiarize native communities with Western style business dealings and thus prepare them for becoming citizens. Seemingly this was the same idea he put forth to resolve confusion over land possession at Tyendinaga, so it is unclear whether the council had agreed to this policy, or whether Dr. Oronhyatekha took it upon himself to make this suggestion. As was seen at Tyendinaga, not all believed a system of land registration to be the solution because it undermined the traditional communal ownership of land.

The General Council also protested the loss of Indian status for women who married white men and the subsequent loss of property, annuities, and band membership for them and their children. Dr. Oronhyatekha argued that intermarriage with other nationalities should be encouraged because marriage within bands of a small population size could cause mental and physical infirmities. Further, he had observed that this clause actually *caused* immorality; to avoid losing status, native women lived with non-native men without being married. Finally, Dr. Oronhyatekha pointed out that communities were more likely to agree to any future legislation if they were consulted beforehand and their suggestions seriously considered. Instead, they were suspicious of the government's intent.[31]

The Grand River community continued to debate these issues, partly resulting in the establishment of a select House of Commons committee to inquire into the conditions of the reserve. In May 1874, the committee tabled their report, which contained testimony from missionaries (though Nelles seemed to be absent), Indian Agent Gilkison, local doctors, various members of the Grand River community, and Dr. Oronhyatekha, who was still the chairman of the Grand Council. First, Dr. Oronhyatekha logically suggested, each native group should be dealt with separately rather than under the blanket legislation of 1869. Although he acknowledged it would be impossible to have an act for each, he nevertheless argued that legislation should be suitably elastic to cover differences in each community. With that proviso, again he advocated that all natives should be given legal ownership of their land and suggested a land registration system. Interestingly, this time he specified that records of land changes should be kept by members of the community appointed by its council. This idea perhaps indicated the level of community frustration with obtaining information from the government, often a tedious, lengthy, and confusing process. Dr. Oronhyatekha also acknowledged government fears that the ability to sell land could result in an accumulation of property by a small number of native individuals, leaving the rest poorer, but said that this was easily solved by a process of council oversight. Further, he argued that any man without children had little incentive to improve upon his land since it would revert to the band after his death, rather than to family. This "iniquitous enactment" was the real reason, he stated, that the government found First Nations indifferent to providing for their future, another common stereotype in the nineteenth century.

Regarding enfranchisement, Dr. Oronhyatekha could "hardly conceive it possible to frame an Act which would ... more effectually bar any Indian from seeking" it. Anyone enfranchised must surrender all rights, in exchange for paying taxes and being open to be sued for debts, neither of which was the case for those with Indian status. But he was convinced that many would want to be enfranchised if they received their land in fee simple and their portion of the community capital that was invested by the government of their behalf. Last, Dr. Oronhyatekha repeated his assertion that the clause that took away a native woman's status once married to a white man promoted immorality.[32] While only one of many who appeared before the select committee, Dr. Oronhyatekha's beliefs were commonly expressed by others as well.

That following summer, the Grand General Indian Council met at Sarnia to further discuss these and other issues stemming from the new legislation.[33] Delegates from the Grand River, the Oneida of the Thames, and most of the Anishinabe reserves in southern and central Ontario attended. The first order of business was the election of the council's executive. Two members of the Grand River party nominated Dr. Oronhyatekha to be council president. With four nominees to choose from, the delegates ultimately voted for the Reverend Henry P. Chase, an Anishinabe missionary, with Dr. Oronhyatekha coming in second place. Next, the council read the 1869 Enfranchisement Act clause by clause, pausing to discuss each at length. As represented by the printed council minutes, Dr. Oronhyatekha remained uncharacteristically silent.

Gilkison, the Grand River Indian agent, wrote after the Sarnia meeting that he believed hardly anyone from his community agreed with the council recommendations since it was largely made up of Anishinabe. However, many at the Grand River objected to parts of the new legislation, so he suggested that all of the Indian Acts be repealed and replaced by one that would be generally satisfactory.[34] It is unknown if Gilkison's interpretation of the Grand River community reaction to the events at Sarnia is correct, but certainly there had been tension between it and Anishinabe council delegates since 1870. Disagreement between the two groups continued at the 1874 meetings, and in fact a number of delegates withdrew altogether. [35] If Dr. Oronhyatekha also left, that would explain the lack of comments from him in the minutes. Further, it appears as if he was part of a group from the Grand River that formally petitioned the government, stating that the recommendations of the council did not represent their views.[36] Two years later, no Grand River delegates attended the Grand Council meeting, and in 1878 its deputation withdrew once again over political disagreements with Anishinabe representatives. The Grand River community hosted the meeting in 1880, but the 1882 council seems to be the last one attended by its representatives.[37] Although the issues that concerned Dr. Oronhyatekha were debated and modified over the next few decades, these contentious policies embodied in various incarnations of Indian legislation remained until the mid to late twentieth century.

Oddly, despite his characterization of the enfranchisement legislation as a hindrance — not encouragement — to First Nations, in October 1872, Dr. Oronhyatekha wrote to Joseph Howe asking to be enfranchised. He also wished to receive a sum from the money held in trust for the Haudenosaunee in lieu of the allotment of fifty acres of land that he would receive in due course following enfranchisement. This is likely because he did not envision ever returning to live on the reserve. Further, he believed that the land would be more valuable to the Grand River community if it remained as part of its reserve, rather than split from it as would happen under the enfranchisement legislation. Money would be of more use to him and his family, he wrote. The exact amount of money he was willing to let Howe decide upon, but he noted that white farms adjacent to the Grand River reserve sold for thirty to sixty dollars per acre depending upon the improvements made upon the land. He also calculated his life interest in the trust fund, based on the previous year's interest of fifteen dollars and fifteen cents, to be about $400. Elias Hill, the only other Grand River member to apply for enfranchisement, had been offered $300 eleven years earlier when the yearly interest totalled about ten dollars. One month later, Dr.

Oronhyatekha asked the department to also enfranchise Ellen and their children, who were members of the Tyendinaga band. With the money obtained from enfranchisement, he proposed to build a flax and grist mill at Tyendinaga and thus encourage the Mohawk community to farm flax. In the end, however, Dr. Oronhyatekha never finalized his application.[38] Whether this was due to political or financial reasons is unclear, although several years later, he was part of the group of Grand River men who protested enfranchisement. It was, they said, illogical. It targeted their most educated and skilled men, but by taking away their band membership and ability to live on the reserve, it meant that the rest of the band could not benefit from their experience. Furthermore, they felt that were becoming more "civilized" on their own under their own rules.[39]

BAND MEMBERSHIP

Among his deliberations about enfranchisement, Dr. Oronhyatekha also considered the matter of his band membership. In 1865 or 1866, Dr. Oronhyatekha had been struck off the Six Nations of the Grand River list because of his long absence from the reserve. On appeal to the Indian Affairs office in Ottawa, he was restored to the list, only to be struck off again by Gilkison when he moved to Frankford to set up his medical practice. Again he appealed and was restored to the list in 1870 at the order of the Indian Affairs office. In 1873, he transferred to the Tyendinaga band list. In 1875, now living in Buffalo, he applied to be restored to the Six Nations list. The Grand River council deliberated and agreed that Dr. Oronhyatekha should be restored to its list, but Gilkison objected. He felt that no one absent from the reserve, especially someone who lived outside of Canada, should be a member. Chief Josiah Hill wrote to Dr. Oronhyatekha informing him that most of the chiefs, with the exception of a few of the Mohawk ones, were tired of Gilkison interfering in their deliberations, this being just one more example. If Gilkison refused to act, Hill encouraged Dr. Oronhyatekha to write to Indian Affairs to complain.

In response, Gilkison undermined Hill's letter by describing Hill as a drunk who had committed numerous immoral and illegal acts. Gilkison also accused Hill, the council interpreter, of deliberately transmitting an inaccurate account of the council discussion about Dr. Oronhyatekha's application to be placed on the Grand River list. Gilkison also made his dislike, even contempt, of Dr. Oronhyatekha clear. He was "out of all patience, in having to write of Dr. Martin, or, his assumed Indian name (with which he deludes the public) as *I know him*, from his shameless conduct, to be quite unworthy of credit & notice, — that, even his own people discard him." He paid "flying visits" to the reserve during which he influenced some of the chiefs, Gilkison continued, in a way that confounded Gilkison's political advice to the council. This included Dr. Oronhyatekha's attempt to oust Dr. Dee and take his position for himself, though this seems to have only been a rumour. Even one of his teachers — likely Nelles — called Dr. Oronhyatekha *"clever, crafty, & false."* These were not reasons to deny him band membership, Gilkison said, but since he and his family were on the Tyendinaga list, he could not be on another. This argument was rather disingenuous, since it would have been easy enough to remove the family from the Tyendinaga list in the same way Dr. Oronhyatekha had been transferred to it several years earlier. Gilkison also asserted that since Dr. Oronhyatekha now lived in the United States, the matter was moot. Finally, Gilkison noted at the council meeting during which the chiefs approved Dr. Oronhyatekha's return to the Grand River list, a number of chiefs were absent. In these instances, Gilkison said, he disallowed such decisions as they were not truly representative of the council. The real crux of the matter lies in Gilkison's opinion that "It would, under the circumstances, prove unfortunate to authority, were Martin's application granted." Gilkison, like many other Indian agents, struggled to uphold their positions within native communities and thus disliked anyone who challenged their authority.

In response, Dr. Oronhyatekha stated that while his office was located in Buffalo, his family had not moved to the United States. As well, other members of the Grand River lived in the U.S. and had not been removed from the list, though Gilkison disputed this as well. He also explained that Gilkison disliked him, a feeling that had intensified since the select House of Commons inquiry. If necessary, Dr. Oronhyatekha wrote, he intended to bring the matter before council once again, or even to court.

At first, Indian Affairs agreed with Gilkison's decision. But one year later in 1876, when Dr. Oronhyatekha no longer practised in Buffalo, it instructed Gilkison to bring the matter to the Grand River council for resolution. Seemingly, Gilkison did not, for several months later the office again ordered that Dr. Oronhyatekha and his family should be placed on the Grand River list. The matter lay unresolved until 1879 when Gilkison raised the issue at council, and this time, the council split on the matter. According to protocol, all votes must be unanimous. But the Indian Affairs office instructed Gilkison to put them on the Grand River list anyway, because legislation allowed professional men to live away from a reserve and still retain band membership. Early in 1880, Gilkison protested once again. According to him, the chiefs objected to Dr. Oronhyatekha's return to the Grand River list since he had voluntarily transferred his membership to Tyendinaga and further, he had married into a local family and owned property there. The Indian Affairs office overrode his wishes, however, and placed the Oronhyatekha family on the Grand River list.

There the matter rested until 1891 when Dr. Oronhyatekha asked for his family to be re-transferred to the Tyendinaga list since his family now mainly resided there. As before, his request proved controversial. Following protocol, Dr. Oronhyatekha asked the Tyendinaga Council of Chiefs to approve his request during a meeting; those present did so, but those absent protested saying that because it was a matter of land and money, the general council needed to vote on the issue. There were also personal conflicts. Chief Sampson Green apparently disliked Dr. Oronhyatekha because he had had Green arrested years earlier for embezzlement. Others in the community said Ellen interfered in Anglican Church matters and accused her of bribing the chiefs with bags of apples and clothing for their children. Another part of the community felt it was a matter of reciprocity; Tyendinaga members who had moved to Grand River had been refused band membership, while others pointed out that a number of Grand River members had been admitted to Tyendinaga membership in the past. Dr. Oronhyatekha's supporters argued that the Tyendinaga and Grand River communities came from one people and thus transfers should be possible, and pointed to the fact that he employed band members in the winter when work was needed.

Confused over how to interpret the Indian Act, the DIA was unsure whether the Tyendinaga general council or Council of Chiefs should vote on membership issues. Officials did decide in 1894, however, that they needed to investigate the charges of bribery. Perhaps because he had exaggerated or falsified the charges, Sampson Green refused to participate when the DIA investigator visited the reserve that July. He refused to reveal the names of his witnesses to the acts of bribery and stated he was too busy with farming to talk with the investigator, despite the urging of other chiefs to have the matter resolved. Left with only hearsay, the DIA ignored the charges, and placed Dr. Oronhyatekha and his family on the Tyendinaga list. Green and his supporters petitioned Prime Minister John Thompson, stating that the Conservative party would lose eighty votes if the decision was not reversed. Oddly, Green stated that most of Dr. Oronhyatekha's supporters were liberals, even though Dr. Oronhyatekha himself was a staunch Conservative. The decision stood nonetheless.[40]

Why was Dr. Oronhyatekha's band membership so contentious? First, it seems likely that the controversies of the 1860s continued to linger in the minds of the council chiefs. Band membership also meant a right to share in yearly interest money, and as native communities found their annuities mismanaged by Indian Affairs, such as in the Grand River Navigation Company debacle, councils became increasingly concerned about the number of band members sharing the remaining income. Finally, this issue seems to have become a test case in the struggle for power and personal conflict between council chiefs, and between chiefs and the DIA, which often interfered in local politics.

A MOVE TO LONDON

During the initial debates over his band membership, Dr. Oronhyatekha moved to London in 1875 and re-established his medical practice there. He was also appointed as physician to the nearby Oneida of Thames reserve. Like his appointment to Tyendinaga, this appointment may have resulted from his friendship with John A. Macdonald, although Macdonald was no longer prime minister (after 1874). Clearly they were still friends. Dr. Oronhyatekha wrote to congratulate Macdonald on his re-election to the seat of Kingston, and asserted that his return to the office of prime minister was just a matter of time. In conclusion, Dr. Oronhyatekha said he and his family all loved the name of "Sir John." In fact, if his recently born baby girl, Annie Edith, had been a boy, he would have named him John Alexander as an expression of his feelings.[41]

However the appointment arose, Dr. Oronhyatekha visited the Oneida reserve every week for over a decade[42] and opened a private medical practice in downtown London. Little is known of his practice there, but he became well known in the city, attested to by his entry in a local history. The author wrote that the

> pleasant results that have followed his practice warmly testify to his ability and popularity as a physician; and to his natural qualifications as a medical practitioner he brings a mind well stored with medical learning, and an experience which others might well desire. A clever student, he avails himself of the latest and most popular works of medicine, keeping thoroughly posted with the progress of this science. Not only professionally, but as a citizen, in both private and public circles, the doctor has become well and favorably known.

Another London publication stated that Dr. Oronhyatekha was "almost too well known as to require comment."[43]

Part of his fame stemmed from the controversial letters he wrote to newspapers, largely in defence of First Nations culture and society. A reader of the *Toronto Mail* wrote a letter to the editor in November 1875 ridiculing the idea that prohibition improved society. He used native society as proof of his argument. "The North American Indians enjoyed perfect prohibition," he wrote. "They were certainly not industrious; their morality was questionable; their treachery and inhumanity were proverbial," he concluded.

Dr. Oronhyatekha's response was typically humorous but scathing. He assumed the author of the letter, a Mr. R.W. Phipps, was a white man, because all the statements he made except for one were false, and "that, according to our experience, is about the average truthfulness of the average white man." Native peoples, while not "'hewers of wood and drawers of water,'" were assiduous and perseverant in their occupations as warriors and hunters. In fact, the Haudenosaunee, he said, commanded the respect of all native groups from the Atlantic to the Mississippi and from the Great Lakes to the Ohio River. Their confederacy was an "enduring monument to their wisdom, patriotism, and statesmanship," and their constitution "might well have been copied by the framers" of Canadian confederation. As for immorality, Dr. Oronhyatekha continued, certainly it had increased, but that stemmed from contact with white men. "Let Mr. Phipps visit the Six Nations, and he will find that a simple stick or broom placed against the door of a house, indicating that there is nobody at home, more effectually protects the property in that house than all the locks and bars, watchmen, and police are able to do for property in the city of Toronto. Then, again, an Indian cannot curse and swear till he has learned the English or some other language than his own." Still, he didn't think that Canadians were especially immoral, but certainly he thought that "the Indians are ten-fold better than they are, and in the earlier times ... the Indians were ten-fold better than they are now." The Haudenosaunee had a golden rule, Dr. Oronhyatekha wrote: "'Do unto others as they do unto you;' and if Mr. Phipps or any other white man has ever suffered treachery or inhumanity at the hands of Indians, it has been in consequence of the above *Golden Rule.*"

A further exchange appeared from "B.A." of Peterborough, attacking native treatment of women. Both Dr. Peter E. Jones and Dr. Oronhyatekha responded. It was true that Haudenosaunee women worked while the men were hunting or at war, Dr. Oronhyatekha agreed, but they never made them "do all the drudgery while we were engaged in drinking and carousing in some neighbouring beer-shop ... at any rate not till the 'average' white man taught us their superior way of treating women." He asked if B.A. knew that hundreds of women worked in mills and factories in England in drudgery to support their husbands. In comparison, Haudenosaunee women were the holders of political power; they determined who became chief and were consulted by council about matters that concerned the confederacy. In fact, the Haudenosaunee were "so much better than white people owing in a measure to the exalted and untrammelled position our women occupy."

Nevertheless, Dr. Oronhyatekha was "liberal enough to admit that there are some white men who very nearly approach the high standard of morality and true nobility of the Indians." But when he saw his people slandered in a newspaper, he was compelled to show that "the Indian has always been, is now even in his degenerate days, and ever will be, better than any white man on the face of the earth." In fact, he offered his "cordial sympathy" to B.A. "for having been so unfortunate as not to have been born an Indian."[44]

In 1877, he drew media attention in the *St. Thomas Journal* for his comments on the so-called discovery of the grave of Tecumseh, a Shawnee leader who was most known in Ontario as an ally of the British in the War of 1812. In the nineteenth century, there were numerous attempts to locate and excavate Tecumseh's bones. The idea of finding Tecumseh's burial ground originated with supporters of William Henry Harrison, during his American presidential campaign of 1840, who wished to honour him by collecting artifacts from his military triumphs over native groups. The resulting excavation in Ontario was met with outrage, although it seemed unlikely that the bones found were, in fact, Tecumseh's. Subsequently, various communities and historical societies took up the cause to erect a monument near Tecumseh's grave or at a place deemed honourable for his re-interment. One of these groups was the United Canadian Association, whose general mandate aimed to boost Canadian nationalism. Members of this association conferred with Chief George H.M. Johnson, Dr. Oronhyatekha's cousin, who apparently owned a map that indicated the location of Tecumseh's burial based on oral tradition. These directions indeed led to *a* grave, which the United Canadians excavated. They called upon Daniel Wilson, Dr. Oronhyatekha's old professor from Toronto University, to examine the bones and verify that it was Tecumseh. Instead, Wilson pronounced the bones to be an assortment of human and animal bones, likely buried as a decoy.

Not all Canadians believed that Tecumseh should be immortalized with a monument, and several wrote to the *St. Thomas Journal* deriding such an idea. Author "E.D.H." called Tecumseh and other natives savage, pagan, cruel, cowardly, lazy, thieving, and dirty. Dr. Oronhyatekha answered back in anger. If some natives now possessed the traits listed, it was because of the contact they had had with white men, he wrote. In fact, countered Dr. Oronhyatekha, "many of the most cruel and diabolical outrages ... are done by *white men disguised as Indians* — by white men who, *perhaps*, are able to discern only a little less between right and wrong, between justice and intolerant bigotry," than E.D.H. himself. With another sharp dig, he said he was "quite prepared to admit that my race are not what they once were —*brave, just* and *honest*; but my only wonder is that having been in more or less constant intercourse with white gentlemen like 'E.D.H.' for a century or so they are not ten times worse than they are." Further, he cited prominent anthropologists of the time who argued that First Nations possessed many admirable traits. In response, E.D.H. acknowledged that there were exceptions to his characterizations, including Dr. Oronhyatekha himself who had accomplished much.[45]

In 1879, Dr. Oronhyatekha again appeared in local newspapers during his temporary appointment as physician to the Moraviantown reserve during a smallpox outbreak.[46] At first, it was not recognized as smallpox, delaying the use of quarantine. Moraviantown's physician, Dr. George Tye, began to vaccinate everyone, but when some refused to be quarantined, he resigned. Other local doctors also refused to visit the reserve. Chief C.M. Stonefish and the Indian Agent Thomas Gordon called upon the Department of Indian Affairs to ask Dr. Oronhyatekha to attend the community. Ellen and the children worried that he would also fall sick, and, in fact, Dr. Oronhyatekha did not feel safe. But he did not see how he could refuse, since all other doctors had deserted them.

Over a number of days in late May, Dr. Oronhyatekha finished vaccinating most of the Moraviantown residents, but the disease had already spread. In June, to create an effective quarantine, he established a twelve-bed temporary hospital at the home of Jeremiah Stonefish, the brother of the chief, with Stonefish and his wife as attendants. The local band council also appointed Stonefish as a constable so that he could enforce sanitary regulations and ensure that all the sick were moved to the hospital. Council also enacted a bylaw forbidding visits to homes that had sick individuals, enforced by a fine ranging from two to ten dollars. To supervise the hospital and the general disinfection of homes and the clothing of the sick, Dr. Oronhyatekha hired Dr. Kenwendeshon (John C. Maracle), a Tyendinaga Mohawk who practised in Syracuse, New York. Kenwendeshon was a nephew through Ellen's family and had apprenticed with Dr. Oronhyatekha in London; out of desperation for assistance, Dr. Oronhyatekha asked him to leave his practice temporarily. Leaving Maracle in charge of the day-to-day hospital operations, Dr. Oronhyatekha checked in each week and also visited families who needed medical treatment unrelated to smallpox. They were afraid, they told him, to see Maracle at the hospital in case they contracted the disease. Dr. Oronhyatekha's own practice in London suffered because his patients feared exposure to smallpox.

Even though diphtheria and tuberculosis killed more Ontarians than smallpox — there had been just over one hundred deaths in the previous two years — smallpox epidemics were met with widespread dread. Edward Jenner had invented a vaccine in the 1790s, but supplies could be contaminated or ineffective. Further, the public feared that the vaccine actually caused the disease and resisted vaccination. Without compulsory vaccination, public health authorities could only rely on the goodwill of the public and the establishment of quarantine to quell an outbreak. For those who fell sick, all Dr. Oronhyatekha could do was dose them with cream of tartar and extract of malt, typical treatments of the time.[47]

Public fear meant it was impossible to get food and other supplies for the hospital or for the Moraviantown residents. Merchants refused to deliver goods or to allow residents inside their shops. In the end, Chief Stonefish donated one of his cows to the hospital to provide much needed milk for patients. By late June, local politicians were so concerned that they jointly wrote to the Department of Indian Affairs expressing their fears. These concerns made the local papers, including London's *Free Press*. Little had been done, it said. The sick had not been quarantined, and Dr. Oronhyatekha only visited occasionally and then only to vaccinate those not sick. It also described how the sick washed their clothes in streams and rivers, the very same water that other communities used. Very quickly, however, the *Free Press* printed an apology, describing Dr. Oronhyatekha's establishment of quarantine and his arrangement for the hospital to be under the constant charge of Dr. Kenwendeshon. The implication that Moraviantown residents had poisoned local water was untrue, it backtracked. Shortly thereafter, Indian Agent Gordon and Dr. Oronhyatekha met with local politicians to reassuringly explain their course of action.

By late July, Dr. Oronhyatekha reported that there were only six patients at the hospital, and several of these would be discharged shortly. There were no new cases, so he hoped that the outbreak was almost over. The hospital closed in mid-August, although Dr. Kenwendeshon stayed two more weeks just in case. In the end, forty-two fell ill with smallpox and of these, thirteen died, but these deaths occurred before the hospital had been established.

Even Dr. Oronhyatekha's role in stemming the outbreak of small-pox turned political. Originally, he had quoted a fee of twenty-five dollars per visit, but when he realized he would have to continue to visit Moraviantown to treat families who did not have smallpox, he changed his price to a more affordable monthly charge of one hundred and fifty dollars. The Department of Indian Affairs questioned this change, asking why he needed to visit the community so often since Dr. Kenwendeshon was in charge of daily hospital care. This query prompted Chief Frank Wampum to write to Indian Affairs, describing Dr. Oronhyatekha as a "sharp man" who had clearly conspired with Chief Stonefish to increase his profits. Agent Gordon also reported that he had charged for visits not made and that some described him as unprincipled. In the end, however, at a Moraviantown council meeting attended by all chiefs, Gordon, and Dr. Oronhyatekha, these misunderstandings were cleared up, and the chiefs agreed to pay his outstanding charges.

Dr. Kenwendeshon or John C. Maracle.

FAMILY TRAGEDY

In the summer of 1881, the Oronhyatekha family suffered a blow from which it never recovered. For the Grand River community, May 24, or Victoria Day, is one of the most celebrated days of the year. At its inception in 1862 on the occasion of her Silver Jubilee, Queen Victoria granted a special gift to the Haudenosaunee, announcing that her loyal allies would never go hungry on the anniversary of her birth. The British Crown presented every man, woman, and child with a gift of a loaf of bread and a pound of cheese. The Haudenosaunee acknowledged this gift from the Crown as a re-affirmation of their longstanding nation to nation relationship.

Like in most towns throughout Ontario, Londoners marked the occasion with picnics and special events. Ellen and Dr. Oronhyatekha took their young family to the celebrations in London. Bena was now sixteen, Acland almost twelve, and Henry, or Sorie as he was nicknamed, was ten. Another son, named Albert Edward after the Prince of Wales, had died as an infant in 1873, and Annie Edith (Kajijunhaweh), the child who would have been named after John A. Macdonald if she had been a boy, had died of typhoid pneumonia in the spring of 1876 just before her second birthday.[48] With their three children in tow, the family attended a picnic in London's Springbank Park; however, Dr. Oronhyatekha was called away to attend to a patient. At 5:00 p.m. Ellen and the children embarked on the pleasure steamer *Princess Victoria* to return to downtown London at the forks of the Thames River. The passengers numbered about eight hundred, but the steamer was only cleared for one hundred. Overcrowded, taking on water from a hole scraped in the hull, and with people rushing from one side to another to wave at passing boats, the *Victoria* eventually capsized. The boiler, not fully bolted to the floor, tipped over and smashed through the boat. The upper deck fell onto those standing on the lower deck. Acland was thrown into the water but managed to climb onto the capsized boat. Ellen was found clasping Henry to her, but he had drowned, along with 182 men, women, and children on board. Ellen appeared dead but was resuscitated.

Another boy, S.F. Lawrason, had been sitting with the Oronhyatekha boys on a pile of wood used to stoke the boiler. Lawrason recounted that when the passengers noticed two sculls racing each other, they rushed to that side of the boat for a better view. A wave of water washed over the wood pile.

As the boat tipped, the crowd fled to the other side, and the boiler broke free. Lawrason lost consciousness but awoke momentarily to see Sorie and his schoolmates from the Colborne Street School form a chain of hands toward the banks of the Thames River. But the clay banks were slippery and as people climbed out of the water, they were often pulled back by those struggling in the water behind them. Henry was one who drowned in this way.[49]

Henry's death devastated Ellen, so much so that she never fully recovered. At this time Ellen was pregnant with their sixth child, who was born in early January 1882. Unfortunately, the baby, John Alexander Herbert, named after John A. Macdonald and Henry Acland, died at the age of two.[50] These tragedies made Ellen reclusive and overly protective of her remaining two children. She did not want to stay in London any longer. She and the children returned to their home in Tyendinaga and rarely left it thereafter. Dr. Oronhyatekha needed to make a decision. Should he return to Tyendinaga with his family, even though his previous experiences there proved controversial, or should he stay with his successful practice in London and endure the long train ride between him and his family? Many months after Ellen's departure, he decided to remain in London. Their relationship endured long periods of separation for the rest of their lives, but the greatest toll was born by his first son, Acland, who as a young man succumbed to alcoholism.

Dr. Oronhyatekha may have questioned his decision to stay in London when in 1885 he was once again charged with non-attendance, this time by members of the Oneida of the Thames community. Like at Tyendinaga a decade earlier, several chiefs and community members petitioned the government to remove him from his post as medical attendant. At a council meeting early that year, a man named Elijah Ninham accused Dr. Oronhyatekha of providing insufficient notice of his intent to vaccinate the community. When a number of chiefs provided evidence to the contrary, Ninham then alleged general negligence. He said Dr. Oronhyatekha was only present Saturday night to Sunday morning, and stayed most of the time in bed. He also charged Dr. Oronhyatekha with removing large amounts of cord wood from the reserve for his personal use in London. Finally, he asserted that Dr. Oronhyatekha was immoral because he boarded with a widow who lived with a married man who had deserted his family. Further, the widow's sister stayed in the same room as Dr. Oronhyatekha and accompanied him on his medical visits.

Fortunately for Dr. Oronhyatekha, he attended this council meeting and ably addressed these charges and was supported by numerous other chiefs. Reporting to Indian Affairs, Dr. Oronhyatekha's supporters described Ninham as troublesome. The doctor, they said, had fulfilled his duties and more. He had assisted in the erection of a new council house and temperance hall, the latter largely paid for by Dr. Oronhyatekha and his fraternal colleagues. Further, the council had originally agreed to pay his travelling expenses between London and the reserve and agreed that the sick would pay for their own medicines. But this had not occurred for many years, and Dr. Oronhyatekha estimated he was out of pocket approximately $1,200. For that reason, the council had agreed to compensate him with cord wood for home use.

Addressing the charges of immorality, Dr. Oronhyatekha stated that he boarded at the late Chief William Cornelius's home because it was centrally located and near the council house. In fact, the chiefs had chosen this location for him. An addition to the house served as his office. The widow's sister had lived there since she was a small child, and thus was not there as a companion to Dr. Oronhyatekha. Instead, he had trained her as a nurse of sorts, able to provide medicines for common diseases. This arrangement proved a great convenience, the chiefs reported. The real issue, they wrote, was that Dr. Oronhyatekha had promised to remove Ninham from the community, a move that many people desired.

In the end, satisfied with the information provided at the council meeting, many of the individuals who signed Ninham's petition removed their names, but the petition was still sent to Indian Affairs with a number of names, including those of a few chiefs.[51]

BECOMING A BUSINESSMAN

The 1880s were a transitional decade for Dr. Oronhyatekha. Seeking approval and acceptance but finding only controversy and strife at the Grand River, Tyendinaga, and with Indian Affairs officials, his political activities tapered off; instead he dedicated more of his time to fraternal organizations. Dr. Oronhyatekha's last real foray into politics occurred in 1885 around the issue of the right of First Nations to vote. The 1885

Electoral Franchise Bill proposed that First Nations men in central and eastern Canada who met the property qualifications should be able to vote. John A. Macdonald, once again prime minister and superintendent general of Indian Affairs since 1878, realized that native communities had largely rejected the idea of enfranchisement embodied in the earlier Indian Acts. This bill was Macdonald's compromise, and it was welcomed by some native individuals because it allowed them to keep their native rights *and* gave them the additional right to vote.

The debate raged in Parliament — both within and between the Conservative and Liberal parties — and in newspapers across Canada. Politicians questioned how natives who, legally characterized as wards of the government under the Indian Act, could be entrusted to vote responsibly. Were they even "persons" as defined by the Franchise Bill? Since they had refused the duty of citizenship through enfranchisement, why should they receive the vote? Some proponents of women's suffrage were outraged that First Nations might receive the vote before they did. Others wondered if they would be able to vote freely; that is, without interference by Indian agents. As well, the Riel Uprising had just broken out in the northwest, and some feared the franchise would be extended to include those who were currently fighting government troops. The Liberal MP for Brant County raised another issue. Many members of the Grand River community argued they were allies, not subjects, of the British Crown, and thus were not citizens to whom the vote could be extended. Many Haudenosaunee agreed; they had their own political organizations. They also worried that voting would compromise their special Indian status because in the past voting had been linked to enfranchisement. Others, however, hoped their rights would be better represented in Parliament if they voted.[52]

As he had done during the changes to Indian legislation in the 1870s, Dr. Oronhyatekha visited reserves to explain the Franchise Bill, though it is unknown whether he did this of his own volition or at Macdonald's behest. In late 1885, he attended a council at the Oneida of the Thames, which numerous Grand River chiefs also attended. While Dr. Oronhyatekha assured those present that they should support the Conservatives and his old friend John A., the chiefs felt they did not understand the provisions of the act well enough. They feared that the vote might be linked with enfranchisement, a principle they rejected, or that it might undermine their traditional government. Some disliked the Conservative government more generally. Several months later, Dr. Oronhyatekha visited Tyendinaga. At a council meeting there, he advised the chiefs to form a political organ- ization to guard their interests. Like the Grand River, Tyendinaga's large population could substantially influence the vote in their respective coun- ties. In fact, opponents of the bill pointed out in the House of Commons debates that Dr. Oronhyatekha, a loyal Orange lodge supporter, was organ- izing Orange lodges on reserves, and that Orangemen also voted conserv- ative and were anti-French. They charged that these were the real reasons that Macdonald wanted natives to vote.[53]

Dr. Oronhyatekha also made his opinions clear in a letter to the *London Advertiser*, which was picked up by other papers such as the Montreal *Gazette* and the Toronto *Mail*, and noted by politicians during the debates over the bill in Parliament. This bill, he said, was the "most important measure ever submitted to Parliament having in view the ele- vation of the Indian and the removal of all distinctions between him and the other citizens of this Dominion."

Earlier attempts at enfranchisement through assimilation had failed because it stripped First Nations of their culture and divided their com- munities. Dr. Oronhyatekha described the type of individuals that the bill proposed to give the vote. Those living at Tyendinaga and the Grand River were capable and intelligent. They were successful farmers and proven loyal allies. These two communities had schools and churches. Residents paid for road and bridge maintenance and contributed to the salaries of ministers, teachers, and even some Indian Affairs staff. Their yearly annuities were not gifts from the government but interest on their own money. In other words, they were responsible tax-payers who deserved the vote. Dr. Oronhyatekha reassured readers that the vote would not be given to participants in the Riel Uprising and that native communities would not allow Indian Affairs to interfere in voting. His arguments fell on many deaf ears. The *London Advertiser* responded that even though Dr. Oronhyatekha claimed First Nations were superior to whites, most took his assertion as humour, not truth. Londoners did not believe that "savages" fighting with Riel were "more entitled to the franchise than the artizans [sic] and dwellers on individual holdings, who pay taxes and help support the Government and these same Indians."[54] The bill passed, but there was no agreement among First Nations communities or among the national political parties, and in 1898 with the Liberal return to power, First Nations lost the right to vote until the 1960s.

With a reduction in his political activities, Dr. Oronhyatekha devoted more time to fraternal organizations. In London he belonged to the International Order of Good Templars, the Loyal Orange Association, the Masons, and in particular, the Independent Order of Foresters (IOF). In 1878, he joined London's Court Dufferin of the IOF, and in 1879 the membership elected him the High Chief Ranger of the Ontario High Court and Supreme Chief Ranger in 1881. When the head office of the IOF relocated from London to Toronto in 1889, Dr. Oronhyatekha closed his practice, resigned his position as medical attendant to the Oneida of the Thames community, and moved to Toronto. Despite rumours that he would run for a Conservative seat in Toronto, he believed that as head of the IOF, he should not be partisan.[55] After 1889, his focus turned to the management and expansion of the Foresters, transforming it from a small and internally conflicted group into an international business.

CHAPTER 5

SECURITY, JUSTICE, AND EQUALITY

A "JOINER"

The Victorian era (1837–1901) produced a generation of people who believed a firm commitment to God and an unrelenting duty to work and the betterment of mankind were rewarded by immortality in the afterlife. While expressed differently, these were recognizable values inherent in Mohawk society. Through their institutions and beliefs, the Haudenosaunee held a deep and fundamental commitment to what they believed the Creator had given to them and the duties with which he had charged them. In their world, the practice of extending respect to all living things ensured that they would be provided for in return. These reciprocal relationships applied to other people as well as to the natural environment. The Haudenosaunee's Great Law preached peace, power, and righteousness. They were to secure and maintain peace among people. If their actions were guided by righteousness, they would remain in a position of power, and economic and spiritual survival would be assured for the next seven generations. It became Dr. Oronhyatekha's personal mission to marry these two diverse cultural perspectives into a complementary, contiguous whole through his work in fraternal societies, particularly the Independent Order of Foresters, whose underlying purpose was the promotion of the similar ideals of liberty, benevolence, and concord. In a society that denied the worth of traditional native values, Dr. Oronhyatekha nevertheless expressed them through the IOF's principles and the beliefs of Victorian society to achieve security, justice, and equality for thousands of men and women.

Fraternal societies existed in virtually every village, town, and city in North America and the United Kingdom. Members could travel freely and still find a warm and friendly greeting at the numerous courts, lodges, and social clubs of the societies to which they belonged. Most societies claimed benevolence to be their major purpose. Duties of members included visiting the sick, attending the funerals of their fraternal brothers, and patronizing each others' businesses. Societies also collected money for members who had been injured and unable to work or for families whose breadwinner had died. These funds could be an informal passing of the hat, or a formal subscription to life and sickness insurance paid by monthly dues.

Beyond benevolence, membership in these societies was an integral component in the arsenal of any ambitious young man. Society members were drawn from both the working and the middle class, but membership symbolized pursuit of economic and social mobility. The values of duty, self-improvement, and industrious leisure were a bulwark of the respectable middle class. Further, societies based their rituals and ceremonies upon biblical stories and characters, Christianity comprising another essential element of respectability. With a hierarchical structure of "degrees," some with as many as ninety-six, a doctor, lawyer, or a labourer by day could become something much grander and more important — a Prince of Mercy or a Knight Templar — within the rank and file of their respective lodges. These rituals and degrees promoted a sense of brotherhood and masculine belonging, a factor some historians see as key to promoting membership at a time when the home was becoming more feminized. The resulting networks could be useful in business, but also served as a substitute to the increasingly fractured extended family as rural out-migration and urban employment increased. While each lodge had different versions, their regalia, badges, secret signs and passwords, oaths, and symbols lent a sense of spiritualism but also of mystery and spectacle. Outside of the rituals, fraternal lodges also clearly provided a source of entertainment, but one viewed as virtuous and productive, an important distinction in this time when even leisure activities were meant

[ASSESSMENT SYSTEM]

.. THE ..

I. O. F.

IS A
FRATERNAL BENEFIT
SOCIETY
*whose Canadian birthplace
was London.*
Was organized in 1874.
Has been in business 26 years.
Has a membership of about 170,000.
Has a surplus fund of over $4,150,000.
Has paid over $8,500,000 in benefits.
Members' ages average 35 years.
*Is the Fraternal Society that furnishes
insurance on plans similar to the
level premium system of the Old
Line Insurance Companies at two-
thirds their rates*

No Assessments at Deaths.

For further information, write
ORONHYATEKHA, S.C.R
(A London Old Boy)
TEMPLE BUILDING.   TORONTO

Nineteenth-century business often depended on connections made in social and fraternal organizations. Dr. Oronhyatekha's association with the London Old Boys' Association is included in this ad for the organization's souvenir publication in 1900.

to improve individuals. Those who became officers of societies, like Dr. Oronhyatekha, also were able to travel widely on business.[1]

Like many young men seeking success and influence, Dr. Oronhyatekha joined a number of fraternal organizations, including the Knights of the Maccabees, the Old Boys' Association of London, the United Order of Workmen, the Loyal Orange Association, or Orange Order, several branches of freemasonry, the Independent Order of Good Templars, and the Independent Order of Foresters.[2]

Soldiers fighting in the War of 1812 transplanted the Orange Order to Canada, and Irish immigration to Upper Canada in the early 1830s further spread its influence. While Protestant Orangeism endorsed anti-Catholic sentiments, the intense religious rivalry that materialized in street brawls and skirmishes had mostly ended before Oronhyatekha joined mid-century. The order became more respectable as the nineteenth century progressed, and by its end, one in every three men belonged.[3] Its membership thus broadened from Irish immigrants to reflect the diverse ethnic, religious, and class composition of the communities in which the organization was rooted. Lodges organized at the local, district (township), county, and provincial level under the Grand Lodge of British North America, which was established in 1830.[4]

Why would Dr. Oronhyatekha join an organization formed in the context of the Protestant-Catholic rivalries of British colonialism, and one seemingly divergent from native culture and goals? Read differently, the Orange Order's other aims — to promote loyalty to the British Crown and to retain Canada within the British Empire — converged with those of the Mohawk. Influenced by his grandfather, George Martin, a staunch British loyalist, and raised in the Haudenosaunee culture, which understood its treaties to have been made with the British Crown, not with Canadian politicians, Dr. Oronhyatekha found value in these goals, as did other Mohawks. In fact, the Loyal Orange Lodge 99 on the Tyendinaga reserve opened in 1848, and Haudenosaunee established other lodges at Ohsweken on the Grand River reserve and at Oneida of the Thames.[5] Politically, Dr. Oronhyatekha supported the Conservatives, and around the time of his joining, many Tories were Orangemen, including his friend and soon-to-be prime minister of Canada, John A. Macdonald. As well, like other fraternal organizations, the order offered social activities and political and economic connections that proved useful in early Canada.

However, Dr. Oronhyatekha seems to have been involved less in the Orange Order than in the Masonic Order, the International Order of Good Templars, and, of course, the Independent Order of Foresters. By 1869, Dr. Oronhyatekha had been elected the District Master for the Loyal Orange Lodge of South Hastings.[6] In the summer of 1873, the time when he was accused of medical non-attendance by some in the Tyendinaga community, he attended the triennial meeting of the Imperial Grand Orange Council of the World in Glasgow, Scotland. More than just a meeting, the council treated Dr. Oronhyatekha and the other Canadian delegates to visits to places of significance to Orangeism. In England, they visited Birmingham and Liverpool, where a feast was thrown in their honour. In July, they visited Derry in Ireland. Taking the train to Armagh, Northern Ireland, they were greeted by cheering Orangemen. The group then paraded through the town to its meeting place, marching through crowds of supporters and streets lined with flags and orange lilies. The *Belfast Newsletter* reported that the number of people was so great that the procession took over an hour. Dr. Oronhyatekha and the other delegates were called upon to make a speech in Armagh. He noted that Canadian Orangemen were loyal to the British Crown and determined to be forever connected with their mother country, England, as were the Orange Irish. In fact, he said, Canadians would lay down their lives on her behalf.

The Canadians had also been scheduled to attend a lodge meeting in Antrim the next month, but Dr. Oronhyatekha received word that his son Albert Edward, only three months old, had died, and he rushed home instead to be with his family.

During his time in London, Ontario, Dr. Oronhyatekha joined Lodge 303 and served as both District and County Master in 1888, and while living in Toronto, he belonged to Lodge 342. He also helped organize the Orange Mutual Insurance Society of Ontario in 1881. Drawing upon his experience with the Foresters, this arm of the order aimed to provide funds for sick Orangemen and the families of those who passed away.[7]

FREEMASONRY

The Haudenosaunee had been associated with the Masons as early as 1798 when they established Lodge 11. Joseph Brant himself had been an official of this lodge, and he also belonged to Lodge 10 in Hamilton.[8] While a student at the Toronto Medical School, Oronhyatekha joined the Masons through King Solomon's Lodge 22, a Scottish Rite lodge in the city. He was initiated on October 12, 1865, and "raised" on January 25, 1866. He also joined King Solomon's Lodge 8 of the Royal Arch (York Rite) branch of masonry.[9]

Once based upon the medieval craft of stone masonry, free-masonry evolved into a fraternal organization before it appeared in North America. Masons developed several branches, including the York (or American) and the Scottish Rite. Both began with the three common degrees of the Blue Lodge, but diverged in their higher levels. The Scottish Rite encompassed a further thirty degrees, while masons following the York Rite progressed through an additional ten degrees. The Royal Arch lodges conferred the fourth through seventh degrees, the Royal and Select Masters the eighth through eleventh levels, and the Knights Templar lodges the final two levels.[10]

After leaving university in Toronto, Dr. Oronhyatekha continued to be actively involved in various Masonic organizations and seemed unperturbed by their differing practices, and in some cases, outright challenges to the legitimacy of fellow organizations. During his early years of medical practice, he was the organist for the St. Mark's chapter of Royal Arch Masons, Lodge 26 in Trenton. In 1871, he acted as Pursuivant for the Grand Lodge of Canada (Scottish Rite), announcing all applicants for admission and supervising the regalia of the lodge; he may have also belonged to the Franck Lodge 127 of Frankford. After moving to Stratford, he joined the Tecumseh Lodge 144, also of the Scottish Rite.[11]

As he did in other fraternal organizations, Dr. Oronhyatekha served in official positions beyond his local lodge. While living in London, he was elected the Inspector General of the Georgian Division, a large area that encompassed Simcoe and Grey counties and the Muskoka, Parry Sound, and Algoma districts under the York Rite. Having achieved the 33rd degree, the highest of the Scottish Rite, in 1884 he was made an honorary member of the newly established Supreme Grand Council of Britain and Ireland. He also served as Thrice Illustrious Master (TIM) of the Shekinah Council of the Royal and Select Masters that year, and thus as the Immediate Past TIM in 1885. In 1888, he was the Medical Director for the Dominion Masonic Benefit Association.[12]

He also supported the formation of several chapters of the Rose Croix under another Masonic organization, the Egyptian Rite of Memphis, although officials of the Scottish Rite rejected it as a spurious rival. By 1882, he was elected a Past Grand Master General and Grand Lecturer in the Egyptian branch, two positions he held several times in the 1880s. In 1884, he was created a member of the Imperial Grand Council of the World for Egyptian rites, and the year after he was elected Associate Grand Secretary of the Executive Council of the Sovereign Sanctuary, the body with jurisdiction over Canada.[13]

In the mid-1880s, he also served as an officer of the Rosicrucian Society of Canada, an organization established at Orillia, and successively as Junior General and Grand Senior General of the Constantinian Order of Canada.[14]

After moving back to Toronto, Dr. Oronhyatekha rejoined King Solomon's Lodge 22 in 1893. His son Acland was now also a member. Like his father, Acland had joined this lodge two years earlier while a medical student at Trinity University. In June of the next year, Dr. Oronhyatekha was "parachuted" into the Scottish Rite Richardson Lodge in Stouffville, a small town north of Toronto, and a far distance from Dr. Oronhyatekha's home in the city. Made its Worshipful Master, he was perhaps chosen to firmly establish the lodge, which had had a difficult time in the recent past.[15]

Ultimately, Dr. Oronhyatekha achieved the highest degrees in several of the Masonic branches. He reached the 33rd degree (Sovereign Grand Inspector General) in the Scottish Rite, the 96th degree in the Egyptian Rite of Memphis, and the 90th degree in the Rite of Misraim. In the York Rite, he achieved the penultimate 12th (Knight Templar) by 1900 and may have obtained the last one before his death in 1907. He was also the editor of the *Masonic Tablet*, a publication out of London.[16]

TEMPERANCE

In 1854, while still a teenager, Dr. Oronhyatekha joined the Independent Order of Good Templars (IOGT), an organization of men and women that believed in personal abstinence from spirits and the prohibition of the sale of all alcohol. The IOGT motto, Faith, Hope and Charity, additionally suggests its religious and moral underpinnings. Like many fraternal organizations of the nineteenth century, the IOGT also served a social purpose, with local lodges meeting monthly.

Dr. Oronhyatekha believed in temperance and prohibition based upon the problematic history of native peoples with alcohol. At one IOGT meeting in Guelph, with a mix of his trademark humour and pride in his people, he stated he was pleased that "white people were getting up where the Indians were one hundred years ago." At that time, native people realized the detriment of alcohol and asked the government to prohibit the sale of liquor to them. Since then, he continued, native homes and families had been protected.[17]

This message had also been at the heart of Dr. Oronhyatekha's speech at the centennial celebration of the publication of Dr. Benjamin Rush's *An Inquiry into the Effects of Ardent Spirits upon the Human Mind and Body*. With this treatise, Rush, a Philadelphia physician and pioneer of the temperance movement, began an educational campaign about the deleterious effects of alcohol. In 1885, the American National Temperance Society invited other organizations and churches to celebrate this anniversary in Philadelphia, and published the speeches given at the event. Representing the Six Nations Temperance Society and the Victoria Worrell Lodge of Good Templars (London), and as a vice-president of the National Temperance Society itself, Dr. Oronhyatekha spoke at the two-day Centennial Conference in September. He was "anxious that ... it should go on record that you are simply following the teachings and example of my people," he said to the audience. "Among white races and among other nations, from time immemorial, intoxication has existed in some form or other, except among the Indian races," he continued, but with "the advent of white men upon our continent, intemperance began to appear among our people." His people had petitioned their chiefs in the 1660s to enact a law to ban the sale of alcohol. We "are succeeding very well in civilizing the whites ... I think upon the whole they are a little further advanced upon this question than you are, and I hope before many years we shall be able to get them up to our level," he quipped.[18]

Dr. Oronhyatekha's belief in temperance and prohibition was typical of many middle class professionals — doctors, lawyers, business owners, preachers — in mid to late nineteenth-century Canada. The middle class feared that drinking was on the rise and that Canadians chose strong spirits more often than beer or cider. Prices for rum and whiskey had fallen and the companies manufacturing and selling alcoholic beverages had become more sophisticated in their marketing. As the population grew, so did the number of taverns, places the middle class saw as sites of dangerous self-indulgence and violence. The rise in immigration increased stereotypical fears of certain ethnicities that supposedly drank excessively. Doctors debated the efficacy of treating medical and psychological ailments with alcohol. As other beverages such as tea and milk became cheaper and more widely available, alcohol became increasingly associated with leisure rather than an accompaniment to meals.

Temperance groups arose in Upper Canada in the 1820s, but as the nineteenth century progressed, they began to consolidate efforts, bringing together individuals who approached these issues from a variety of perspectives. Churches saw alcohol as leading to immorality and vice. Business owners saw a reduction in drinking as a way to control their labour force and improve work efficiency. Many in the middle class believed in the value of self-help, of which temperance was part, as a path to upward moral, social, and economic mobility. Social reformers focused on the use of alcohol by men as the cause of poverty, child neglect, and violence toward women. At first efforts relied on moral persuasion to convert drinkers into abstainers, but as it became clear that this approach had a limited effect, organizations lobbied for prohibition as the only means to stop Canadians from drinking. The focus also shifted from individual consumers to the manufacturers and sellers of alcohol.[19]

Founded in New York State in the early 1850s, the Independent Order of Good Templars spread to Canada a few years later, meeting in Hamilton in 1854. Oronhyatekha joined that same year at the age of thirteen or fourteen, and it is possible that through the IOGT he met Dr. John W. Fergusson, with whom he worked before attending the Toronto School of Medicine. Fergusson was elected Grand Worthy Chief Templar of the Grand Lodge of Canada (Ontario), the highest position in the province, in 1859 and 1860, and then served as Grand Worthy Secretary for several years thereafter.[20]

It is impossible to tell if Dr. Oronhyatekha attended the annual meetings of the Grand Lodge of Canada, although certainly they were held in southwestern Ontario cities geographically accessible to him in the 1850s and early 1860s. An early history of the organization noted that Dr. Oronhyatekha first appeared in the records of the international Right Worthy Grand Lodge as an attendee of the 1865 annual meeting held in London. He steadily rose in rank and importance within the IOGT. In 1868, as the Grand Worthy Chief Templar of the Ontario Grand Lodge, he attended the annual meeting of the Grand Lodge of North America in Indiana with Dr. Fergusson, who was the secretary. In 1872, Dr. Oronhyatekha again served as Grand Worthy Chief Templar, a post he held three more times. This position oversaw all other officials, enforced the constitution and by-laws, decided on appeals or questions

of procedure, visited district lodges, and presided at the annual meetings of the Grand Lodge of Canada (Ontario).[21] During this time, he
helped build a temperance hall for the Good Templars at the Oneida of
the Thames reserve and intended to establish a lodge at the Grand River
as well, though it is unclear if he did so.[22]

At a joint meeting of the IOGT and the Sons of Temperance in February
1868, Dr. Oronhyatekha and Dr. Fergusson, among others, called for a
meeting to organize a consolidated temperance organization. One year
later, officials of various groups in Ontario and Quebec formed the Canada
Temperance Union (CTU). The CTU aimed to educate the public about the
evils of alcohol through churches, distribution of temperance literature, and
public lectures, as well as lobby for prohibition. Dr. Oronhyatekha sat on
several committees, including the constitutional committee, which formu-
lated the goals of the CTU, another to compile statistics on alcohol manufacturing and on "crime, insanity, and other evil effects" caused by alcohol,
one to consider the need for an inebriate asylum, and a fourth to explore the
possibility of a temperance publication. The CTU membership nominated
him to serve as a vice-president, but in the end he was not elected.[23]

In 1870, the CTU acknowledged it could only focus on Ontario
and renamed itself the Ontario Temperance and Prohibitory League.
But it continued to press for consolidated efforts towards prohibition.
Legislation at that time only allowed for the possibility of locally controlled prohibition. In Ontario, the Canada Temperance Act (1864), more
commonly known as the Dunkin Act, gave local authorities the power to
hold a popular vote on whether to allow the sale of liquor. The act also set
restrictions on the amount of liquor to be sold at any one time and the
hours during which storekeepers could sell it. Compared to earlier local
option laws, the Dunkin Act was more stringent, but not encompassing
enough for advocates of true prohibition.

After Canadian confederation in 1867, prohibitionists lobbied for
national legislation. In 1873, temperance societies petitioned to have the
issue introduced to Parliament. John A. Macdonald referred the matter to a
House of Commons select committee. As a result, the Ontario Temperance
and Prohibitory League lobbied for political supporters. All parties agreed
to research prohibition in other countries to explore how it might be implemented in Canada. After presenting their report to Parliament, they met

again in 1875, this time in Montreal. The approximately 285 delegates and politicians from central and eastern Canada formally resolved that alcohol caused crime, poverty, and immorality and thus the only way to proceed was total prohibition of the manufacture, sale, and importation of all liquor. Attendees also decided that a national organization was still needed, and in 1876 the Dominion Alliance for the Total Suppression of Liquor Traffic was founded. Dr. Oronhyatekha served as an Ontario council member. However, the Alliance only recommended to Parliament that a local option law be implemented for all of Canada. Parliament deferred the issue since it was unclear whether prohibition was a national or provincial matter.[24]

In the meantime, in Ontario, the Liquor License, or Crooks Act of 1876 tightened up control over who could sell alcohol. It established a provincially appointed board of commissioners to decide who received a liquor licence. The act also restricted how many licences could be given in a local area, increased the licence fee, and required the inspection of any business selling liquor. In London, where Dr. Oronhyatekha was living, the city council proposed to raise licence fees. Beer manufacturers such as John Carling and temperance advocates including Dr. Oronhyatekha attended the council meeting to argue their respective positions. In the end, the council narrowly voted to increase the fees.[25]

Two years later, in 1878, Parliament enacted The Canada Temperance or Scott Act, a national law similar to Ontario's Dunkin Act in that it allowed local jurisdictions to vote in restrictions on alcohol. Prohibition advocates in Ontario found the Scott Act to be temporarily and unevenly successful at best. Twenty-five counties and two cities in the province voted for local prohibition, however all of them repealed it within a few years.[26]

Some temperance workers believed that if the Liberals and Conservatives would not support prohibition, a third political party should be created. In 1887, a national Prohibition Party was founded, but not all temperance advocates supported it. The Dominion Alliance, for instance, preferred to back any politician who believed in prohibition. A Conservative supporter, Dr. Oronhyatekha argued that temperance societies should put forth their own candidates, but he was unsure if this necessitated the creation of a third political party.[27]

Continued pressure resulted in the establishment of a Royal Commission to Investigate Liquor Traffic in 1892. The IOGT suggested to

the Canadian government that Dr. Oronhyatekha be one of the commissioners, but to no avail.[28] Unfortunately for prohibitionists, in 1895 the
commission advocated tighter controls on the sale of alcohol but not an
outright ban, and even these recommendations were ignored. One year
earlier in Ontario, the provincial government had consented to a popular
vote on prohibition, but voter turnout was so low that it was reluctant to
act. A national plebiscite on prohibition in 1898 resulted in a similar situation. Liberal Prime Minister Wilfrid Laurier believed prohibition was
too divisive to impose on Canadians.

Reflecting on the Royal Commission, Dr. Oronhyatekha noted that
the more than one thousand Canadian doctors consulted agreed that
abstinence led to better health, with fewer than three hundred physicians
dissenting. To opponents, he argued that Christianity was full of prohibi-
tive measures. He also drew attention to the types of prohibition already
in place with which Canadians approved. It was illegal to sell alcohol to
natives, he noted, and statistics clearly showed that there was less crime
in native communities compared to the rest of Canada. "Of course, some
credit must be given to our innate honesty and peaceable lives," he said
humorously, but he did believe prohibition was one of the causes. One
couldn't buy liquor between Saturday night and Monday morning, or on
election days — a kind of prohibition, he suggested, and no one objected
to *that* law. "Now, let us just add a few more days to these prohibitionary
days," he concluded. He gave this speech in support of the "yes" vote during the 1902 Ontario referendum to further restrict the sale of alcohol.[29]
While the majority voted yes in 1902, again voter turnout was too low for
implementation. Dr. Oronhyatekha would never see total prohibition as
Canadians did not embrace it until the First World War.

The temperance movement was also divided by racial issues. One of
Dr. Oronhyatekha's most remembered roles in the IOGT was his proposal
of the "Oronhyatekha substitute," or a compromise regarding the admission of African-Americans to the order. While the IOGT was unusual
among fraternal organizations because it allowed female members and
even elected female officials, it was divided over black membership.
After Abraham Lincoln's Emancipation Proclamation of 1863 freed black
slaves, and the U.S. Civil War ended in 1865, African Americans sought to
establish local IOGT chapters and to be represented at the Grand Lodge

or state level. In Canada, by 1877, Ontario possessed fifteen black lodges that totalled several thousand members.[30]

Contention arose in 1868 when the Kentucky Grand Lodge protested the existence of several all-black lodges in that state. The overarching body, the Right Worthy Grand Lodge (RWGL) appointed a committee to resolve the issue; it affirmed racial equality within the organization but allowed the state Grand Lodges to determine the eligibility of membership within their own jurisdictions. Like many compromises, it satisfied no one. The Grand Lodges in Tennessee and Kentucky called for the formation of a separate organization called the Colored Templars of North America, while the Grand Lodge of England demanded equality for black members. The issue arose again at the 1872 annual meeting, which many southern state representatives attended. Once again, they proposed a separate order and the subsequent transfer of all black members to that order, which would ultimately become independent of the IOGT altogether. Another special committee agreed on the establishment of a separate organization but only under the supervision of the IOGT. It also decided that the revocation of black membership could only result from constitutional violations such as the non-payment of dues, and not because of race. Worried that black lodges would form in states that did not have any white lodges — and thus control the state Grand Lodge — southern members rushed to form lodges throughout their jurisdictions.

Black membership became more contentious in the 1870s as the number of members from England and the southern states increased dramatically. In 1873, the black lodges in North Carolina petitioned the RWGL for a duplicate state Grand Lodge, since the existing one refused to recognize them. It also would not send the black lodges the requisite password; the password was changed regularly, and no member would be admitted to a meeting without uttering that password. Essentially, the Grand Lodge hampered the ability of the black lodges to meet and refused representation of its members. A third special committee on black membership ordered all Grand Lodges to share passwords, but decided against the formation of duplicate Grand Lodges in the United States. However, after 1875, the IOGT allowed some duplicate black Grand Lodges if several local lodges already existed, a decision it revoked after several British officials resigned. In 1876, the Grand Lodge of England, headed by Joseph

Malins, issued an ultimatum: it would organize Black lodges in states if Grand Lodges refused to do so. Southerners accused Malins of a desire for power rather than believing in black equality.

The IOGT did not have a chance to vote on the British ultimatum at its annual meeting in Louisville in May 1876. Instead, Dr. Oronhyatekha pointed to a number of earlier decisions that barred exclusion based on race and offered a new resolution: the Right Worthy Grand Lodge would revoke any lodge charter that violated this principle, but that the state Grand Lodges held the power to determine which local lodges should receive charters.[31] Called to a vote, the IOGT membership agreed to Dr. Oronhyatekha's "substitute," though it was not unanimous. Malins and the other British representatives withdrew from the meeting, and in protest formed the separatist Right Worthy Grand Lodge of the World.

Contemporaries and historians disagree over the motivation of Dr. Oronhyatekha's compromise. Williams Wells Brown, a former slave, writer, and IOGT member, accused him of racism. He recounted a story from the 1874 annual meeting in Boston as proof. Malins asked Dr. Oronhyatekha to sit for a photo of all three men together, showing the diversity of races accepted by the IOGT. According to Malins, Dr. Oronhyatekha replied, "No ... I don't mind coming down to have my portrait taken with a white man, but I will never come down so low as to be photographed with a Nigger."

Malins used this story against Dr. Oronhyatekha, and the two men became bitter opponents. Malins and Brown expressed contempt for the "substitute," calling it a "subterfuge." On the other hand, Jessie Forsyth, an English IOGT official who truly believed in equal rights for blacks, became fond of Dr. Oronhyatekha. Is it likely she would feel so if Dr. Oronhyatekha did not share this belief? American historian David Fahey points out that the Oronhyatekha "substitute" outlawed overtly excluding members based on their race, but allowed it to occur in practice. However, he also argues that Dr. Oronhyatekha didn't view the schism as centring on the issue of white supremacy.[32]

Despite Malins's and Dr. Oronhyatekha's dislike of one other, the IOGT almost immediately dispatched Dr. Oronhyatekha and John Hickman, the Right Worthy Grand Templar, to begin reconciliation, but to no avail. The IOGT subsequently ordered Hickman and Dr. Oronhyatekha to go to England to negotiate with the British leaders, even though the two men disagreed over the best approach. Dr. Oronhyatekha wanted to deliberately establish a black lodge in the southern U.S. to symbolize the IOGT's power to do so. Hickman, originally a member from Kentucky, the state most antagonistic to black membership, feared this move would only further alienate southern lodges. In England, Hickman ignored Dr. Oronhyatekha and instead turned to Samuel Capper, a British member of the IOGT, for assistance.

The three men met with Malins and his colleagues in October to discuss reconciliation. Unaware that the southern lodges had already rejected the idea, Hickman proposed that the white Grand Lodges of the southern states allow the Right Worthy Grand Lodge to organize segregated duplicate local and state level Grand Lodges for its black members.[33] But the conference broke up over a completely different issue. While many lodges in Wales and Scotland supported Malins, some British and Irish lodges refused to secede from the Right Worthy Grand Lodge, and instead sided with the North Americans, partly because of Dr. Oronhyatekha's status as an Orangeman. Others remained in the RWGL because they harboured a personal dislike of Malins. To make matters worse, Dr. Oronhyatekha had organized a new lodge on the Isle of Man before the conference, a defiant symbol of the power of the North American RWGL. The next year he returned to organize more lodges in the United Kingdom.[34]

In 1878, the RWGL changed its constitution to explicitly state that African Americans had the right to be members through separate lodges, but by then the Malinites demanded total desegregation of the organization. It was not until 1886 that another serious attempt at reconciliation occurred, this time in Boston. Jessie Forsyth recorded that meeting in her memoirs, noting that the North American representatives arrived more than an hour late, thus creating tension among the gathered British officials. Forsyth wrote that she had been "extremely anxious to see Dr. Oronhyatekha and at the same time just a little afraid of him." She was not sure what she expected to see, "certainly not exactly a 'big chief' in feathers and war paint, but at the same time [she] was hardly prepared to meet a handsome, kindly, genial gentleman who, as events proved, was just as anxious to 'bury the hatchet' as anyone could be."[35] In fact, Malins and Dr. Oronhyatekha, once enemies, seemed determined to achieve a reunion. It was agreed that black lodges would remain temporarily separate where necessary but no new duplicate Grand Lodges would be created.

In 1887, the IOGT met in New York State to ratify the Boston agreement. Jessie Forsyth praised Dr. Oronhyatekha as having been among the officials who "strove hard to maintain the good feeling with which the sitting had opened." She felt that members could "never sufficiently admire and appreciate his attitude in the circumstances, because he had been the worst-abused of all the RWGL leaders during the years of disruption" by the British secessionists.[36]

Although reunited, IOGT members still disagreed over black membership and the new constitution. How long would the "temporary" separation of black lodges last? Could there really be desegregated lodges in the American south? Some British members felt the new constitution to be racist, but accepted it to keep the order united, while others continued to press for integration. Some southern lodges simply died out as members voted with their feet against the new constitution. In fact, the next few decades saw the decline of North American lodges and the rise of new international lodges in Europe.

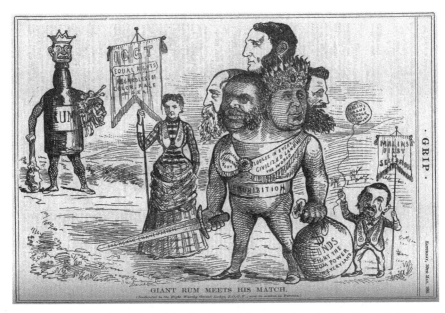

"Giant Rum Meets His Match." Dr. Oronhyatekha is depicted with other officials of the IOGT. Note Malins in the corner representing the secessionists. *Grip* published this cartoon during the 1885 meeting of the Right Worthy Grand Lodge in Toronto.

Between 1883 and 1885, Dr. Oronhyatekha served on an international level as the Right Worthy Grand Counsellor, an advisory role to the Chief Templar. The following year he acted as the Right Worthy Grand Vice Templar. In 1887, when the RWGT, John Finch, suddenly passed away, the constitution directed all officials to move into the higher role left vacant. Vice Templar Jessie Forsyth should have become the counsellor, but instead decided to nominate Dr. Oronhyatekha for the position. As a close adviser to Finch and a prominent North American member, she felt he was the best choice for the position. He continued on in that role between 1889 and 1891.[37]

In 1888, to fulfill Finch's wishes, Dr. Oronhyatekha established a monthly magazine, the *International Good Templar*. Never a financial success, the publication cost more in printing and mailing costs than it generated in subscriptions and advertising revenue. Typically, Dr. Oronhyatekha and other officials paid for these expenses out of their own pockets, only reimbursed a small portion by the IOGT. Dr. Oronhyatekha also served for a number of years on the Literature Committee, which

Bena often attended meetings of the IOGT with her parents. *The International Good Templar* featured her picture as of one of the daughters of its leaders.

oversaw the distribution of information on the issues of temperance and prohibition, including the *Good Templar*, and acted as the Superintendent of Missions for North America, a position that charged him with opening new lodges and finding new members.[38]

In 1891, he travelled overseas to the IOGT annual meeting held in Edinburgh. By now, Jessie Forsyth was quite friendly with the Oronhyatekha family. She had met his wife, Ellen, at the 1889 meeting in Chicago, and on her way home to England had spent several days with the family at their Toronto home. On the 1891 trip to and from Scotland, she shared a state room with his daughter Bena. The whole family, she wrote in her memoirs, nursed a man with pneumonia and a large number of their party suffering from seasickness. At the Edinburgh meeting, Dr. Oronhyatekha reached the pinnacle of the organization when the membership elected him the Right Worthy Grand Templar, nominated surprisingly by Joseph Malins himself. In 1893, due to his pressing work with the Independent Order of Foresters, he declined a further nomination to continue on as Chief Templar.[39]

Like his work with the Independent Order of Foresters, Dr. Oronhyatekha's roles within the IOGT allowed him and his family to travel to places and meet people that few Haudenosaunee people could at that time. Besides travelling to Chicago in 1889 and Edinburgh in 1891, Bena and Ellen (also a member) accompanied Dr. Oronhyatekha to the 1893 gathering in Iowa, and stopped off to visit the World's Fair in Chicago on the way home. The fair organizers had declared one day "Good Templars Day." While in Chicago, Dr. Oronhyatekha also delivered an address on the history of temperance in Canada to the World Temperance Congress, which was meeting at the same time the fair was going on. They also travelled to Zurich, Switzerland, for the IOGT's 1897 annual meeting, which included a garden party at the Château Au, the home of the Baroness von Sulzer-Vart. As part of their travels, they also stopped in London and Paris.[40]

The IOGT also provided Dr. Oronhyatekha with an arena to practise his debating and negotiating skills. Members T.F. Parker and S.B. Chase, who wrote a history of the organization, noted that his "distinct personality and large ability" gained him official positions, and they described him as "imperturbably cool in debate, never losing his temper; he is as difficult an opponent as is often met with in a deliberative assembly."[41] He demonstrated these skills as he rose to prominence in the Independent Order of Foresters.

FORESTRY

The Independent Order of Foresters, or IOF, had its roots in England. Like other fraternal organizations, the IOF stemmed from the medieval guild system. The men who tended the woodlands of reigning monarchs — stewards, wardens, and foresters — loosely organized themselves into groups. Should tragedy befall them, they pooled their meagre resources to bury their comrades and provide relief for the families. These loose-knit groups were later immortalized in English folklore and personified by Robin Hood and his band of merry men.

In 1745, at Knarsborough, Yorkshire, these men organized themselves into the Royal Order of Foresters and formalized a system of mutual aid and assistance through local lodges or "courts." Like other guilds in England, they developed secret rituals known only to their members, enabling them to identify one another. In 1834, the name formally changed to the Ancient Order of Foresters (AOF). By the time Oronhyatekha joined, the organization acted more as a fraternity than a guild of working foresters, although its titles, regalia, and rituals were inspired by its medieval past.

In 1864, the AOF opened its first court in North America, Court Brooklyn in New York. By 1871, the American branch of the AOF had become frustrated by the extremely slow response of the English head court, both in settling internal disputes and processing the claims of its members. After petitioning to be allowed to establish a subsidiary high court in the U.S., to no avail, AOF members seceded from the British body and formed the Independent Order of Foresters. The founder of the new IOF was Colonel Alonzo B. Caldwell, and he assumed the title "Most Worthy High Chief Ranger," a name that harkened back to the organization's roots in forestry. At the 1875 annual meeting, Caldwell introduced the ten-cent endowment plan, which provided the beneficiary of a deceased member ten cents from each member, the total benefit of which could not exceed $1,000.[42] It was this endowment that Dr. Oronhyatekha grew into an immense yet controversial amount over the next three decades.

This 1892 *Independent Forester* magazine shows the values of Liberty and Benevolence, symbolized by two women, and Concord, shown by clasped hands. The all-seeing eye represented an omniscient and omnipresent God and the religious underpinnings of the order.

The IOF instituted Court Hope, the first Canadian court, in London in 1876. By 1878, Robert Cordes had replaced Caldwell as Chief Ranger, and it was Cordes who admitted Dr. Oronhyatekha to Court Dufferin during his visit to London, even though the constitution restricted membership to adult white males. Cordes recorded this notable event in his annual report. Upon "the solicitation of nearly every member," he said, he issued a "special dispensation ... to initiate one Doctor Oronhyatekha, a gentleman of Indian parentage, who was highly recommended by everyone who knew him. This act I have never regretted as he is one of the hardest workers in the Order in Canada, and by his labors, Independent Forestry is spreading throughout the Dominion." Speaking two decades later of his motivation to join, Dr. Oronhyatekha said "They told me that an Indian could not be a member ... That was enough for me; I had to get in."[43]

Dr. Oronhyatekha moved swiftly up the IOF ranks. At his own expense, he established many more courts under the IOF banner of

Liberty, Benevolence, and Concord. He served briefly as the Vice Chief Ranger of Court Dufferin before he and others organized another London court, Court Victoria, and he moved his membership to it. He also served as court physician, meaning he examined potential members to see if they boasted good enough health to meet the insurance requirements mandatory to join. After the formation of the Right Worthy High Court of Ontario in 1878, the jurisdiction that immediately oversaw local courts, he was elected its Right Worthy high chief ranger, a position he held almost continuously until 1882.[44]

DISSENT AND SECESSION

Dr. Oronhyatekha's early years with the IOF were filled with contention.[45] In 1879, treasurer Henry Griffin absconded with some $17,000. The newly centralized collection of member dues for death benefits, rather than by each local lodge, allowed the accumulation of such a large endowment under his control. Calls to have members pay a second time led to rebellion. Several American courts wished instead to keep membership dues by state, and when the IOF executive refused, the Illinois courts seceded.

As High Chief Ranger of Ontario, Dr. Oronhyatekha called an emergency meeting of the provincial court to discuss rumours of Canadian secession from the IOF Supreme Court. Twenty courts wished to separate while only six expressed their willingness to repay their dues. Dr. Oronhyatekha refused to allow secession and instead asked for an amicable separation of Canadian endowment funds from American ones. If he hadn't prevented widespread secession, the IOF in Canada would have collapsed; in the month following the special meeting, a number of members died, and the remaining members could not have covered the payment of death benefits.

The endowment issue continued to be contentious. Members disagreed about whether death duties should be levied each month, or at the time of death, but the decision was postponed until the annual convention of the international Supreme Court to be held in London that fall. Dr. Oronhyatekha reaffirmed, however, that he would not consider secession from the IOF, only the separation of Canadian and American endowments.

The 1879 annual meeting of the Supreme Court tested Dr. Oronhyatekha's leadership. He presented his proposal for separation of monies, but it was denied, resulting in the High Court of Ontario representatives voting to secede from the IOF. Ever the compromiser, Dr. Oronhyatekha suggested that the decision be deferred, but his motion was struck down. The next day, Dr. Oronhyatekha and a loyal minority found that the Supreme Court had assumed the Ontario court dead. Dr. Oronhyatekha instead believed that the remaining courts loyal to the IOF still constituted a legal authority. Constitutionally, only five courts were needed, and ten remained. The Supreme Court executive quickly agreed, and the membership elected Dr. Oronhyatekha as Ontario High Chief Ranger once again.

Dr. Oronhyatekha faced a struggle to rebuild the IOF. After secession, only 196 Ontario members remained, there were no funds for death benefits, and the reputation of the organization had been tarnished by Griffin's embezzlement. Secessionists further attacked its reputation. They established a rival body, the Canadian Order of Foresters (COF), and for the next few years the two waged a war of words. Using newspapers and the COF publication, the *Canadian Forester*, it characterized the IOF as a "Yankee" organization, accused it of charging excessive rates, spread rumours of further IOF defections, and impugned Dr. Oronhyatekha himself because he was native. Using his position as editor of the *Independent Forester*, the IOF publication, Dr. Oronhyatekha rebutted such claims.

Court Chatham presented another challenge when it decided to join the COF. In seceding, the membership took its IOF regalia and furniture with them. Dr. Oronhyatekha filed a law suit to recover the property. Under cross-examination, counsel for the COF attempted to have the case thrown out of court on the grounds that Dr. Oronhyatekha was not a legitimate member of the IOF because of his native background. The lawyer read aloud the clause that stipulated members must be white. "Then, sir," the lawyer asked, "as a matter of fact, you were never a member of this Order, and you are not now a member?" Dr. Oronhyatekha disagreed. "Well, in view of this section of the Constitution, I don't see how you could be a member," the lawyer pressed. Dr. Oronhyatekha's response showed his deftness and acumen for debate:

You see you don't understand the law. The Constitution which you have quoted was only intended to exclude applicants who belonged to a race ... inferior to the white race. If you will look on page 145 ... (pointing to the minutes of the proceedings of the M.W.H. Court), you will find that ... [it] legalized my admission because they recognized the fact that I belonged to a race which was superior to the white.[46]

Following a great deal of laughter from the crowd, the lawyer apologized, assuring him that he had not meant to cast any aspersions on his background. However, the IOF lost its suit due to a technicality.

The 1881 annual meeting of the Supreme Court was another fateful one for Dr. Oronhyatekha. Even though his son Henry had drowned less than a month before, Dr. Oronhyatekha travelled to New York City to attend. Among other issues to be settled, the Dr. McConkey claim brought controversy. McConkey had been a member of Court Kempenfeldt in Barrie, Ontario, a lodge instituted by Dr. Oronhyatekha in 1880. When McConkey died shortly afterwards of typhoid, the IOF refused to pay his death benefit, claiming the court had never been registered. Dr. Oronhyatekha pointedly referred to the records of the last annual meeting, which had recognized the creation of Court Kempenfeldt. Nevertheless, the Supreme Court denied the claim.

Eight days after the New York meeting closed, Dr. Oronhyatekha opened the annual convention of the High Court of Ontario. He summarized the business conducted at the Supreme Court meeting, a report which initiated a stunning resolution. It was moved that "the Supreme Court has thereby proved itself recreant to the fundamental principles of the Independent Order of Foresters, and as it therefore no longer represents the Order, it is hereby resolved that we will stand by the old flag of Independent Forestry, and carry out in their entirety the principles upon which rests the foundation of the Order." The representatives at the meeting voted unanimously to approve this resolution. In essence, the High Court of Ontario had declared itself the true IOF, and accused the Supreme Court of abrogating its duties.[47]

Beyond its refusal to pay the McConkey claim, the Ontario representatives expressed concern over a number of other issues raised at the

Supreme Court meeting. First, it had changed the name of the organization to the United Order of Foresters. Second, it had become increasingly secular; the Supreme Court had done away with the position of chaplain and now allowed courts to meet on Sundays.

The High Court of Ontario reorganized itself as the "true" IOF. Dr. Oronhyatekha, surely still grieving for his son Henry, declared his retirement from office in order to devote himself to his medical practice, but he was persuaded that he could not leave during this time of crisis. The membership re-elected him as high chief ranger. Since the High Court of Ontario represented the entire order in Canada at that time, Dr. Oronhyatekha essentially functioned as the supreme chief ranger.

Dr. Oronhyatekha assumed the position of supreme chief ranger at the IOF's weakest moment. With but a remnant of its membership and verging on bankruptcy, the future of the IOF looked bleak.[48] Dissenters challenged his leadership the very next year at the 1882 annual meeting. He again had intended to retire from office, having shepherded the IOF through the crucial first year after its separation from the American order. But upon learning that a small party believed that his native background hindered the development of the IOF, not only did he stand for re-election, but he challenged his main opponent to run against him. Dr. Oronhyatekha was re-elected as supreme chief ranger.

During the 1882 meeting, Secretary Edward Towe rose and accused Dr. Oronhyatekha of using improper proxy votes to be elected, and charged that he and the Executive Council had used endowment funds saved for death benefits to pay off the organization's debts.[49] Dr. Oronhyatekha responded by stepping down temporarily from office and asking for a committee to investigate. The next day, the committee exonerated Dr. Oronhyatekha, and Towe retracted his accusations.

But one week later, while Dr. Oronhyatekha was caring for Ellen, who was sick at home at Tyendinaga, Towe and other IOF members visited the various London courts, repeating the charges and encouraging defection to the COF. Court Dufferin, the original lodge that Dr. Oronhyatekha had joined in 1878, invited him to a meeting with the intent of surrendering their charter to him, thus appearing to have voluntarily left the IOF rather than be expelled. Hearing about this scheme in advance, Dr. Oronhyatekha arranged for a loyal Dufferin member to object to the presence of the dissenters at the meeting, and he suspended them; since they were suspended, their presence violated the constitution, and thus Dr. Oronhyatekha could revoke the court charter before it could secede. Most of Court Dufferin joined the COF as the aptly renamed Court Defiance, but to Dr. Oronhyatekha's satisfaction, they did so as expelled IOF members. Further, Towe was charged with mishandling claim money.

The COF reacted by sending a circular to newspapers for publication. It characterized Dr. Oronhyatekha as having brought nothing but "contention and strife" to the IOF. They stated that he had falsified membership numbers and the amounts of assets and liabilities and had used the *Independent Forester* as his personal publication. Worse, when challenged, he had expelled members and closed down Court Dufferin, it said. The pamphlet invited all IOF members to join the COF and rob Dr. Oronhyatekha of his power by doing so. How many members did so is unknown, but in London, Court Maple defected shortly thereafter. According to Dr. Thomas Millman, one of Dr. Oronhyatekha's local supporters, the IOF was all but dead in the city.[50]

The COF and IOF continued to attack each other through their respective publications, comparing finances and challenging the legitimacy and morality of the other. The war continued in person. In 1885, COF officials disrupted meetings to institute IOF courts in Ontario and Quebec. At a meeting in Sebringville, Ontario, one COF member accused Dr. Oronhyatekha of falsely claiming to have banked $10,000 with the Canadian government as a security, a requirement for traditional insurance companies to operate legally in Canada. While the IOF was not required to do so, this was part of Dr. Oronhyatekha's plan to bring increased legitimacy to IOF insurance benefits. In response, Dr. Oronhyatekha secured a letter from the Ottawa bank superintendent and had it sent to the Sebringville meeting. Using his tongue-in-cheek humour to deflect COF criticisms, he wrote that the "I. O. F. is well able to defend itself, that the task is so easy that even 'an Indian' has little difficulty in coming out successfully in any contest which they may invite."[51]

Another confrontation occurred at Arkona. The COF held a meeting in which they repeated their accusations. IOF members in attendance telegraphed Dr. Oronhyatekha asking if he had been invited to respond to such claims. He answered that he had not, but would be happy to attend a future meeting. At this meeting, which lasted until 2:00 a.m., both Dr. Oronhyatekha and Towe of the COF spoke about the other's accusations. COF members charged Dr. Oronhyatekha with irresponsibly instituting a court in Watford without requiring medical exams. While regrettable, Dr. Oronhyatekha replied that this had been the policy under the old IOF, and in fact as soon as he had been elected the high chief ranger of Ontario, he had implemented mandatory medical exams. Towe also brandished a blank cheque signed by Dr. Oronhyatekha as a sign of his financial irresponsibility. Dr. Oronhyatekha noted, quite reasonably, that whenever he went away, he left a few cheques with Towe, the former IOF treasurer, so that any death claims that might arise could be paid immediately. Further, he insinuated that Towe's possession of this cheque showed his own lack of morality because all IOF property should have been returned after his expulsion.

COF representatives also raised the controversial Oates case. Benjamin Oates had been a member of Court Maple in London, which had defected to the COF. He died shortly after of consumption. Oates had paid his IOF dues up to the date of secession, but the COF had never turned the money over to the IOF, thus the IOF deemed Oates a lapsed member and his widow not entitled to his death benefit. The Oates family brought the case to court, and the judge ruled that the IOF must pay the claim. Really a case born from the confusion surrounding the secession controversy, the COF and the IOF used it to point fingers at each other. The COF accused the IOF of refusing to pay legitimate claims unless forced to do so by the courts. The IOF said that the COF's admittance of Oates, a dying man, demonstrated that it had loose medical exams and thus poor financial practices in extending him insurance.

Dr. Oronhyatekha told the Arkona audience that he had been previously cleared of all of Towe's charges, and that Towe himself had mishandled IOF insurance claims. Dr. Oronhyatekha also used his sharp wit to allay the accusations at the Arkona meeting. Speaking of the 1882 meeting when Towe had first charged Dr. Oronhyatekha, he pointed out that in his annual secretary's report, Towe had contradictorily attributed the IOF's success that year to Dr. Oronhyatekha. Towe then alleged that Dr. Oronhyatekha had written the report himself. "In other words that he had not brains enough to write a simple report, and had to come to me to furnish him with a little brains," Dr. Oronhyatekha remarked. Notably, Dr.

Oronhyatekha said, it was not until Towe was defeated in his bid for the position of supreme treasurer that he made his accusations.

The Arkona meeting finally ended after the majority of the audience agreed that the IOF was cleared of any wrongdoing in the Oates case. However, the COF published a circular provocatively entitled *The Perfidious Conduct of Dr. Oronhyatekha and some of the Officers of the I.O.F. Exposed.* Dr. Oronhyatekha tabled this report to the Supreme Court along with his resignation. Upon further examination, it exonerated Oronhyatekha, and he was elected by acclamation to his post as supreme chief ranger for another year.[52]

Another challenge from within the IOF came in 1890. The high chief ranger of the Court of Michigan attempted to secede from the IOF, partly because of Dr. Oronhyatekha's native background. The IOF Executive Council tried and found him guilty of treason and libel and expelled him. The remainder of the Michigan High Court vowed its loyalty. In writing about the event, Dr. Oronhyatekha turned the issue by saying, "it is true that it is my good fortune to be an Indian, but as it is inherited I ought not to be censured for belonging to that race. Under existing circumstances I had much rather be the 'Indian of Toronto' than the House in Saginaw," he finished with humour.[53]

EXPANSION

In 1881, when the Canadian IOF courts broke away from the American order, it was a turning point for both the organization and the now forty-year-old Dr. Oronhyatekha. He quickly recognized that renewed interest and significant enhancements in membership benefits were required if the IOF was to survive. Despite the controversies and challenges to his leadership, Dr. Oronhyatekha steadily increased membership and improved the IOF's structure and finances. In 1882, he travelled to the young province of Manitoba and instituted a high court. This trip marked the beginning of a twenty-five-year effort that would take Dr. Oronhyatekha around the world. By 1890, Dr. Oronhyatekha reported the IOF had spread to all provinces and territories in Canada and to thirteen states in the U.S., as well as Hawaii.

In 1891, during his travels for the IOGT, he established the first British court in Liverpool. Two years later, during another IOGT trip, he and his son Acland instituted courts in Scotland, Ireland, and Wales, as well as in several places in England. He relied on his IOGT networks, securing his former enemy Joseph Malins as one of the high chief rangers.[54] In 1898, the IOF expanded to Norway and Sweden, again using Dr. Oronhyatekha's IOGT contacts. In 1900, Dr. Oronhyatekha travelled to Australia and New Zealand to establish the IOF. That year, courts also opened in India and France, the latter no doubt helped by the IOF winning a gold medal in the Paris Exhibition for its display of their fraternal work. Eventually, Dr. Oronhyatekha instituted courts in Belgium, Ceylon, Holland, Germany, Denmark, and Egypt. Speaking of the IOF's rapid expansion, a fellow member wrote that he would not be surprised to hear that Dr. Oronhyatekha had "instituted a high court of the I.O.F. on the very [North] Pole itself." With the exception of the U.K., Norway, and Sweden, however, IOF courts in these countries only lasted a few years. It proved too expensive to maintain the order in relation to the members recruited and income generated.[55]

Acland graduated from Trinity University in 1891. He was admitted to the IOF as a minor under special dispensation in 1881, awarded the Supreme Court degree in 1885, and appointed Supreme Messenger in 1886 and High Junior Woodward in 1888. As a deputy supreme chief ranger and assistant secretary to the Medical Board in the early 1890s, he was placed in charge of extending the IOF in the U.K.

The Supreme Court often feted Dr. Oronhyatekha after he returned home from his travels.

Starting with a low of 369 members, IOF membership numbered near 250,000 worldwide by the time of Dr. Oronhyatekha's death in 1907.[56] This tremendous growth partially resulted from Dr. Oronhyatekha's links with his fraternal brothers in the IOGT, the Masons, and the Orange Order. These associations also enabled Dr. Oronhyatekha to access political and business leaders around the world, many of whom joined the IOF. Such members included American president William McKinley, Sir Wilfrid Laurier, a prime minister of Canada, Sir Charles Tupper, a father of Confederation, H.R. Emmerson, a premier of New Brunswick, George W. Ross, a premier of Ontario, Dr. Walter H. Montague, a secretary of state and minister of agriculture, George Kirkpatrick, a lieutenant governor of Ontario, and assorted members of Parliament. In turn, their names lent further legitimacy to the organization.

Dr. Oronhyatekha also used savvy advertising and recruitment techniques. In 1896, he placed lithographs of his picture in IOF uniform in every Canadian Pacific Railway station. He often offered prizes to top-recruiting courts or individuals. For example, he announced in

As a way to build a sense of belonging at mass initiations, the IOF issued souvenir coins and medals. This medal commemorated the joint initiation of 1,001 members at Massey Hall in Toronto.

Dr. Oronhyatekha pictured in his IOF uniform.

October 1888 that the court with the most new members recruited during the remainder of the year would receive a full set of officers' sashes, valued at twenty dollars. The court in second place would be awarded a full set of officers' badges, and the third place winner a framed copy of a picture of the Supreme Court officials. Other prizes included an IOF banquet lamp or souvenir spoon, morocco-bound copies of his *History of the IOF*, and even cash awards. Occasionally, he reduced initiation rates for specific periods of time, or allowed the fees to be paid in installments as an incentive. He also initiated large groups at one time. In 1902, he offered membership to all Torontonians without fees if they joined in January or February. On February 19, he inducted 505 new members at a large ceremony, and another 300 a few months later in April. The next year he initiated over 3,000 new members in only five cities, and in 1904 another 2,500 during three meetings.[57]

An obvious way to expand membership was to open the IOF to the wives and children of members. In 1888, Dr. Oronhyatekha established the first Juvenile Foresters court in London, but for years the Supreme Court resisted his emphatic belief that women should be able to join. Finally, in 1898, women-only Companion Courts were formally approved.[58] Tapping into the popularity of marching and drilling at that time, Dr. Oronhyatekha also created the Royal Foresters, a uniformed arm of the IOF that formed "encampments" rather than courts. To receive this advanced "Royal and Chivalric Degree," initiates needed to be Foresters first. Entitled Sir Knight, a Royal Forester needed to possess honour, chivalry, courage, and self-sacrifice for the benefit of the weak, emulating the nobleman of the forest, like the legendary Robin Hood.[59]

The mystique of secret rituals, of course, drew in members. Interestingly, in 1868, Dr. Oronhyatekha proposed that the Good Templars abolish all degrees and rituals as "an unnecessary and troublesome encumbrance and a fruitful source of embarrassment."[60] As IOF supreme chief ranger, however, he clearly saw the value of rituals, and rewrote them a number of times. These prescribed the proper protocols to be admitted to meetings, the order of business, initiation, installment, and other ceremonies, oaths and obligations of the officers, signs and salutes, and odes and prayers.

Like many other fraternal societies, the IOF drew inspiration for its rituals from the Old Testament, but it also turned to its legendary forestry-based past. For example, in its 1899 initiation ceremony, potential candidates were allegorically treated as strangers found wandering in a forest. The senior and junior woodwards blindfolded and bound the wrists of the applicant. The senior woodward then knocked on the meeting room door three times, to raise an "alarm," answered by three more knocks by the senior beadle on the other side. Upon opening the door, the beadle asked "[W]hat is the cause of this alarm?" The senior woodward replied, "While the Junior Woodward and myself were in the outskirts of our Forest, we came upon *a stranger* whom we forthwith captured; and *he informs* us that *he desires* to become *a member.*" The chief ranger then beckoned the applicant to enter, saying "the captive *stranger asks* a great privilege at our hands ... *His* fidelity of purpose must be demonstrated, and the brethren must be satisfied of *his* fitness and worthiness." To do so, the candidate was conducted around the room as members sang an initiation ode. The orator recited the Ten Commandments, and the vice chief ranger instructed the applicant on the purpose and duties of the order. Under dimmed lights, the members joined hands and formed a circle of concord around the candidate. As the woodwards removed the applicant's blindfold, the orator proclaimed, "And God said, let there be light; and there was light." The candidate then swore an oath of duty and secrecy. As all the members chanted, the supreme chief ranger flashed the symbolic "great light," or salt sprinkled with alcohol. The chief ranger then provided more "light" or further instruction on the principles of Liberty, Benevolence, and Concord and the signs and passwords of the order. The circle of concord formed around the applicant once again, and he was proclaimed a member.[61]

Dr. Oronhyatekha also promoted social events and engineered showy spectacles that brought widespread public attention to the IOF and attracted new members. Members organized court activities such as dances, Christmas banquets, masked balls, smoking concerts, cake walks, and basket socials. In 1887, the London Foresters hosted the public at the city roller rink. The evening's entertainment included refreshments, music, and the installment of officers — a secret ceremony not normally seen by non-members. In 1889, the IOF courts of Hamilton and area entered the society parade contest at the local carnival. Decorated with evergreens, flowers, and a beribboned stuffed elk and carrying young girls dressed in white who symbolized the Canadian provinces, the IOF float won the prize for best exhibit. Dr. Oronhyatekha and other officials followed in full regalia, parading to Dundurn Park, where the main activities of the day took place. In 1892, he and his son Acland participated in the "Meeting of Nations," a "Grand Historical Tableaux," a fundraiser for the Women's Christian Temperance Union. Demonstrating the progress of native people with a tongue-in-cheek "before and after," Acland pretended to scalp a dead soldier while his father presented a Forester widow with an insurance cheque for $3,000.

In 1899, Dr. Oronhyatekha and the Royal Foresters descended upon Barrie to celebrate Dominion Day. Residents gathered to watch as they marched through town, performed military drills, and competed against the Barrie lacrosse team. That night a celebration at the opera house included welcome speeches and a musical and literary program. On the Sunday, seated conspicuously at the front with town residents behind them, the Foresters attended church. Even the sermon lauded the work of the IOF. Part of the annual meeting of the High Court of Central Ontario in 1900 was held in a public park in Owen Sound and more than three thousand people attended to hear Dr. Oronhyatekha and other officials speak.

In 1902, attending the triennial Supreme Court meeting in Los Angeles, Dr. Oronhyatekha and other Foresters marched in the floral parade for La Fiesta, a week-long celebration of the city's multicultural history.

Even his return from vacation in the Middle East in 1898 was celebrated with a procession of members, Royal Foresters, and a band, from his home on Carlton Street in Toronto to the IOF building on Bay and Richmond, some thirty minutes away by foot, as a prelude to an evening reception. Such spectacles could hardly help be noticed by the press and by the public.[62]

Among other fraternal organizations, the IOF staffed a tent as part of "Society Row" during the annual Toronto Exhibition. Here, IOF members dressed in regalia advertised the benefits of membership and gave away tokens with IOF symbols. The *Globe* described its tent in 1905 as "magnificently-furnished" with carpets, upholstered chairs, and a dressing room for the ladies. "There, where the cool breezes sweep across the blue waters of Lake Ontario," visitors rested to contemplate what they had seen at the fair. In 1892, a large oil portrait of Dr. Oronhyatekha formed part of the art gallery exhibit at the Toronto fair. At least one year, the Mohawk band from Deseronto performed; dressed in buckskin, their exoticness

This 1902 membership certificate signed by Dr. Oronhyatekha shows the symbols of Liberty, Benevolence, and Concord, as well as a moose, the king of the forest. According to the ritual of the Royal Foresters, the moose was the "lordly ranger of the forest, a king of his kind, and his head is to us a symbol of excellence, and should stimulate us to try and excell [*sic*] in all good works, but especially in those connected with our Order."[63]

The IOF created "jewels" or pins, and badges and ribbons to wear as part of its uniform.

Visitors to the Toronto Exhibition relax at the IOF tents.

attracted a crowd. In 1898, the IOF held its triennial meeting of the Supreme Court at the same time as the Toronto Exhibition, and members competed in a fancy drill and a band competition at the fairgrounds.[64]

Dr. Oronhyatekha used the royal visit of the Duke and Duchess of Cornwall and York (later King George V and Queen Mary) to Toronto in October 1901 as another opportunity for flamboyant advertising. Like other fraternal societies, the IOF took out prominent advertisements in several souvenir publications. These may have reached tens of thousands of people, if not more; the number of people who flooded the streets to see the Duke and Duchess in Toronto numbered almost a quarter of a million. Calling itself the "best fraternal benefit society in existence," the ads proudly informed readers that it had 187,000 members, almost five million in funds, and had distributed over ten million in benefits. These ads also showcased the impressive new IOF headquarters, the Temple Building, only four years old at the time.[65]

Unsurprisingly, Dr. Oronhyatekha joined Toronto's planning committee for the royal visit. He had plenty of opportunity to showcase the IOF. On October 11, like other buildings flanking the royal procession route, the Temple opened its rooftop to visitors seeking a good vantage point. Near the Temple, the IOF erected a massive arch under which the royal carriage and procession passed. Only one of two arches made for the occasion, the IOF spared no expense, dedicating several thousand dollars to its construction. The four-fronted arch stood five storeys high and spanned Bay Street at Richmond. Its four pillars were ornamented with plaster of Paris crowns, shields, and pine cones, and were surmounted by a dome painted a sky blue underneath. Atop the arch's dome rose a gold Tudor crown twenty-five feet in diameter and bejewelled with coloured glass globes lit with electric lights. The whole of the arch was lighted in red, blue, and white so that it could be seen at night. As the royal carriage approached the arch, one hundred uniformed Royal Foresters of the Temple Encampment standing on the columns and dome presented swords while the Trumpet Band played a fanfare. The duke and duchess bowed in acknowledgment to the Foresters' lavish welcome.

The Toronto *Globe* called the Foresters' arch the "most elaborately decorated and the most skilfully designed" of all the arches under which the royal couple had passed during their entire trip, and in case any Torontonian had not seen it in person, the paper printed a sketch of it for its readers. Together with the illuminated Temple Building, which featured fourteen thousand incandescent lights surrounding each window and its tower, the arch lit up the night sky until almost midnight, forming one of the "Centres of Attraction" for the thousands milling about in the city streets. In 1902, the IOF donated the arch to the city of Toronto and moved it to the exhibition grounds next to the location of its yearly open house tent. Upon its gift, Dr. Oronhyatekha joked that when he became mayor of Toronto, he would make the fair truly international, and when he became the president of the exhibition itself, he would have stately homes, not just tents, for foreign visitors; when it was "international in character ... it will become the Mecca of Foresters of all kindreds and tongues."[66]

But this royal visit must have meant more to Dr. Oronhyatekha than simply an opportunity to bring attention to the IOF. In 1901, the Duke visiting Canada was the son of the Prince of Wales who had visited Canada in 1860, and his visit must have reminded Dr. Oronhyatekha of how his life had changed so significantly since then. He, who professed himself a Mohawk ally many times in his life, must have also seen the visit as another opportunity to express his loyalty.

The Temple Building and the IOF arch lit up the night during the royal procession in 1901. Note the Royal Foresters standing on the arch itself.

Beyond such spectacles, part of the draw to join the IOF was Dr. Oronhyatekha himself. His humour and boyish charm disarmed the public. A showman, he personally connected with individuals even in crowds. At one high court meeting in Australia, Dr. Oronhyatekha announced to the large gathering, "Brethren, I would like to shake hands with you all. Hold up your hands, everyone." When a "forest of hands" went up, he called out "Shake!"[67] For good or for bad, his native background fascinated the public. In the nineteenth century, the public considered native people exotic, and since he did not fit the stereotype of a backwards savage, his achievements and in particular his connection to British royalty appeared even more unusual. Standing over six feet tall, the press often remarked on his large and imposing presence and the size of his head, which he claimed was the largest on the North American continent. Journalists also frequently complimented his eloquence, his quick wit, and his skill in debate.[68]

In 1893, the *Toronto Daily Mail* published an extended biographical sketch. Noting his many fraternal associations, the *Mail* quipped that as "a Mason he ... has long since passed the third degree, the mirth-destroying stage, that once reached ... destroys the desire and capacity to smile. But those who know Oronhyatekha, have seen his genial smile and heard his hearty laughter ... Without the adventitious aid of birth or fortune," the *Mail* continued, "he has pushed his way by dint of energy and ability to the front.... The elements that have contributed to this success are not far to seek.... He has studied books much, he has studied men more.... He wields the pen of a ready writer.... An English periodical speaks of him as being 'calm, courteous, imperturbable, clear and decisive. He is a master in debate. His weapon is as smooth and incisive as a Damascus scimitar; his dexterity in wielding it, and his quickness in watching the fence of an opponent, are extraordinary and admirable.'"[69]

Certainly, many IOF members expressed great appreciation for his leadership. After its difficult reorganization, the membership made a special presentation to him at the High Court of Ontario meeting in June 1883. The previous supreme chief ranger, Edward Botterell, presented him with a gold watch engraved with the IOF crest to mark the "gratitude of the entire membership for [his] never tiring zeal and indefatigable energy in advancing the interests of our beloved order." He had quadrupled the membership roll, Botterell continued, "and you have never considered yourself, or the interests of those dear to and dependent on you, in your great work for us ... we can never repay you for all you have done in placing our Order in so prosperous a condition." Dr. Oronhyatekha cherished this gift for the rest of his life, as a symbol representing "the friendship, the sincerity and integrity of the men who worked with him."[70]

Twenty-two years later, the IOF again celebrated Dr. Oronhyatekha's leadership. In 1905, he had been re-elected by acclamation as supreme chief ranger for twenty-five years running. In honour of the occasion, the membership presented him with a unique "jewel," or pin, consisting of three bars of gold connected by small chains. Rubies spelled out "1881" on the first bar, diamonds formed his name on the second bar, and the third bar had sapphires arranged in the date, 1906.[71]

FINANCIAL REORGANIZATION

"Fraternity plus insurance" branded the IOF. By the early 1900s, the IOF provided "cradle to grave" benefits, including life and disability insurance, a pension, sick benefits, and a sum to pay for funerals. At this time, most Canadians obtained insurance through fraternal societies rather than commercial companies. As the nineteenth century progressed and Canada became increasingly industrialized, more and more men and women migrated from rural farms to urban centres and took on wage labour jobs. With little safety legislation in place, some of these factory jobs could be dangerous. The loss of a daily wage when sick or disability from losing a hand or limb could be financially devastating. As well, the extended kin network began to break down as family members were no longer as likely to live in the same area, and recent immigrants might not have family in Canada. Perceptions of medical care also changed over the nineteenth century; once cared for in the home, the ill and dying were increasingly treated in hospitals, making it more expensive to be sick. Burials also became more expensive. In the almost complete absence of a social safety net, the Foresters offered security in the form of fraternalism and financial aid. Fraternal insurance was also popular because aid in a time of need was seen as a right of membership, rather than charity, which was viewed as a symbol of moral failure or a poor work ethic. By 1900, many fraternal societies had let their insurance plans lapse, but the IOF continuously improved its policies and expanded its membership base to make it the most successful fraternal insurance in Canada. Starting with a debt of $4,000 in 1881, by Dr. Oronhyatekha's death in 1907, the IOF had accumulated over 10 million dollars in funds. Like other fraternal organizations with insurance plans that survived the nineteenth century, the IOF became more like commercial insurance companies but maintained its fraternal rituals.[72]

Conscious of the attacks from outside and within the IOF, Dr. Oronhyatekha spent much of his time bolstering the legitimacy of the organization, both in financial and legal matters. Like many other fraternal groups, the IOF had changed from a purely assessment model — collecting a flat fee of ten cents from each member after a death — to one with monthly charges based on the cost of risk and an estimated number of deaths per year.[73] This happened in 1879. Two other major changes to the endowment laws occurred that year. First, the Supreme Court adopted age grading for all new members, meaning that members joining at an older age paid higher dues than younger ones. A common practice in commercial insurance, age grading aimed to balance the higher health risks and shorter lifespan of older members with higher payments. Second, the Supreme Court introduced two other benefit classes, $2,000 and $3,000, for which members had to pay dues above those of the original $1,000 policy.

In 1881, during the reorganization of the Supreme Court, this latter change proved controversial, but Dr. Oronhyatekha threatened to block all proposed endowment law changes unless members approved this clause. That year, the allowed age of members slightly expanded from between ages twenty and fifty to eighteen and fifty-five. The age grading was further refined by every two years, rather than every five, as had been the case in 1879. Rates also more than doubled for most new members, and now included the cost of management expenses. Optional sickness and funeral benefits were also established in 1881. For an enrollment fee and monthly dues, the IOF provided its members with free medical attendance, a weekly allowance during an illness, and a lump sum for funerals upon death.

In 1891, monthly endowment dues rose substantially for members over age fifty, and a new clause stipulated that no one could join after age fifty if they worked in a career considered hazardous. In 1896, a $500 endowment class was created, resulting in a shift in rates, with some of the costs for older members in other classes rising quite significantly. Two higher endowment classes of $4,000 and $5,000 were also established, a change Dr. Oronhyatekha had wanted since 1886 but which had been resisted by the provincial Superintendent of Insurance. Rates for new members were adjusted again in 1898, and costs for most age categories increased.[74]

Beyond paying fees, members had to proclaim a belief in a supreme being and live a moral life. Applicants also needed a medical exam. While the IOF had used a cursory medical questionnaire, Dr. Oronhyatekha introduced a more rigorous assessment. This tightening of requirements aimed to keep insurance rates within reach of the average wage earner and to improve IOF finances; it was more expensive to carry members who had a pre-existing condition that might result in sickness or early death.

Before 1878, the IOF's original medical examination consisted of one compound question: "Have you ever had spitting of blood, bronchitis, asthma, rheumatism, gout, scrofula, spinal disease, fistula, rupture, disease of the kidneys, bladder, heart, chronic diarrhea, dysentery, or a protracted cough, or any disease that would have a tendency to shorten life?" Dr. Oronhyatekha implemented a new two-page medical exam that included questions about an applicant's age, weight and height, vaccination status, family history of illness, any disabilities, as well as an expanded list of diseases for screening. Applicants with heart or lung conditions, rheumatism, tuberculosis, or even "General bad health" were rejected. The court physician was also expected to examine the applicant's heart, respiration, and internal organs. In 1880, the medical exams tightened again. Instead of merely asking about an applicant's health, the new regulations specifically banned individuals with certain histories of disease. In 1884, urine testing became mandatory to further screen out the sick. Dr. Oronhyatekha even attempted to have social members — those who did not take out insurance — pass a medical exam.[75]

Under Dr. Oronhyatekha, the IOF also tightened up its description of the hazardous classes. In 1883, the Supreme Court ordered a study on dangerous professions, such as mining or policing, reasoning that those employed in such professions were more likely to fall ill or die early because of their work. These members paid higher insurance premiums. A staunch prohibitionist, Dr. Oronhyatekha recommended in 1887 that the extra hazardous class should include saloon and hotel keepers. These men had a lower life expectancy, he said, just as lead and coal miners did. In fact, the medical board often recommended that even individuals who drank alcohol should be banned, though this extreme opinion was never officially approved. By 1898, the constitution banned coal, lead, and copper miners, individuals working with explosives, and anyone manufacturing or selling alcohol from membership. By 1902, the latter provision was made even more specific, including anyone carting or bottling liquor. Any existing member who took up one of these careers would be downgraded to a purely social membership, without the benefit of life insurance.[76]

Another step towards legitimacy involved provincial incorporation under the Ontario Benevolent Societies Act in 1881. Its charter listed the IOF's purpose as the provision of funds to widows and heirs or to those reaching the age of seventy, and to the sick, as well as the "mutual assistance, enjoyment, entertainment and improvement of members, socially and morally, by the practice of provident and benevolent usages." However, as time passed, Dr. Oronhyatekha wished the IOF to be treated similarly to commercial insurance companies in that the federal government would regularly inspect its finances. In 1884, the federal government in fact considered a bill that required fraternal societies offering insurance to fall under the Consolidated Insurance Act, which governed commercial companies. Under this act, companies needed to be licensed and make a deposit of fifty thousand dollars with the government. Originally, since most fraternal societies simply levied assessments upon a member's death, no funds accumulated. But when they changed, as the IOF did, to monthly premiums, larger amounts accumulated, which opened up opportunities for fraud. Thus some politicians believed the government should regulate such organizations. Introduced by Finance Minister Leonard Tilley, the bill proposed that fraternal societies should obtain a licence and make annual financial reports but not be required to make a deposit. Dr. Oronhyatekha travelled to Ottawa to urge Tilley to require all fraternal societies to establish a reserve fund, the amount to be based on membership numbers, until a deposit of $50,000 had accumulated. It was too late, however, in the parliamentary session to modify the bill. Although it was hotly contested, the amendments to the Insurance Act passed, but allowed fraternal societies to choose whether they would be governed by it.[77]

Dr. Oronhyatekha insisted that Tilley accept a ten-thousand-dollar deposit in the government bank in Ottawa. Ever watchful of the IOF, the COF also attempted to do the same but it was refused; normally, the bank only opened accounts for individuals and only to a maximum of one thousand dollars. Tilley finally bowed to Dr. Oronhyatekha's wishes, likely because of his personal connections with John A. Macdonald and other politicians. A special committee of the IOF deliberated what to do next. It again attempted to deposit fifty thousand under the supervision of the government's department of insurance, but this was repeatedly refused since the new legislation did not require it. As a result, Dr. Oronhyatekha decided to not register under the new act as it would cost money and achieve no benefit.[78]

By 1888, Dr. Oronhyatekha had decided to privately incorporate the IOF, especially since the organization was Canada-wide, not just in Ontario. Joseph Jamieson, a member of Parliament and fellow Forester, promoted the incorporation bill in Parliament. The AOF and COF protested, claiming the public would be confused by the use of the name "Foresters" by multiple groups, only one of which would be incorporated. A more general bill dealing with fraternal societies loomed on the horizon and some groups felt IOF incorporation should wait until then. In opposition, Dr. Oronhyatekha believed that the AOF and COF protested because they would be further disadvantaged by the growth resulting from IOF incorporation. Despite Dr. Oronhyatekha's argument to the contrary, the government superintendent of insurance also protested incorporation because he felt that the IOF rates were too low to be sustainable and worried that insurance plans offered by fraternal societies were too risky.[79]

Nevertheless, the bill to incorporate the IOF passed. For his support, the IOF proclaimed Jamieson a chevalier of the Grand Cross of Merit and presented him with the according "jewel." During an evening celebration and dinner, Senator David Reesor, another IOF champion, received a gold-headed cane and an honorary membership for his support. Now incorporated, the IOF was allowed to hold $100,000 of property, soon to be of use in building its new headquarters in Toronto, and to invest its funds in various ways. Originally, Dr. Oronhyatekha wanted to submit annual financial reports for inspection, but the government decided this would place the IOF in a too similar status to commercial companies without requiring the mandatory deposit of $50,000. Despite this, Dr. Oronhyatekha stated that it was clear the IOF was not afraid of inspection as commercial companies had accused.[80]

He continued to try to have the IOF placed under the Insurance Act. In 1892, he and two politicians, both of whom were IOF members, met with the minister of justice to discuss the issue. But it was not until 1896 that IOF powers and accountability expanded. The year before, the IOF had applied to amend its act of incorporation. Again, Dr. Oronhyatekha wished to have the IOF licensed, fall under federal government inspection, be able to hold an increased amount of property, deposit money with the government as a security, increase the maximum mortuary benefit from three thousand to five thousand dollars, and to be allowed to invest money internationally. William Fitzgerald, the superintendent of insurance, protested. He felt that the IOF rates were too low for long-term sustainability. Whether it was the influence of John A. McGillivray, the supreme secretary, now an M.P., or Dr. Oronhyatekha's single-minded persistence, in 1896 the government passed the revised act with all of the amendments Dr. Oronhyatekha wanted. The IOF now fell into a special category. It was licensed by the Insurance Act as required for commercial companies, but was exempt from maintaining a reserve, which commercial companies had to do.[81]

In 1889, the IOF relocated its headquarters from London to Toronto, the financial centre of the province. Dr. Oronhyatekha decided to build a suitable headquarters rather than continuing to rent office space for his ever-growing staff, and purchased land at the corner of Bay and Richmond in downtown Toronto. Designed by architect and fellow Forester George Gouinlock, on May 30, 1895, the governor general, the Earl of Aberdeen, laid the cornerstone of the Temple.

As Dr. Oronhyatekha focused on improving the finances and reputation of the IOF, his career revolved more around business and less on medicine. Until 1886, as high chief ranger of Ontario and then supreme chief ranger, he only received a small sum voted to him by the membership, usually two hundred dollars a year. Even this amount he often declined because he knew the IOF was financially vulnerable. In 1886, the amount jumped significantly to fifteen hundred and the next year, an official salary of two thousand dollars was instituted for the position of supreme chief ranger, with the stipulation that Dr. Oronhyatekha "devote all his time for the benefit of the Order." By 1891, he received an annual salary of six thousand dollars and by 1905, fifteen thousand.[82] After relocation to Toronto, he still advertised his medical practice, but he must have had limited time to see patients.[83]

LIBERTY, BENEVOLENCE, AND CONCORD

The Haudenosaunee valued collectivity. At the same time, the social gospel movement was well in hand. Largely driven by Christian principles, social gospellers believed in political and social reform to address child labour, racial tension, crime, alcohol abuse, economic inequality, and poverty. They advocated for institutional or government intervention to solve these issues. Merging traditional and contemporary values, Dr. Oronhyatekha made humanitarianism a cornerstone of the IOF. As he built the organization, he tried to demonstrate that its motto, "Liberty, Benevolence and Concord," was more than mere words. As the *Independent Forester* proclaimed, the IOF was "based on the broadest principles of mutual aid and fraternal intercourse in all the social and business relations of life." Beyond providing for the sick and families of the deceased, its "grand object [was] to unite in one *true brother-hood* all good men, without regard to sectarian creeds, political dogma, or conditions of life ... to foster a spirit of co-operation in all departments of labour and commerce; assist the unfortunate and relieve the distressed." The principles of the order taught all Foresters to be *"Sober, Upright* and *Conscientious* — willing to help, ready to relieve, and obedient to the laws of the country, so as to command respect from their fellow-men." The IOF ritual book also explained the meaning of its motto. To glorify God, members should strive for liberty from ignorance and vice. Liberty also symbolized the brotherhood of man; one could disagree with one's fellow man, yet still respect liberty of thought. Liberty also meant freedom to choose political, national, and religious beliefs. Benevolence was one of God's virtues, and the brother-hood of man acted as its "keystone." IOF members should seek to improve the wellbeing of others, by visiting the sick, burying the dead, and shunning personal gratification. Benevolence and Concord linked "brother to brother in the bonds of Faith in God." Concord, the belief that members should do unto others as they should do unto them, promoted peace and harmony.[84]

Dr. Oronhyatekha believed in the equality of men and women. Contrary to the common nineteenth-century stereotype that depicted native women as mere drudges, many Haudenosaunee women held power-ful political and social positions. Dr. Oronhyatekha witnessed this in his own family, having grown up with several influential women, such as his paternal aunt Nellie Martin Johnson, a clan mother. Although presented jokingly and ironically, invoking the language Indian Affairs used when discussing First Nations, at the 1885 Christmas banquet, Dr. Oronhyatekha suggested that the presence of women there showed a "gradual increase of the civilization of the Foresters." He hoped such progress would continue until the white members had reached the higher level of civilization now occupied by the Haudenosaunee.[85] By the end of the nineteenth-century, mainstream society increasingly accepted women's role in social reform, and the IOGT provided a strong example of the benefit of including women as members and officials. Not surprisingly then, in 1882, only one year into his tenure as supreme chief ranger, Dr. Oronhyatekha advocated the admission of women as full members of the IOF, a proposal that was soundly defeated. In 1884, he reintroduced the issue in a more strategic way, suggesting that female members be accepted in the United States as they had before the 1881 reorganization. Further, to counter the argument that women's health was more precarious than men's, he suggested that they pay the increased rates of the hazardous class. In 1885, he tried a different tack, presenting statistical evidence that women actually lived longer than men. He also noted that banning women from membership would hamper the IOF's expansion into the northern United States.

In 1891, a special committee studied the issue and recommended that women be allowed to join, but in separate courts. Objectors characterized insuring women as experimental and worried about what might define "total disability" for a woman since their bodies were weaker. Further, the mandatory physical exam required applicants to be stripped to the waist so that the physician could thoroughly examine the heart and lungs. The report suggested such an exam was improper for women and that doctors were "hampered by the conformation of the female chest." How could they be properly examined? Ineffective exams would lead to the admittance of less than healthy members, jeopardizing IOF finances. At the very least, the benefit rates needed to be modified because of the special diseases that only women contracted. These arguments persuaded the majority of voters. The issue was raised again in 1893 at the High Court of New Brunswick annual meeting. Dr. Oronhyatekha explained that he had promised not to bring up the topic again, but since another member had done so, he gladly noted that it had to be referred to the Supreme Court. This victory, Dr. Oronhyatekha believed, resulted from the number of Good Templars members present at the meeting. Nevertheless, it took several more years for the admission of women, and then it was only as social, not beneficiary, members, and only in separate "companion" courts.

At the turn of 1897, Dr. Oronhyatekha reported that eighty companion courts existed throughout North America and Britain, and he hoped that there would be 10,000 members by the fall of 1898. He also wished that in the following year the Supreme Court would accept an insurance plan for women. If not, he planned on recommending a separate Supreme Court for women. In 1898, the IOF executive finally agreed to provide insurance benefits if women chose. However, companion courts remained segregated, and although Dr. Oronhyatekha recommended it, not all high courts accepted female representatives at their meetings.[86]

Despite the IOF membership's acceptance — even celebration — of Dr. Oronhyatekha's native ancestry, applicants with ethnic or racial backgrounds other than White generally fared less well. Although the clause banning non-whites from joining was not reinstated during the 1881 reorganization, there is little discussion of race in IOF documents. Of course, Dr. Oronhyatekha had witnessed firsthand the long-standing and contentious division of the Good Templars over the issue of race. Although some members protested, in 1898 an IOF committee charged with considering the issue recommended against "in future" the admission of members of Chinese, Japanese, African descent. There were clearly already some non-white members however; one month before the committee recommended against such admission, the *Independent Forester* featured the biography of Moy Loy, a state interpreter in Vermont, who had joined the previous January and taken the highest amount of insurance in the $5,000 class.[87]

Unlike the Orange Order, which required members to defend Protestantism, the IOF accepted members of other religions. In 1896, two Jewish courts formed, one in Toronto and one in North Dakota. Competing for members in Quebec, particularly against the Catholic Order of Foresters, the IOF sought to institute courts in French-speaking Roman Catholic areas of the province. Dr. Oronhyatekha wrote in his history of the IOF in the 1890s that the organization experienced difficulty in recruiting French-speaking Roman Catholic Quebeckers, but that at the time of publication there existed both purely French and mixed English and French courts. Quebec members elected Dr. T. Cypihot as the first French-Canadian representative to the Supreme Court in 1891. As a recruitment measure, the IOF translated its rituals into French the following year, and the *Independent Forester* in 1897. The IOF also invited prominent clergymen and members of the Saint-Jean-Baptiste Society to its events as a way to market itself.[88]

Under Dr. Oronhyatekha, the IOF also expanded its benefits for the aged. The Haudenosaunee valued the elderly for their life experience and wisdom while social gospellers advocated for reform to ensure care for the aged. After 1881, members reaching the age of seventy received one-tenth of their benefit annually until the whole had been paid out. Dr. Oronhyatekha later recommended that members aged seventy and older should be exempt from dues, with the exception of sickness and funeral fees. In 1898, he introduced an Old

Age Pension Benefit that provided a yearly income. At that time, care for the aged experiencing financial need was transitioning from the home to specialized institutions, some of which had less than ideal conditions. In 1903, Dr. Oronhyatekha announced that he would donate his home on Foresters' Island, an island near Deseronto that he owned, to be a retirement home for elderly IOF employees. In 1905, he proposed a similar home in California.[89]

Dr. Oronhyatekha also rewarded the sacrifices made by members who voluntarily joined military service. During the Spanish-American War (1898) and the Second Boer War in South Africa (1899–1902), the IOF reduced rates for all serving soldiers and sailors. Normally, the IOF classed these professions as hazardous, thus requiring higher monthly dues, but for the duration of these wars they fell under the ordinary class. As loyal as any Anglo-American and proud of his members' collective heroism, Dr. Oronhyatekha believed it his duty to ensure volunteers were not placed at any further disadvantage. He may have also been inspired by his son's application to serve in South Africa. Now thirty-one and a physician himself, Acland applied to be a surgeon during the Boer War. In 1900, Dr. Oronhyatekha proudly welcomed home about three hundred IOF members who had returned from South Africa, throwing them a special banquet at the Temple, which he decorated in bunting and electric lights for the occasion.[90]

The IOF also raised money to treat members suffering from tuberculosis, or consumption as it was more commonly called. Doctors usually recommended isolation and rest at a sanatorium, particularly in a location with bracing country air, which was thought to be good for the lungs. In 1897, the National Sanatorium Association opened the Muskoka Cottage Hospital near Gravenhurst, Canada's first TB institution. Built on the cottage plan, patients were housed in smaller buildings around a central hospital. Despite the term "cottage," which today conjures up a rustic building, these dwellings were closer to more lavish Victorian-style homes. By 1898, the *Independent Forester* solicited a few cents from every member to build a six-room cottage at the hospital specifically for IOF members. Dr. Oronhyatekha personally contributed ten dollars. A collection was also taken at the annual celebratory church service. Although an IOF staff member visited the site in 1898, it seems as if the cottage was never built. Individual IOF courts did, however, donate money to the institution for the next decade.[91]

The IOF also participated in humanitarian relief efforts after the 1906 San Francisco earthquake. Early in the morning of April 18, the San Andreas fault ruptured, causing widespread destruction. Still considered one of the worst natural disasters to occur in the United States, the quake and several days of resulting fires destroyed almost 80 percent of the city and left half to three-quarters of the population homeless. Upon hearing of the disaster, Dr. Oronhyatekha immediately wired $2,500 to establish a Forestric relief fund and sent a circular to all courts worldwide asking for donations to help its San Francisco members. Altogether IOF members sent $15,000 in aid. The executive also decided to waive the dues for several months while maintaining benefits for such members.[92]

Dr. Oronhyatekha also wanted the IOF to make further provisions for children. In 1888, he instituted the first juvenile court, Court Excelsior, in London. This was an experiment, but one successful enough that the Supreme Court shortly approved the Juvenile Branch of the IOF. Members needed to be between ages twelve and eighteen, and pledge not to smoke, swear, or drink and to obey their parents. Juvenile courts could also establish tactical drills or other activities for physical exercise.[93]

Postcard of the Orphans' Home, Foresters' Island, circa 1906.

This postcard shows Dr. Oronhyatekha with the children of the orphanage. These two postcards may have been part of the set sold to generate income for the orphanage.[94]

Inspired by Masonic orphanages in Ireland, in 1903 Dr. Oronhyatekha introduced plans for the construction of a home for orphans of deceased Foresters to be built on Foresters' Island, having donated the land to the IOF for that purpose. He wished to care for and educate these children "as a father would train and care for his own offspring." All orphans over the age of four were eligible and those with one parent, if unfit, also qualified. Education would follow the Ontario public curriculum closely, and Dr. Oronhyatekha anticipated that students would learn practical skills in farming, and gardening, and in the workshop and kitchen. If a student had an aptitude for another trade or avocation, the orphanage would try to adapt its training, he said. Reverend A.H. Creegan was appointed head of education.

Dr. Oronhyatekha believed the orphanage was the crowning achievement of his fraternal career; he would rather be remembered by the orphaned children who would live here, he declared, than in the fields of politics, science, or literature. It was the "dearest project of his life."

The IOF threw a number of concerts to raise money for the orphanage, but members were also expected to give generously. If every member gave ten cents, Dr. Oronhyatekha said, it would be enough to construct a building for one hundred children. Donations appear to have been slow, however; in 1905, the *Independent Forester* chided members' lack of contributions by stating perhaps they did not understand the value of Dr. Oronhyatekha's gift. Dr. Oronhyatekha then recommended that each member should give one cent monthly for the maintenance of the orphans. He also created the IOF match box, an item made of oxidized nickel, to be purchased for fifty cents, with all proceeds going to the home. In addition, he paid many of the orphanage's expenses out of his own pocket.

Dr. Oronhyatekha turned the first sod in the summer of 1903, and the cornerstone was laid in 1904. Thousands of Foresters, government officials, and church dignitaries attended a lavish ceremony that August. As he had for the Temple Building, Dr. Oronhyatekha contributed to the orphanage's architectural design. Unhappy with the estimates he had received, he decided to oversee its construction himself. Typically, the result was lavish and impressive. At its completion in November 1905, the orphanage was a massive structure with ornamental steel sheeting covering concrete walls. Each corner of the orphanage was fitted with battlement towers, and a central tower rose eighty feet in height. Two verandas extended across the front and both sides of the building at the second and third storeys. Like the Temple Building, the orphanage featured state-of-the-art conveniences and safety measures, including water and sewage systems, its own power plant, fire hydrants on the roof, in the baths, and on each floor, and steam heaters throughout.

Dr. Oronhyatekha constructed a wharf to allow lake steamers to dock in front of the orphanage. From the dock, the main entranceway was through a porch supported by massive Corinthian columns, and an oak stairway stood in the centre of the reception hall, thirty by twenty feet. It was flanked by a dining hall more than double in length. The girls' dormitory was situated on the lower floor, along with the superintendent's apartments and office space. Classrooms and the boys' dormitory were situated on the third floor. Also included was a parlour, an auditorium that could hold a thousand people, a library, and recreation and convocation halls. A fourth storey was anticipated to accommodate more children at a later date as was a three-storey annex, but these were never built.

Able to house 250 children, the orphanage accepted its first charge, a five-year-old girl from London, England, in November 1905. But several months after Dr. Oronhyatekha's death, the home only housed twenty-nine children, with few pending applications. The cost to run the institution outweighed this small number. By the end of 1907, the Supreme Court closed the home for the winter and sent the children to other orphanages. Under a burgeoning debt, almost as high as $250,000 according to some, it never reopened. In 1908 the IOF officially decided to divest itself of the Foresters' Island facilities, including closing the orphanage and re-establishing it in a more appropriate location. The building was sold in 1908 and slowly demolished over time. The IOF opened a second orphans' home in Oakville in 1909.[95]

Despite his hopes, the orphanage was the least successful of his efforts as supreme chief ranger. But it was only one of a number of monumental projects he completed at the turn of the century.

CHAPTER 6

MONUMENTS

ELEGANT LIVING

Dr. Oronhyatekha adopted a lifestyle befitting his middle-class success as a medical practitioner and his standing in the fraternal societies popular in Victorian Canada. Being "Oxford-trained" may have also created an expectation of a luxurious life. Coupled with the Martin family history, such a lifestyle appeared appropriate. His wife Ellen fully appreciated these desires; her family had a birthright, expressed in terms of land and social prominence at Tyendinaga. As Dr. Oronhyatekha's fortunes and reputation mounted, so too did the need for surroundings that reflected his success.

No matter where else they lived during Dr. Oronhyatekha's early career, he and Ellen always considered Tyendinaga to be their home. Their first house was a modest one. Between 1864 and 1867, while Oronhyatekha attended the Toronto School of Medicine, he and Ellen built a double log cabin on 160 acres at Tyendinaga. They began to farm and raise beef cattle. The cabin soon gave way to a larger and more gracious house known as The Pines. Of all of the homes Dr. Oronhyatekha owned, he described this one as "nearest his heart."[1] It was surrounded with large barns for cattle and other livestock, farm implements, and feed sheds. By 1890, he possessed over 250 acres of land.[2] Because he was away from Tyendinaga much of the time, Dr. Oronhyatekha employed his brother, Simeon, to supervise the farm and grounds.

Inside, Dr. Oronhyatekha and Ellen decorated The Pines in Victorian fashion, likely influenced by their visits to England and Europe. Like most educated and well-travelled Victorians, they assembled an eclectic collection of natural history pieces, taxidermy animals, fine china, Asian artifacts, and native items of cultural significance. Joseph Malins, Dr. Oronhyatekha's IOGT colleague, visited The Pines in 1893 and described it as "the most beautifully furnished house" he had seen in North America. James Mavor, another friend and University of Toronto economics professor, also visited Deseronto. Mavor and Dr. Oronhyatekha were met at the train station by a sleigh drawn by four plumed horses and travelled to The Pines wrapped in buffalo robes, which Mavor described in his memoirs as "commodious." While the living room was plain, "the great room of the house was the drawing-room." Mavor wrote that "Never had I, nor have I since, seen such an amazing apartment. There were collected everything that barbaric taste and ample means could provide. Oronhyatekha … had accumulated on his travels the things that struck his fancy … He had extraordinary pictures on the walls, which were covered with the thickest of embossed papers in brilliant red … and dominating everything, a life-sized statue of Oronhyatekha himself in plaster painted to look like life."[3]

"The Pines" at Tyendinaga.

Amidst all of this was an assemblage of live exotic animals. He collected live reindeer and exotic birds from foreign lands, including a talking parrot, but what seems to have entranced the local people the most was his monkey. Eva Maracle, the daughter of one of Dr. Oronhyatekha's estate caretakers, recalled as a child that children from the reserve would often go to The Pines to see the monkey, which he apparently kept near the entrance to his home.

Maracle also remembered that Dr. Oronhyatekha permitted only the Mohawk language to be spoken there. For the very occasional private visitor to The Pines, this would have added more exoticness to their experience, but to Dr. Oronhyatekha, it was a method to remind himself and those around him that he was still a Mohawk.

Ellen's family also held what was known as Captain John's Island, a low-lying island of some five acres of scrub brush and trees in the Bay of Quinte across from Deseronto. People rarely ventured out to this island during the warm summer months as it was populated primarily by black rat snakes. Amphibious and prone to climbing trees, these huge python-like snakes, while not poisonous and generally non-aggressive, still had an ominous presence. Characteristically, Oronhyatekha saw this island as an opportunity for the IOF, renamed it Foresters' Island, and opened it up to visitors in 1894.

Dr. Oronhyatekha obtained these matching Qing Dynasty vases made for the export market during a visit to China. Bena sold these, among other items, at auction after her father's death.

Acland and Bena at one of their family homes circa 1907. The woman on the left may be Acland's second wife, Therese.

He cleared the island of snakes by unleashing pigs, their natural enemy, and ferrets, which pursued any other unwanted vermin. Dotted with a mix of stately oaks and maple trees, the island had a park-like environment once Dr. Oronhyatekha cut away the underbrush. Here, he constructed a second stately Georgian-style mansion, which he called "The Wigwam." In 1901, he decided to build a modest cottage, which eventually turned into a thirty-room building named "The Castle," with a large, onion-shaped golden dome that rose above the treeline and glistened in the sun. Harking back to the medieval Forestric past, he referred to this home as "Sherwood Forest Castle," which he instructed should be converted into a seniors' home for retired IOF members after his death. The *Forester* magazine described the house as having "every modern convenience," including a hot-water heating system and telephones. The thirty rooms included a billiard room, a smoking room, a photographic darkroom, and a library.[4] Photographs show The Castle to be a gracious Victorian-style home.

The Wigwam.

The Castle in 1902. It was surrounded by a small wood called "Sherwood Forest."

The sitting room at the Castle.

The Castle dining room. Note the frieze of tipis and individuals with headdresses.

The very names The Pines and The Castle are regal, echoing the English-ness that had been replicated in colonial Canada, but they are also remin-iscent of a Haudenosaunee past. The pine, specifically the white pine, sym-bolizes the Great League of Peace that brought together the Haudenosaunee Confederacy of Five (later Six) Nations. Buried beneath the pine were the weapons of past wars between them, and the pine's roots offer a path to those seeking the peace and protection offered by a confederacy. Standing watch atop the great white pine perches an eagle that cries at the sight of any impend-ing danger. The Castle brings to mind the term the Haudenosaunee called their settlements in their lost homelands in upper New York State. Long ago fortified with wooden palisades, these villages had been referred to as castles.

Dr. Oronhyatekha's first act of clearing away the snakes that inhabited Foresters' Island echoed the actions of Hiawatha, one of the founders of the Great League of Peace. A Mohawk orator, Hiawatha brought the message of peace to the Five Nations. To convince the Onondaga nation of the value of joining the Great League, he first had to comb out the snakes entangled in the hair of Tadadaho, a particularly vicious and fearsome chief, so that his mind would be clear and he might hear Hiawatha's message of peace.

These homes met Dr. Oronhyatekha's need to find a peaceful refuge from the rigours of his world. Foresters' Island was a place apart, and one over which he had total control. According to Eva Maracle, Oronhyatekha spent most of his time at home at The Castle. She remembered that he would sweep into The Pines like a whirlwind, generating activity. But he stayed there for only a little while before going to Foresters' Island.

FORESTERS' ISLAND

Dr. Oronhyatekha also viewed the island as a place for his fellow Foresters to rest, relax, and be entertained. It was soon dotted with cottages, and over the years he constructed a wharf, a hotel, a dining hall, a bandstand, and a pavil-ion called Foresters' Hall. He expanded The Castle to include a ballroom, a dining hall, and more bedrooms.[5] With all these amenities, he hosted large groups, many of whom included influential politicians, church leaders, gov-ernment officials and business leaders of the day. In 1894, for example, he hosted the Indian Rights Association, a mostly American group concerned with the treatment and conditions of native peoples.[6]

Dr. Oronhyatekha seated on the lawn on Foresters' Island.

The island and hotel were also open to tourists, and Bena helped manage it for her father.[7] By the mid to late 1800s, the nearby St. Lawrence River and the Thousand Islands had become a popular vacation destination. Over the late nineteenth century, the average work week decreased in hours, and workers increasingly expected some vacation time. Often unable to afford lengthy or expensive travel to England or Europe, the middle class looked to areas nearer to their homes. Foresters' Island was conveniently located a few hours away by train from Toronto, and on the way to the Thousand Islands region. At the same time, the back-to-nature movement meant that Canadians valued outdoor trips to natural or wilderness areas as a way to invigorate one's health, particularly for urban dwellers concerned about living in cities with poor sanitation and sewage systems. Romanticism, a movement that rejected urbanization and industrialization and portrayed nature as picturesque, untouched, and a place to have a spiritual experience, also led more Canadians to seek out nature. This movement cast native peoples as primitive but noble upholders of ancient preindustrial customs, again as a rejection of modernization. The fact that a native family owned and ran the island hotel only increased its exoticism in the eyes of tourists.[8]

❧ "Isle Hotel" - Foresters' Island ❧ Park. ❧

SEASON OF 1897.

❧ ❧ ❧ ❧

THE "ISLE HOTEL" occupies an ideal site on Foresters' Island Park, a beautiful spot in the far-famed Bay of Quinte, Ontario. The Island lies opposite the Town of Deseronto, and about midway between the Hastings and Prince Edward's shores. At Deseronto is the terminus of the Bay of Quinte Railway, which connects with all the trains of the Grand Trunk Railway; it also connects with the C. P. R. at Tweed. The steamers of the Richelieu and Ontario Navigation Company call daily. The steamers Alexandria and North King make regular trips. All the boats plying on the Bay of Quinte call at Deseronto or the Park. Telegraph and Telephone connections with all points.

As a Summer Resort, the "Isle Hotel" is pre-eminently well located. It is cool, healthy and easily accessible. It offers delightful, interesting and restful advantages for physical and mental recreation. Conducted on American and European plans. Rates $1.50 and upwards per day. Liberal discount for parties staying for a protracted period. For further information as to rates, etc., apply to

❧ First-class Boat Livery   ORONHYATEKHA,
   in connection . . .   Deseronto, Ontario.

The waterfront Isle Hotel was open to all tourists, not just IOF members.

But most often, Foresters' Island served as a retreat for the executives, staff, and members of the IOF. Fond of grand gestures and opulent displays, Dr. Oronhyatekha staged picnics and events on the island, inviting performers, both native and non-native, to put on productions for his guests. These concerts often featured local Mohawk singers, and sometimes Dr. Oronhyatekha's daughter Bena sang and recited poetry in both Mohawk and English. The Mohawk brass band from the Grand River, made up of many of Dr. Oronhyatekha's nephews, including his namesake nephew Peter W. Martin, also frequently played for guests.

In 1894, the same year that Foresters' Island officially opened, the IOF surplus passed the million dollar mark, and Dr. Oronhyatekha threw a celebration in August. Even though the weather was poor, about three thousand people still attended the gala, which included games, speeches, and musical performances. The next year, between five and six thousand members and families from all over Ontario and the American Northeast and Midwest gathered on the island to celebrate the IOF's twenty-first anniversary over three days in June. A formal ceremony on the Monday afternoon included speeches by various officials and a formal presentation to Colonel A.B.

Caldwell, the American founder of the organization. As thanks for hosting the celebrations, the IOF presented Ellen with an elaborate set of china and Bena a set of gold-enamelled buttons. The Oronhyatekha family's love of music was evident during the weekend. As part of the anniversary service, Bena led the Mohawk choir in singing hymns in both Mohawk and English. The Mohawk, Deseronto, and Picton bands also performed. Lit by hundreds of Chinese lanterns, the celebrations closed on Monday evening with a concert, fireworks, and dance that lasted into the early morning hours.[9]

The dock at Foresters' Island. After 1904, visitors accessed the island via *The Mohawk Queen*, a steamer Dr. Oronhyatekha had built as a ferry between it and Deseronto.[10]

The Mohawk Brass Band from the Grand River often played at IOF celebrations on Foresters' Island.

Dr. Oronhyatekha had a zoo, which included this tame moose.

The IOF pavilion at Foresters' Island.

The anniversary celebration became an annual tradition. In 1896, more than ten thousand people attended, many arriving on a special eight-car train that ran from Toronto to Deseronto. Along with the usual speeches, dance, anniversary service, and musical performances by the Mohawk band and choir and the Oronhyatekha family, the festivities included athletic games and a regatta, all with prizes. The boat races featured a competition between former world champion sculler Ned Hanlan and James Rice, another competitive rower. Hanlan also judged all the other water events. The games on land included foot, potato, candle, and sack races, the long jump, and a Canada vs. the United States tug of war.[11]

For its annual celebrations, the IOF arranged for special excursion trains to take members from Toronto to Deseronto. Note the large portrait of Dr. Oronhyatekha on the front of the train.

Poster for the IOF annual picnic and regatta in 1896.

An IOF gathering on Foresters' Island. Dr. Oronhyatekha and Ellen are in the middle of the second row.

THE TEMPLE

As the IOF fanned out across North America, its need for office space grew. It had twice moved to different quarters in London, but Toronto had become the financial centre of Ontario. Near the end of 1888, the issue of a new headquarters arose. Dr. Oronhyatekha wrote that the IOF reluctantly decided to leave London, the "cradle of Independent Forestry in Canada," and "so many tried and true Foresters" who had stood by the organization in its early years of turmoil. In 1889, the IOF bade farewell to London. Dr. Oronhyatekha himself, now forty-eight years old, moved to 724 Yonge Street and by 1900 to an apartment at 209 Carlton Street. The IOF moved to new offices, first at the corner of King and Bay over John Treble's long-established gentlemen's clothing shop and later to the nearby Dominion Bank Building at King and Yonge streets, both in downtown Toronto. By 1893, Thomas Millman, the supreme physician, reported these offices to be crowded. Two years later, the IOF contemplated purchasing the Temperance Hall, but ultimately decided to buy a plot of land on the northwest corner of Bay and Richmond streets and construct its own building. This was a propitious location, near the proposed new city hall.[12]

Perhaps the only rival the orphanage could have had for Dr. Oronhyatekha was the Foresters' Temple, the IOF's world headquarters. In 1895, George Gouinlock, a deputy supreme chief ranger and Toronto architect, won the competition to design it. When the Temple Building opened in 1898, it was heralded as the tallest building in the British Empire.[13]

The Earl of Aberdeen and governor general of Canada ceremoniously laid the Temple cornerstone on a very hot day in late May 1895. Both he and his wife were honorary members of the order. The afternoon began with a banquet in his honour at the Queen's Hotel. To begin the ceremony, the pipe band and guard of honour of the 48th Highlanders marched down Queen Street to Bay, where a huge platform decorated with bunting and the flags of Great Britain and the United States stood. There a crowd awaited the arrival of the governor general and Dr. Oronhyatekha, who followed by carriage. After speeches, the governor general used a ceremonial silver and onyx trowel and a gavel made of cherry from the historic Mount Vernon, former home of George Washington, to lay the granite cornerstone. The granite had been obtained from Aberdeenshire

The Foresters' Temple as planned in 1895.

The governor general, the Earl of Aberdeen, addresses the crowd at the cornerstone ceremony.

to honour the governor general. A time capsule with IOF documents, membership certificates, badges, and copies of the *Independent Forester* magazine, were underneath. A reception followed the ceremony.[14]

Despite the positive press coverage of the festivities, the Temple drew controversy. The *Monetary Times*, a Toronto financial newspaper that frequently attacked fraternal insurance, suggested that Dr. Oronhyatekha had built it as a monument to celebrate himself. Further, the *Times* revealed, the IOF act of incorporation allowed the organization to own $100,000 of property but the Temple was valued at over $250,000. To skirt this issue, the *Times* suggested the IOF had resorted to shady dealings — the IOF had transferred ownership of the land to Dr. Oronhyatekha's personal secretary, Jessie Bayly, who then extended a mortgage to the Foresters. Some IOF members opposed to the Temple accused Dr. Oronhyatekha of being a dictator rather than the leader of a democratic organization dedicated to serving its members. In fact, one member sued the IOF executive based on the costly construction of the Temple along with assorted charges of financial mismanagement. However, it was at this time that Dr. Oronhyatekha and the IOF executive had introduced into Parliament revisions to the IOF's act of incorporation, which included an increase in the amount of property it could legally hold. These revisions were passed in the spring of 1896, blocking any further accusations.[15]

The Temple was significant for reasons beyond its height. The relocation of City Hall to Bay and Queen and the subsequent building of the Temple marked the beginning of the transformation of Bay Street from a warehouse zone and a home to small commercial structures to the heart of a high-density financial centre of Toronto. The Temple spawned the construction of a host of other skyscrapers around it.[16]

At its completion in 1897, the Temple stood ten storeys with an additional two storeys in the central tower, which was open to the public for viewing the city. The *Globe* described it as dwarfing the surrounding buildings into "comparative pigmies." Court meeting rooms took up part of the fourth and fifth floors. A two-storey assembly room for seven hundred people was located on the sixth and seventh floors, while the mostly female clerical staff worked on the eighth floor. The two highest storeys consisted of lodge and committee rooms, a kitchen, and a banquet hall that sat three hundred people. The lower storeys offered more office space, much of which

The Temple's lavishly decorated marble entrance hall could be accessed from Richmond Street, as shown here, or from Bay Street.

The Assembly Hall.

was rented out to other businesses. As a 1901 city directory shows, the Temple rented to an abundance of professionals and businesses, including telegraph and loan companies, banks, booksellers, solicitors, printers and publishers, insurance and real estate agents, engineers, architects, a barber, and a baker. The Masons and the Independent Order of Oddfellows also rented rooms. The IOF even had its own newsstand and cigar store. The basement housed bicycle storage, two smoking lounges, and a reading room.

Gouinlock designed the Temple in the Romanesque revival style, which was popular in the late 1900s for public buildings. Of massive construction, Romanesque buildings were costly and thus usually constructed by the wealthy, the government, or by large organizations. Gouinlock included the style's characteristic semicircular arches, deep windows, and recessed entrances, rounded corner turrets capped with cupolas, a square tower on the roof, and a variable stone and brick façade with belt courses, a purely decorative layer of stone that separated each floor. To provide more light in the higher storeys, he used bay windows rather than the deeply recessed ones of the Romanesque style as on the lower floors.

Dr. Oronhyatekha in his office on the seventh floor of the Temple.

Like just about every other facet of Dr. Oronhyatekha's work, the Temple Building was constructed using state-of-the-art technology. On the way to California in 1896, he and Bena stopped in Chicago to tour the mechanical systems of the city's greatest new buildings to see what should be implemented in the Temple. Chicago architects had been experimenting with new methods such as steel frame construction, pioneered only a few years earlier for the twelve-storey Tacoma Building. The first Toronto building with a steel structure was constructed in 1889. Not thoroughly convinced that a steel skeleton could support the weight of such a tall structure, Gouinlock reinforced the steel girders with masonry walls of red brick and Credit Valley stone. Each stone was pressure-tested before it was used, and at the foundation the walls were more than four feet thick, thinning to eighteen inches at the top floor. So well-built was the Temple that in the early twentieth century when the Guaranty Trust Company wanted to expand its space in the basement, it found it impossible. The construction company discovered an impenetrable basket-weave of iron rods inside the stone walls.

Much thought went into making the building completely fireproof. Dr. Oronhyatekha may have been struck by the recent destruction of the newly built Simpson's department store by fire only a few blocks away from the Temple site. Further, the taller the building, the more important it became to plan for fire safety, since people would be farther from ground-level exits. The Temple had three brick firewalls running the height of the building to prevent flames from spreading within the structure. Polished to an antique copper finish, steel was used for all doors and even for the wainscoting on the walls. Fireproof terracotta tiles lined all of the steel construction inside the building. This was so well-planned that if there was a fire, only the window frames and sashes and the hardwood floors could burn. In order to protect the Temple from fires from surrounding buildings, Dr. Oronhyatekha had two fire hydrants installed on the roof.

When finished, the Temple Building boasted the largest isolated electrical plant in Toronto at a time when only the wealthy and a few large companies could afford to buy electricity. Housed in the basement, the plant produced all the electricity and steam needed to light and heat the building. To ventilate the building, air from the rooftop was drawn in and forced through either a refrigerator room or a hot chamber before it circulated

The electrical plant of the Temple.

throughout the building. A refrigerating apparatus in the basement cooled all the tap water for drinking. Each floor had a mail chute that directly connected to a city mailbox. The Temple also boasted three elevators — devices that allowed buildings to become taller than ever since workers would not have to climb stairs. Elevators were new to buildings in the late 1890s.[17]

Dr. Oronhyatekha planned not just one, but three celebrations for the completion of the building. The first two were openings in August and December 1897, and the third was a formal dedication in the late summer of 1898. The August ceremony served IOF members, many of whom came from across Ontario, Quebec, and the northeastern United States. The afternoon began with a procession through the streets of downtown Toronto, the band of the 48th Highlanders leading the way, followed by the uniformed Royal Foresters and twelve carriages of visiting IOF officials. In the evening, everyone gathered in the assembly hall, which was decorated with flags and coloured draperies and brilliantly lit with electric lights. Dr. Oronhyatekha formally declared the Temple open and invited the audience to tour the rest of the building although it was not fully finished. A dance rounded out the evening.

The December celebration functioned as a "citizens' day," allowing Torontonians to see the new building. According to the *Globe*, ten thousand people attended despite the disagreeable weather. That evening, Dr. Oronhyatekha paraded in with the Royal Foresters and a band. Frederick Barlow Cumberland, a deputy supreme chief ranger and the superintendent of works for the Temple, declared the building open. Cumberland and Dr. Oronhyatekha gave speeches outlining the history of the IOF, particularly noting that Prime Minister Wilfrid Laurier had recently joined — a sign of its stability. Dr. Oronhyatekha then revealed a life-size painting of Laurier to grace the Temple. But, he said, the IOF was as proud to have members of prominence as it was to have workingmen. More speeches, recitations, and musical solos completed the evening. A few days later, the supreme secretary presented to the staff and membership a life-size portrait of their supreme chief ranger to hang in the Temple. Painted in secret by Brantford artist John C. Whale from a photograph, Dr. Oronhyatekha was surprised by the reveal.[18]

The formal dedication of the Temple was a two-day event at the end of August 1898, after the annual meeting of the Supreme Court. Once again the building was lavishly decorated, but this time the electric lights spelled out "Welcome Home." Dr. Oronhyatekha and the other officers of the IOF entered the hall under an arch of swords held aloft by the Royal Foresters outfitted in their black and gold lace uniforms. Supreme Counsellor Judge William Wedderburn ceremoniously turned the key to the Temple over to Dr. Oronhyatekha, and supreme secretary John McGillivray presented him with a gold, silver, and ivory gavel from the IOF staff in thanks. Following the IOF rituals for public dedication ceremonies, Dr. Oronhyatekha dedicated the Temple to the "principles of liberty and benevolence and concord, and to works of charity. May peace, harmony and goodwill towards men ever reign within these walls." Then he returned the key, symbolizing that the Temple was now the possession of all the members. The next day, members marched down to the Canadian Exhibition grounds. There the IOF hosted a band competition and the Royal Foresters participated in a fancy drill contest. At stake was $1,800 in prizes.[19]

As early as 1899, the Temple began to expand. The IOF built a five-storey annex, which was connected to the Temple by a bridge. It contained a café, a ladies lunchroom, and the "blue room," which was

The Temple café opened in 1900 and advertised itself as the "Finest Equipped Restaurant in Canada." With both table d'hôte and à la carte service, it was open from 7:00 a.m. until "after the Opera." Dr. Oronhyatekha believed the café would popularize the Temple Building and make its offices more attractive to renters. However, it was unprofitable, and closed in 1901.[20]

for private dining. In 1901, the rounded roof turrets were removed and replaced with an eleventh floor to accommodate the demand for more office space. The Temple amenities proved popular. During 1899, for example, it hosted nearly three hundred Masonic and other fraternal meetings as well as a number of banquets.[21]

Ever ready to mock the IOF, in May 1895 the *Monetary Times* sarcastically remarked that the proper adornment for the new Temple Building under construction would be "a statue of Dr. Oronhyatekha at the top, or better still, a life-size medallion of the doughty doctor in imperishable brass somewhere on the outer walls."

In fact, in 1896, IOF officials decided to commission a life-size bronze statue of Dr. Oronhyatekha for the Temple rotunda. Rather than in jest as the *Times* suggested, the statue symbolized member loyalty, acknowledged his hard work, and celebrated the upcoming twenty-fifth anniversary of the IOF (1899). Each member was asked to contribute ten cents toward the cost. The *Independent Forester* noted that even those members who had not met Dr. Oronhyatekha contributed; this was seen as proof of their loyalty.

Walter S. Allward won the competition to design the statue. A Toronto artist and an IOF member, Allward had previously sculpted part of the monument to the volunteers who served in the Riel Uprising and the statue of Upper Canada governor John Graves Simcoe, both of which stood in Queen's Park. Allward would go on to create many other memorials, most notably the Canadian National Vimy Memorial in Vimy, France. Bronzed by the Bureau Brothers company, one of the United States's best art foundries, Allward finished the statue of Dr. Oronhyatekha in time for the 1899 annual meeting in mid-June. Supreme Physician Thomas Millman wrote in his diary that it was a "splendid likeness."

The IOF threw a party for the unveiling of the statue. F. Barlow Cumberland, the chair of the statue committee, read a formal address expressing his admiration of Dr. Oronhyatekha's activities in working for the benefit of humanity. Later that night, the IOF members reassembled at the Temple for a musical concert and speeches, including one from IOF founder Colonel A.B. Caldwell. By 1904, the statue was on display in the Oronhyatekha Historical Rooms and Library, located in the Temple Building itself.[22]

THE ORONHYATEKHA HISTORICAL ROOMS AND LIBRARY

In 1901, Dr. Oronhyatekha gifted his collection of objects, previously on display in his homes, to the IOF. In September of the following year, the Oronhyatekha Historical Rooms and Library opened in the Temple Building to a varied audience, including members of the Mohawk community. The *Toronto Star* heralded it as "The Beginning of a Very Valuable Museum."[23]

Oronhyatekha had been exposed to collectors and the idea of collecting as early as 1862. While at Oxford, he visited the British Museum and the Ashmolean, and he contributed to Henry Acland's personal collection. As a student at the Toronto Medical School, he was exposed to the early Canadian Institute museum, the Museum of Natural History and

Fine Arts (later the Ontario Provincial Museum), and Daniel Wilson's anthropological collection at University College.

In his travels as an aspiring young physician, and later as IOF's supreme chief ranger, Dr. Oronhyatekha did as all good Victorians did — he collected. These souvenirs symbolized the prestige and status accorded a world traveller, and the wealth needed to travel. Collecting was also seen as a sign of industrious learning at a time when the middle class believed that even leisure activities needed to be educational. The late 1890s in Ontario witnessed the rise of historical and scientific society museums.[24]

Like most nineteenth-century museums, Dr. Oronhyatekha's collection was as random as it was eclectic. It combined objects for serious study with items that were simply exotic or bizarre. The deed of gift to the IOF describes the collection as "rare and interesting articles and utensils illustrating the life, art and handicraft of the Indian Nations" and objects from the "old French wars," the American Revolution, the War of 1812, including "battle flags, weapons, uniforms and accoutrements … decorations, medals and other rewards for valour and meritorious service and tokens of esteems" presented by the British and French governments to members of Dr. Oronhyatekha's family and "other noted chiefs and warriors." His gift also included all of the paintings, books, documents, photographs, and souvenirs related to the founding of the IOF that he had collected over the years.

Dr. Oronhyatekha had a number of motivations for his donation to the IOF. He wished to see these artifacts "preserved safely for all time." The newly constructed fireproof Temple Building was an ideal location; no public museum at this time had such safety precautions. Displaying his collection at the building also increased its accessibility, and he hoped it would be "useful" to students and the general public "in order to stimulate interest in the history of the countries and peoples concerned, and that the memory of the brave deeds of bygone days may not wholly perish, but may serve as a fresh bond of union between the descendants of the old-time combatants." An educational purpose was important. Cumberland, charged with preparing the collection's catalogue, wrote in it, "Education, increased interest in history, nature, and art, and beyond all, thought and reading in the Home, the centre of every Forester's heart, may, it is hoped, be helped by a short study in this collection and so

gladden the generous donor who has transferred his valued treasures."
Finally, always thinking about publicity, Dr. Oronhyatekha believed that
his collection promoted a good corporate image, attracting tourists to the
Temple. It would "thereby contribute to make more widely known the
noble and beneficent work of the Order." In return, the IOF agreed to have
the objects arranged and provided with explanatory "cards," to have free
public admission, and to publish a catalogue. He also instructed the IOF
to collect a sample of documents, regalia, medals, and other items from
his personal effects to add to the collection as a "memorial" to him and his
lifelong work for the order after his death.[25]

Although Dr. Oronhyatekha personally collected many of the items,
others had been gifts. For example, the Earl of Enniskillen had presented him with part of King William of Orange's travelling chest used
in the Battle of the Boyne in Ireland in 1690 — likely a symbolic gesture
because of Dr. Oronhyatekha's membership in the Orange Order.[26] Dr.
Oronhyatekha also purchased collections and commissioned collectors
to assist him.

George Mills McClurg, a lawyer for Ontario native groups, collected
objects from his clients, although his ability to obtain items partly stemmed
from the trust that they placed in Dr. Oronhyatekha. McClurg also prepared descriptions of these objects, relying heavily on associated oral
histories to do so. Cumberland arranged the collection in the historical
rooms, and with McClurg and naturalist J.B. Williams, prepared the 1904
catalogue that accompanied it. Cumberland also contacted antiquities
dealers to purchase items to augment the collection. Mary Rose Holden, a
member of the Wentworth Historical Society in Hamilton, may have also
collected or helped organize the museum; in 1900, she wrote that she was
at the beck and call of the Foresters under Dr. Oronhyatekha.[27]

The 1904 catalogue shows the museum contained at least thirty-four
cases of approximately two thousand artifacts, although not all objects were
included in the catalogue.[28] Some of these charted the institutional history
of the IOF and the important moments in Dr. Oronhyatekha's career. Such
items included the gavel used by founder A.B. Caldwell at the 1874 institution of the IOF, samples of IOF jewels, an ebony and gold gavel given to
Dr. Oronhyatekha as president of the National Fraternal Congress, and a
loving cup presented to him at Christmas by the IOF in 1903.[29]

Over the years, Dr. Oronhyatekha also collected many objects during his world travels. Egypt, the Middle East, India, and Asia became popular tourist destinations in the late nineteenth century. The construction of the Suez Canal and rail lines between Alexandria and Cairo eased travel within Egypt, and archaeological excavations by the British Museum stimulated the public's curiosity about the country's antiquities. Rising interest in visiting locations mentioned in the Bible resulted in increased tourism to Jerusalem and Palestine. As in Egypt, the British presence in India opened up the country to English-speaking tourists. In fact, these destinations were so popular that travel companies such as the ubiquitous Thomas Cook began to organize tours. Dr. Oronhyatekha visited Cairo, Alexandria, Palestine, and Jerusalem in the summer of 1898 and the spring of 1899, both trips meant to build up his weakening health. In 1900 and 1905, he travelled to India on IOF business and at least once purchased "curios" from a "peddler."[30]

A mummy was the gem of any Egyptian collection. Dr. Oronhyatekha's mummy was a child "from the Nile." While in Cairo, Dr. Oronhyatekha also purchased a few replicas of scarabs, which were often placed within the wrappings of mummies. Less exotic items included screens to sequester women, a brass and silver bowl, bead necklaces, a scabbard made from an alligator head, a gong, and a metal club and spears. Now a cryptic catalogue entry, Cumberland described object 694 as a "Decorated Dagger of an Egyptian lady. Presentation made to Hon. Dr. Oronhyatekha."

Among other Indian items, Dr. Oronhyatekha collected brass flower jars from Jeypore, a "beggars' bowl" used by monks to collect food donations, a wooden shield, elephant goads, statues of Hindu gods, and various pieces of Benares brasswork, a popular tourist item. He also purchased an alabaster model of the Taj Mahal. Dr. Oronhyatekha may have seen this piece, as the catalogue suggested, as "evidence of the high civilization of a race of coloured men while many whites of Western Europe were only emerging from primeval condition and America was still in the backwoods."[31]

Japan remained an isolated country until the mid-nineteenth century, when various nations negotiated trade agreements. Increased international trade led to the building of steamships and railways and installation of telegraph wires, all of which stimulated tourism. Westerners avidly read the increasing numbers of books published on the history and culture of

An exhibit in the Oronhyatekha
Historical Rooms.

Japan, the most famous being *Madame Chrysanthème*, better known as
Madame Butterfly. Exhibits at World's Fairs, such as the 1893 Columbian
Exposition in Chicago, included Japanese art and artifacts, inspiring a
collecting craze of Asian objects. This *Japonisme* movement continued to
be popular until the early years of the twentieth century. The tourist trade
was thus booming by the time Dr. Oronhyatekha visited Japan in 1900
and 1901 while on IOF business trips to and from Australia. His souvenirs
are typical of the time, and include a dragon-embellished bronze flower
holder, shoes for both "wet days" and "dry days," silk embroidered fans,
lacquerware, a pair of chopsticks, a temple bell, and two jade carvings.[32]

Presumably, Dr. Oronhyatekha also collected the models of famous
buildings and statuary during his European travels. Discredited in the early
twentieth century because of a new emphasis on originality and authenticity,

plaster casts or marble replicas of Greco-Roman and Italian Renaissance art pieces were widely exhibited in Victorian museums. Curators believed that viewing even replicas of these masterpieces facilitated a sense of artistic taste and an appreciation for beauty. Most Canadians could not afford the time or money to travel to Europe, so museums brought such art to them. In fact, many European museums produced their own casts for sale. North American museums eagerly ordered these replicas as a way to obtain a comprehensive collection, which would have been impossible otherwise, both because of the singularity of the originals and their value. Casts were cost effective, and even wealthy individuals purchased them to demonstrate their good taste and education to family and friends.

Dr. Oronhyatekha's collection contained five replicas of various statues of Venus, including the Venus de Milo housed at the Louvre in Paris and the Venus de Medici at Uffizi Palace in Florence. He also possessed an Apollo and an Augustus Caesar, the originals of which the Vatican owned, and a bronze model of the statute of St. Peter, also from Rome. A bust of Queen Victoria and a marble one of Dr. Oronhyatekha himself sculpted by Guglielmo Pugi, an Italian artist, rounded out this representation of venerable individuals.

Casting also allowed large-scale buildings or monuments to be made in miniature and thus displayed in museums. Dr. Oronhyatekha collected models of the campaniles of San Marco (Venice), Giotto (Florence), and Pisa, the columns of St. Theodore and of the Winged Lion (Venice), the Lateran Obelisk (Rome) — the largest standing Egyptian obelisk in the world — and temple columns from the Forum. The catalogue suggested the columns gave visitors "some idea of … the glory of Rome when the Roman nation were [sic] the conquerors and rulers of the then known world."[33]

Like many collectors of the time, Dr. Oronhyatekha salvaged items feared to be otherwise lost. For example, his collection contained pieces from the old parliament buildings in Toronto. In 1886, construction began on a new building in what became Queen's Park. The old buildings on Front Street stood vacant until they were gradually demolished between 1900 and 1903. Dr. Oronhyatekha collected a matchbox and inkstand once owned by Sir Oliver Mowat, the third premier of Ontario and later lieutenant-governor. He also collected the original dais and background for the throne used by provincial governors as far back as 1832, the speakers's card trays, and the division bell that called members to vote. The catalogue copy described the latter nostalgically:

> Though silent now, the tinklings ... have "called in the Members" on many an epoch-making occasion.... Motions such as in the Parliamentary embroglios of [William] Lyon Mackenzie ... the threatened duel between John A. Macdonald and Col. Rankin ... the removal of the Union Parliament of Upper and Lower Canada to Quebec in 1839, and the opening of the Provincial Legislature of Ontario after the confedera- tion of Canada in 1867. At the call of this Division Bell, from the struggles of 1837, the attaining of Responsible Government in 1842, and the advent of Provincial Home Rule at Confederation in 1867, the representatives of a Free people have recorded their votes in Parliament.

Other items — keys, door plates and signs, a fire shovel, and an MP nameplate from the 1830s — were actual parts of the old buildings.[34]

Case 15 contained objects salvaged from the old Jesuit fort Sainte Marie among the Hurons II, located on Christian Island in Georgian Bay. This village was the last bastion of the Jesuit missionaries and their Wendat (Huron) congregation as they fled from successive Haudenosaunee attacks in the 1640s. As an archaeological site, it had been known to Canadians as early as the 1840s, and with no preventative legislation, relic hunters combed the site for souvenirs.[35] On his way to the upper lakes to explore archaeological sites and burial mounds, George McClurg excavated the old fort and shipped 250 pounds of material to Toronto in the fall of 1902. Some of the objects ended up in Dr. Oronhyatekha's collection, including iron and stone tools, silver jewellery, and door hinges and key locks from the fort itself.[36] These items may have held additional meaning for Dr. Oronhyatekha since it was his ancestors who had driven out the Jesuits and the Wendat. In this sense, these items could be seen as objects of conquest.

The late nineteenth century witnessed an explosion of natural hist- ory museums. Not surprisingly, Dr. Oronhyatekha owned a large number of natural history items such as urchins, stuffed birds, botanical samples, and fish and reptile specimens. About one thousand of the total objects consisted of shells, sponges, and corals. Some of these items also touched on the idea of salvage, but in the context of animal extinction. The catalogue entry for a Bird of Paradise from New Guinea, for example, featured this witty exchange, "Moral: Reproachful aunt (to boy who has been stealing birds' eggs): 'Ah! cruel boy, what will the poor mother bird say when it comes back and finds the eggs have been taken from its nest?' Observant boy: 'It won't say nuthin', 'cause it's in your hat.'"[37]

In the nineteenth century, many Canadians saw the study of natural history as a way to understand God's rational design of the universe and to appreciate its beauty and complexity. Not merely an educational pursuit at the time, the study of natural sciences possessed a spiritual underpinning. Collecting and inventorying natural resources also allowed Canadians to make sense of the unknown, particularly in comparison to Europe. Unlike most of the other objects described, the catalogue classified tropical shells, corals, and sponges according to taxonomic and other scientific categories based on the works of well-known naturalist John George Wood.[38]

The collection also included the Australian platypus, then an almost extinct animal whose physical oddity attracted the public. Seemingly part fish, bird, and quadruped, it confounded naturalists' taxonomies and drew much speculation over its origins. At first, naturalists even considered the animal to be a hoax. Still fascinated by the creature a century after its discovery, collectors displayed them in their museums during the Victorian age. Featured in Case 18, "Curios from Foreign Parts," along with an assortment that included a branch from a Jamaican lace tree, a Ceylon tortoiseshell comb, and an emu egg, Dr. Oronhyatekha's platypus received this understated introduction, "This little animal has excited the greatest interest on account of its extraordinary shape and singular habits."[39]

Like the platypus, there were other singular pieces, oddities that many Victorian collectors enjoyed. These included a pipe carved by Boer prisoners held in Ceylon, a cane made from sheets of paper stuck together by a convict, and a vase made from a brass shell.[40]

Native artifacts dominated Dr. Oronhyatekha's collection, and in an unusual twist for the time, they were exhibited as if native peoples and their leaders were the mainstream culture. Dr. Oronhyatekha asserted that First Nations, particularly the Haudenosaunee, had and would continue to have an equal place in a world of nations; his people did not face extinction as projected in the common stereotypes of the time. In comparison, objects from other cultures, most situated away from the North American continent, were relegated to otherworldliness.

Many of the military objects recalled a time of imperial-aboriginal allegiance, especially during the War of 1812, and of active participation by native nations in defence of the British Crown while establishing Canada's borders.[41] Not surprisingly with his shooting skills, Dr. Oronhyatekha collected a variety of guns and assorted paraphernalia. For example, Case 30 displayed powder horns once owned by Anishinabe Chief Kegedonce, Joseph Brant's pistol and musket, and an English dueling pistol from Chief Petowegesic of Walpole Island. Other military items included a knife and scabbard once belonging to Oshawana, Tecumseh's chief warrior in the War of 1812, an early 1800s Chippewa tradition belt marking loyalty to British and American allies, war clubs, a war headdress, a military messenger's saddlebag, medals commemorating colonial wars, and flags from the outposts at Drummond Island, Michilimackinac, Detroit, and Fort Malden, the latter having also belonged to Oshawana. Cumberland used the Detroit flag to tell the story of the fort's surrender in 1812 under pressure from Isaac Brock, the commander of the British forces, and Tecumseh, his ally.[42]

The average visitor to the Oronhyatekha Historical Collection may have viewed these military items as further proof of the stereotype of First Nations as savage warriors. Members of historical societies would have viewed these objects as part of their dearly held United Empire Loyalism, which dominated their early museums. Only partly based on historical fact, the Loyalist myth portrayed those who left the American colonies during the Revolution as having sacrificed their homes and territory, all for their loyalty to the British. Forced to eke out a living in the harsh Upper Canadian wilderness, they saw the Loyalists as the founders of the province. And then, during the War of 1812, the Loyalists rose again to defend their new homes against American attacks.[43] Historical societies also praised native leaders for helping to found and protect Upper Canada during the Revolution and the War of 1812, creating a kind of "imagined community" with them. Yet society members also believed native peoples to be a culture that was fading in the midst of supposedly superior pioneer stock or as communities whose survival depended on assimilation.[44]

Some native peoples saw themselves as Loyalists, as well as the *original* founders of the territory that became Upper Canada. But unlike non-native Loyalists, they firmly believed in their equality and autonomy; they were allies, not subjects, of the British. Consequently, Dr. Oronhyatekha interpreted many of the items on display based on these meanings.

Medals, for example, symbolized loyalty. Government officials presented native men with medals to mark important events such as treaty signings and renewal of alliances. Often accompanied with certificates avowing recipients' loyalty and status, medals also confirmed their authority. While all medals were highly prized, George III medals were particularly significant to native men in Canada; those who kept them were British allies during the American Revolution and the War of 1812, while men who backed the American side had their medals replaced by U.S. presidential ones. As well, native communities often displayed their medals to the Canadian government as proof of their status as allies, not citizens, when officials violated their understanding of treaties. The Oronhyatekha collection included George III medals given to Puckeshinwa, Tecumseh's father, Delaware Chief John Tomigo, Na-bon-a-au-boy, the son of Chief Wa-be-chechake of Sault Ste Marie who died during the War of 1812, and Chief Oshawana; a Treaty Six medal once belonging to Siksika (Blackfoot) Chief Crowfoot; and a War of 1812 medal awarded to "Chief Naudee, "Warrior, Guide and Scout," who was likely John Naudee, otherwise known as Oshawana. Tecumseh's George III belt medal, awarded by Sir Isaac Brock, was also part of the Oronhyatekha collection.

Gift-giving in general was an important ritual between colonial and First Nations that often preceded trade or political negotiations. The Oronhyatekha museum displayed a broadcloth skirt given to the wife of Chief Kiagesis in 1793 "by order George III," along with a compass and a tomahawk peace pipe attributed to Tecumseh. Three other tomahawk pipes in Dr. Oronhyatekha's collection once belonged to the Anishinabe Chief Miskokoman, and Chiefs Kiageosh and Macounce of Walpole Island. The iconic British military red coat also symbolized alliance and goodwill. These were also given to chiefs during treaty negotiations in the Canadian northwest in the late nineteenth century. Featured in Case 29, the two in the Oronhyatekha collection once belonged to Oshawana and to George King, a warrior of the Chippewa of the Thames nation in Ontario.[45]

Like Western museums that prized items attributed to politicians and military men such as George Washington or John A. Macdonald, Dr. Oronhyatekha's museum emphasized First Nations leaders such as Joseph Brant, Shingwauk, Tecumseh, Oshawana, and Crowfoot. These objects all declared their prowess in military campaigns and recognized their statesmanship in forming alliances. By juxtaposing the artifacts of his own life, Dr. Oronhyatekha angled to ensure his own immortality as a leader.

Some objects spoke directly to the relationship between native and British nations, and the sovereignty each possessed. In 1887, McClurg obtained the Penn wampum belt from Chief Waubuno (John B. Wampum). Native people viewed treaties as an agreement between two sovereign nations. This belt, depicting in white two men clasping hands on a field of purple beads, symbolized the treaty between William Penn and the Muncey in 1682 when the land that became the state of Pennsylvania passed to Penn. When Waubuno had visited Queen Victoria in England in 1886, he showed it to her, a common gesture to remind the British Crown of its historical obligations.[46]

The museum also featured ceremonial clothing worn by First Nations when they met royal representatives. Their addresses to royal visitors to Canada acted as a ritualistic and symbolic part of maintaining their alliance with the Crown, and thus such items of clothing and decoration carried these meanings. While the public may have seen these objects as merely exotic, to native peoples they symbolized their autonomy as nations who dealt with the Crown on equal terms. In 1860, as representatives of the Muncey and Oneida of the Thames reserves, John Tecumseh Henry, the president of the Ontario Grand Council of Chiefs, and his wife presented an address to the Prince of Wales. Their outfits, consisting of a black beaded coat and leggings, beaded pouches, council belt, and beaded and quilled headdresses, were given to Oronhyatekha. Once belonging to his father, Maungwudaus, Henry's pouch may have represented the passing of hereditary leadership, and thus his authority in representing his community to the future King of England. Similar items included a golden eagle headdress worn by Chief Waubuno when he met Queen Victoria in 1886. The Crown also customarily presented medals to aboriginal peoples as symbols of their loyalty during such visits. The Oronhyatekha museum contained a Victoria silver medal given to Waubano by the Prince of Wales and another medal presented by the Duke and Duchess of York in Calgary during their 1901 tour.[47]

Victorian culture celebrated royalty, although for different reasons. The collection included Maundy money — coins given by sovereigns to the poor — and a number of commemorative medals struck for coronations and jubilee celebrations.[48] One of the most spectacular of the objects associated with royalty was a replica of the British coronation chair, the original of which had been most recently been used on August 9, 1902, for the coronation of King Edward VII, the man whom Dr. Oronhyatekha had met forty-two years earlier during his royal tour of Canada. Evidence as to whether Dr. Oronhyatekha attended the 1902 coronation is conflicting. His name does not appear in the published list of attendees, and Thomas Millman, the IOF supreme physician, wrote in his diary that Dr. Oronhyatekha returned from a trip to England on July 11. However, the collection catalogue includes the very chair reserved for Dr. Oronhyatekha in Westminster Abbey. It seems likely that Dr. Oronhyatekha had been invited to the coronation, which had been originally scheduled to take place on June 26, but delayed because the king needed emergency abdominal surgery. Nevertheless, a service was conducted at St. Paul's Cathedral that was attended by many foreign guests who had already arrived. Dr. Oronhyatekha probably attended this event instead of the later official coronation in early August.[49]

The British coronation chair in Oronhyatekha's museum is an exact reproduction of the original that now sits in St. George's Chapel in Westminster Abbey. The original was constructed in 1296 for King Edward I to enclose the Stone of Scone, the stone used in the coronation of Scottish kings and captured by Edward as a spoil of war. Commissioned by Dr. Oronhyatekha, the English firm Hampton and Sons crafted the replica, which arrived sometime around January 1904. As the collection catalogue noted, "No previous copy had ever been made, but as a special concession to this Canadian collection, permission ... was granted." Even the graffiti etched into the oak by Westminster choir boys was copied. Edward's coronation, like that of George VI's in 1937, stimulated a wave of reproductions of the chair. John Ross Robertson, a Toronto newspaperman, politician, and fellow Mason, commissioned a replica as well. A collector of historic chairs, Robertson's coronation chair and ten others were displayed at the 1904 Canadian National Exhibition. Possession of a replica was "seen as a desirable asset by foreign magnates."[50]

With his famous sense of humour, Dr. Oronhyatekha was fond of telling a different version of the story of how he obtained the coronation chair. He always maintained that he had a standing invitation to visit Queen Victoria. During one of many of his visits, he said he was taken on a tour of Westminster Abbey and shown the chair. He expressed his interest to the queen, who responded that she had another one stored away and that since he seemed to like it so much, he could have it. No matter the story, for Dr. Oronhyatekha the coronation chair acted as yet another example of the direct relationship between the British Crown and the Haudenosaunee. His visit to England for the coronation and the chair itself must have also reminded him of meeting Acland and the young Prince of Wales in 1860, and how this event changed his life. For others, it aided the study of English history, the *Toronto Daily Star* said, since few have the money to travel to England to see the original. In "his goodness," Dr. Oronhyatekha had given the chair to all of Toronto.[51]

For a time, the coronation chair sat in the entrance of the IOF orphanage. Today it is usually kept in the foyer of Casa Loma in Toronto.

The museum also offered visitors an opportunity to appreciate the ages-old relationships between native nations before the arrival of Europeans. It included archaeological artifacts from all over Ontario, many of which McClurg had collected. Like natural history artifacts, archaeological collections were also popular in Victorian Canada. These objects were viewed in different ways by the mainstream and native populations. Usually interpreted by the general public as proof of native peoples' coming extinction or assimilation, from the native point of view, these objects offered instead archeological evidence of their North American occupation dating back thousands of years and thus an assertion of their legitimate rights over land, especially as settlement expanded across Canada.

The collection also featured trade silver of tremendous range and variety. Native peoples often purchased silver pieces such as brooches, hatbands, or crescent-shaped gorgets worn at the throat as part of their fur-trade transactions. Until recently, historians interpreted such objects as evidence of the adoption of Western-style clothing. Seen through another lens, trade silver not only reminded museum visitors of a long-standing economic relationship developed over hundreds of years, but also the clever adaptation of artistic designs by native peoples. A round gorget worn at the throat, for instance, was not a wholly new idea, but simply an evolution of the tradition to wear a flat circle of polished shell in the same place. The shininess of the shell or silver possessed spiritual meaning as well. Rather than wearing only one piece of trade silver, native people often covered a piece of clothing all over with silver brooches as a mark of status and wealth achieved from trade. Likewise, they adopted trade beads for decorating clothing but used them in patterns that replicated older painted or porcupine quill designs.[52]

While museums were very popular in Victorian society, traditional Haudenosaunee sometimes frowned upon the collection of objects, in particular human remains, for religious reasons. The Oronhyatekha museum included human remains and grave gifts. The catalogue lists five skulls and two skull gorgets (adornments made from human bone) and gifts of arrowheads and other tools, a pistol, and part of a pipe, all excavated from graves. Displaying native human remains could be seen as analogous to exhibiting mummies — a way to study and appreciate ancient cultures, or alternatively, extremely disrespectful to one's ancestors and a violation of religious beliefs.[53]

Dr. Oronhyatekha's museum also included objects that the Haudenosaunee and other native peoples considered to be sacred, even secret. Normally such items would not be on display for all to see, at least without first conducting the proper protocol. Nor was it thought appropriate to discuss certain spiritual beliefs outside of the native community. Some objects are considered to be animate beings and needed to be treated accordingly. False Face masks, for example, require rigorous care; the keeper of a False Face maintains the spirit's life by feeding it corn mush, rubbing oil or grease on the wood, and blowing tobacco smoke into its mouth. They are only to be viewed at certain ritual times of the year. Disrespect or neglect of them results in illness, death, or other serious repercussions. Thus museum display of such objects could be seen as violating a number of spiritual protocols.

It is unclear how such spiritual objects came to be in the Oronhyatekha collection or why their keepers decided to give them up. For example, while the catalogue gave one False Face mask a lengthy label, it is simply an excerpt from the Ontario provincial archaeological report that described the hesitant donation of another mask by a man from Grand River. No context or suggestion of how this relates to the object is provided. The story attached to another object shows that conversion to Christianity often resulted in the donation of objects. The catalogue stated that Chief Shanghonouse of the St. Clair River area donated a wooden "Little Indian Idol," once belonging to his great-grandfather, to his "friend Mr. McClurg," for this reason.[54] While Dr. Oronhyatekha professed himself to be a Christian, he must have known that some traditionalists found the display of such objects disturbing, even offensive.

The Oronhyatekha Historical Collection and Library was one among many monumental achievements completed by Dr. Oronhyatekha during his tenure as IOF supreme chief ranger. Indeed, the period between 1878 and 1907 was one of personal and professional success. He turned the IOF from a struggling and fractured organization into an international company that merged Haudenosaunee and fraternal values with commercial insurance. He had loyal followers, travelled around the world, met royalty and influential politicians, and appeared widely in the domestic and international press.

But these years were also marked with personal sadness and loss. His son Henry had drowned in the Victoria Day disaster in 1881, and he had lost three other children in their early years. In spring 1900, his wife Ellen was diagnosed with breast cancer and hospitalized for several weeks. That fall, Dr. Oronhyatekha's lifetime mentor, Henry Acland, passed away at his home in Oxford. Ellen died the next summer, in May 1901. She was buried in the Christ Church Anglican Cemetery at Tyendinaga next to her children. After her funeral, Thomas Millman, the IOF's supreme medical examiner, wrote simply that Dr. Oronhyatekha "feels the death of his wife very much."[55]

Perhaps the loss of four children at such young ages made him want to keep his remaining two children close at hand. Bena often travelled with him and Ellen on business, and she also helped manage the Isle Hotel for him.[56] It wasn't until June 1906, at the age of forty-two, that Bena married — an Australian named Percy John Johnson. Acland, his remaining son, followed in his footsteps, both in becoming a physician and joining the IOF. After attending Queen's University in Kingston, Acland attended medical school at Trinity University in Toronto, graduating in 1891 with his M.D. and C.M., or Master in Surgery degree. As early as 1881, Acland was made an honorary IOF member and began to climb through the ranks, no doubt at his father's behest. He eventually became one of the deputy supreme chief rangers. In the 1890s, the IOF appointed Acland as assistant secretary to the Medical Board for Great Britain and Ireland, and he moved to England for several years.[57]

In 1895, he married English actress Natalie Charlotte Desmond, also known by her stage name, Natalie Brande, or Gaygengorah (Fair Flower), as she was later named by the Haudenosaunee. They met while she was acting in the comedic play "The Planter" at the Prince of Wales Theatre in London, England, and honeymooned in Canada, visiting family at Deseronto. As a performer, she often acted and sang as part of the entertainment at IOF celebrations. But Acland's life does not seem to have been entirely a happy one. Community history says he had a drinking problem, hinted at by Thomas Millman, who wrote in his diary that Acland had "not enough stability. Is too fond of knocking about and rather fond of his glass." In 1901, Acland and Natalie parted ways, supposedly divorcing in South Dakota, a state known for only requiring ninety days of residence to do so.

Later that year, Acland was away in Australia on IOF business when his mother died. Dr. Oronhyatekha joined him there several months later, during which time Acland found himself in serious trouble.

Elizabeth James, an IOF typist, accused Acland of indecent assault, which consisted of him kissing her and proposing marriage. She refused. Confusingly, the press reported that James refused partly because he was already married, though Acland suggested he could get a divorce. James later noted that normally Acland acted as a gentleman, but he had been intoxicated at the time. In turn, Acland accused James of kissing him, and other IOF employees believed she was attracted to him. The IOF manager for Melbourne convinced James to keep the charges silent until Dr. Oronhyatekha arrived, but the police received an anonymous letter and investigated. Acland appeared in court and was cleared of the more serious charge of force being used due to lack of evidence, but the jury could not decide if James had been a consenting party. The court remanded Acland for a further trial. The following March he was convicted and sentenced to three months in prison with hard labour.[58]

As difficult as these family crises were for Dr. Oronhyatekha as a father, he was about to experience one of the most stressful events of his business career: testifying at the Royal Commission on Life Insurance in 1906.

CHAPTER 7

THE ROYAL COMMISSION ON LIFE INSURANCE

TOWARD THE ROYAL COMMISSION

In 1905, the New York State government launched an investigation into the life insurance industry. Named after its chair, the four-month Armstrong investigation found several American life insurance companies rife with abuse. Its rulings led the Canadian government to establish the MacTavish Royal Commission on Life Insurance in 1906, which investigated both commercial and fraternal insurance bodies. Like its American counterpart, the Canadian industry contained a great deal of nepotism, conflicts of interest, monopolistic corporate behaviour, "fast and loose investment policies," and a few illegalities. Unlike in the United States, however, policy holders were not generally disadvantaged, because these practices had led to profitable investments.[1]

Judge Duncan B. MacTavish presided over the Canadian commission. The government appointed him and the other commissioners to investigate insurance company expenses, management, and investment of funds. The commission was also to explore the current legislation regulating the insurance industry and make recommendations to improve it. In total, the commission investigated twenty-two commercial life insurance companies and five fraternal benefit societies, including the IOF.[2]

TESTIFYING

Dr. Oronhyatekha had testified before a royal commission in 1888, when the Commission on the Relations between Labor and Capital had called him to speak about mutual benefit societies.

He first appeared before the MacTavish Commission on September 13, 1906.[3] W.H. Hunter, the IOF counsel, also occasionally answered questions. Together they appeared before the judges for seven grueling days. At first the commission's main counsel, George Shepley, asked Dr. Oronhyatekha to explain the founding of the IOF, its constitution and insurance policies, and his own history with the organization.

Shepley next asked about the opposition to IOF incorporation in 1889. In response, Dr. Oronhyatekha submitted figures prepared by the federal actuary, A.K. Blackadar, which had been the basis for the opposition. Blackadar had projected that the IOF would be bankrupt by 1910 owing to what he characterized as an insufficiency of the rates charged. In response, Dr. Oronhyatekha proclaimed that the IOF had a surplus of more than ten million dollars at that moment, and that each year it grew by about one million. This, he said, disproved actuarial claims about the unsustainability of IOF rates. Throughout the days of testimony, Shepley asked many times about actuarial calculations that suggested the IOF did not collect high enough premiums, but each time Dr. Oronhyatekha steadfastly defended IOF rates and demonstrated their similarity to those approved by the National Fraternal Congress, an American umbrella organization for fraternal societies. As well, he compared Blackadar's rates with the rates calculated by J. Howard Hunter, the Ontario insurance registrar, which were lower and closer to IOF rates. Further, he said, if needed, though he never expected it to be necessary, the IOF had the constitutional power to levy additional assessments to pay outstanding claims if the surplus ran out. This was a provision that he had explicitly inserted into the constitution as a safety measure.[4]

Dr. Oronhyatekha also emphasized the importance of the money accumulated from lapses in IOF membership. Essentially, money paid by former IOF members would not be used to pay their claims upon death or illness. Instead it sat in IOF accounts, gathering interest. This amount, Dr. Oronhyatekha argued, was more than his opponents realized. Further, the IOF needed much less in operating expenses; Dr. Oronhyatekha stated that the IOF used just $2 per insurance policy compared to the $15 per policy used by commercial insurance companies. In addition, the medical examination reduced the cost of risk by weeding out unhealthy individuals. Not all actuarial tables included this factor, Dr. Oronhyatekha pointed out. As well, the IOF terminated policies if members lived an unhealthy or immoral life, which non-fraternal companies could not do; this also reduced the cost of risk. Nor did the IOF have shareholders who expected yearly dividends or a large staff that drew a salary, like traditional insurance companies. While there were some sales commissions in later years, most IOF officials outside of the Supreme Court executive voluntarily led courts and recruited new members. Fraternal and commercial insurance, Dr. Oronhyatekha argued, should not be compared, but rather accepted as two totally different systems.[5]

Next Shepley turned to IOF expansion overseas, particularly in Australia, where it had been contentious. In 1900, several politicians had called for an inquiry into the IOF, which Dr. Oronhyatekha suspected to have been instigated by jealous commercial insurance companies. Dr. Walter H. Montague, a former MP and federal minister of agriculture, who headed up the Australian expansion, requested a royal commission in order to prove the IOF a reputable company. However, around the same time, Montague had given a $50 subscription to the party in power to be used in its next election campaign. Opponents labelled this bribery. Montague claimed it was a personal gift of thanks to Sir Alexander Peacock, the premier of Victoria, for his help. Peacock had invited him to many government functions and introduced him to prominent men so that Montague could promote the IOF. Dr. Oronhyatekha confirmed that this fifty dollars had not come out of IOF funds, and further, he had known nothing about it. Montague was also charged with giving money to a candidate running for Parliament. Eventually, the Australian government did strike a royal commission in 1904. The judge found Montague guilty of attempting to bribe a politician to have the royal commission established, though in 1906, Shepley indicated that the bribery was actually intended to stop the commission. When Shepley questioned Dr. Oronhyatekha about his culpability in hiring Montague, he said he could not be held responsible if Montague had acted outside of his responsibilities. "If he had stolen sheep out there in Australia, surely we could not be held responsible for that act," he argued.[6]

Shepley also spent a great deal of time asking questions about past IOF deficits. Operation expenses, especially for expansion, were normally financed by the general fund, but they had run so high that the IOF had tapped into the funds used to pay member claims. The construction of the orphanage had also mostly been financed by the illness and funeral funds. As recommended by William Fitzgerald, the federal superintendent of insurance, Dr. Oronhyatekha had therefore curtailed expansion outside of North America, cut back on advertising, and reduced the frequency of the *Forester* magazine in order to pay down these deficits. Yet, Dr. Oronhyatekha noted, the mortuary fund still had many millions above those needed to pay *all* of the IOF death claims.[7]

Another line of questioning centred on IOF investments in other companies as a way to grow its endowment. In 1882, the IOF founded the Foresters Colonization Society of Canada, intending to survey and settle a tract of land on the Red Deer River in what would become the province of Alberta several decades later. Typical of similar settlement schemes, the company planned to provide financial support to prospective settlers in return for interest payments on the land. This land had been recently opened up for purchase by the Canadian government, which had appropriated it through a treaty with the Niitsitapi (Blackfoot), Tsuu T'ina (Sarcee), and Assiniboine nations in 1877. The area had been recently explored by naturalist John Macoun, who, visiting the area during a period of unnaturally high rainfall, mistakenly concluded it to be rich farming land. Thus the colonization society advertised that wheat, oats, barley, and sugar beets could be raised and that sheep ranching could be established. It also noted coal beds as another source of potential profit for settlers. Ambitiously, it further proposed to provide or promote saw and grist mills, a general store, assistance in building houses, and a rail line. Registered under the *Canada Joint Stock Companies Act*, the directors intended selling stock worth $500,000. But by the close of 1883, the company had broken up, possibly because of the COF secession — one of the directors was Edward Towe — and seemingly, the IOF never did purchase this land.[8]

The IOF also invested in mortgages and debentures, in utility companies such as the Hamilton Cataract Power, Light and Traction Company, in lumber and coal companies, and in building the Alexandra Palace Apartments, one of Toronto's first apartment buildings.[9] In 1898, the IOF considered purchasing enough shares in the Provincial Trust Company of Ontario to gain a controlling interest. The IOF re-formed this company as the Union Trust in 1901. Establishing a separate company with financial experts, the IOF believed, would result in more strategic investments than IOF officials could make on their own. While Dr. Oronhyatekha was nominally its president, George Foster, a former minister of finance and recently defeated Conservative MP, really managed the Union Trust. It invested in timber limits, saw mills, and lands in the northwest for speculative purposes, sometimes through third party companies. Like with its earlier plans, the IOF intended to settle Foresters on part of this land. By 1905, however, the IOF questioned the wisdom of investing its surplus through the Union Trust and the ethics of the board members personally profiting from investments. These issues, plus the implementation of new laws in New York after the Armstrong investigation, compelled the IOF to sell off its land holdings under the Union Trust.

Shepley's questions to Dr. Oronhyatekha, Foster, now an opposition MP, and to Elliott Stevenson, the IOF supreme counsellor, centred on possible conflicts of interest, and probed whether the directors of the Union Trust borrowed money from the IOF to make personal investments. In fact, the bulk of the examination related to the Foresters focused on the Union Trust and its investments through third-party companies. The commission questioned various officials of these companies well into October 1906.[10]

The purchase of the property on which the Temple sat also came under question. Shepley asked why Jessie Bayly, Dr. Oronhyatekha's secretary, personally purchased the land. He suggested this arrangement meant the IOF could skirt around the limit of property value it was legally allowed to own as stipulated by its act of incorporation. Dr. Oronhyatekha explained that his real estate broker suggested that if the seller knew the IOF was interested, the price of land would be jacked up, and therefore a more anonymous individual should act as the buyer. After the IOF's act of incorporation changed in 1896 to allow it to hold a greater amount of property, some of the land was transferred to the IOF. The rest, because it was still valued at an amount higher than the IOF could legally hold, was transferred to the Ontario Realty Company, a body established by the IOF. This subsidiary also owned part of the Temple Building, the other part being owned by Union Trust. This arrangement was necessary as the final cost of the Temple lay just under one million, not the $350,000 that the IOF was allowed to own. Shepley again insinuated the IOF had purposely evaded its act of incorporation. Dr. Oronhyatekha responded instead that in order to comply with the act, he had had to establish this new company.[11]

After the IOF examination ended, the *Independent Forester* reported that "It only remains to say that both the S.C.R. and the S.C [Supreme Counsellor] express satisfaction with the manner and thoroughness of the Commission's examination of the Order; that the Order has come through the examination with honor to itself and its officers is generally acknowledged by everyone." Later it reported that Dr. Oronhyatekha had closed his testimony by quoting a line from Tennyson: "Whatever record leaps to light I never shall be shamed."[12] At a gathering at the Temple in January, the speeches to welcome Dr. Oronhyatekha presented the IOF as triumphant. "There was not a Forester but who could read with pride the evidence of the Chief before the commission," the Toronto *Globe* summarized. Robert Mathison, the new supreme secretary, said of the IOF that "no institutions investigated by the commission has been shown so generally sound in its system of insurance and its conduct of business, and the evidence of no directors or managers has been so favorably commented on as that of our supreme chief ranger and Supreme Counsellor." Dr. Oronhyatekha's speech argued that fraternal insurance in general had been finally recognized as legitimate, and since 43,000 new applications had been submitted in 1906, the public had not found the IOF wanting either.[13]

THE FINDINGS

The Royal Commission was less kind to the IOF in its report, and found several problematic practices in the insurance industry as a whole. Speculative investments using policy holders' premiums, the proportion of which exceeded safe limits, were common. Business dealings evidenced deception, cronyism, and conflicts of interest between the heads of insurance companies and the companies in which the money was invested. In fact, some boards of these were identical. Rather than acting as trustees protecting their policy holders' premiums, insurance company executives borrowed money to make investments for their own personal gain. In essence, the policy holders took all of the risk while the executives could potentially rake in the profits. The commission also believed that the government never intended it to be possible under the *Insurance Act* for insurance companies to hold controlling stock in another company as a way to create a subsidiary, or investment arm. Operating expenses, particularly to attract new policy holders and to build the Temple, even if partly rented out to others, had become extravagant, it said. Regarding the IOF specifically, the commission reported it to be

> the largest ... and the widest in geographical extent of all those fraternal organizations with which the Commission has been concerned. Its methods have been aggressive, its accumulation of funds and its distribution of insurance benefits remarkable, its expenditure enormous. It illustrates in a singular degree the possibility of supreme control becoming vested in an individual. Its management has been characterized by extravagance which, in the pursuit of geographical expansion became recklessness. It has succeeded hitherto in inducing Parliament to accord it exceptional recognition as a fraternal society from the insurance standpoint and has incidentally broken through nearly all the barriers interposed by the Department of Insurance in the attempt to keep the statute law of insurance upon an intelligible an[d] consistent footing.[14]

The report noted the IOF's anomalous status; the government had recognized it as if it were a commercial insurance company but without the legal reserve required. In that sense, it had all the advantages but none of the disadvantages of true commercial companies. It also recapitulated how expensive it had been to extend the IOF to the UK, Europe, India, and Australia. The IOF had spent more than it had received in membership income, and Dr.

Oronhyatekha's efforts to reduce expenses had come too late. This resulted in taking from the mortuary, funeral, and sickness funds, the profits from membership lapses, and any accrued interest above 4 percent to pay down the deficit. The commission report noted that little had been paid back to these funds though the IOF executive had resolved to do so.[15]

In the final analysis, the commission cleared the IOF of any illegalities but deemed some of its business transactions unfavourable. The commissioners judged the complicated land purchases around the construction of the Temple to be deceptive and purposely evasive of the IOF's act of incorporation. Similarly, the commissioners believed that the Union Trust — which was not bound by the Insurance Act — was a method to evade its restrictions on investments. To protect policy holders, the act stated that money held by an insurance company could be invested in mortgage securities, debentures, and certain stocks, but not in land or other ventures considered speculative.[16]

The report also addressed fraternal insurance more generally. It credited fraternal groups with bringing cost effective insurance to the "home of the humblest" and stated that their "social element ... has made for the betterment of their members in many ways."[17] However, the commissioners found problematic the fact that whenever rates increased, they only applied to new members. They also examined the number of lapses in the IOF, and found them inadequate to produce the amount of surplus needed to augment lower rates. Ultimately, the commissioners recommended implementing the rates of the National Fraternal Congress.[18] Overall, to resolve the problems it found in the insurance industry, the commissioners drafted a new insurance bill, an amended version of which passed into law in 1910.

In the meantime, accusations of the Union Trust's improper business dealings re-emerged in 1907, squarely aimed at George Foster, who stood for federal re-election for the Conservative party. An anonymously authored pamphlet entitled *Frenzied Finance and the Foresters* called his dealings one of the "boldest schemes ever devised by a party of speculators for enriching themselves at the expense of other people," that is, the widows and orphans who relied upon the IOF. The Union Trust, it said, had been created specifically to evade the provisions of the Insurance Act, which forbid speculative investments using policy-holders' money. The pamphlet insinuated that Foster had used his speculative profits to fund his successful 1904 campaign. Worse, Foster and many of his political colleagues, deemed by the pamphlet as "plotters," might be called into Conservative cabinet positions. In particular, Foster's opponents feared if re-elected in 1908, he would return to his previous position as minister of finance.[19]

In 1907, Foster stood up in Parliament to defend his name. He also published a written response to the accusations bluntly subtitled, "How a Commission to Investigate Insurance was Turned into a One-Sided Political Inquisition," which argued that the commission stepped outside its powers in order to discredit the Conservative party. Foster also accused Shepley of making false assertions; most of the Conservative politicians involved with the Union Trust had no relationship with the IOF and, he stated, he had made a handsome profit for the Union Trust. Foster denied that he had received any commissions from the sale of lands owned by the Union Trust. He also correctly pointed out that it was quite common for directors of a company to sit on the board of another company with which it had business, that the types of investment he made were common to most large trust companies, and that bank directors frequently lent themselves money for business investments. Despite his opponents' attempts to discredit him, Foster won re-election in 1908.[20]

THE INSURANCE INDUSTRY

Foster accurately stated that the Union Trust's investments in utility companies and western land for settlement were common choices for insurance companies. He was also right that the Union Trust operated similarly to many insurance and other companies in Canada. But both the American and Canadian commissions need to be seen within the context of the changing attitudes towards big business around the turn of the century. Whereas the public had once viewed business leaders as honourable men, it now became more suspicious, particularly as the gap in wealth between owners and policy holders grew. Insurance company heads argued that interlocking companies with shared executives, like that of the IOF and the Union Trust, made good business sense, but society began to view these arrangements as a conflict of interest and the creation of unfair monopolies. Rather than relying on personal integrity, the public began to prefer state regulation of big business, leading to increased transparency and stricter reporting and investment regulations.[21]

Were the IOF rates unsustainable, as the royal commission proclaimed? Certainly the orphanage proved unsustainable, and IOF overseas expansion cost more than the expansion tax each member paid, and most of the non-North American courts failed by the end of the First World War. But without having the full numbers associated with membership and insurance classes, or more information about its investments, it is impossible to tell whether the IOF collected enough money to cover its claims. The *Forester* frequently published the number of members and the total amount of the surplus, but without knowing the ages of each member — and thus his or her life expectancy — and the class of insurance in which each member enrolled, full calculations are impossible. Further, while rates increased several times over the years, these only applied to new members. One would need to know how many members fell under which set of rates.

We are left, then, with only interpretations of the numbers, and these vary widely, depending upon whether one was an IOF supporter or opponent. Under the editorship of James Alexander Hedley, Toronto's *Monetary Times* weighed in on the IOF rates. A long-time enemy of fraternal insurance generally, the *Times* frequently demonstrated its contempt of what it believed to be unsustainable financial practices beginning in the 1880s.[22] Indeed, the *Times* had attacked Dr. Oronhyatekha in its pages for over twenty years by the time the royal commission began. In 1887, one article argued that the low monthly premiums charged by the IOF had been sufficient so far, but only because the membership was fairly young. By the time it aged, the *Times* said, there would not be enough money to cover its claims. Those running insurance plans needed a reserve and adequate rates for those reasons, neither of which the IOF had, the *Times* concluded. Like he would do many times in the future, Dr. Oronhyatekha responded in writing to these claims, his letters printed by the *Times* in full or paraphrased by its editor. His responses never won over Hedley. In 1887, he concluded the figures Dr. Oronhyatekha provided were jumbled and absurd. "Perhaps they are in the Ojibway dialect, or is it the Seneca, or the Iroquois?" he mocked.[23] The *Times* rarely acknowledged that Dr.

Oronhyatekha had increased IOF rates several times because he was also concerned about long-term sustainability.

Hedley's attacks were also personal, and often tinged with racism. In 1893, the *Times* reprinted an article about the IOF travelling to England and its attendant costs:

> The faithful followers of the Indian deity, Oronyhatekha [*sic*], have hired a ship with which to make a pilgrimage to England ... worshippers have been summoned to accommodate the red god across the ocean ... This is as it should be. We could make no more [r]easonable suggestion, unless it be to buy a ship with the insurance money of the policy-holders, and let the Foresters ... sail round and round the world continuously, doing homage night and day to their deity ... This idea of a portable deity is capital. It costs a lot of money, but it must be had.[24]

In 1898, the *Times* poked fun at the IOF's costly social gatherings by saying that "mankind owes a great debt of gratitude to Dr. Oronhyatekha for what he has done to amuse them by means of his game of Forestry. He deserves to rank with the founder of the Kindergarten, the inventor of golf, the author of poker ... hang the expense; our 80,000 members will stand it."[25]

During the royal commission, the tone of the *Monetary Times* changed slightly. While it had earlier portrayed Dr. Oronhyatekha as an autocrat who had hypnotized his sycophantic followers, now it reported that he seemed unaware of all of the investments made with IOF money and that directors of the Union Trust had disobeyed his wishes. Hedley was unsympathetic however. Referring to Foster, the *Times* concluded that the "Doctor [had] used politicians for the benefit of the I.O.F. Scarcely to be wondered at, that they found that two could play at that game, and repaid the compliment."[26]

The Canadian Fraternal Association (CFA) and the National Fraternal Congress (NFC) also debated insurance policy rates. In 1896, J. Howard Hunter, the first inspector of insurance and registrar for fraternal societies in Ontario, proposed that the CFA adopt a rate table higher than that used by fraternal insurance, a suggestion that met with resistance. Dr. Oronhyatekha brought the IOF into the National Fraternal Congress and also served as its vice president in 1899–1900. The next year he became its president. In early 1891, the NFC advocated that all fraternal insurance assessment rates should be based on standard mortuary tables. After consulting actuaries, in 1899, an NFC special committee recommended use of rates derived from the mortuary tables approved in 1891. In 1900, under Dr. Oronhyatekha's presidency, the congress embedded these rates into its Uniform Bill, stating that no member society should possess rates lower than it advised. Hunter found these rates to be very similar, if not identical for some ages, to the rates he recommended to be incorporated into the Ontario Insurance Act. Another table of rates, these calculated by A.K. Blackadar, the federal government actuary, was likewise very similar. By the fall of 1900, IOF rates were not identical but were very close.[27]

Historians also disagree about the sufficiency of fraternal rates. Martin Daunton has judged the NFC rates too low compared to other actuarial standards used at the time, and Michael Bliss agrees that most fraternal societies were unsound. After the 1930s, employer and government insurance supplanted fraternal insurance, and historians have interpreted this as proof that fraternal rates were unsustainable. Studying the Independent Order of Odd Fellows, J.C. Herbert Emery argues instead that fraternal rates along with other sources of income were sufficient. If enough money could be accumulated while members were young enough (and thus healthy), their claims as they grew older could be met. This is the reverse of the argument often presented by the opponents of fraternal insurance in the early 1900s. While there were flaws in the fraternal system, Emery also acknowledges many of the benefits that Dr. Oronhyatekha himself proclaimed: the lodge structure meant fewer employees and thus minimal overhead; age-graded fees discouraged older and presumably less healthy individuals from joining; the medical exam reduced the number of physically risky members; and the close social network prevented "morally" hazardous members and the making of false claims.[28]

Whatever the truth may have been, Elliott Stevenson, the supreme chief ranger in 1910, accepted the royal commission's interpretation of the IOF rates as being unsustainable. In part, this was because the new insurance act forced the separation of funds paid by old and new members. Each time the IOF had increased its rates, the increase had only applied to new members, but the funds had been kept together. This meant that newer members subsidized the older members, whose rates were less sustainable. With the forced separation of funds, this discrepancy became perilous. This meant that the rates of the older members needed to be adjusted, a fact that contributed to a decline in membership, as Dr. Oronhyatekha had always feared.[29]

A MUCH-NEEDED REST

During his testimony at the royal commission, Dr. Oronhyatekha displayed his wit, sarcasm, and sometimes a self-deprecating humour to diffuse intense exchanges. One magazine noted that he seemed to enjoy being centre stage although he appeared weary and under "nervous strain." In fact, the commissioners stopped the proceedings several times to accommodate his health. Four days into Dr. Oronhyatekha's testimony, Shepley asked to adjourn early because the "weather is so oppressive, and the doctor is not strong physically." The next day, the commission adjourned for a longer afternoon break than usual, again to allow Dr. Oronhyatekha to rest.[30]

Struggling with diabetes and its complications for years, Dr. Oronhyatekha appears noticeably gaunt in this picture.

Dr. Oronhyatekha on his way to the pyramids in Egypt.

Dr. Oronhyatekha's health had been failing since 1896. He suffered from diabetes, for which no cure or treatment other than dietary restrictions had yet been discovered, and complications including heart disease had taken their toll. James Hughes, one of his friends, remembered Dr. Oronhyatekha's first cardiac event. They were travelling together on a train when Dr. Oronhyatekha suddenly "pitched forward and fell into [his] lap. 'Jim,' he said, 'there's something wrong with my heart.'"

Over the next few years, he had taken a number of vacations to warmer climates to rest and restore his health. In December 1902, the *Forester* magazine reported that he had finally consented to see a specialist in New York City, who recommended that he take several months off from work. Dr. Oronhyatekha agreed to vacation overseas but only while conducting IOF business. In 1904 and 1905, his health required him to take more time off. His once-massive frame had become frail, and during the commission he needed assistance to and from his chair. In January 1907, the *Globe* reported him to be in "feeble physical condition," so much

Bena and Ellen on holiday.

so that he had to read his address at an IOF gathering, rather than deliver it off the cuff as usual. This was his last IOF event. His doctors advised him to go south to recuperate in a warmer climate. Taking their advice, he said his farewells, first to his staff at the Temple and then at Tyendinaga. He left for Savannah, Georgia late in February, and it is said he stopped off for a week in Washington to visit President Teddy Roosevelt, an IOF member, at the White House. Almost as soon as he arrived in Savannah, his condition deteriorated. After receiving word, Acland hurriedly left Toronto to see his father once more, but did not make it in time. Dr. Oronhyatekha died on March 3, 1907, of a heart attack at the DeSoto Hotel.[31] He may never have heard the official findings of the royal commission, which were not published until February 22, 1907.

EPILOGUE

LEGACY AND MEMORY

THE ORONHYATEKHA FAMILY

Dr. Oronhyatekha and Ellen had six children, only two of whom, Acland and Bena, lived into adulthood. Acland and his first wife Natalie Brande parted ways in the early 1900s. He claimed he had divorced her, but she claimed abandonment after he left for Australia on business. She had been forced to take employment in an office in New York City. The matter rose to a head when, in late May 1907, she accidently encountered him coming out of a hotel in New York, on the way to the Netherlands to join his second wife, Theresa Henrekke Hansen, whom he had met in 1905 in Norway on IOF business. The ensuing court case for abandonment ended on a technicality when the judge ruled that Brande was a resident of New Jersey, and thus out of the court's jurisdiction. One month later, and only four months after his father's passing, Acland suffered a heart attack at home at The Pines, dying just days before his thirty-eighth birthday. Brande's claims that they had never divorced complicated his estate. Hansen was unfortunately visiting her former home at the time of Acland's death, but she returned to Canada, dying in 1922 after an operation. They had no children. That left only Bena. She had married Percy John Johnson, an Australian goldsmith, at The Castle on Foresters' Island in June 1906. While Dr. Oronhyatekha disapproved of Johnson, he did employ him as manager of the orphanage.

Bena and Percy had no children, and at some point Johnson permanently returned to Australia alone. Bena passed away in 1939, leaving no direct descendents. Nevertheless, Dr. Oronhyatekha had so many brothers and sisters that there are numerous distant relatives, as well as those of Ellen, in their home communities of Tyendinaga and the Six Nations of the Grand River. The Oronhyatekha name also lives on in other varied ways, from flowers to fiction to founding myths.[1]

COMMEMORATIONS

One of the first commemorations was proposed as early as 1912. With his focus on helping the needy, Dr. Oronhyatekha would have been delighted to know that the IOF suggested building a hospital in his name at the Grand River. A Mrs. K.C. Steele, an IOF member from Ohio, contacted the Department of Indian Affairs and proposed that if the Grand River council could contribute $5,000, she would collect $10,000–15,000 through public donations. The community had indeed desired a permanent hospital for some years, since it operated in tents, even in the winter. Indian Affairs, however, disapproved of Steele's proposed method of collecting subscriptions, perhaps because she intended to take a percentage as a commission. Nevertheless, the council invited Steele to explain her plans, appointed several chiefs to form the Oronhyatekha Memorial Hospital Association, and invited representatives from the two local IOF courts to join. In the end, however, the council rejected the plan since it feared the long term maintenance of the hospital would be too expensive.[2]

In 1966, Dr. Oronhyatekha, along with Tom Longboat, a champion long-distance runner, was inducted into the Canadian Indian Hall of Fame. The previous year, the Canadian National Exhibition, supported by the Inuit-Eskimo Association of Canada, had created this portrait gallery as a way to honour accomplished native individuals for their contributions to Canadian society. Now housed by the Woodland Cultural Centre, Dr. Oronhyatekha's portrait hangs with other prominent individuals such as Tecumseh.[3]

More recently, Dr. Oronhyatekha's story inspired Joseph Sagaj, an Anishinabe visual artist best known for designing the Royal Commission

Joseph Sagaj's interpretation of Dr. Oronhyatekha's life graces the Miziwe Biik
Employment and Training Centre in Cabbagetown, Toronto.

on Aboriginal Peoples logo, to paint a mural of his life on the Miziwe
Biik Employment and Training Centre in Toronto. Sagaj read about Dr.
Oronhyatekha in Ethel Brant Monture's biographical *Canadian Portraits*.
Intrigued, Sagaj visited the Royal Ontario Museum, the Foresters, and
Dr. Oronhyatekha's grave to learn more about his life. His mural incor-
porates images of Oronhyatekha in his traditional costume and his
presentation to the Prince of Wales in 1860, his university graduation
photograph, the IOF Temple and orphanage, his home at 209 Carlton
Street, IOF medals and a wampum belt.[4]

But other communities claim Dr. Oronhyatekha as one of their own. This diversity of commemorations speaks to the wide-ranging and cross-cultural nature of his achievements. In 1956, the Ontario Archaeological and Historic Sites Board (now Ontario Heritage Trust) approached the Reverend Walter Smith of Christ Church at Tyendinaga to suggest Dr. Oronhyatekha as a suitable candidate for the then new provincial plaquing program. Smith presented the idea to the Tyendinaga band council, which approved. The board installed the plaque in 1957, near the Oronhyatekha family graves, as a part of the larger celebrations of the landing of the loyalist Mohawk at the Bay of Quinte after the American Revolution. This plaque mistakenly denotes him as a chief, a common description of him during his lifetime, and focuses on his early years; it includes his attendance at Oxford and the University of Toronto, his presentation to the Prince of Wales, his place on the Wimbledon shooting team, and his election as president of the Grand General Indian Council.[5]

In 1995, the Toronto Historical Board (now Heritage Toronto) honoured Dr. Oronhyatekha with a plaque in Cabbagetown's Allan Gardens. Supported by the Woodland Cultural Centre, this one is more inclusive — calling him a "physician, philanthropist, mason, fraternalist and collector" — but also included his education and his role in the 1860 royal visit. It also notes Ellen's illustrious heritage as the great-granddaughter of Joseph Brant. The inclusion of the translation of his name — Burning Sky — was welcomed as a gesture to the Mohawk speakers at Grand River and their interest in language preservation. (The 1957 plaque did not mention the meaning of his name or his baptismal name, Peter Martin). The Toronto plaque is also the only one that mentions that the IOF donated the Oronhyatekha collection to the Royal Ontario Museum (ROM) after his death.[6]

In 2001, the Historic Sites and Monuments Board (HSMB) began to discuss commemorating Dr. Oronhyatekha. A division of Parks Canada, the HSMB has designated people, places, events, and buildings with national historic significance since 1919. Suggestions for designations can be submitted by members of the public. The Woodland Cultural Centre and the chief and council of Tyendinaga initiated the proposal, with support from the Foresters and the Six Nations of the Grand River. Dr. Oronhyatekha easily fit into the HSMB's categories of "economic leaders who have made a definitive ... contribution to Canadian life," and "ethnic leaders whose contribution ... had an impact ... beyond the ethnic community." In 2005, the HSMB also erected its plaque near Dr. Oronhyatekha's grave at Christ Church. Compared to previous plaques, the main emphasis for national designation was his fraternal and philanthropic work. While acknowledged, his native background is not central. Visitors to Christ Church can also view the altar cross donated by Bena. Her father had purchased this olivewood cross with inlaid mother of pearl in Jerusalem. Bena also followed through with her father's intention to donate a stained-glass window to the church. This large window by the noted McCausland Company, depicting Jesus with a flock of lambs, rises above the altar.[7]

Various organizations have remembered Dr. Oronhyatekha. Past Master Clifford Rich of the Masons presented a biographical paper at the 1973 biennial meeting of the now defunct Canadian Masonic Research Association. This paper was later printed in its publication series. The Knights Templar also published a biographical profile in its *Knight Templar Magazine*, as has the Orange Order on its historical website. In 2007, the Bay of Quinte branch of the United Empire Loyalist Association of Canada inducted him into their Loyal Americans Hall of Honour, citing his family's loyalist roots through his grandfather George Martin, his mother Lydia Loft, and his wife, Ellen Hill. Founded in 1914, this organization aims to "enrich the lives of Canadians through fostering public awareness of our national history, and, in particular, of the United Empire Loyalists and their contributions to Canada, while also celebrating their memory and perpetuating their heritage as an integral part of the Canadian identity." Among its other activities, the Bay of Quinte branch established its Hall of Honour in 2003. Other luminaries keeping Dr. Oronhyatekha company in the hall include John Babcock, Canada's last surviving veteran from the First World War, inventor Thomas Edison, and Lester Pearson, former prime minister of Canada.[8]

BUILT HERITAGE

Dr. Oronhyatekha spent years designing elaborate buildings, many of which, unfortunately, have since been destroyed. Like the orphanage, the Temple did not survive. In 1950, the Foresters sold the building when the company decided to build new offices. In the late 1960s, the new owners decided to demolish the Temple. Once the tallest building in the city, it was now dwarfed by modern-day skyscrapers. "The Temple Will Fall," proclaimed the *Toronto Daily Star*.

In today's heritage climate, the Temple would likely be a designated building and protected from demolition. But in 1970, the *Star* reported that only Eric Arthur, the former dean of the school of architecture at the University of Toronto, protested its demolition. Further, the Temple's downtown location and high tax rates made it "economically impractical" to preserve. This was also a time when office space was in high demand and new buildings were cropping up everywhere. "Today, the only sounds are of workmen … removing … debris," the *Star* lamented. "An all-white door with a hand-engraved elk leans against a ground-floor wall, smudged and marked, its elaborate brass handle hanging askew … The walls are marked with graffiti and the passageways are littered with plaster and wood … construction scaffolding surrounds the building where once, in 1905, a giant arch [for the royal visit] spanned Bay St." Demolition took six months to complete.

Some parts remain. The IOF restored the time capsule for display, and the wall panels and furnishing of the original executive boardroom were re-installed at its new headquarters, Foresters' House. Herbert Spencer Clark, once owner of Guild Inn in Toronto and architectural salvager of buildings facing the wrecking ball, collected and restored part of the façade of the Temple. Today it can be seen at the Guildwood Sculpture Garden in the Beaches area of Toronto.[9]

Time has been kinder to the homes in which the Oronhyatekha family lived. After moving several times within London, in the early 1880s the family moved to an apartment building on Litchfield Street (now Central Avenue). Shortly after, they moved just down the street to 172 Litchfield. Described by an 1889 local history as a "fine residence," their new home was an elegant two-storey Italianate yellow brick house. A 1988 local heritage home walking tour noted several of its unusual features, including its three foot thick foundation walls, triple-layered brick walls, and the rafters made from halved tree trunks. As with the Temple, Dr. Oronhyatekha preferred his buildings solidly constructed.[10]

After the IOF moved its headquarters to Toronto in 1889, Dr. Oronhyatekha lived alone while the rest of the family resided at Tyendinaga.

Dr. Oronhyatekha boarded
with the Barker family at 209
Carlton Street.

He lodged at 209 Carlton Street, a semi-detached Second Empire style
home, with the Barker family, whose daughter Lillian worked as a clerk at
the Foresters. In 1976, the city of Toronto designated this house a heritage
property as part of the wider Cabbagetown Heritage Conservation District,
although its association with Dr. Oronhyatekha is only briefly mentioned.

In 2008, the Cabbagetown Preservation Association proposed to
rename the area's public lanes — "unique heritage elements of the Victorian
plan and existing historic streetscapes" — to commemorate historic individuals, places, and events and to "strengthen neighbourhood identity."
As a result, Lane A was renamed "Dr Oronhyatekha Lane." The house,
lane, and plaque in Allan Gardens feature in a number of area walking

Doctor O Lane in the
Cabbagetown Heritage
Conservation District,
Toronto.

tours. While most simply note his presence and briefly describe his career, the First Story Toronto Bus Tour is different. It aims to emphasize the long occupation of the area by First Nations and to reclaim the city as indigenous space. It thus uses Dr. Oronhyatekha's residence to point out that native individuals have "continuously occupied" the area, rather than thinking of native peoples and cities as incongruous.[11]

At Tyendinaga, Acland inherited The Pines and its 150 acres of farmland, and Bena, The Castle. Both were later demolished as were all the buildings on Foresters' Island. Dr. Oronhyatekha left most of Foresters' Island to the IOF; even the land he had given Acland passed to the IOF on Acland's death. In 2005, the Foresters turned the island back over to the Mohawks of the Bay of Quinte.[12]

The buildings of Foresters' Island under demolition.

POPULAR CULTURE

Dr. Oronhyatekha's well-known personae inspired individuals to create eponymous objects such as the Oronhyatekha chrysanthemum. In the early 1900s, Toronto's Miller and Sons florists, the company that supplied the Temple, created this new variety. The New York Peter Henderson and Company garden catalogue described the flower, also known as a Yellow Eaton, as "A bright yellow 'sport' from Timothy Eaton. It has the perfect habits of the Timothy Eaton, but lacks the coarseness sometimes attributed to that variety. Splendid for every purpose." In turn, Dr. Oronhyatekha sponsored a challenge cup at the inaugural Provincial Fruit, Flower and Honey show in Toronto in 1904 for the best exhibit of his namesake flowers.[13] Thomas Ball, a long time IOF member, created a new hybrid muskmelon for Dr. Oronhyatekha. He forwarded a few samples to the Temple, and after having it tested by horticulturalists and "veteran gourmets," Dr. Oronhyatekha declared the species would be the "official melon" of the orphanage gardens.[14]

Dr. Oronhyatekha's interests in shooting and sailing have also been commemorated. A rifle shooting competition named after him began in Napanee in the 1980s. Merchant Andrew McGee of Back Bay, New

Brunswick, presumably a friend or IOF colleague, named one of his six ships after him. The *Oronhyatekha* was a forty-foot wooden schooner. After McGee's death, his daughter Blanche sold it to Robert George of Nova Scotia in 1950, although shortly thereafter it was left to become derelict on the riverbank near Upper Pereau.[15] As evident from the boating competitions held during IOF celebrations on Foresters' Island, Dr. Oronhyatekha was fond of water sports. In 1906, he commissioned the Oronhyatekha Cup, to be awarded in a sailing competition on the Bay of Quinte. He died, however, before establishing the event. In the 1970s, the Prince Edward Yacht Club in Picton revived the idea, and the Mohawk chiefs of Tyendinaga agreed that the cup, then held by an Oronhyatekha family member, be the prize for this competition. The inaugural Oronhyatekha Challenge Cup took place in 1976. Today the club holds an annual Viking 28 Challenge competition, which "continues in the spirit of the original desires of the Cup's founder."[16]

Dr. Oronhyatekha's time at Oxford appears in Canadian author Guy Vanderhaeghe's 2002 fictional *The Last Crossing*, which won CBC's annual Canada Reads competition in 2004. This book tells the story of the three Gaunt brothers, two of whom go searching for the third who had disappeared in North America. Simon Gaunt had been studying at Oxford in the 1860s at the same time as Oronhyatekha. In order to meet him, Simon wangled an invitation to a gathering at which Oronhyatekha was the honoured guest, or "principal attraction," as Vanderhaeghe describes it. The two men spent most of the evening in conversation, and to his brother Charles's dismay, Simon consequently donated twenty pounds to a subscription for Oronhyatekha's tuition. When Charles intimated that Oronhyatekha couldn't possibly benefit from an Oxford education, Simon stated that Oronhyatekha's desire for education was clear. "When one feels a lack, one must take steps to remedy it," Simon replied, implying that he, too, might be seeking purpose in his own life. Charles disdained the growing friendship between his brother and Oronhyatekha, and saw Simon as an innocent needing protection. In treating Oronhyatekha as an equal, Simon made himself look ridiculous to the amusement of other Oxford students: "They strolled arm in arm through the quadrangles. He gave the Indian private lessons in his rooms, fed him biscuits and tea. He taught Oronhyatekha to ride a velocipede, a comedy fully appreciated by all who witnessed it." Charles saw an impossible and even comedic disjunction between what he saw as Indian-ness and the culture of British Oxford.

One night, Oronhyatekha and Simon met at a local establishment. Seeing them, Charles hid in case Simon insisted on introducing him to his new friend. During their conversation, Simon witnessed Oronhyatekha touching a lock of Simon's blond hair, as if he was unable to help himself. While Charles could forgive a "savage" having poor manners, he was so disturbed that his brother would allow such a familiarity that he decided to inform their father about the friendship. Their father ordered Simon to cut off his new friend, and when Simon refused, he forbade him to return to Oxford. Eventually, Simon decided to become a native missionary, partly because of his contact with Oronhyatekha. Horrified, Charles accused Simon of pining for "more Oronhyatekhas ... because they cannot see you for what you are — preposterous." Nevertheless, Simon departs for the United States and is reported missing after a blizzard on the western prairies of Montana Territory. In the end, Charles finds his brother living with the Crow people. While met with suspicion by much of the Crow village, Simon has formed his own family and refuses to return to England.

Vanderhaeghe came across the real Dr. Oronhyatekha during his background research on Oxford University and felt that the historical descriptions of his time there were indicative of how many nineteenth-century individuals regarded First Nations. Certainly, Charles's assumption of ignorance, backwardness, and an inability to fit into "modern" life were typical. Plus, Vanderhaeghe acknowledged, he found Oronhyatekha's story just too good not to include.[17]

Dr. Oronhyatekha's time at Oxford also appears in travel literature. In its entries for St. Edmund Hall, the latest version of *Lonely Planet Great Britain* noted that Dr. Oronhyatekha studied here, and in a romantic twist, that he "eloped with the principal's daughter."[18]

He is also profiled in the young teen book *Canadian Boys Who Rocked the World* (2007). Whitecap, the publisher, describes the premise of the book like this: "30 lives that achieved greatness before age 20. No one ever said you had to be a grown-up to do something great ... these boys have shaken the planet with their achievements." Those selected for the book are described as "born with strength, determination, and an unstoppable sense of adventure."[19]

Dr. Oronhyatekha's life and more specifically his accomplishment in building the Temple was the focus of a spoken word performance in summer 2014. Called "Stand Up, Stand Out," it formed part of the Restless Precinct project, which asked "participants to consider how culture grows out of intersections and collisions between different perspectives ... [T]he exhibition proposes a model for diversity that celebrates communication across difference." The curators wanted to "privilege Indigenous ... perspectives, as a way of uncovering the many untold histories of ... Canada." Located in Guildwood Park, historian Victoria Freeman conducted her performance on top of the Temple Building fragment in between photos of Dr. Oronhyatekha. According to Freeman, her "performance/collage" juxtaposes the Temple façade fragment with two texts: the museum catalogue of the Oronhyatekha Historical Rooms and letters Dr. Oronhyatekha wrote to the editor of the Toronto *Daily Mail* in 1875, responding to the racist debate over native peoples and prohibition in 1875.[20] The performance was complemented with a tour of the First Peoples gallery at the Royal Ontario Museum (ROM) by Keith Jamieson and Trudy Nicks, who co-curated *Mohawk Ideals, Victorian Values*.

Historian and writer Victoria Freeman performs "Stand Up, Stand Out" on top of the Temple fragment in summer 2014.

INSTITUTIONAL MEMORIES

Dr. Oronhyatekha's twenty-nine-year career with the IOF continues to influence the Foresters. Even after his death, the organization featured Dr. Oronhyatekha's image and accomplishments in its advertising. Today, the IOF remembers Dr. Oronhyatekha as a "charismatic leader" who pulled the organization's "shattered fragments" together and "led it to incredible new heights" in thirty-five countries. Through his "pioneering spirit and indomitable will," he provided the IOF "a solid and lasting foundation." The organization also describes him as a "man ahead of his time" who "championed the rights of women, children and minorities." In concluding the section on Dr. Oronhyatekha, the IOF's 1997 history states, "There is an important message to be learned from our early years and our first leader ... He helped us see that we can transcend our differences by focusing on values we share ... like protecting our children ... keeping families together ... helping those less fortunate ... and knowing others will extend that help to us in our time of need."

Photographs, artifacts, and other ephemera related to Dr. Oronhyatekha and the IOF more generally are housed at Foresters' House, the IOF's headquarters in Toronto. The IOF also established a memorial scholarship for First Nations students attending medical school in honour of Dr. Oronhyatekha.[21]

Despite his brief time there, St. Edmund Hall at Oxford University includes Dr. Oronhyatekha as one of its distinguished students. To commemorate the connection between Oxford and the Foresters, Supreme Chief Ranger Louis Probst commissioned Canadian artist C.W. Kettlewell to paint a portrait of a young Oronhyatekha in his 1860 ceremonial dress. In 1968, the IOF presented the hall with this portrait. In the course of the speeches that followed, the principal of St. Edmund Hall displayed Oronhyatekha's tomahawk, which he had given to Thomas Marshall, the student under whom he had been placed in 1862. This, along with other artifacts from his stay, is on display in the Oronhyatekha Room at St. Edmund's Hall, and although the year given is 1861, rather than 1862, Dr. Oronhyatekha's matriculation is listed among the significant events in the hall's online historical timeline.[22]

Over the last two decades, the University of Toronto has recognized Dr. Oronhyatekha as a distinguished alumnus. He was included in the article "Leaders and Mavericks," in a 2000 volume of *U of T Magazine*, one of the institution's alumni publications. The university made much of Dr. Oronhyatekha during 2002, the year of its 175th anniversary. The same publication called him one of three "trailblazers" who "challenged the prejudices of their day and changed the profession of medicine." The other two individuals were Augusta Stowe-Gullen, one of Canada's first female physicians, and Anderson Abbott, the first African-Canadian doctor. Dr. Oronhyatekha's graduation was also included in the historical timeline of important events and innovations featured in the university's *National Report*, a publication distributed with the *Globe and Mail*. Finally, the university hung banners throughout Toronto with the photographs of the "great minds" affiliated with it. Dr. Oronhyatekha's banner focused on his early career before joining the IOF. In spring 2014, *U of T Medicine* magazine selected Oronhyatekha for its "Old School" portrait feature, displaying his photograph and a brief biography. Most recently, he was noted as someone who changed the field of medicine in the dean's welcome message to incoming fall 2015 students.[23]

In 1911, the IOF donated the Oronhyatekha Historical Collection to the Royal Ontario Museum, then a part of the University of Toronto. As one of the founding artifact donors of the museum, Dr. Oronhyatekha was thanked at the opening of the ROM in 1914.[24] Its first director, Dr. Charles T. Currelly, however, dismissed much of the collection. He categorized it as:

(1)   A collection of Indian stone implements and pipes, which are of no particular value but which we should be very glad to have.

(2)   A collection of personal historical things of Toronto, etc. for which we have no place in the constitution of the museum, with the exception of a piece or two ...

(3)   The third section of objects picked up in travel, mainly in Egypt, are not only worthless but are objects which would have to be so labeled that they would bring discredit upon those from whom they came. There are two or three exceptions in this class that we would be glad to keep, and

my private advice would be for the complete destruction of the remainder as they are not even copies of real things, but are fantastic creations ...

(4)   The fourth class is a series of marble carvings from the modern Italian factories, and one of the objects of the Museum is to educate people away from things of that kind.[25]

Needless to say, Dr. Oronhyatekha would have been unimpressed with such an assessment. He had purchased objects from cultures around the world, those which he probably believed best represented them, and brought them home to show his people.

Today his collection has been re-evaluated. Items purchased as souvenirs, once dismissed as copies, kitsch, commercially produced, or not truly representative of the culture that produced them, shed light on the historical preferences of tourists and mark their experiences. While the local history items did not fit the more global mandate of the ROM, this does not make them less important to the history of Toronto. The objects collected from native individuals still make a statement about political sovereignty, as Dr. Oronhyatekha intended, and in particular can assist in retrieving information about native participation in the War of 1812. The significance of the collection is best appreciated as a whole, representative of Dr. Oronhyatekha's experiences and accomplishments. Middle-class Victorian men made such collections as symbols of their education, status, and success, and the collection as a whole should be viewed as such. It is also a personal expression; it tells us much about his stylistic preferences, his travels, allegiance with royalty, how he negotiated both the Victorian and Mohawk worlds, and his belief in the importance of First Nations and their contributions to Canada.[26]

In the museological ethos at the time of the donation, the ROM dispersed the artifacts into departmental collections according to geographical location of origin. In 2001, the ROM and the Woodland Cultural Centre (WCC) reintegrated many of Dr. Oronhyatekha's artifacts in their exhibit *Mohawk Ideals, Victorian Values: Oronhyatekha M.D.*, which explored his life and career. As is increasingly common in museum practice, the ROM and the WCC hoped to present a diversity of voices.

While there are no direct descendants from Dr. Oronhyatekha and Ellen Hill, many from the Grand River and Tyendinaga hold memories of the family. Indeed, their collaborative approach resulted in the sharing of stories at Grand River and Tyendinaga, and the discovery of other objects once owned by Dr. Oronhyatekha and the family. More than just a biographical look at one individual, the exhibit also revealed the repressive and manipulative state of nineteenth-century government–native relations, and the challenges native people faced as a result. Dr. Oronhyatekha, as a case study, showed how one person could successfully combine elements from both the native and the non-native worlds, thus disproving the common nineteenth-century stereotype of the "dying Indian." As curator Trudy Nicks writes, for the Haudenosaunee, the exhibit "represented a statement of agency, cultural strength, and identity."[27]

NOTES

INTRODUCTION

1. "Many Tributes to Oronhyatekha," *Globe*, March 7, 1907, 14.
2. Donald Brearley, "Physicians: A Database of Short Character Sketches about Physicians from the Belleville Area (Roughly 45 Mile Radius) in Ontario who Graduated before 1940." Quinte Branch, Ontario Genealogical Society, 2012, 51, www.rootsweb.ancestry.com/~canqbogs/pdf_files/Physicians_DrBrearley.pdf, accessed March 6, 2013.
3. "Canadian Indian Doctor Led Independent Order of Foresters," *Toronto Star*, October 18, 1980, G9; "Dr. Oronhyatekha Funeral to Be Held on Thursday," *Toronto Star*, March 4, 1907, 1; "Honor the Dead Chief," *Globe*, March 1907, 5; "Dr. Oronhyatekha Dead," *Boston Daily Globe*, March 4, 1907, 4; "Dr. Oronhyatekha Dead: Full-Blood Indian Who Founded the Order of Foresters," *Washington Post*, March 4, 1907, 1; "Head of Foresters Dies in Georgia," *Chicago Daily Tribune*, March 4, 1907, 4; "Dr. Oronhyatekha: The Remarkable Wilbraham Graduate Who Died in Savannah, Ga.," *Hartford Courant*, March 9, 1907, 14; "Supreme Chief Ranger Is Dead: Hon. Dr. Oronhyatekha Passes Away at Savannah, Was Very Noted Canadian," *Atlanta Constitution*, March 4, 1907, 2; *British Medical Journal* 1, 2414 (April 6, 1907): 846; "Oronhyatekha, M.B.," *Canadian Practitioner and Review* 32, 5 (1907): 308; "Anthropologic Miscellanea," *American Anthropologist* 9, 1 (1907): 244; "Death of Dr. Oronhyatekha," *IGT* 20 (1897): 123; "The Late Dr. Oronhyatekha, P.I.C.T.," *IGT* 20 (1897): 144–45; National Fraternal Congress,

Journal of Proceedings 21 (1907): 135. His funeral service is also recorded in *Memorial Service, Hon. Dr. Oronhyatekha, J.P., Supreme Chief Ranger, Independent Order Foresters, Massey Hall, Toronto, Canada, Wednesday, March 6th, 1907, at 7:30 p.m., conducted by Rev. F. Wilkinson, Rector St. Peter's Church, Toronto* (Toronto: Hunter, Rose, 1907?); "Oronhyatekha," *IF* 28, 4 (April 1907): 72; and "Oronhyatekha Dead," *IF* 28, 3 (March 1907): 34–40. The quote "sorrowing thousands" is found on page 34 of this latter article. The IOF order for mourning is "Proclamation," *IF* 28, 3 (March 1907): 43.

4. Oronhyatekha was sometimes translated as Burning Cloud, Heavens on Fire, or Sun of the Morning.

5. The consul appointment is noted in "Independent Order of Foresters," *Toronto Daily Star*, May 25, 1901, 13.

6. "Remarkable Oronhyatekha," *Winnipeg Tribune*, March 7, 1907, 3; Gold Hills advertisement, *Canadian Miner* 1, 3 (1897): 2.

7. *Canadian Patent Office Record* 15, 7 (1887): 343.

8. Robert Ker, ed., *St. George's Parish Church, St. Catharines: Jubilee Celebration and Historic and Centenary Review* (St. Catharines: Star Print, 1892?), 185–86; Appendix No. 16, *Transactions of the Buffalo Historical Society* 3 (Buffalo: Courier Co., 1885), 90; National Educational Association, *Journal of Proceedings and Addresses, Session of the Year 1891 Held at Toronto, Ontario, Canada* (New York: J.J. Little & Co., 1891), 26, 234–38; "Notes," *IF* 12, 2 (August 1891): 58. He was also on the general organization committee for the 1884 centennial; see United Empire Loyalists Centennial Committee, *The Centennial of the Settlement of Upper Canada by the United Empire Loyalists, 1784–1884: the Celebrations at Adolphustown, Toronto and Niagara, with an Appendix, Containing a Copy of the U.E. List, preserved in the Crown Lands Department at Toronto* (Toronto: Rose Publishing Co., 1885), 51.

9. *Minutes of the Fifteenth Session of the Synod of the Diocese of Huron, Held in London, on Wednesday, Thursday and Friday, June 5th, 6th and 7th, 1872* (London: Herald Printing Establishment, 1872), 472.

10. Quote is from David M. Fahey and Jon S. Miller, eds., *Alcohol and Drugs in North America: A Historical Encyclopedia* (Santa Barbara: ABC-Clio, 2013), 281.

11. E.J. Dunn, *Builders of Fraternalism in America*, Vol. 1 (Chicago: Fraternal Book Concern, 1924), 223–24, 237, 228, 262, 263.

12. Gerald Anglin, "The Strangest Insurance Company in the World," *Maclean's*, 64, 3 (1951): 10, 44.

13. Brendan F.R. Edwards, "Ethel Brant Monture: 'A One-Woman Crusade,'" Historical Perspectives on Canadian Publishing, McMaster University

Library, http://hpcanpub.mcmaster.ca/case-study/ethel-brant-monture-one-woman-crusade, accessed September 28, 2014; Ethel Brant Monture, *Canadian Portraits: Brant, Crowfoot, Oronhyatekha* (Toronto and Vancouver: Clarke, Irwin and Company, 1960), 131, 141–42.

14. Keith R. Miller, "Beyond Indian Leadership," *Tawow* 2, 2 (1971): 12.

15. For a focus on the IOF, see Gayle M. Comeau-Vasilopoulos, "Oronhyatekha," *Dictionary of Canadian Biography* 13 (1901–10): 791–95; David T. Beito, *From Mutual Aid to the Welfare State: Fraternal Societies and Social Services, 1890–1967* (Chapel Hill: University of North Carolina Press, 2000); Darren Ferry, *United in Measures of Common Good: The Construction of Liberal Identities in Central Canada, 1830–1900* (Montreal and Kingston: McGill-Queen's University Press, 2008); Colin Vollick, "Oronhyatekha, the Independent Order of Foresters, and the Forester Island Orphanage," *Lennox and Addington Historical Society Papers and Records* 17 (1987): 55–75; "The Good Works of Dr Oronhyatekha," *Medical Post*, 32, 2(1996): 41. His role in other societies is less well covered, but for the Masons, see Clifford E. Rich, "Dr. Peter Martin, M.D. (Oronhyatekha)," *Canadian Masonic Research Association* 107 (1973): 12–22. For the International Order of Good Templars, see David M. Fahey, *Temperance and Racism: John Bull, Johnny Reb, and the Good Templars* (Lexington, KY: University Press of Kentucky, 1996). For the Orange Order, see Cecil J. Houston and William J. Smyth, *The Sash Canada Wore: A Historical Geography of the Orange Order in Canada* (Toronto: University of Toronto Press, 1980).

16. Warren Potter and Robert Oliver, *Fraternally Yours: A History of the Independent Order of Foresters* (London: Queen Anne Press, 1967), 14–15, 82; Marianne Gerdes, *Shaping Our Future Together* (Don Mills: Foresters, 1997), 15–16.

17. Allan Sherwin, *Bridging Two Peoples: Chief Peter E. Jones, 1843–1909* (Waterloo: Wilfrid Laurier University Press, 2012).

18. Trudy Nicks, "Dr. Oronhyatekha's History Lessons: Reading Museum Collections as Texts," *Reading Beyond Words: Contexts for Native History*, 2nd ed., eds. Jennifer S.H. Brown and Elizabeth Vibert (Toronto: University of Toronto Press, 2009), 459–89; Keith Jamieson, "Oronhyatekha," *Rotunda* (Fall 2002): 32–37; *Mohawk Ideals, Victorian Values*, on exhibit at the WCC, Brantford, Ontario, July–December 2001 and at the ROM, Toronto, Ontario, March–August 2002; Trudy Nicks, "The War of 1812 as Remembered in the Oronhyatekha Historical Collection," *American Indian Art Magazine* (Summer 2012): 60–69.

19. *One Hundred Years of Temperance: A Memorial Volume of the Centennial Temperance Conference Held in Philadelphia, PA., September, 1885* (New York: National Temperance Society and Publication House, 1886), 106.

20. "The Late Dr. Oronhyatekha," *The Lancet*, March 16, 1907: 752.

21. For the concept of cultural brokers, see Margaret Connell Szasz, ed., *Between Indian and White Worlds: The Cultural Broker* (Norman, OK: University of Oklahoma Press, 1994).

22. Michele Horton, phone interview with Michelle Hamilton, September 2, 2014.

CHAPTER 1: AMBITIONS

1. Alexander, Simeon, Anthony and Elizabeth are noted in *The History of the County of Brant, Ontario: Containing a History of the County its Townships, Cities, Towns, Schools, Churches, etc; General and Local Statistics; Portraits of Early Settlers and Prominent Men; History of the Six Nation Indians and Captain Joseph Brant (Thayendanegea); History of the Dominion of Canada, Miscellaneous Matters, etc., etc., etc.* (Toronto: Warner, 1883), 688. Simeon is noted in Alma Greene, *Tales of the Mohawks* (Canada: J.M. Dent & Sons, 1975), 154. Harry is noted only through family history. Catherine, Alexander, and Elizabeth are included in the Haudenosaunee Project on Ancestry.ca, http://wc.rootsweb.ancestry.com/cgi-bin/igm.cgi?op=GET&db=erikj&id=I32927, accessed June 2, 2012. George P., Simon, Ann, and Margaret are recorded in Dr. Oronhyatekha's will. George P., Jessie, Alex, Elizabeth, and Emma are named in the diary of their nephew, also named Peter Martin, 1879–84, typescript, page 1, private collection. The National Anthropological Archives of the Smithsonian Institution hold photos that are described as Jesse (oldest brother); Margaret (sister); Emma (sister); Lydia (oldest sister); George (brother); William (brother); and Elizabeth (sister), among other family members. Alexander, Elinor, Emily, Lydia, Margaret, Mary, Rebecca, Simon, and William are recorded in *Mohawk Chapel, Indian Baptisms, 1827–1840s* (Brant County Branch, Ontario Genealogical Society), Publication #187. The early dates provided here are baptismal dates and may not reflect birth years. A handwritten family tree from the Grand River community notes George, Alex, Simeon, Maggie, Lizzie, Emma, and a half-sister Kate Newhouse. The latter may be Catherine, born 1820 before Peter and Lydia married, who married Nicholas Newhouse. University of Oxford, *Alumni Oxonienses, the Members of the University of Oxford, 1715–1886: Their Parentage, Birthplace,*

and the Year of Birth, with a Record of their Degrees. Being the Matriculation Register of the University, Alphabetically Arranged, Revised and Annotated (Nendeln, Liechtenstein: Kraus Reprint, 1968), 1045 records Oronhyatekha as the sixth son.

2. Lydia Martin is recorded as the head of the household in Canada, 1852 census, Brant County, Tuscarora Township, page 13, C-949, SC, RG 31, LAC.

3. Lydia Loft Martin's death date is recorded as September 20, 1884, in the parish register, 1829–1943, page 151, Her Majesty's Chapel of the Mohawks, PREG 912, Diocese of Huron Archives, Huron University College, London, Ontario. Here, she is listed as age eighty-four, making her birth year 1800; however, she is recorded as age forty-five in the 1852 census (born 1807), sixty in Canada, 1871 census, Brant County, Tuscarora township, page 54, C-948, SC, RG 31, LAC (born 1811) where she was found living with her children and other extended family members. Lyman Draper records her as age seventy-seven in 1879, making her birth year 1802. See 13F33, Joseph Brant Papers, Draper Manuscripts, State Historical Society of Wisconsin. Their marriage year is 13F37, Brant Papers, Draper Manuscripts, State Historical Society of Wisconsin.

4. For more about the Martins, see David T. MacNab, "George Martin," *Dictionary of Canadian Biography* 8 (1851–60): 619–21; Evelyn H.C. Johnson, "The Martin Settlement," *Some of the Papers Read During the Years 1908–1911 at Meetings of the Brant Historical Society* (Brantford: Courier, 1913), 55–64.

5. Children listed as attending the Martin school in 1846 likely lived in the settlement. Their last names were Hill, Maracle, Clause, Smith, Doctor, Miller, Loft, Carloe, and Green as recorded in NEC, *Report by a Committee of the Corporation Commonly Called the New England Company, of their Proceedings for the Civilization and Conversion of Indians, Blacks, and Pagans, in the British Colonies in America and the West Indies, Since the Last Report in 1840* (London: J.P. Gibson, 1846), 98.

6. Charles M. Johnston, *The Valley of the Six Nations: A Collection of Documents on the Indian Lands of the Grand River* (Toronto: Champlain Society, 1964), passim. For more about the complicated nature of land claims at Grand River, see NEC, *Report by a Committee of the Corporation Commonly Called the New England Company* (1846), 101–56; Charles M. Johnston, "The Six Nations in the Grand River Valley, 1784–1847," *Aboriginal Ontario: Historical Perspectives on the First Nations*, eds. Edward S. Rogers and Donald B. Smith (Toronto: Dundurn Press, 1994), 167–81; Sidney L. Harring, *White Man's*

Law: Native People in Nineteenth-Century Canadian Jurisprudence (Toronto: University of Toronto Press, 1998), 35–61.

7.   NEC, *Report by a Committee of the Corporation Commonly Called the New England Company* (1846), 47, 98.

8.   For more about Upper Canada education and the Irish National Reader series, see *A Brief History of Public and High School Text-Books Authorized for the Province of Ontario 1846–1889* (Toronto: Warwick and Sons, 1890); Robert J. Graham, "The Irish Readers Revisited: The Power of the Text (book)" *Canadian Journal of Education* 14, 4 (1989): 414–26; Susan E. Houston and Alison Prentice, *Schooling and Scholars in Nineteenth-Century Ontario* (Toronto: University of Toronto Press, 1988); Violet Elizabeth Parvin, *Authorization of Textbooks for the Schools of Ontario* (Toronto: University of Toronto Press, 1965); Alison Prentice, *The School Promoters: Education and Social Class in Mid-Nineteenth Century Upper Canada* (Toronto: McClelland and Stewart, 1977); George S. Tomkins, *A Common Countenance: Stability and Change in the Canadian Curriculum* (Vancouver: Pacific Educational Press, 2008); E.T. White, *Public School Text-Books in Ontario* (London: Chas. Chapman Co., 1922). The textbooks discussed here are *First Book of Lessons for Use in Schools* (Montreal: Armour and Ramsay, 1845); *Second Book of Lessons for the Use of Schools* (Montreal: Campbell Bryson, 1849); *Sequel to the Second Book of Lessons, for the Use of Schools* (Toronto: Brewer, McPhail and Co. 1853); *Third Book of Lessons for the Use of Schools* (Montreal: Armour and Ramsay, 1846).

9.   Canada, 1852 census, Brant County, Brantford, sub-district 5, page 185, C-948, SC, RG 31, LAC.

10. *Fourth Book of Lessons for the Use of Schools* (Edinburgh: G. and J. Grierson, 1851), 134, 138–41.

11. For Oronhyatekha's description of his life at the Mohawk Institute, see Oronhyatekha to Acland, March 24, 1862, A-2081, Sir Henry Wentworth Acland Papers, R10912-0-6-E, LAC. See also Elizabeth Graham, *The Mush Hole: Life and Two Indian Residential Schools* (Waterloo: Heffle Publishing, 1997), Jennifer Pettit, "From Longhouse to Schoolhouse: The Mohawk Institute, 1834–1970," MA Thesis, University of Western Ontario, 1993, and for general information on residential schools in Canada, J.R. Miller, *Shingwauk's Vision: A History of Native Residential Schools* (Toronto: University of Toronto Press, 1996).

12. "Physiology and Phrenology at the Town Hall," *Conservative Expositor*, Brantford, April 18, 1854, 3.

13. A. O'Leary, *Delineation of Character as Determined by the Teachings of Phrenology, Physiology, and Physiognomy* (Boston: Bradley, Dayton and Co., 1860).

14. Oronhyatekha to Acland, March 24, 1862, A-2081, Acland Papers, LAC.

15. Oronhyatekha to Acland, March 24, 1862, A-2081, Acland Papers, LAC.

16. Indeed, there was an O'Leary family living in Wilbraham, but it is not known if this is the same family that hosted Oronhyatekha. See Chauncey E. Peck, *The History of Wilbraham Massachusetts* (Wilbraham? 1914?), 265, 398.

17. "Oronhyatekha was a Wilbraham Boy," *Hartford Courant*, June 7, 1907, 11.

18. Peck, *History of Wilbraham*, 225.

19. See, for example, "Death of Dr. Oronhyatekha at Savannah on Sunday," *Globe*, March 4, 1906, 1; G. Mercer Adam, "Dr. Oronhyatekha, M.D.," *Prominent Men of Canada: A Collection of Persons Distinguished in Professional and Political Life, and in the Commerce and Industry of Canada* (Toronto: Canadian Biographical Pub. Co., 1892), 44; Ethel Brant Monture, *Canadian Portraits: Brant, Crowfoot, Oronhyatekha* (Toronto and Vancouver: Clarke, Irwin and Company, 1960), 133.

20. David M. Fahey, ed., *The Collected Writings of Jessie Forsyth 1847–1937: The Good Templars and Temperance Reform on Three Continents* (Lewiston: Edwin Mellon Press, 1988), 371.

21. Monture, *Canadian Portraits*, 134.

22. Reverend David Sherman, *History of the Wesleyan Academy, at Wilbraham, Mass. 1817–1890* (Boston: The McDonald and Gill Company, 1893), 24.

23. For the history of Wesleyan Academy, see Sherman, *History of the Wesleyan Academy* and Peck, *History of Wilbraham*, 220–26.

24. For Oronhyatekha's description of his time at Wesleyan, see Oronhyatekha to Acland, March 24, 1862, A-2081, Acland Papers, LAC.

25. "National Fraternal Congress. Report of the President," *IF* 22, 1 (January 1901): 1.

26. "Great Success of the Foresters," *Globe*, December 18, 1900, 6.

27. NEC, *Report of the Proceedings of the Corporation Commonly Called the New England Company, for the Civilization and Conversion of Indians, Blacks, and Pagans, in the British Colonies in America. Since the Last Report in 1849, to the End of the Year 1858* (London: J.P. Gibson, 1859), 51, 53. For Oronhyatekha's description of his time at Kenyon, see Oronhyatekha to Acland, March 24, 1862, A-2081, Acland Papers, LAC.

28. George Franklin Smythe, *Kenyon College: Its First Century* (New Haven, CT: Yale University Press, 1924), 167, 39; *General Catalogue of Kenyon College, Gambier, Ohio* (Toledo, OH: Franklin Printing and Engraving, 1899), 100.

29. NEC, *Report of the Proceedings of the Corporation Commonly Called the New England Company, for the Civilization and Conversion of Indians, Blacks, and Pagans, in the British Colonies in America. Since the Last Report in 1849*, 54; Heywood to Acland, November 7, 1862, A-2081, Acland Papers, LAC.

30. For a history of this early legislation, see John S. Milloy, "The Early Indian Acts: Developmental Strategy and Constitutional Change," *As Long As the Sun Shines and the Water Flows: A Reader in Canadian Native Studies*, eds. Ian A.L. Getty and Antoine S. Lussier. (Vancouver: University of British Columbia Press, 1983), 56–64; Darlene Johnson, *The Taking of Indian Lands in Canada: Consent or Coercion?* (Saskatoon: University of Saskatchewan Native Law Centre, 1989), 44–61; and eds. John Leslie and Ron Maguire, *The Historical Development of the Indian Act*, 2nd ed., (Ottawa: Indian and Northern Affairs Canada, 1983).

31. Province of Canada, *An Act to Encourage the Gradual Civilization of the Indian Tribes in this Province, and to Amend the Laws Respecting Indians*, Ch. 26, 20 Vict., 1857.

32. Sally Weaver, "The Iroquois: The Consolidation of the Grand River Reserve in the Mid-Nineteenth Century, 1847–1875," *Aboriginal Ontario*, eds. Rogers and Smith, 199–200.

33. William Budd Bodine, *The Kenyon Book*, 2nd ed. (1891), 317.

34. *Catalogue of the Theological Seminary of the Diocese of Ohio, and Kenyon College. 1857–58* (Gambier: Theological Seminary Press, 1858), 22, 23.

35. A.D. Rockwell, *Rambling Recollections: An Autobiography* (New York: Paul B. Hoeber, 1902), 85–87.

36. Oronhyatekha, *History of the Independent Order of Foresters* (Toronto: Hunter, Rose and Company, 1895), 62.

37. For Milnor Hall, see *Kenyon College, Gambier, Ohio. From an Article, With Additions. Reprinted from Scribner's Monthly for March 1878* (Columbus: Cott and Hann, 1878?), n.p.; *Kenyon College* (Gambier, 1844), 2; *Kenyon College* (Gambier, circa 1880), 39–41; *Catalogue of the Theological Seminary of the Diocese of Ohio, and Kenyon College. 1857–58*, 29–30, 33.

38. Bodine, *The Kenyon Book*, 248; *A Memento of the Donors and Founders of the Theological Seminary of the Protestant Episcopal Church in the Diocese of Ohio, and Kenyon College; Being the Report of a Committee of the Board of Trustees, Presented September 27, 1860* (Cincinnati: Moore, Wilstach, Keys and Co., 1860), 79.

39. *Catalogue of the Theological Seminary of the Diocese of Ohio, and Kenyon College. 1859–60* (Gambier: Cincinnati Gazette Company, 1860), 35–36; Grade Book, 1850–1860, GSCA.

40. Grade Book, 1850–1860, GSCA; Thomas Greenslade to Dr. George Pearce, July 7, 1990, Allan Gale File, GSCA. The textbooks from which Oronhyatekha studied can be found in Kenyon College catalogues.

41. Expenses can be found in *Catalogue of the Theological Seminary of the Diocese of Ohio, and Kenyon College. 1857–58*, 33–34; *Catalogue of the Theological Seminary of the Diocese of Ohio, and Kenyon College. 1859–60*, 38–39; *Kenyon College, Gambier, Ohio. From an Article, With Additions. Reprinted from Scribner's Monthly for March 1878*, n.p.; *Kenyon College* (Gambier, circa 1880), 40–41. Boarding assignments are found in *Catalogue of the Theological Seminary of the Diocese of Ohio, and Kenyon College. 1857–58*, 23; *Catalogue of the Theological Seminary of the Diocese of Ohio, and Kenyon College. 1858–9* (Gambier: Cincinnati Gazette Company, 1859), 21; *Catalogue of the Theological Seminary of the Diocese of Ohio, and Kenyon College. 1859–60*, 19. Grade Book, 1850–1860, GSCA, shows Oronhyatekha's absence in the fall term of 1859.

42. Oronhyatekha to Acland, March 24, 1862, A-2081, Acland Papers, LAC. Oronhyatekha said the grant was thirty pounds a year for two years, while Heywood to Acland, November 7, 1862, A-2081, Acland Papers, LAC gives the amount of fifteen dollars a year for three years. The 1859 NEC report, page 2, states that Nelles gave 150 dollars to Oronhyatekha in 1858.

43. See, for example, "A Prominent Member of the Medical Profession," *Canadian Journal of Medicine and Surgery* 3, 2 (1898): 117–18 and "Dr. Oronhyatekha, P.R.W.G.T," *IGT* 7 (1894): 258.

44. Princess Viroqua's newspaper reports and ads include "Princess Viroqua's Work," *New York Times*, November 16, 1888, 8; "Mohawk Indian Princess Pays a Visit to Milwaukee," *Milwaukee Journal*, June 21, 1899, 5; "Princess Viroqua, M.D.," *Los Angeles Times*, August 16, 1902, 10.

45. Oronhyatekha to City Council, August 6, 1860, M-233, 24140-24143, Lennox and Addington Historical Society Records, R14133-0-7-E, LAC.

46. Alpha Delta Phi, *Catalogue of the Alpha Delta Phi Society* (Utica: Curtiss and Childs, 1870), 188; *Kenyon Reveille* 4, 1 (December 1859), n.p.; *Kenyon Reveille* 4, 2 (June 1860), n.p. The list of members of the Kokosing Tribe appeared regularly in the *Kenyon Reveille*. Oronhyatekha's file at the Kenyon archives includes such a list, presumably because of its relevance.

47. See the minutes of the Philomathesian Society, GSCA.

48. John B. Hattendorf, *A Dusty Path* (Canton: Consolidated Graphic Arts, 1964), 37; "Memorabilia Kenyonensia: Burial of Homer," *Kenyon Collegian* 5, 2 (November 1859), 84-7; "Burial of Homer! By the Class of '62, Kenyon:

June 29, 1859," Pamphlet, Humor at Kenyon File, GSCA; "Burial of Homer! Class of '62," invitation, Gale file, GSCA.

49. Matriculation Book, GSCA; *Catalogue of the Theological Seminary of the Diocese of Ohio, and Kenyon College. 1858–59*, 21; *Catalogue of the Theological Seminary of the Diocese of Ohio, and Kenyon College. 1859–60*, 19; *General Catalogue of Kenyon College, Gambier, Ohio*, 49.

50. Oronhyatekha to Acland, March 24, 1862, A-2081, Acland Papers, LAC; "Olla Podrida," *Kenyon Reveille* (June 1860): 2; "Memorabilia Kenyonensia: The Concert and the Third Kenyon Rebellion," *Kenyon Collegian* (March 1860), 279–83.

51. Kenyon College, *Twentieth Anniversary of the Class of 1862* (Rushville, IN: Republican Book and Job Office, 1882), 22, 40–1.

CHAPTER 2: THE ROYAL VISIT

1. Oronhyatekha to Acland, March 24, 1862, A-2081, Sir Henry Wentworth Acland Papers, R10912-0-6-E, LAC.

2. For more about the Six Nations of the Grand River during this time period, see Sally M. Weaver, "The Iroquois: The Consolidation of the Grand River Reserve in the Mid-Nineteenth Century, 1847–1875," *Aboriginal Ontario: Historical Perspectives on the First Nations*, eds. Edward S. Rogers and Donald B. Smith (Toronto: Dundurn Press, 1994), 182–212.

3. Veronica Strong-Boag and Carole Gerson, *Paddling Her Own Canoe: The Times and Texts of E. Pauline Johnson* (Toronto: University of Toronto Press, 2000), 48; Charlotte Gray, *Flint and Feather: The Life and Times of E. Pauline Johnson, Tekahionwake* (Toronto: HarperFlamingo Canada, 2002), 36-7; Horatio Hale, Chief George H.M. Johnson, "Onwanonsyshon, His Life and Work among the Six Nations," *Magazine of American History* 13, 2 (1885): 137–8; Vol. 841, C-15112, 23–5, 29–30, DIA, RG 10, LAC.

4. Pennefather to Thorburn, July 6, 1860, Vol. 545, C-13358, 451–2, DIA, RG 10, LAC; "Address of the Chiefs, Sachems, and Warriors of the Six Nations Indians Residing on the Grand River, Done in General Council, August 20, 1860, Vol. 1, Office of the Governor General, RG 7, G 23, LAC; Johnson to Thorburn, August 23, 1860, Vol. 842, C-15113, 169-70, DIA, RG 10, LAC. Emphasis in italics is mine.

5. Ethel Brant Monture, *Canadian Portraits: Brant, Crowfoot, Oronhyatekha* (Toronto and Vancouver: Clarke, Irwin and Company, 1960), 134.

6. Monture, *Canadian Portraits*, 136.

7.   Oronhyatekha to Acland, March 24, 1862, A-2081, Acland Papers, LAC.

8.   Acland's accounts of his meetings with Oronhyatekha can be found in J.B. Atlay, *Sir Henry Wentworth Acland, Bart., K.C.B., F.R.S. Regius Professor of Medicine in the University of Oxford: A Memoir* (London: Smith, Elder and Co., 1903), 283–86 and more fully in Acland's letterbook, "Letters from North America," 113–18, 123–25, Acland Papers, LAC.

9.   George Franklin Smythe, *Kenyon College: Its First Century* (New Haven, CT: Yale University Press, 1924), 29.

10. Ian Radforth, *Royal Spectacle: The 1860 Visit of the Prince of Wales to Canada and the United States* (Toronto: University of Toronto Press, 2004), 145–48. The correspondence regarding the planning of the Six Nations of the Grand River meeting with the prince is found in Vol. 841, C-15113, 451–52; Vol. 842, C-15113, 58–59, 235, 265–66, 268–70, 279, 297–99, 311–14, 347–50; and Vol. 545, C-13358, 115–16 all in DIA, RG 10, LAC. For the Sarnia ceremony, see Radforth, Royal Spectacle, 221–22, 228, 233–35, 237, 308.

11. *The History of the County of Brant, Ontario: Containing a History of the County its Townships, Cities, Towns, Schools, Churches, etc; General and Local Statistics; Portraits of Early Settlers and Prominent Men; History of the Six Nation Indians and Captain Joseph Brant (Thayendanegea); History of the Dominion of Canada, Miscellaneous Matters, etc., etc., etc.* (Toronto: Warner, 1883), 338–41; "The Prince's Progress," *Globe*, September 15, 1860, 2; "Movements of the Prince of Wales," *Daily Leader*, September 15, 1860, 2; Title missing, *Brant Expositor*, September 14, 1860, 3.

12. Oronhyatekha, "Address from the Six Nations of Indians, in Canada to H.R.H. Prince of Wales," A-2081, Acland Papers, LAC.

13. F. Douglas Reveille, *History of the County of Brant* (Brantford, ON: Hurley Printing Company, Limited, 1920), 63.

14. Radforth, *Royal Spectacle*, 209, 70; Title missing, *Brant Expositor*, September 14, 1860, 3.

15. Oronhyatekha to Acland, February 28, 1861, A-2081, Acland Papers, LAC; Radforth, *Royal Spectacle*, 231–32.

16. Radforth, *Royal Spectacle*, 232–39.

17. Ruth B. Phillips, "Making Sense Out/of the Visual: Aboriginal Presentations and Representations in Nineteenth-Century Canada," *Art History* 27, 4 (2004): 600.

18. F. Barlow Cumberland, *Catalogue and Notes of the Oronhyatekha Historical Collection* (Toronto: Hunter, Rose Company, 1904), 21–22, 24, 25, 26, 90; Collection records, File Natural History Museum — L.A. County, Dr.

Oronhyatekha Exhibit Papers, Woodland Cultural Centre, Six Nations of the Grand River; Phillips, "Making Sense Out/of the Visual," 603–06.

19. Oronhyatekha to Acland, September 14, 1860, A-2081, Acland Papers, LAC.

20. Oronhyatekha to Acland, February 28, 1861, A-2081, Acland Papers, LAC.

21. Letterbook, "Letters from North America," 114, 124, 125, Acland Papers, LAC.

22. Oronhyatekha to Acland, February 28, 1861, A-2081, Acland Papers, LAC.

23. For more about the company, see Bruce Emerson Hill, *The Grand River Navigation Company* (Brantford, ON: Brant Service Press, 1994).

24. Oronhyatekha to Acland, February 26, 1862 and March 24, 1862, A-2081, Acland Papers, LAC.

25. Weaver, "The Iroquois: The Consolidation of the Grand River Reserve," eds. Rogers and Smith, *Aboriginal Ontario*, 201–02.

26. Oronhyatekha to Acland, February 28, 1861 and March 24, 1862, A-2081, Acland Papers, LAC.

27. Oronhyatekha to Acland, February 4, 1863, A-2081, Acland Papers, LAC.

28. See, for example, *Glasgow Herald*, March 11, 1862, 2; *Reynolds's Newspaper*, March 16, 1862, 6; *Bristol Mercury*, March 15, 1862, 1; *Caledonian Mercury*, Edinburgh, March 10, 1862, 3; *Boston Daily Advertiser*, February 10, 1862, 2; *Vermont Chronicle*, Bellows Falls, March 4, 1862, 36; *New York Evangelist*, March 6, 1862, 4.

CHAPTER 3: ORONHYATEKHA, M.D.

1. Met Office, Historical Station Data, Oxford, www.metoffice.gov.uk/climate/uk/stationdata/oxforddata.txt, accessed July 17, 2012; "Monthly Metereological Register," Canadian Institute, *Canadian Journal of Industry, Art and Science* 7 (1862): 232–33.

2. Based on data provided through www.VisionofBritain.org.uk, accessed August 16, 2016, which uses historical material copyrighted by the Great Britain Historical GIS Project and the University of Portsmouth.

3. Thomas F. Plowman, *In the Days of Victoria, Some Memories of Men and Things* (London: John Lane, The Bodley Head, 1918), 71–73. We are indebted to author Guy Vanderhaeghe for this reference.

4. MSMuseum 417, 13315, Sarah Acland Photograph Album, Museum of the History of Science, Oxford; Heywood to Acland, May 7, 1862 and Oronhyatekha to Acland, February 4, 1863, A-2081, Sir Henry Wentworth Acland Papers, R10912-0-6-E, LAC.

5. Heywood to Acland, February 25, 1861, A-2081, Acland Papers, LAC.

6. Heywood to Acland, February 25, 1862, A-2081, Acland Papers, LAC.

7. Nelles's charges and Oronhyatekha's responses to them are found in Gilkison to Bartlett, August 24, 1864, MS 2604, George Mills McClurg Correspondence, A.E. Williams/United Indian Bands of the Chippewas and the Mississaugas Papers, F 4337-10-0-4, AO; Oronhyatekha to Acland (two letters), February 26, 1862; Heywood to Acland, November 7, 1862; and Oronhyatekha to Acland, February 4, 1863, A-2081, Acland Papers, LAC.

8. MSMuseum 417, 13315, Sarah Acland Photograph Album, Museum of the History of Science, Oxford; *St. Edmund Hall Magazine* (1968–9): 15; University of Oxford, *Alumni Oxonienses, the Members of the University of Oxford, 1715–1886: Their Parentage, Birthplace, and the Year of Birth, with a Record of their Degrees, Being the Matriculation Register of the University, Alphabetically Arranged, Revised and Annotated* (Nendeln, Liechtenstein: Kraus Reprint, 1968), 898.

9. Oronhyatekha to Acland, November 13, 1864, A-2081, Acland Papers, LAC.

10. Oronhyatekha to Acland, February 26, 1862, February 4, 1863, and November 13, 1864, A-2081, Acland Papers, LAC.

11. Beresford Hope did not specify whether he meant King's College in London or at the University of Cambridge.

12. Oronhyatekha to Acland, February 4, 1863; Hope to Acland, February 26, 1862; and March? 1, 1862, A-2081, Acland Papers, LAC.

13. F. Max Müller, *The Life and Letters of the Right Honourable Friedrich Max Müller*, Vol. 1 (London: Longmans, Green, 1902), 252, 260.

14. Oronhyatekha to Acland, February 26, 1862; Müller to Acland, March 3, 1862?; and March 6, 1862?, A-2081, Acland Papers, LAC.

15. Heywood to Acland, February 25, 1862; Oronhyatekha to Acland, February 4, 1863; and Heywood to Acland, April 30, 1862, A-2081, Acland Papers, LAC.

16. "A Mohawk at Oxford," *London Review and Weekly Journal of Politics, Literature, Art and Society* (March 15, 1862): 255–56.

17. Head to Acland, March 3, 1862, A-2081, Acland Papers, LAC; Turner to Thorburn, March 12, 1862, and Copy, Retallack to Thorburn, March 12, 1862, Vol. 847, C-15114, 476–8, DIA, RG 10, LAC.

18. Gilkison to Bartlett, August 24, 1864, MS 2604, McClurg Correspondence, A.E. Williams/United Indian Bands Papers, AO.

19. Oronhyatekha to Acland, March 24, 1862, A-2081, Acland Papers, LAC.

20. Oronhyatekha to Acland, July 8, 1872, A-2081, Acland Papers, LAC.

21. The debate over the existence and content of these letters can be found in Oronhyatekha to Acland, March 24, 1862; Head to Acland, April 6, 1862; Oronhyatekha to Acland, June 6, 1862; Oronhyatekha to Acland, May 5, 1863; Lang to Oronhyatekha, April 21, 1863; and Oronhyatekha to Acland, June 6, 1862, A-2081, Acland Papers, LAC.

22. Heywood to Acland, May 7, 1862, A-2081, Acland Papers, LAC.

23. University of Oxford, *Alumni Oxonienses*, 1045.

24. Heywood to Acland, May 7, 1862, A-2081, Acland Papers, LAC.

25. Charles Edward Mallet, *A History of the University of Oxford*, Vol. 3, Modern Oxford (New York: Longmans, Green and Co., 1928), 334, states that tuition in the 1870s was about twenty-one pounds a year.

26. Müller to Acland, n.d., A-2081, Acland Papers, LAC.

27. Oronhyatekha to Acland, June 6, 1862, A-2081, Acland Papers, LAC.

28. Oronhyatekha to Acland, March 24, 1862; and Wilson to Acland, November 18, 1866, A-2081, Acland Papers, LAC.

29. "24th Anniversary of the I.O.F.," *IF* 19, 1 (July 15, 1898): 4–5.

30. The letters relevant to this time period and his intention to become a medical doctor are Heywood to Acland, July 17, 1862; Oronhyatekha to Acland, July 28, 1862; Oronhyatekha to Acland, September 6, 1862; Rolph to Oronhyatekha, October 9, 1862; Heywood to Acland, November 7, 1862; Heywood to Acland, December 6, 1862; Heywood to Acland, December 24, 1862; Heywood to Acland, January 3, 1863; Oronhyatekha to Heywood, January 10, 1863; Heywood to Acland, January 20, 1863; Heywood to Acland, February 3, 1863; Oronhyatekha to Acland, February 4, 1863; Lang to Oronhyatekha, April 21, 1863; Oronhyatekha to Acland, May 5, 1863; and Heywood to Acland, July 24, 1863, A-2081, Acland Papers, LAC.

31. *The Ontario Medical Register* (Hamilton: C.E. Stewart and Co., 1872), 50; James Sutherland, *Sutherland's City of Hamilton and County of Wentworth Directory for 1868–9* (Hamilton: A. Lawson and Co., 1868?), 75, 348.

32. Canada, 1861 census, Tyendinaga, page 34, C-1034, SC, RG 31, LAC; Canada, 1852 census, Tyendinaga, page 15, C-11727, SC, RG 31, LAC. Ellen Hill is called "Deyorouseh" in Canada, 1871 census, Stratford, page 48, C-9940, SC, RG 31, LAC.

33. Gayle M. Comeau-Vasilopoulos, "Oronhyatekha," *Dictionary of Canadian Biography* 13 (1901–10): 791 has the marriage date as August 28, but the Oronhyatekha family Bible, private collection, records the date as September 14.

34. Oronhyatekha to Bartlett, February 4, 1864, Vol. 420, C-9624, DIA, RG 10, LAC; Oronhyatekha to Bartlett, November 7, 1865, Vol. 424, C-9625, DIA, RG 10, LAC.

35. Joseph Malins, "A Visit to the Oronhyatekhas," *IF* 14, 3 (September 1893): 72, 73; "Foresters Celebrate," *IF* 15, 4 (October 1894): 98; Lady Meg, "Oronhyatekha," *IF* 22, 1 (January 1901): 53; "The Chief's Wife Laid to Rest," *IF* 22, 6 (June 1901): 273–75; "The Late Mrs. Oronhyatekha," *IF* 22, 6 (June 1901): 275–76.

36. For the history of the University of Toronto see University of Toronto, *The University of Toronto and Its Colleges, 1827–1906* (Toronto: University Library, 1906); Martin L. Friedland, *The University of Toronto: A History* (Toronto: University of Toronto Press, 2002); W. Stewart Wallace, *A History of the University of Toronto 1827–1927* (Toronto: University of Toronto Press, 1927).

37. January 31, 1842, Order-in-Council — Crown to King's College — Brantford Township 1,265 acres, *Six Nations of the Grand River, Land Rights, Financial Justice, Creative Solutions* (Six Nations of the Grand River, 2006), 60. www.caledoniawakeupcall.com/documents/ClaimsBooklet.pdf, accessed January 1, 2016.

38. Heywood to Acland, December 30, 1867, A-2081, Acland Papers, LAC.

39. University of Toronto, *University of Toronto and Its Colleges*, 259, states that twenty-six degrees were awarded in 1866, the year that Oronhyatekha graduated with his MB.

40. Allan Sherwin, *Bridging Two Peoples: Chief Peter E. Jones, 1843–1909* (Waterloo: Wilfrid Laurier Press, 2012).

41. For more about medical education in the nineteenth century, see R.D. Gidney and W.P.J. Millar, *Professional Gentlemen: the Professions in Nineteenth-Century Ontario* (Toronto: University of Toronto Press, 1994). Quote is from page 356.

42. "Students—Session 1863-4," *Annual Announcement of the Toronto School of Medicine in Affiliation with the University of Toronto, 22nd Session, from Oct. 1st., 1864, to April 1st, 1865* (Toronto: Globe Steam Book and Job Press, 1864), 9; University of Toronto, *Class and Prize Lists, 1864* (Toronto: Henry Rowsell, 1864), n.p.

43. Bartlett to Gilkison, August 23, 1864, 237, and Bartlett to Anderson, September 3, 1864, 260, Vol. 548, C-13359, DIA, RG 10, LAC; Gilkison to Bartlett, August 24, 1864, MS 2604, McClurg Correspondence, A.E. Williams/United Indian Bands Papers, AO.

44. *Class and Prize Lists, 1864*, n.p.; University of Toronto, *Class and Prize Lists, 1866* (Toronto: Henry Rowsell, 1866), n.p.

45. Ethel Brant Monture, *Canadian Portraits: Brant, Crowfoot, Oronhyatekha* (Toronto and Vancouver: Clarke, Irwin and Company, 1960), 142.

46. D.R. Keys, "Oronhyatekha, M.D.," *University of Toronto Monthly 7*, 7 (May 1907): 168.

47. Province of Canada, Appendices, *Report of the State of Militia of the Province of Canada, Sessional Paper* 4, 29–30 Vict., 1866, 32, 33, 36.

48. "The Late Dr. Oronhyatekha, P.I.C.T.," *IGT* 20 (1907): 145.

49. Clifford E. Rich, "Dr. Peter Martin, M.D. (Oronhyatekha)," *Canadian Masonic Research Association* 107 (1973): 17.

50. November 13, 1884, Daniel Wilson journal transcript, H.H. Langton Fonds, B65-0014/004, University of Toronto Archives; Daniel Wilson, *The Huron-Iroquois of Canada: A Typical Race of American Aborigines* (Ottawa?: 1884), 90, 91; Daniel Wilson, *The Lost Atlantis and Other Ethnographic Studies* (Edinburgh: D. Douglas, 1892), 291, 296, 298, 302. For Wilson's biography, see Marinell Ash, *Thinking with Both Hands: Sir Daniel Wilson in the Old World and the New*, ed. Elizabeth Hulse (Toronto: University of Toronto Press, 1999).

51. Oronhyatekha, "The Mohawk Language," *Canadian Journal of Industry, Science, and Art* 10, 57 (May 1865): 182–94. He delivered a second article to the institute in 1876. See Oronhyatekha, "The Mohawk Language," *Canadian Journal of Science, Literature, and History* 15, 1 (April 1876): 1–12.

52. Canada, 1871 census, Stratford, page 48, C-9940, SC, RG 31, LAC; "A Visit to the Oronhyatekhas," *IGT* 6 (1893): 243.

53. University of Toronto, Class and Prize Lists, 1866, n.p.

54. Oronhyatekha to Acland, November 13, 1861, A-2081, Acland Papers, LAC.

55. Oronhyatekha to Acland, May 5, 1866, Vol. 2, photostat letter, Acland Papers, LAC.

56. University of Toronto, Class and Prize Lists, 1866, n.p. Specific requirements for achieving the MB can found in *Annual Announcement of the Toronto School of Medicine in Affiliation with the University of Toronto, 22nd Session, from Oct. 1st, 1864, to April 1st, 1865*, 13–14.

57. Province of Canada, *Report of the State of Militia of the Province of Canada, Sessional Paper* 4, 29–30 Vict., 1866, 32, 36; *Canada Gazette* 24, 33 (August 19, 1865): 2; *Canada Gazette* 24, 39 (September 30, 1865): 1; *Canada Gazette* 24, 17 (April 29, 1865): 1; Nominal roll, March 1866, Queen's Own Rifles Museum and Archives, Casa Loma, Toronto.

58. For more about the Queen's Own Rifles of Canada, see Lieutenant-Colonel Reginald Pellatt, *A Guide to Riflemen of the Queen's Own Rifles of Canada* (Toronto: Arthurs-Jones, 1924); Queen's Own Rifles of Canada, *Book of Remembrance, 1866–1918* (1932); and Ernest J. Chambers, *The Queen's Own Rifles of Canada: a History of a Splendid Regiment's Origin, Development and Services: Including a Story of Patriotic Duties Well Performed in Three Campaigns* (Toronto: E.L. Ruddy, 1901). For more about the Battle of Ridgeway and the Fenian Raids of 1866 in general, see Hereward Senior, *The Last Invasion of Canada: The Fenian Raids, 1866–1870* (Toronto: Dundurn Press in collaboration with the Canadian War Museum, 1991); Peter Vronsky, *Ridgeway: the American Fenian Invasion and the 1866 Battle that Made Canada* (Toronto: Allen Lane, 2011); and John A. Macdonald, *Troublous Times in Canada: A History of the Fenian Raids of 1866 and 1870* (Toronto: W.S. Johnston and Co., 1910).

59. "Honouring the Noble Dead," *Globe*, June 3, 1891, 11.

60. "University of Toronto," *Journal of Education for Upper Canada* 19, 11 (1866): 175.

61. Wilson to Acland, November 18, 1866, A-2081, Acland Papers, LAC; Macdonald to Wilson, July 2, 1866, Letterbook 9, page 381.5, Vol. 512, part 2, C-24 and August 16, 1866, page 155103-4, Vol. 339, C-1709, John A. Macdonald Papers, MG 26, LAC.

62. "Toronto University," *Journal of Education for Upper Canada* 20, 7 (July 1867): 126; historical register, College of Physicians and Surgeons, Toronto, Ontario.

63. Sherwin, *Bridging Two Peoples*, 35.

CHAPTER 4: A SEARCH FOR INFLUENCE

1. Mackenzie Bowell, *1868–69: Directory of the County of Hastings* (Belleville: Intelligencer Office, 1869), 239, 81; Royal College of Physicians and Surgeons, *The Ontario Medical Register, 1870* (Hamilton: C.E. Stewart and Co.), 77. Oronhyatekha is also listed as a bookseller in Henry McEvoy, ed., *The Province of Ontario Gazetteer and Directory* (Toronto: Robertson and Cook, 1869), 162. For Frankford, see Walter Lewis and Lynne Turner, *By Bridge and Mill: A History of the Village of Frankford* (Kingston: Lake Ontario Regional Library, 1979), especially 33–35, 44. Walter S. Herrington, *History of the County of Lennox and Addington* (Toronto: Macmillan Company of Canada, Ltd., 1913), 232, says he moved to Napanee in 1866, but this date

may be incorrect. The medical register for Upper Canada in 1867 does not list Oronhyatekha, and unfortunately the medical registers for Ontario in 1868–69 are not extant.

2. NEC, *History of the New England Company, from its Incorporation, from the Seventeenth Century, to the Present Time Including a Detailed Report of the Company's Proceedings for the Civilization and Conversion of Indians, Blacks, and Pagans in the Dominion of Canada, British Columbia, the West Indies, and S. Africa, during the Two Years 1869–70* (London: Taylor and Co., 1871), 113, 147.

3. Herrington, *History of the County of Lennox and Addington*, 232.

4. *Canada Medical Journal and Monthly Record of Medical and Surgical Science* 4 (1868): 574, 575; *Canada Medical Journal and Monthly Record of Medical and Surgical Science* 7 (1871): 47.

5. NEC, *Report of the Proceedings of the New England Company for the Civilization and Conversion of Indians, Blacks and Pagans in the Dominion of Canada, South Africa and the West Indies during the Two Years 1871–1872* (London: Taylor and Co., 1874), 192; Oronhyatekha to Acland, April 25, 1872, A-2081, Sir Henry Wentworth Acland Papers, R10912-0-6-E, LAC; Adelaide Leitch, *Floodtides of Fortune: The Story of Stratford and the Progress of the City Through Two Centuries* (Stratford: City of Stratford, 1980), 188–89; F.B. Kennedy, "Stratford Has Had Splendid Lot of Practitioners Since Settlers Came 100 Years Ago," R. Thomas Orr Scrapbook, 104, Stratford-Perth Archives; James Anderson to Editor, *Canadian Antiquer and Collector*, August 2, 1988, Oronhyatekha Clipping File, Stratford-Perth Archives. According to Anderson's letter, Oronhyatekha and his family first lived just outside of town in 1871, and then moved to a brand new house in Stratford in 1872. Royal College of Physicians and Surgeons, *The Ontario Medical Register, 1872* (Hamilton: C.E. Stewart and Co., n.d.), 80, still listed Oronhyatekha as located in Frankford.

6. *Napanee Pictorial Almanac and Lennox and Addington Book of Reference for 1873, Containing a Short Sketch of the Rise and Progress of the Town, an Alphabetically Arranged Directory of the Inhabitants, with much other Useful and Valuable Information for the People, also, Advertisements from Several of the Leading Businsss [sic] Men of the Town and a Large Amount of very Interesting and Instructive Reading Matter* (Prescott: Beeman Bros., 1872?), n.p.; Richardson and Punchard, *Directory of the City of Kingston with the Villages of Barriefield, Portsmouth and Cataraqui, and Towns of Gananoque and Napanee for 1873–4* (Napanee: Henry and Bro's. Steam Book and Job

Printers, 1873), 126. Royal College of Physicians and Surgeons, *The Ontario Medical Register, 1874* (Toronto: Monetary Times, n.d.), 84, still lists Oronhyatekha as practising in Stratford.

7. Herrington, *History of the County of Lennox and Addington*, 232; Macdonald to Casey, September 30, 1872, Letterbook 18, page 583, C-31, John A. Macdonald Papers, MG 26, LAC; File 1866, Vol. 1897, C-11107; File 1058, Vol. 1879, C-11105; File 2390, Vol. 1909, C-11109; File 1455, Vol. 1888, C-11106; File 756, Vol. 1873, C-11105; File 1847, Vol. 1897, C-11107; Vol. 422, C-9624, 462–79; Vol. 424, C-9625, 129–39; Vol. 429, C-9629, 203–06; and Vol. 431, C-9630, 90–93, DIA, RG 10, LAC. The reference to his campaigning for the Liberal-Conservative party is in Leitch, *Floodtides of Fortune*, 189. Dr. Oronhyatekha's quote about the 1872 election is from "Great Success of the Foresters," *Globe*, December 18, 1900, 6.

8. Ethel Brant Monture, *Canadian Portraits: Brant, Crowfoot, Oronhyatekha* (Toronto and Vancouver: Clarke, Irwin and Company, 1960), 140–41. His salary for the period April 1, 1873 to March 31, 1874 is recorded in Department of the Interior, Annual Report, 1874 (1875), 72.

9. More details about this complicated and lengthy matter can be found in Oronhyatekha to Campbell, September 14, 1873, File 2390, Vol. 1909, C-11109; M File, Vol. 422, C-9624, 62–79; and File 4485, Vol. 1954, C-11120, DIA, RG 10, LAC.

10. File 3141, Vol. 1942, C-11117, DIA, RG 10, LAC.

11. W.C. Venning to Dr. Oronhyatekha, March 10, 1875, Vol. 7928, A-288, 443, NEC Papers, R10819-0-8-E, LAC.

12. "Medical," *Evening Courier and Republic*, January 20, 1875, 2. See also *Buffalo City Directory for the Year 1875* (Buffalo: Courier Company, 1875), 531.

13. "An Indian Ranger," *Buffalo Express*, January 31, 1890, 6.

14. *History of the County of Middlesex, Canada, from the Earliest Time to the Present, Containing an Authentic Account of Many Important Matters relating to the Settlement, Progress and General History of the County, and including a Department Devoted to the Preservation of Personal and Private Records, etc., Illustrated* (Toronto: Goodspeed, 1889), 954–55, states Oronhyatekha moved to London in 1875. He is not listed in city directories until W.H. Irwin and Co., *City of London Annual, Alphabetical, General Miscellaneous and Subscribers' Classified Business Directory for 1876-'77 — to Which Is Added Directories of Strathroy, Park Hill, Lucan and Ailsa Craig* (London: Advertiser Steam Presses, 1876?), 151. His correspondence shows that he still lived in Buffalo in May 1875 but was in London by early December 1875,

as evidenced by his letter to the *Toronto Mail*, December 4, 1875, 3. His name first appears in the Indian Affairs annual reports as physician to the Oneidas in the DIA report for 1876.

15. The following information can be found in Jacalyn Duffin, *Langstaff: A Nineteenth-Century Medical Life* (Toronto: University of Toronto Press, 1993) and R.D. Gidney and W.P.J. Millar, *Professional Gentlemen: the Professions in Nineteenth-Century Ontario* (Toronto: University of Toronto Press, 1994).

16. For the history of rifle-shooting in Canada, see K.B. Wamsley, "Cultural Signification and National Ideologies: Rifle-Shooting in Late Nineteenth-Century Canada," *Social History* 20, 1 (1995): 63–72; R. Blake Brown, *Arming and Disarming: A History of Gun Control in Canada* (Toronto: University of Toronto Press, 2012), 35–52; and Alex Lord Russell, *Illustrated Hand Book of Rifle Shooting, with an Appendix* (Toronto: Hunter, Rose, 1869), 1–9.

17. Province of Canada, Appendices, *Report of the State of Militia of the Province of Canada*, Sessional Paper 4, 29–30 Vict., 1866, 32, 36; Canada, Report of the State of the Militia of the Dominion of Canada for the Year 1868, *Sessional Paper* 10, 32 Vict., 1869, 32, 33; "Dominion Prize Meeting," *The Volunteer Review and Military and Naval Gazette* 3, 39 (September 27, 1869): 626; "Dominion of Canada Rifle Association," *The Volunteer Review and Military and Naval Gazette* 4, 38 (September 19, 1870): 602; "Hastings Rifle Association," *The Volunteer Review and Military and Naval Gazette* 5, 37 (September 11, 1871): 582; "Rifle Matches," *The Volunteer Review and Military and Naval Gazette* 6, 42 (October 14, 1872): 505; "Rifle Competition," *The Volunteer Review and Military and Naval Gazette* 8, 44 (November 3, 1874): 521; *The Volunteer Review and Military and Naval Gazette* 5, 9 (February 27, 1871): 134. His full militia career is unclear. According to the *Canada Gazette* 17, 39 (March 29, 1884): 12, and the *Canadian Militia Gazette* 1, 4 (June 2, 1885): 31, he retired from the militia in 1884, when he was second Lieutenant of the 26th Battalion, Company No. 5, in Lucan, Ontario. "Official Visit of the Supreme Chief Ranger," *Brisbane Courier*, November 12, 1901, 2, reported him as saying he had been in the forces for twenty-five years, rising to the level of lance corporal but had "lost his stripe" because of the bad behaviour of his squad but was later promoted to captain.

18. *History of the County of Middlesex*, 955; "The Wimbledon Team," *Canadian Illustrated News*, July 29, 1871, 66; *The Volunteer Review and Military and Naval Gazette* 5, 22 (May 29, 1871): 347; *The Volunteer Review and Military and Naval Gazette* 5, 31 (July 31, 1871): 487; "Wimbledon," *Globe*, July 29, 1871, 4; "Life in England," *Globe*, July 27, 1871, 2; "Life in England," *Globe*,

August 2, 1871, 4; "The Wimbledon Meeting," *Globe*, August 3, 1871, 2; "The Wimbledon Meeting," and "The Canadians at Wimbledon," *Globe*, August 10, 1871, 2; "The Canadian Volunteers at Wimbledon," *Globe*, August 14, 1871, 2; "Banquet to Canadian Volunteers," *Newcastle Courant*, July 7, 1871, 6; "The Wimbledon Meeting," *Birmingham Daily Post*, July 18, 1871, 5. For the association of Arthur with the Grand River community, see Pauline E. Johnson, *Legends of Vancouver* (Toronto: McClelland, Goodchild and Stewart, 1911), 157–65.

19. Acland's birthdate is noted in Oronhyatekha, *History of the Independent Order of Foresters* (Toronto: Hunter, Rose and Company, 1895), 788.

20. Oronhyatekha to Acland, April 25, 1872 and July 8, 1872, and Tappan to Oronhyatekha, June 20, 1872, A-2081, Acland Papers, LAC.

21. "Oronhyatekha is Chief," *Toronto Daily Star*, December 29, 1906, 4.

22. Alma Greene, *Tales of the Mohawks* (Canada: J.M. Dent & Sons, 1975), 122–26.

23. NEC, *History of the New England Company, from its Incorporation, from the Seventeenth Century, to the Present Time Including a Detailed Report of the Company's Proceedings for the Civilization and Conversion of Indians, Blacks, and Pagans in the Dominion of Canada, British Columbia, the West Indies, and S. Africa, during the Two Years 1869–70*, 113, 145, 283; NEC, *Report of the Proceedings of the New England Company for the Civilization and Conversion of Indians, Blacks and Pagans in the Dominion of Canada, South Africa and the West Indies during the Two Years 1871–1872*, 188, 192, 195–98, 295–97.

24. NEC, *Report of the Proceedings of the New England Company for the Civilization and Conversion of Indians, Blacks and Pagans in the Dominion of Canada, South Africa and the West Indies during the Two Years 1871–1872*, 192–93, 195.

25. NEC, *Report of the Proceedings of the New England Company for the Civilization and Conversion of Indians, Blacks and Pagans in the Dominion of Canada, South Africa and the West Indies during the Two Years 1871–1872*, 15–21, 23–8, 76–77. Quotes are from page 19 and 26. It is not clear what happened since the matter seemed to be in question still in 1875; see W.C. Venning to Dr. Oronhyatekha, June 30, 1875, Vol. 7928, A-288, 530, NEC Papers, LAC.

26. For an overview of the development of Indian legislation in Canada, see eds. John Leslie and Ron Maguire, *Indian and Northern Affairs, The Historical Development of the Indian Act*, 2nd ed. (Ottawa: Indian Affairs and Northern Development, 1983). *An Act for the gradual enfranchisement of Indians, the better management of Indian affairs, and to extend the provisions of the Act*

31st Victoria, Chapter 42, www.aadnc-aandc.gc.ca/ DAM/DAM-INTER-HQ/ STAGING/texte-text/a69c6_1100100010205_eng.pdf, accessed April 11, 2013.

27. NEC, *Report of the Proceedings of the New England Company for the Civilization and Conversion of Indians, Blacks and Pagans in the Dominion of Canada, South Africa and the West Indies during the Two Years 1871–1872*, 199.

28. NEC, *History of the New England Company*, 282–83.

29. NEC, *Report of the Proceedings of the New England Company for the Civilization and Conversion of Indians, Blacks and Pagans in the Dominion of Canada, South Africa and the West Indies during the Two Years 1871–1872*, 79–84, 393. Quotes are from pages 80, 82, 83.

30. The 1870 report is *The General Council of the Six Nations and Delegates from Different Bands in Western and Eastern Canada, June 10, 1870* (Hamilton: The Spectator, 1870?). For a general history of the council, see Norman Shields, "The Grand General Indian Council of Ontario and Indian Status Legislation," *Lines Drawn Upon the Water: First Nations and the Great Lakes Borders and Borderlands*, ed. Karl S. Hele (Kitchener: Wilfrid Laurier Press, 2008), 205–18; and Norman D. Shields, "Anishinabek Political Alliance in the Post-Confederation Period: The Grand General Indian Council of Ontario, 1870–1936" (Queen's University, MA Thesis, 2001).

31. File 3541, Vol. 1934, C-11114, DIA, RG 10, LAC.

32. The report is contained in File 3589, Vol. 1935, C-11114, DIA, RG 10, LAC. Dr. Oronhyatekha's comments are recorded on pages 10–11. More complaints made by the Grand River community can be found in this file.

33. The report can be found in File 4103, Vol. 1942, C-11117, DIA, RG 10, LAC.

34. Gilkison to Superintendent General of Indian Affairs, July 18, 1874, File 3589, Vol. 1935, C-11114, DIA, RG 10, LAC.

35. Shields, "Anishinabek Political Alliance in the Post-Confederation Period," 31–48.

36. File 4324, Vol. 1949, C-11118, DIA, RG 10, LAC.

37. Shields, "Anishinabek Political Alliance in the Post-Confederation Period," 60–72; Shields, "The Grand General Indian Council of Ontario and Indian Status Legislation," 206.

38. File 849, Vol. 1875, Reel C-11105, DIA, RG 10, LAC.

39. File 4324, Vol. 1949, Reel C-11118, DIA, RG 10, LAC. In 1891, however, Lawrence Vankoughnet, the deputy superintendent general of Indian Affairs, considered Dr. Oronhyatekha to be "ipso facto" enfranchised because he was a "professional man." See Vankoughnet to Dewdney, September 26, 1891, File 4618, Vol. 1956, C-11120-21, DIA, RG 10, LAC.

40. See File 347, Vol. 426, C-9627, 375–77; G file, Vol. 418, C-9621; and File 4618, Vol. 1956, C-11120-21, DIA, RG 10, LAC. Gilkison's quotes are from his letter to E.A. Meredith, April 12, 1875, File 4618, Vol. 1956, C-11120-21, DIA, RG 10, LAC.

41. Oronhyatekha to Macdonald, January 20, 1875, Vol. 346, C-1711, 158737-38, Macdonald Papers, LAC.

42. In 1886, the Oneida council petitioned the DIA to also appoint Dr. Oronhyatekha as their magistrate because they felt the need for such an official who could speak their language. The DIA denied this request, based on a lack of funds and the fact that their agent, Thomas Gordon, had the power to act as magistrate. See File 72,790, Vol. 2361, C-11208, DIA, RG 10, LAC.

43. *History of the County of Middlesex*, 955; London Old Boys' Association, *Souvenir Programme, International London Old Boys at Home* (London: A. Talbot and Co., 1903), 27.

44. "Communications," *Toronto Mail*, November 30, 1875, 3; "Communications," *Toronto Mail*, December 4, 1875, 3; "Communications," *Toronto Mail*, December 14, 1875, 2.

45. Guy St. Denis, *Tecumseh's Bones* (Montreal and Kingston: McGill-Queen's University Press, 2005), 38–43. Dr. Oronhyatekha's letter is "An Indian Vindicates his Race," *St. Thomas Journal*, February 8, 1877, 5.

46. The smallpox outbreak and Dr. Oronhyatekha's role is recorded in File 13288, Vol. 2088, C-11154, DIA, RG 10, LAC and *Periodical Accounts Relating to the Missions of the Church of the United Brethren established among the Heathen*, Vol. 31 (London: G. Norman and Son, 1880), 301–2. The latter states that forty-seven fell ill and eleven died.

47. Statistics can be found in William B. Spaulding, "The Ontario Vaccine Farm, 1885–1916," *Canadian Bulletin of Medical History* 6, 1 (1989): 47. For the development of public health measures and legislation regarding smallpox, see Barbara Lazenby Craig, "State Medicine in Transition: Battling Smallpox in Ontario, 1882–1885," *Ontario History* 75, 4 (1983): 319–47 and Paul Adolphus Bator, "The Health Reformers versus the Common Canadian: The Controversy of Compulsory Vaccination Against Smallpox in Toronto and Ontario, 1900–1920," *Ontario History* 75, 4 (1983): 348–73.

48. Canada, 1871 census, Stratford, page 48, C-9940, SC, RG 31, LAC; Canada, 1881 census, London, page 47, C-13270, SC, RG 31, LAC; Oronhyatekha to Macdonald, January 5, 1882, Vol. 390, C-1759, 185028, Macdonald Papers, LAC; "Births, Marriages, and Deaths," *Canadian Journal of Medical Science*

1, 5 (May 1876): 183; Edward Marion Chadwick, *A Genealogy of the Brant Family from Ontarian Families* (Toronto: Rolph, Smith and Co., 1894), 4.

49. *History of the County of Middlesex*, 277–81; Warren Potter and Robert Oliver, *Fraternally Yours: A History of the Independent Order of Foresters* (London: Queen Anne Press, 1967), 61; Catherine B. McEwen, ed., *The Carty Chronicles of Landmarks and Londoners* (London: London and Middlesex Historical Society, 2005), 48–51; "The Victoria Disaster," *IF* 1, 9 (June 10, 1881): 68–69.

50. Oronhyatekha to Macdonald, January 5, 1882, Vol. 390, C-1759, 185208, Macdonald Papers, LAC. The Oronhyatekha family Bible, private collection, states that John Alexander Herbert was born January 3, 1883, not 1882 as according to the previous letter.

51. File 56, 897, Vol. 2283, C-11194, DIA, RG 10, LAC.

52. Malcolm Montgomery, "The Six Nations Indians and the Macdonald Franchise," *Ontario History* 57, 1 (1965): 13–17; Donald B. Smith, "Macdonald's Relationship with Aboriginal Peoples," *Macdonald at 200: New Reflections and Legacies*, eds. Patrice Dutil and Roger Hall (Toronto: Dundurn Press, 2014), 77–80; J.R. Miller, "Macdonald as Minister of Indian Affairs: The Shaping of Canadian Indian Policy," *Macdonald at 200*, 328–29; Julie Evans, Patricia Grimshaw, David Philips and Shurlee Swain, *Equal Subjects, Unequal Rights: Indigenous Peoples in British Settler Colonies, 1830–1910* (Manchester: Manchester University Press, 2003), 113–34; Sally Weaver, "The Iroquois: The Grand River Reserve in the Late Nineteenth and Early Twentieth Centuries, 1875–1945," *Aboriginal Ontario: Historical Perspectives on the First Nations*, eds. Edward S. Rogers and Donald B. Smith (Toronto: Dundurn Press, 1949), 235–6.

53. "A Tory Tutor Among the Oneidas," *London Advertiser*, December 23, 1885, 4; "Tyendinaga Reserve," *The Indian*, April 14, 1886, 79; Canada, House of Commons, *Debates*, 1885, 48–49 Vict., 2121–22.

54. "Personal and Political," *London Advertiser*, May 13, 1885, 4; "The Indian Franchise," *Gazette*, May 8, 1885, 5; "Indian Franchise," *Mail*, Toronto, May 6, 1885, 4–5.

55. File 97,758, Vol. 2470, C-11226, DIA, RG 10, LAC; untitled, *Toronto Daily Star*, August 24, 1900, 1; Oronhyatekha, *History of the IOF*, 66.

CHAPTER 5: SECURITY, JUSTICE, AND EQUALITY

1. For more about fraternal societies, see Christopher J. Anstead, "Fraternalism in Victorian Ontario: Secret Societies and Cultural Hegemony," (Ph.D.

Dissertation, The University of Western Ontario, 1992); Mark C. Carnes, *Secret Ritual and Manhood in Victorian America* (New Haven, CT: Yale University Press, 1989); Mary Ann Clawson, *Constructing Brotherhood: Class, Gender and Fraternalism* (Princeton: Princeton University Press, 1989); Darren Ferry, *United in Measures of Common Good: The Construction of Liberal Identities in Central Canada, 1830–1900* (Montreal and Kingston: McGill-Queen's University Press, 2008), 136–69.

2. Knight of the Maccabees, *Constitutions and Laws of the Knights of the Maccabees of the World, Governing the Supreme Tent, Gt. Camps & Subordinate Tents* (London: Southam and Brierley, 1881), records Dr. Oronhyatekha as the Great Medical Examiner. He appears in the Old Boys' Association souvenir publications for 1900, 1901, 1903, 1905. "General News of the City," *Globe*, July 19, 1897, 12 and "London was their Home," *Globe*, March 26, 1901, 2 list him as a member of the Old Boys Association, and the *Special Report by the Bureau of Education. Educational Exhibits and Conventions at the World's Industrial and Cotton Centennial Exhibition, New Orleans 1884-'85* (Washington: Government Printing Office, 1886), notes that he joined the United Order of Workmen and had served as a Grand Workman.

3. Cecil J. Houston and William J. Smyth, *The Sash Canada Wore: A Historical Geography of the Orange Order in Canada* (Toronto: University of Toronto Press, 1980), 3.

4. For more about the Orange Order in Canada, see Gregory S. Kealey, "The Orange Order in Toronto: Religious Riot and the Working Class," *Essays in Canadian Working Class History*, eds. Gregory S. Kealey and Peter Warrian (Toronto: McClelland and Stewart, 1976), 13–34; Hereward Senior, *Orangeism: The Canadian Phase* (Toronto: McGraw-Hill Ryerson, 1972).

5. Houston and Smyth, *The Sash Canada Wore*, 95.

6. Mackenzie Bowell, *1868–69: Directory of the County of Hastings* (Belleville: Intelligencer Office, 1869), 34.

7. Imperial Grand Orange Council of the World, The Imperial Grand Orange Council, Dublin, 1903, *Report of Proceedings* (1903?), 53, 54, 55, 59, 63; William Johnson, "Imperial Grand Orange Council. From 1866 to the Present Time," *Belfast News-Letter*, December 28, 1896, 7; "The Canadian Delegates in Armagh — Grand Orange Demonstration," *Belfast News-Letter*, July 24, 1873, 3; "Orange Meeting in Antrim," *Belfast News-Letter*, August 16, 1873, 4; Grand Orange Lodge of Ontario West, *Report of the Proceedings of the Right Worshipful Grand Lodge of the Loyal Orange Association of Ontario West Assembled in the Opera Hall, Strathroy on the 21st and 22nd Days of February, 1882,*

http://canadianorangehistoricalsite.com/GOLofONTARIOWEST1882.php; Grand Masters and Secretaries of the Grand Lodge of British America and Provincial Grand Lodges, 1888, http://canadianorangehistoricalsite.com/ CANADIANORANGELODGEOFFICERS1888.php, "Oronhyatekha," http:// canadianorangehistoricalsite.com/index-29.php, all accessed December 27, 2014; Houston and Smyth, *The Sash Canada Wore*, 132.

8. J. Ross Robertson, *The History of Freemasonry in Canada, from its Introduction in 1749, Compiled and Written from Official Records and from MSS Covering the Period 1749–1185, in the Possession of the Author* (Toronto: George N. Morang and Company, Limited, 1900), 690, 687.

9. *By-laws and History of King Solomon's Lodge, A.F. & A.M., No. 22, G. R. C.* (Toronto, 1896), 68; Clifford E. Rich, "Dr. Peter Martin, M.D. (Oronhyatekha)," *Canadian Masonic Research Association* 107 (March 1973): 17.

10. Carnes, *Secret Ritual and Manhood*, 5, 167–8. For more on the establishment of freemasonry in Canada, including various schisms, see Special Committee on Publications, Grand Lodge A.F. & A.M. of Canada in the Province of Ontario, *Beyond the Pillars: More Light on Freemasonry* (Hamilton: Masonic Holdings, 1973); Osborne Sheppard, *A Concise History of Freemasonry in Canada*, 3rd ed. (Hamilton: R. Duncan and Co., 1924); Walter S. Herrington and Roy S. Foley, A *History of the Grand Lodge A.F.& A.M. of Canada in the Province of Ontario, 1855–1955: the First One Hundred Years* (Toronto: McCallum Press Ltd., 1955). For more about the first three degrees, see Thomas Sargant, *The Freemason's Manual Containing the First, Second and Third Degrees of Freemasonry; Embellished with Symbolical Illustrations, Together with Installation, Consecration, and Dedication Ceremonies, Etc. Also, Rules and Regulations for Masonic Trials, Forms for Minutes, By-Laws, &c.* (Toronto: Masonic Publishing Co., 1880).

11. Bowell, *1868–69: Directory of the County of Hastings*, 402; Grand Lodge of Ancient, Free and Accepted Masons of Canada, *Proceedings* (Hamilton? 1872), 1; Grand Lodge of Ancient, Accepted and Free Masons of Canada, *Proceedings of the Grand Lodge of Ancient, Accepted and Free Masons of Canada, At a Special Communication, held at the Village of Trenton, on the 24th day of Sept., A. D. 1873, A. L. 5873. Also at Its Nineteenth Annual Communication, Held at Toronto, Ont, on the 8th & 9th days of July, A. D. 1874, A. L. 5874* (Hamilton: Spectator Steam Printing Press, 1874), 701.

12. J. Ross Robertson, *The Cryptic Rite: Its Origin and Introduction on this Continent. History of the Degrees of Royal, Select, and Super-Excellent Master; The Work of the Rite in Canada with a History of the Various Grand Councils*

that have Existed from the Inception of the Rite in Canada till the Present Time (Toronto: Hunter, Rose and Co., 1888), 233, 235, 241; "Supreme Grand Council A. & A. Rite, 33°, Great Britain and Ireland," *CCMR* 18, 3 (March 15, 1884): 81–2; "R.S. Masters," *CCMR* 19, 3 (March 15, 1885): 78; Dominion Masonic Benefit Association, File 121, Box 2, Benevolent Societies Corporation Files, RG 55-8, AO.

13. Special Committee of the Supreme Council, *The History of the Supreme Council of the Ancient and Accepted Scottish Rite in Canada, 1868–1960* (Ottawa, 1961), 33–5; "Egyptian Masonic Rite of Memphis, 96°," *London Advertiser*, August 9, 1881, 4; Oronhyatekha to William Peckham, September 8, 1882, William H. Peckham Papers, AR1997.1, Chancellor Robert R. Livingston Masonic Library of Grand Lodge, New York, New York; "The Union of the Sovereign Sanctuaries," *CCMR* 17, 2 (February 5, 1883): 44; "Egyptian Masonry," *CCMR* 18, 7 (July 1884): 210; "Sovereign Sanctuary," *CCMR* 19, 1 (January 15, 1885): 26, 27; "Royal and Oriental," *CCMR* 23, 4 (October 1888): 109; "Royal and Oriental," *CCMR* 24, 2 (August 1889): 52; *CCMR* 18, 2 (February 15, 1884): 63; "Sovereign Sanctuary," *CCMR* 19, 1 (January 15, 1885): 27. For more about Egyptian masonry, see *Ritual of the A. and A. Egyptian Rite of Memphis 96°*. Also *Constitution and By-Laws of the Sovereign Sanctuary, Valley of Canada* (1889) and Calvin C. Burt, *Egyptian Masonic History of the Original and Unabridged Ancient and Ninety-Six (96°) Degree Rite of Memphis. For the Instruction and Government of the Craft* (Utica: White and Floyd, Printers, 1879).

14. "Rosicrucian Society of Canada," *CCMR* 18, 12 (December 15, 1884): 372; "Grand Imperial Council of the Constantinian Order of Canada," *CCMR* 19, 8 (August 15, 1885): 243; "Annual Meeting of the Red Cross of Constantine," *CCMR* 19, 11 (November 15, 1885): 341.

15. *By-laws and History of King Solomon's Lodge* (Toronto, 1896), 68, 51; William Sanders, "The History of the Richardson Lodge No. 136, G.R.C.," *Proceedings of the Heritage Lodge 730* 33 (2010): 97; Grand Lodge of Ancient, Free and Accepted Masons of Canada, *Proceedings of the Grand Lodge of Ancient Free and Accepted Masons of Canada, in the Province of Ontario, at Special Communications Held at Cayuga, 28th September, A. L. 5894, and at Napanee Mills, 16th May, A. L. 5895, also at the Fortieth Annual Communications Held at the City of Toronto on the 17th and 18th July, A. D. 1895, A. L. 5895* (Hamilton: Spectator Printing Co., 1895), 162.

16. "The Union of the Sovereign Sanctuaries," *CCMR* 17, 2 (February 5, 1883): 44; "Gathering of I.O.F. at Foresters' Island," *Mail and Empire*, July 16, 1900, 7; *IF* 8, 1 (June 1887): front cover.

17. Letitia Youmans, *Campaign Echoes: the Autobiography of Mrs. Letitia Youmans, the Pioneer of the White Ribbon Movement in Canada. Written by Request of the Provincial Woman's Christian Temperance Union of Ontario* (Toronto: W. Briggs and Montreal: C.W. Coates, 1893?) 145-7.

18. *One Hundred Years of Temperance: A Memorial Volume of the Centennial Temperance Conference Held in Philadelphia, Pa., September, 1885* (New York: National Temperance Society and Publication House, 1886), 60, 659, 106-7.

19. For temperance and prohibition in Canada, see Craig Heron, *Booze: A Distilled History* (Toronto: Between the Lines, 2003); Jan Noel, *Canada Dry: Temperance Crusades Before Confederation* (Toronto: University of Toronto Press, 1995); Darren Ferry, "'To the Interests and Conscience of the Great Mass of the Community': The Evolution of Temperance Societies in Nineteenth-Century Central Canada," *Journal of the Canadian Historical Association* 14 (2003): 137-63.

20. "Now Is the Time to Close the Barroom," *Globe*, November 26, 1902, 1-2; Isaac Newton Peirce and Silvanus Phillips Thompson, *The History of the Independent Order of Good Templars* (Birmingham Grand Lodge of England,1873), 52, 157, 168, Appendix C.

21. T.F. Parker and S.B. Chase, *History of the Independent Order of Good Templars, from the Origin of the Order to the Session of the Right Worthy Grand Lodge of 1880. Together with an Exposition of the Order* (New York: Phillips & Hunt, 1882), 122; Peirce and Thompson, *History of the Independent Order of Good Templars*, 129, 156, 168, Appendix C, 225, 235. Dr. Oronhyatekha is noted as the GWCT in Ruth Elizabeth Spence, *Prohibition in Canada* (Toronto: William Briggs, 1919), 105. Two of Oronhyatekha's letters to Henry Acland in 1872 are written on stationary from the Office of the Grand Worthy Chief Templar. The article "Oronhyatekha, the Right Worthy Grand Counsellor," from the August 1888 *IGT* and reprinted in David M. Fahey, ed., *The Collected Writings of Jessie Forsyth 1847-1937: The Good Templars and Temperance Reform on Three Continents* (Lewiston: Edwin Mellon Press, 1988), 373 notes he served as GWCT four times. According to David M. Fahey, *Temperance and Racism: John Bull, Johnny Reb, and the Good Templars* (Lexington, KY: University Press of Kentucky, 1996), 92, one of these times was in 1876. The IOGT, *Journal of Proceedings of the Twentieth-Fourth Annual Session, of the R.W.G. Lodge Held at Minneapolis, Minn., May 28, 29, 30 and 31, 1878* (Napanee: Canada Casket Steam Printing and Publishing House, 1878), 197 notes he was GWCT in 1877. The duties of officials can be found in IOGT, *Constitution of the Grand and Subordinate Temples, of the I.O.G. Templars, Canada* (Napanee:

Henry and Brother, 1874), 6–7. Dr. Oronhyatekha's rulings on constitutional matters can be found in Thomas Lawless, *The Canada Digest, IOGT*, 2nd ed. (Hamilton: Thomas Lawless, 1872) and Thomas Lawless, *The Canada Digest, IOGT*, 3rd ed. (Hamilton: Thomas Lawless, 1875).

22. DIA, *Annual Report, 1884* (1885), 5; NEC, *Report of the Proceedings of the New England Company for the Civilization and Conversion of Indians, Blacks and Pagans in the Dominion of Canada, South Africa and the West Indies during the Two Years 1871–1872* (London: Taylor and Co., 1874), 308.

23. Spence, *Prohibition in Canada*, 105–6; Canada Temperance Union, *Proceedings of the Second Session of the Canada Temperance Union held at Toronto, Ontario, September 7th, 8th, and 9th, 1869* (Napanee: Henry Brothers, 1869), 37–8, 4, 26, 13, 34, 35, 40, Appendix 24.

24. *Abstract of Report of the Proceedings of the Prohibitory Conference Held in Ottawa, Wednesday and Thursday, April 22nd and 23rd, 1874* (Ottawa? 1874?); Dominion Alliance for the Total Suppression of the Liquor Traffic, *First Annual Meeting February 14, 15, 16, 1877* (Montreal: Wilson's Printing House, 1887), 16; Spence, *Prohibition in Canada*, 92–4, 107–19.

25. *History of the County of Middlesex, Canada, from the Earliest Time to the Present, Containing an Authentic Account of Many Important Matters relating to the Settlement, Progress and General History of the County, and including a Department Devoted to the Preservation of Personal and Private Records, etc., Illustrated* (Toronto: Goodspeed, 1889), 255.

26. Spence, *Prohibition in Canada*, 122–31.

27. Heron, *Booze*, 169; *One Hundred Years of Temperance*, 107.

28. "Our Grand Lodges," *IGT* 5 (1892): 79.

29. "Now is the Time to Close the Barroom," *Globe*, November 26, 1902, 1–2.

30. Fahey, *Temperance and Racism*, 110. Fahey provides a fuller treatment of race and the IOGT.

31. Joseph Malins, *The Unlawful Exclusion of the African Race* (Birmingham: Grand Lodge Office, 1877), 38–9.

32. Fahey, *Temperance and Racism*, 84, 159; eds. David M. Fahey and Jon S. Miller, *Alcohol and Drugs in North America: A Historical Encyclopedia* (Santa Barbara: ABC-Clio, 2013), 284; Malins, *Unlawful Exclusion*, 25–6. The story about the photograph was repeated in "How Oronhyatekha and Hickman Regard the Negro," *Good Templars' Watchword* (November 15, 1876): 762.

33. A transcription of the 1876 conference can be found in Timothy Needham, *The Negro Question and the IOGT Report of Conference Held in London, October 19, 20, and 21, 1876* (London: Kempster and Co., 1876).

34. IOGT, *Journal of Proceedings of the Twentieth-Fourth Annual Session*, 42, 195, 197, 207, 208; IOGT, *Proceedings of the 30th Annual Session of the R.W. Grand Lodge IOGT, Held at Washington, D.C., U.S.A, May 27th, 28th, 29th, and 30th, 1884* (Lincoln: Journal Company, State Printers, 1884), 146, 149, 154.

35. Fahey, ed., *Collected Writings of Jessie Forsyth*, 131–33.

36. Fahey, ed., *Collected Writings of Jessie Forsyth*, 142.

37. William W. Turnbull, *The Good Templars: A History of the Rise and Progress of the Independent Order of Good Templars* (1901), 92, 113; Frances E. Finch and Frank J. Sibley, *John B. Finch: His Life and Work* (New York: Funk and Wagnalls, 1888), 226; Fahey, ed., *Collected Writings of Jessie Forsyth*, 148–50.

38. "Right Worthy Grand Secretary's Department," *IGT* 7 (1894): 362; "Right Worthy Grand Secretary's Department," *IGT* 13 (1900): 120; Turnbull, *Good Templars*, 136; Fahey, ed., *Collected Writings of Jessie Forsyth*, 153.

39. Fahey, ed., *Collected Writings of Jessie Forsyth*, 158, 161, 169, 175; 183; "Thirty-Sixth Session of the International Supreme Lodge IOGT," *IGT* 6 (1893): 207.

40. Fahey, ed., *Collected Writings of Jessie Forsyth*, 179–80, 214–5; "Obituary," *IGT* 15 (1902): 272; "Right Worthy Grand Secretary's Department," *IGT* 6 (1893): 66; "World's Temperance Congress," *IGT* 6 (1893): 147; Advertisement, *IGT* 10 (1897): 180; "Summary of the Thirty-Eighth Regular Session of the International Supreme Lodge," *IGT* 10 (1897): 3.

41. Parker and Chase, *History of the Independent Order of Good Templars*, 123.

42. Oronhyatekha, *History of the Independent Order of Foresters* (Toronto: Hunter, Rose and Company, 1895), 16, 34, 39.

43. Oronhyatekha, *History of the IOF*, 58–9; "Great I.O.F. Initiation," *Globe*, February 19, 1902, 2.

44. Oronhyatekha, *History of the IOF*, 59, 68, 70.

45. The following conflicts are told in Oronhyatekha, *History of the IOF*, chapters 3, 4. For a briefer version, see Warren Potter and Robert Oliver, *Fraternally Yours: A History of the Independent Order of Foresters* (London: Queen Anne Press, 1967), 45–64.

46. Oronhyatekha, *History of the IOF*, 59–61.

47. Oronhyatekha, *History of the IOF*, 235–36.

48. Oronhyatekha, *History of the IOF*, 222, 234, 242, 257. It is difficult to know how many members actually existed. At the annual meeting in New York, 616 members were listed for Ontario but at the High Court of Ontario meeting just days later it was reported that there were some 1200 members "on paper." The next month, only 369 members responded to the requests for confirmation of numbers. One year later, in June 1882, 1,080 members had been confirmed.

49. Oronhyatekha, *History of the IOF*, 261.

50. "The Foresters' Trouble," *Toronto World*, September 25, 1882, 4; October 3, 1882, Thomas Millman Diary, F 4529, AO.

51. Quote is from Oronhyatekha, *History of the IOF*, 330.

52. Quote is from Oronhyatekha, *History of the IOF*, 349.

53. Quote is from Oronhyatekha, *History of the IOF*, 687.

54. Oronhyatekha, *History of the IOF*, 725, 286, 292–3, 298, 325, 387, 403, 430, 450, 466–68, 717, 720, 721, 723.

55. "Official Proclamation," *IF* 18, 11 (May 15, 1898): 334; *Minutes of the Twelfth Regular Session of the Supreme Court of the Independent Order of Foresters* (Toronto: Hunter, Rose, Co., Limited, 1902), 58, Envelope 8, MU 3926, F. Barlow Cumberland Fonds, F 1132, AO; "Bro. James Marshall's Farewell on the Eve of his Departure to Australia," *IF* 20, 7 (January 15, 1900): 203; "Great Britain," *IF* 21, 3 (September 15, 1900): 78; "Foresters at Owen Sound," *Globe*, August 22, 1900, 2; "Dr. Oronhyatekha," *Advertiser*, March 21, 1900, 4; Canada, *Royal Commission on Life Insurance*, Vol. 3 (Toronto: Warwick Bro's and Rutter), 2240, Vol. 1910, Department of Justice, RG 13, LAC; Australia, *Royal Commission on Life Insurance*, Vol. 3 (Toronto: Warwick Bro's and Rutter), 2332–33, Vol. 1910, Department of Justice, RG 13, LAC. Quote is from "Correspondence," *Belfast News-Letter*, September 20, 1894, 3.

56. Oronhyatekha, *History of the IOF*, 402; "Great Record of the IOF," *Toronto Daily Star*, June 16, 1906, 23.

57. *IF* 17, 6 (December 1896): 173; "Official Circular, No. 5," *IF* 9, 5, (November 1888): 130; *IF* 17, 5 (November 1896): 138; "Official Circular No. 12," *IF* 18, 10 (April 15, 1898): 305; *IF* 18, 12 (June 15, 1898): 368, 369; "Official Circular No. 5," *IF* 13, 3 (September 1892): 77; Oronhyatekha, *History of the IOF*, 254, 259; "Great I.O.F. Initiation," *Globe*, February 19, 1902, 2; "Growth of Independent Forestry," *Globe*, April 22, 1902, 10; "End of Triumphal Tour," *Globe*, December 12, 1903, 25; "Foresters Welcomed the Supreme Chief," *Globe*, April 16, 1904, 12; "Great Meeting of the I.O.F.," *Toronto Daily Star*, November 26, 1904, 9; "Open Initiation," *Los Angeles Times*, October 10, 1904, 5. Prices for regalia and other IOF items is in "I. O. F. Price List," *IF* 8, 5 (November 1887): 16.

58. "Juvenile Foresters," *IF* 9, 6 (December 1888): 170.

59. IOF, *Ritual of the Royal Foresters*, 3, 21, 22.

60. Peirce and Thompson, *History of the Independent Order of Good Templars*, 235.

61. Oronhyatekha, *History of the IOF*, 618, 195, 238; "The New Rituals," *IF* 10, 9 (March 1889): 275. Italics are in the original. The full ritual can be found in

IOF, *The Ritual of the Independent Order of Foresters for Subordinate Courts* (Toronto: Hunter, Rose Co., Limited, 1899), 64–86. Revised rituals were published in 1903 and 1905.

62. "I.O.F. Entertainment," *IF* 8, 4 (October 1887): 3; "The Hamilton Carnival," *IF* 10, 3 (September 1889): 91; December 14, 1892, Millman Diary, AO; "Meeting of Nations," ad, *Globe*, December 10, 1892, 15; "Queen Victoria's Diamond Jubilee," *IF* 18 (July 1, 1897): 4–6; "Foresters at Barrie," *Globe*, July 8, 1899, 4; "High Court of Central Ontario," *IF* 21, 3 (September 15, 1900): 66; "Descriptions of the Floral Beauties," *Los Angeles Times*, May 9, 1902, B2; "The Supreme Chief's Home-Coming," *IF* 19, 1 (July 15, 1898): 7.

63. IOF, *Ritual of the Royal Foresters* (London: Advertiser Print. and Pub. Co., 1892), 20.

64. Keith Walden, *Becoming Modern in Toronto: The Industrial Exhibition and the Shaping of a Late Victorian Culture* (Toronto: University of Toronto Press, 1997), 193–95; "Crowds at Fair Break Record," *Globe*, September 2, 1905, 1; *IF* 17, 3 (September 1896): 77; "The I.O.F. Tent at the Exhibition," *IF* 17, 4 (October 1896): 99; *IF* 17, 5 (November 1896): 149; "Toronto's Great Exhibition," *IF* 18, 1 (July 1897): 9; *IF* 13, 3 (September 1892): 75; September 4, 1896, Millman Diary, AO; "The Supreme Court Meeting and the Industrial Fair," *IF* 19, 2 (August 15, 1898): 34–5.

65. Phillip Buckner, "Casting Daylight upon Magic: Deconstructing the Royal Tour of 1901 to Canada," *The British World: Diaspora, Culture, and Identity*, eds. Carl Bridge and Kent Fedorowich (London and Portland: Frank Cass Publishers, 2003), 177; *Official Programme and Souvenir of the Royal Tour Showing the Progress of Their Royal Highnesses, the Duke and Duchess of Cornwall and York through Quebec and Ontario, 1901* (Toronto: Hunter, Rose, 1901), n.p.; *Official Programme of Events which will take Place in the City of Toronto during the Visit of Their Royal Highnesses the Duke and Duchess of Cornwall and York* (Toronto: Dominion Pub., 1901?), 2.

66. "Will Welcome the Duke," *Globe*, July 6, 1901, 24; J. Castell Hopkins, ed., *Morang's Annual Register of Canada Affairs 1901* (Toronto: George N. Morang and Company, Limited, 1902), 264; "Welcoming the King's Son," *Globe*, October 11, 1901, 1, 2, 4, 5, 11; "Their Tireless Activity," *Toronto Star*, September 13, 1902, 2; "Foresters' Arch Given to the City," *IF* 23, 10 (October 1902): 293–96.

67. Potter and Oliver, *Fraternally Yours*, 78–9.

68. See for example, reports from the *Los Angeles Tribune* in "The Supreme Chief Ranger," *IF* 10, 10 (April 1890): 298; from the *East Saginaw Daily*

Courier-Herald in "The S.C.R. in Michigan," *IF* 10, 7 (January 1890): 221; from the *Calgary Herald* in "The Supreme Chief Ranger," *IF* 10, 11 (May 1890): 331.

69. *Toronto Daily Mail*, April 22, 1893, reprinted in Oronhyatekha, *History of the IOF*, 66, 67.

70. Oronhyatekha, *History of the IOF*, 643–44; Ethel Brant Monture, *Canadian Portraits: Brant, Crowfoot, Oronhyatekha* (Toronto and Vancouver: Clarke, Irwin and Company, 1960), 148.

71. "A Well-Deserved Tribute," *IF* 26, 5 (September 1905): 79.

72. George Emery and J.C. Herbert Emery, *A Young Man's Benefit: the Independent Order of Odd Fellows and Sickness Insurance in the United States and Canada, 1860–1929* (Montreal and Kingston: McGill-Queen's University Press, 1999), 3, 14, 16, 96; Oronhyatekha, *History of the IOF*, 403; "The Great Record of the I.O.F.," *Toronto Daily Star*, June 16, 1906, 23; Dustin Galer, "A Friend in Need or a Business Indeed?: Disabled Bodies and Fraternalism in Victorian Ontario," *Labour/Le Travail* 66 (2010): 9–36.

73. Emery and Emery, *A Young Man's Benefit*, 12.

74. For endowment law changes, see Oronhyatekha, *History of the IOF*, 529–41, 237, 521, 374, 380, 439–40, 458. Rates for each class are recorded frequently in the monthly *IF* magazine, usually on the inside cover.

75. Oronhyatekha, *History of the IOF*, 71, 73, 74–6, 197, 210, 212–14, 217, 300, 386.

76. Oronhyatekha, *History of the IOF*, 289, 385, 389, 391, 379, 406, 470; IOF, *Constitution and General Laws of the Supreme Court of the Independent Order of Foresters also Laws Governing High Courts, Subordinate Courts, Companion Courts, Juvenile Courts and Encampments of Royal Foresters* (Toronto: The Hunter Rose Co., Limited, 1898), 144–45; IOF, *Constitution and General Laws of the Supreme Court of the Independent Order of Foresters also Laws Governing High Courts, Subordinate Courts, Companion Courts, Juvenile Courts and Encampments of Royal Foresters* (Toronto: The Hunter Rose Co., Limited, 1902), 158.

77. Oronhyatekha, *History of the IOF*, 294, 324. The quote is from page 245. The government debates can be found in Canada, House of Commons, *Debates*, 1884, 47 Vict., 764–65, 1652; Canada, House of Commons, *Debates*, 1885, 48–49 Vict., 46, 126–27, 2430–39, 3476. The law itself is published in "Amendment to the Insurance Law," *IF* 6, 5 (September 1885): 2–3.

78. Oronhyatekha, *History of the IOF*, 326, 292–93; Canada, House of Commons, *Debates* 1886, 49 Vict., 1549–50.

79. Canada, House of Commons, *Debates*, 1889, 52 Vict., 322, 754–55, 1233; Oronhyatekha, *History of the IOF*, 761, 397; "Our Act of Incorporation," and "Too Late," *IF* 9, 9 (March 1889), 289–90.

80. Oronhyatekha, *History of the IOF*, 654. The two different versions of the act are in pages 417–28. "Presentation to Senator Reesor and 'At Home' by the Supreme Court, I.O.F., at Toronto," *IF* 11, 5 (November 1890): 130–31.

81. "Notes," *IF* 12, 9 (March 1892): 262; *Canada Gazette* 29, 17 (October 26, 1895): 30–1; "Our Bill," *IF* 16, 8 (February 1896), 272–74; *IF* 16, 11 (May 1896), 341; "I. O. F. Bill," *IF* 16, 11 (May 1896): 347–49; "The Globe and J. A. McGillivray, S.S.," *IF* 16, 8 (February 1896): 247. Fitzgerald's objections are published in *A Statement by the Superintendent of Insurance (Wm. Fitzgerald, M.A.) of Reasons Why the Independent Order of Foresters should not have the Powers Granted them by Parliament* (Toronto: Monetary Times Printing Company, 1895).

82. Oronhyatekha, *History of the IOF*, 634, 641, 262, 291, 302, 381, 392, 413, 460; "Foresters at Atlantic City," *New York Times*, August 6, 1905, SM11.

83. See, for instance, "Dr. Oronhyatekha," *Canadian Presbyterian*, Toronto, March 8, 1893, 1. He is listed in Frederick Smily, *The Medical Directory of Toronto and Suburbs* (Toronto: Murray Printing Company, 1900), 17, but with no office hours.

84. "Independent Order of Foresters," *IF* 4, 5 (March 1884): 7; IOF, *Ritual of the Independent Order of Foresters for Subordinate Courts*, 78–79, 97–8; IOF, *Ritual of the Independent Order of Foresters for Subordinate Courts* (Toronto: Hunter Rose Co., Limited, 1903), 52–3. Italics are in the original.

85. "I.O.F. Eighth Annual Banquet," *IF*, Christmas Supplement (1885): n.p.

86. For the issue of the admission of women, see Oronhyatekha, *History of the IOF*, 298, 300, 370, 381, 409, 433–39, 675–76. The quote is from page 438. "Supreme Chief Ranger's Report," *IF* 6, 5 (September 1885): 3; "Companions of the I.O.F.," *IF* 18, 6 (December 1897): 167–68; "Companions of the I.O.F.," *IF* 18, 7 (January 15, 1898): 197; "Companions of the I.O.F.," *IF* 18, 9 (March 15, 1898): 274; "Supreme Court Session," *IF* 19, 3 (September 15, 1898): 86–94, 100–1; "High Court of New Brunswick," *IF* 20, 2 (August 15, 1899): 43–44.

87. "Supreme Court Session," *IF* 19, 3 (September 15, 1898): 97; "Sound Condition of the IOF Demonstrated," *Evening Star*, September 3, 1898, 5; "A Chinese Brother Forester," *IF* 19, 2 (August 15, 1898): 37.

88. "The Brotherhood of Man," *IF* 17, 5 (November 1896): 133; Oronhyatekha, *History of the IOF*, 667–68, 742–43, 778; Ferry, *United in Measures of Common Good*, 159.

89. Oronhyatekha, *History of the IOF*, 537, 372, 380; "Supreme Court Session," *IF* 19, 3 (September 15, 1898): 78; "The Old Age Benefits of the I.O.F.," *IF* 19, 8 (February 15, 1899): 238; IOF, *Constitution* (1898), 255–56, 261–68; Potter and Oliver, *Fraternally Yours*, 81; "A Beneficent Project," *IF* 26, 2 (February 1905): 20.

90. "Supreme Court Session," *IF* 19, 3 (September 15, 1898): 92–3; "Free Admission to the I.O.F. Offered to Members of the Canadian Contingent," *IF* 20, 5 (November 15, 1899): 146; Application for the position of Surgeon in the South African Police, File 19907, Vol. 338, Ministry of Militia and Defence, RG 9, LAC; "Soldiers Dined by the Foresters," *Toronto Daily Star*, November 6, 1900, 8.

91. "Foresters' Cottage," *IF* 18, 7 (January 15, 1898): 197; "Foresters' Cottage," *IF* 18, 8 (February 15, 1898): 235; "Foresters' Cottage for Consumptives," *IF* 18, 9 (March 15, 1898): 267; "24th Anniversary of the I.O.F.," *IF* 19, 1 (July 15, 1898): 5. For more on the institution, see Annemarie Adams and Stacie Burke, "'Not a Shack in the Woods': Architecture for Tuberculosis in Muskoka and Toronto," *Canadian Bulletin of Medical History* 23, 2 (2006): 429–55. For donations from the IOF, see the annual reports of the National Sanatorium Association. After Dr. Oronhyatekha's death, the IOF opened a TB sanitarium in New York State in 1910 and another near Los Angeles in 1912.

92. Potter and Oliver, *Fraternally Yours*, 81; "Fraternity," *Globe*, April 28, 1906, 13.

93. "Juvenile Foresters," *IF* 9, 6 (December 1888): 170; Oronhyatekha, *History of the IOF*, 481, 653–54; IOF, *Constitution* (1898), 292–98.

94. "Souvenir Postal Cards," *IF* 28, 7 (August 1907): 104.

95. "Forestric Homes and Schools to be Established," *IF* 24, 7 (July 1903): 132; "Foresters Welcome Chief at Fair," *Globe*, September 6, 1904, 7; "Foresters' Orphans Home," *IF* 27, 8 (December 1906): 118–19; "How the I. O. F. Cares for Orphans," *Globe*, May 6, 1911, 9; "Orphans' Home," *IF* 26, 5 (September 1905): 73; "Foresters' Orphans' Home," *IF* 26, 5 (September 1905): 78; "Orphans' Home," *IF* 32, 2 (December 1911): 128; Canada, *Royal Commission on Life Insurance*, Vol. 3 (Toronto: Warwick Bro's and Rutter), 2804, Vol. 1910, Department of Justice, RG 13, LAC; "Foresters Initiate New Philanthropy," *Globe*, August 29, 1904, 8, 12; "The Formal Opening of the I.O.F. Orphans' Home by its Great Founder," *Toronto Daily Star*, August 29, 1904, 5; "Formal Opening of the IOF Orphan's Home," *Toronto Daily Star*, August 8, 1905, 4; Potter and Oliver, *Fraternally Yours*, 81, 86, 203; Reports of Officers, Triennial Session of the Supreme Court, Independent Order of Foresters, Toronto, Canada, June 16, 1908, 22–23, Envelope 16, MU 3927, Barlow Cumberland Papers, AO; "The Foresters' Orphan Home," *IF* 29, 5 (July 1908): 53.

CHAPTER 6: MONUMENTS

1. Mary Temple Bayard, "Dr. Oronhyatekha," *Canadian Magazine* (June 1896): 140.

2. "The Supreme Chief Ranger," *IF* 10, 10 (April 1890): 298.

3. Joseph Malins, "A Visit to the Oronhyatekhas," *IF* 14, 3 (September 1893): 72; James Mavor, *My Windows on the Street of the World*, Vol. 1 (Toronto: J.M. Dent and Sons, Limited, 1923), 317–18.

4. "The Annual Outing to Foresters' Island Park," *IF* 23, 8 (August 1902): 230–32; "Forestric Homes and Schools to be Established," *IF* 24, 7 (July 1903): 129–32.

5. July 23, 1894, July 4, 1903, August 11, 1906, Thomas Millman Diary, F 4529, AO.

6. October 1–2, 1894, Millman Diary, AO.

7. July 26, 1902, Millman Diary, AO.

8. Patricia Jasen, *Wild Things: Nature, Culture and Tourism in Ontario, 1790–1914* (Toronto: University of Toronto Press, 1995), 3–20, 56.

9. Warren Potter and Robert Oliver, *Fraternally Yours: A History of the Independent Order of Foresters* (London: Queen Anne Press, 1967), 71–2; July 24, 1894, June 17, 1895, Millman Diary, AO; "Of Age," *IF* 16, 1 (July 1895): 14–23; "A Million and Eighteen Thousand!" *IF* 15, 3 (September 1894): 71; "Foresters' Park," *IF* 15, 3 (September 1894): 72; "Foresters Celebrate," *IF* 15, 4 (October 1894): 97–109. The anniversary service can be found in IOF, *The Ritual of the Independent Order of Foresters for Subordinate Courts* (Toronto: Hunter, Rose Co., Limited, 1899), 114–19.

10. Mohawk Queen, Ship Registration Index, Vol. 1434, C-2470, Department of Transport, RG 42, LAC.

11. "Twenty-Second Anniversary of the I.O.F.," *IF* 16, 12 (June 1896): 381–2; "Twenty-Second Anniversary of the Order," *IF* 17, 1 (July 1896): 5–14; "24th Anniversary of the I.O.F.," *IF* 19, 1 (July 15, 1898): 4–5; "Ontario," *IF* 20, 1 (July 15, 1899): 21–3.

12. Oronhyatekha, *History of the Independent Order of Foresters* (Toronto: Hunter, Rose and Company, 1895), 398; *Province of Ontario Gazetteer and Directory, Including the City of Montreal, P.Q. 1895* (Toronto: Murray Printing Co., 1895), 1560; Frederick Smily, *The Medical Directory of Toronto and Suburbs* (Toronto: Murray Printing Company, 1900), 17; March 5, 1889, October 2, 1893, January 4, 1895, January 30, 1895, Millman Diary, AO; Potter and Oliver, *Fraternally Yours*, 67; "Foresters' Temple, Toronto," *IF* 16, 1 (July 1895): 5. Treble's store was identified using *Illustrated Toronto: The Queen City of Canada* (Toronto: Acme Publishing and Engraving, 1890), 181.

13. Linda Shapiro, ed., *Yesterday's Toronto, 1870–1910* (Toronto: Coles Publishing Co., 1978), 15.

14. May 29–30, 1895, Millman Diary, AO; Potter and Oliver, *Fraternally Yours*, 73; "The Earl of Aberdeen," *IF* 16, 1 (July 1895): 2; "Foresters' Temple, Toronto," *IF* 16, 1 (July 1895): 5–13; "The Foresters' Temple," *IF* 16, 1 (July 1895): 32.

15. 'Sic Venit Gloria,' Etc.," *MT*, Toronto, June 7, 1895, 1580–81; "The Foresters' Temple," *Canadian Architect and Builder* 8, 12 (1895): 145; "The Foresters' Temple of Fame," *MT*, December 13, 1895, 756; Canada, *Royal Commission on Life Insurance*, Vol. 3 (Toronto: Warwick Bro's and Rutter), 2377, Vol. 1910, Department of Justice, RG 13, LAC; "From the Other Side," *Globe*, February 10, 1896, 9; "I.O.F. Executive Sustained," *Globe*, February 8, 1896, 8.

16. William Dendy, *Lost Toronto: Images of the City's Past* (Toronto: McClelland and Stewart, 1993), 129, 131.

17. "Temple Building," *IF* 17, 7 (January 1897): 202–3; "The Foresters' Temple," *Globe*, December 4, 1897, 16; Eric Ross Arthur, *Toronto: No Mean City* (Toronto: University of Toronto Press, 1986), 156, 163, 184, 188–89, 208; "Supreme Court Session," *IF* 19, 3 (September 15, 1898): 70–77; *The Toronto City Directory 1901* (Toronto: Might and Co., 1901), 209; "The Boudoir of My Lady Nicotine," *IF* 20, 3 (September 15, 1899): 71; Dendy, *Lost Toronto*, 129, 131; "The Supreme Chief Ranger in California," *IF* 17, 5 (November 1896): 134, 137. Arthur states that the Temple was the last Toronto building to use cast iron construction, but all *IF* notices say it was of steel. The reference to Guarantee Trust's renovation is Lydia Dotto, "Toronto's Temple Building, once empire's tallest, comes down," *Toronto Daily Star*, August 1, 1970, 25.

18. "I.O.F. Temple Building," Globe, August 23, 1897, 10; "Independent Order of Foresters," *Globe*, August 27, 1897, 6–7; "Citizens' Day," *IF* 18, 7 (January 15, 1898): 205–7; "The Foresters Temple," *Globe*, December 18, 1897, 29; "Presentation of a Portrait of the Chief," *IF* 18, 7 (January 15, 1898): 196.

19. "With Due Ceremony," *Globe*, August 31, 1898, 5; Advertisement, *IF* 19, 1 (July 15, 1898): 27–8. The full dedication ceremony can be found in IOF, *Ritual of the Independent Order of Foresters for Subordinate Courts*, 108–13.

20. "The Feast-House of the 20th Century," *IF* 20, 2 (August 15, 1899): 40; *IF* 20, 7 (January 15, 1900): 212.

21. Advertisement, *Acta Victoriana* (May 1901): inside cover; "The Royal Commission," *IF* 27, 7 (November 1906): 100; Canada, Royal Commission on Life Insurance, 2251, Vol. 1910, Department of Justice, RG 13, LAC.

22. "Insurance Matters," *MT*, May 3, 1895, 1424; November 10, 1896, Millman Diary, AO; *IF* 18, 1 (July 1897): 26; *IF* 18, 8 (February 15, 1898): 230; "The

Statue of the Chief is Finished," *IF* 19, 12 (June 15, 1899): 368; "Unveiling the Oronhyatekha Statue at the Temple," *IF* 20, 1 (July 15, 1899): 5–6; June 16, 1899, Millman Diary, AO; "Oronhyatekha," *Globe*, June 17, 1899, 30; F. Barlow Cumberland, *Catalogue and Notes of the Oronhyatekha Historical Collection* (Toronto: Independent Order of Foresters, 1904), 13.

23. "Opening of the Historical Room," *IF* 23, 10 (October 1902): 296–300; "Historic Room in Foresters' Temple," *Toronto Daily Star*, September 10, 1902, 7.

24. For more about the philosophy behind natural science museums, see Carl Berger, *Science, God and Nature in Victorian Canada* (Toronto: University of Toronto Press, 1983). For Ontario historical and scientific societies, particularly those that collected native objects, see Michelle A. Hamilton, *Collections and Objections: Aboriginal Material Culture in Southern Ontario, 1791–1914* (Montreal and Kingston: McGill-Queen's University Press, 2010), 51–78.

25. Cumberland, *Catalogue and Notes*, 10. The deed of gift is reprinted in *Minutes of the Twelfth Regular Session of the Supreme Court of the Independent Order of Foresters* (Toronto: Hunter, Rose Co., 1902), Appendix "B", 1-2a, Envelope 5, Box 18, Barlow Cumberland Papers, F 1132, AO; Trudy Nicks, "Dr Oronhyatekha's History Lessons: Reading Museum Collections as Texts," *Reading Beyond Words: Contexts for Native History*, 2nd ed., eds. Jennifer S.H. Brown and Elizabeth Vibert (Toronto: University of Toronto Press, 2009), 459–89.

26. Cumberland, *Catalogue and Notes*, 100.

27. Nicks, "Dr. Oronhyatekha's History Lessons," eds. Brown and Vibert, 475. The letters are J.C. Ross to McClurg, June 9, 1905 and July 18, 1905, F 4337-1-0-2; John Monague to McClurg, November 18, 1907 and Jerry Monague to McClurg, December 5, 1907, F 4337-1-0-6 and Johnson Paudash to McClurg, May 13, 1904, F 4337-1-0-12, George Mills McClurg Correspondence, A.E. Williams/United Indian Bands of the Chippewas and the Mississaugas Papers, AO. J.B Williams was noted in Trudy Nicks, "' A Token of Remembrance:' The Oronhyatekha Historical Rooms," Recollecting the Nineteenth-Century Museum conference, Ryerson University, May 15, 2015. Cumberland's papers include a 1904 list of "marine curiosities" from a dealer in Nassau, Bahamas. See Envelope 5, Box 18, Cumberland Papers, AO. Holden to David Boyle, October 23, 1900, Box 1, David Boyle Correspondence, ROM, Toronto.

28. Cumberland, *Catalogue and Notes*, 125, 10, 109.

29. Cumberland, *Catalogue and Notes*, 99–100.

30. "The Foreign Business of the IOF," *Toronto Daily Star*, September 19, 1906, 2.

31. "The Supreme Chief's Home-Coming," *IF* 19, 1 (July 15, 1898): 6; *IF* 19, 9 (March 15, 1899): 265 and "Letter from Miss Oronhyatekha," *IF* 19, 9 (March 15, 1899): 281; "Great Britain," *IF* 21, 3 (September 15, 1900): 78; Cumberland, *Catalogue and Notes*, 14–18, 99, 102–4, 125–30. Some of these items may have been in a display at a banquet in August 1900; see "Farewell Banquet to Bro. Lawless," *IF* 21, 2 (August 15, 1900): 59.

32. "Dr. Oronhyatekha," *Advertiser*, March 21, 1900, 4; "Sailed for the Orient," *Globe*, September 10, 1901, 1; Cumberland, *Catalogue and Notes*, 19, 106, 125. For *japonisme* and material culture, see William Hosley, *The Japan Idea: Art and Life in Victorian America* (Hartford: Wadsworth Atheneum, 1990).

33. Alan Wallach, "The American Cast Museum: An Episode in the History of the Institutional Definitions of Art," *Exhibiting Contradiction: Essays on the American Art Museum in the United States* (Amherst: University of Massachusetts Press, 1998), 38–57; Pamela Born, "The Canon Is Cast: Plaster Casts in American Museum and University Collection," *Art Documentation: Bulletin of the Art Libraries Society of North America* 21, 2 (2002): 8; Cumberland, *Catalogue and Notes*, 18, 19, 106–9, 129.

34. Cumberland, *Catalogue and Notes*, 12–13, 101.

35. Arthur Edward Jones, *"8endake Ehen"* or *Old Huronia, Fifth Report of the Bureau of Archives for the Province of Ontario* (Toronto: L.K. Cameron, 1909), 7–8.

36. "Valuable Relics," *Globe and Mail*, October 7, 1902, 5; Cumberland, *Catalogue and Notes*, 33, 68–71.

37. Cumberland, *Catalogue and Notes*, 14, 15, 19, 30, 32, 33, 72, 104–6, 109–25, 128–30. The quote is from page 19.

38. Suzanne Zeller, *Inventing Canada: Early Victorian Science and the Idea of a Transcontinental Nation* (Montreal and Kingston: McGill-Queen's University Press, 2009), 3–9; Berger, *Science, God and Nature*; Cumberland, *Catalogue and Notes*, 109–21.

39. Harriet Ritvo, *The Platypus and the Mermaid and other Figments of the Classifying Imagination* (Cambridge: Harvard University Press, 1997), 3–15; Cumberland, *Catalogue and Notes*, 104–05.

40. Cumberland, *Catalogue and Notes*, 105, 106, 100.

41. Nicks, "Dr. Oronhyatekha's History Lessons," eds. Brown and Vibert, 476–78.

42. Cumberland, *Catalogue and Notes*, 71, 73–7, 21, 28, 30–3, 35, 45–6, 51, 54–7, 65–8, 78–86, 133–5.

43. For the importance of Loyalism in Ontario, see Norman Knowles, *Inventing the Loyalists: The Ontario Loyalist Tradition and the Creation of Usable Pasts* (Toronto: University of Toronto Press, 1997).

44. Benedict R. Anderson, *Imagined Communities: Reflections on the Origin and Spread of Nationalism*, rev. ed. (London and New York: Verso, 2006), 6–7.

45. Francis Prucha, *Indian Peace Medals in American History* (Lincoln: University of Nebraska Press, 1971), xiii–xiv, 34; Cumberland, *Catalogue and Notes*, 83–90, 54–7, 40, 34, 135. For more about how the War of 1812 can be seen through the Oronhyatekha collection, see Trudy Nicks, "The War of 1812 as Remembered in the Oronhyatekha Historical Collection," *American Indian Art Magazine* (Summer 2012): 60–69.

46. Cumberland, *Catalogue and Notes*, 58–9.

47. Cory Silverstein-Willmott, "Object Lessons: An Ojibway Artifact Unraveled. The Case of the Bag with the Snake Skin Strap," *Textile History* 34, 1 (2003): 79; Ruth B. Phillips, "Making Sense Out/of the Visual: Aboriginal Presentations and Representations in Nineteenth-Century Canada," *Art History* 27, 4 (2004): 599–606; Cumberland, *Catalogue and Notes*, 21–22, 24, 25, 26, 86, 90–98.

48. Nicks, "Dr. Oronhyatekha's History Lessons," eds. Brown and Vibert, 475–6.

49. J.E.C. Bodley, *The Coronation of Edward the Seventh: a Chapter of European and Imperial History* (London: Methuen, 1903), 390; July 11, 1902, Millman Diary, AO; Cumberland, *Catalogue and Notes*, 14; "British Cabinet Reconstructed," *Globe*, August 9, 1902, 1.

50. Cumberland, *Catalogue and Notes*, 10–12; "A Coronation Chair in the Foresters Museum," *Globe*, January 30, 1904, 21; "A Coronation Chair in the Foresters' Museum," *IF* 25, 3 (March 1904): 35; *The Coronation Chair of Great Britain and some Other Historic Chairs of Interest to all Subjects of the British Empire, and Especially to Canadians* (Toronto, 1904), 5–8; Warrick Rodwell, *The Coronation Chair and Stone of Scone: History, Archaeology and Conservation* (Oxford: Oxbow Books, 2013), 218–21, xiii. Rodwell assumed that Dr. Oronhyatekha's chair was made in the 1890s for his IOF office, but we have not found evidence of this earlier date.

51. "Wonderful Chair Secured by IOF," *Toronto Daily Star*, January 30, 1904, 2.

52. Cumberland, *Catalogue and Notes*, 33–34, 61–65, 71.

53. Cumberland, *Catalogue and Notes*, 25, 30, 31, 33, 35, 41, 45, 48, 51, 52, 67, 75. For more about responses to human remains and grave goods on display, see Hamilton, *Collections and Objections*, 79–106.

54. Hamilton, *Collections and Objections*, 129–35; Cumberland, *Catalogue and Notes*, 35–37, 58.

55. April 4, 1900, October 29, 1900, May 29–31, 1901, Millman Diary, AO. A condolence address from the Six Nations of the Grand River was printed in "Condolence of the Chiefs," *Toronto Daily Star*, June 20, 1901, 4.

56. July 26, 1902, Millman Diary, AO.

57. *Calendar of Queen's College and University Kingston, Canada, for the Year 1898–99* (Kingston: British Whig, 1898), 245.

58. Oronhyatekha, *History of the IOF*, 788; "Serious Charge Against a Medical Man," *Stratford Beacon-Herald*, May 25, 1907, 5; June 1, 1893, May 2, 1895, Millman Diary, AO; "Big Chief Haled [*sic*] to Court," *New York Sun*, May 23, 1907, 5; "Charge of Assault," *Advertiser*, December 10, 1901, 5; "Melbourne Assault Case," *West Australian*, December 10, 1901, 5; "Mohawk Medico," *West Australian Sunday Times*, December 15, 1901, 16; "Serious Charge Against a Medical Man," *Argus*, December 18, 1901, 9; "Charge Against a Doctor," *Argus*, February 28, 1902, 7; "Charge Against a Doctor," *Argus*, February 28, 1902, 7.

CHAPTER 7: THE ROYAL COMMISSION ON LIFE INSURANCE

1. Michael Bliss, *Northern Enterprise: Five Centuries of Canadian Business* (Toronto: McClelland and Stewart, 1987), 370–71.

2. Canada, "Order in Council ordering investigation into Life Insurance and of Commission issued under said order," *Sessional Paper* 38, 6 Edward VII (1906); Circular, *Royal Commission of Life Insurance*, File Administrative, Vol. 3, Royal Commission on Life Insurance Papers, RG 33, LAC. The other fraternal groups were the Commercial Travellers' Mutual Benefit Society, the Grand Council of the Catholic Mutual Benefit Association, the Canadian Order of Woodmen of the World, and the Subsidiary High Court of the Ancient Order of Foresters. See Canada, Report of the Royal Commission on Life Insurance, *Sessional Paper* 123a, 7 Edward VII (1907), 2–3.

3. Dr. Oronhyatekha's testimony appears in Canada, *Royal Commission on Life Insurance*, Vol. 3 (Toronto: Warwick Bro's and Rutter), 2238-73, 2284-2401, 2803-7, Vol. 1910, Department of Justice, RG 13, LAC. Some correspondence, internal plans for investigation, complaints, and exhibits entered during testimony can be found in File Independent Order of Foresters, part 1, Vol. 1, and part 2, Vol. 2; File Great West Land Company, Vol. 2; File Union Trust Company, Vol. 2; File Exhibits #461-665 (Incomplete), Vol. 2 and 3; File Administrative, Vol. 3, all in Royal Commission on Life Insurance Papers, RG 33, LAC.

4. Canada, *Royal Commission on Life Insurance*, Vol. 3, 2257, 2372, 2288, Vol. 1910, Department of Justice, RG 13, LAC.

5. Canada, *Royal Commission on Life Insurance*, Vol. 3, 2259, 2269, 2286, 2288, 2294, 2350, Vol. 1910, Department of Justice, RG 13, LAC. These and other arguments were presented in greater length by Dr. Oronhyatekha in his paper "Fraternal Beneficiary Society vs. Old Line Insurance System," National Fraternal Congress *Journal of Proceedings* 10 (1896): 164–91.

6. Canada, *Royal Commission on Life Insurance*, Vol. 3, 2323–30, Vol. 1910, Department of Justice, RG 13, LAC. Quote is on page 2329. A more complicated version, one that partly contradicts the Canadian testimony is found in Australia, *Report of the Royal Commission Appointed to Investigate and Report on Allegations Respecting the Acts of Certain Persons Connected with the Independent Order of Foresters, in Relation to Members of Parliament or Candidates for Parliament of the State of Victoria* (Melbourne: Robt S. Brain, 1904).

7. Canada, *Royal Commission on Life Insurance*, Vol. 3, 2334-43, 2350, 2352, Vol. 1910, Department of Justice, RG 13, LAC.

8. April 6, 1882, April 17, 1882, September 1, 1882, December 20, 1883, Thomas Millman Diary, F 4529, AO; *Canada Gazette* 15, 46 (May 13, 1882): 24. The prospectus for the company and associated correspondence is in File 44180, Vol. 276, T-12542, Dominion Lands Branch, Department of Interior, RG 15, LAC. Dr. Oronhyatekha also acted as a vice president for the Gold Hills Exploration and Development Company of Toronto, director for the Canada Mutual Mining and Development Company, and president of the Kootenay-Cariboo Mining and Investment Company, but it is unclear whether he invested IOF funds. See *IF* 17, 7 (January 1897): back cover; *IF* 18, 1 (July 1897): back cover; *IF* 18, 9 (March 15, 1898): 274.

9. "Re the Independent Order of Foresters," *MT*, June 23, 1905, 1714; "The Independent Order of Foresters," *MT*, December 2, 1905, 711; Canada, Report of the Royal Commission on Life Insurance, *Sessional Paper* 123a, 134–5.

10. Extract from Letter to W.N. Tilley, File Correspondence, Vol. 3, Royal Commission on Life Insurance Papers, RG 33, LAC; Canada, *Royal Commission on Life Insurance*, Vol. 3, 2355-71, 2373-75, 2395–6, 2398-2401, 2411, 2805–6, Vol. 1910, Department of Justice, RG 13, LAC.

11. Canada, *Royal Commission on Life Insurance*, Vol. 3, 2375–82, Vol. 1910, Department of Justice, RG 13, LAC. The cost of the Temple is from Canada, *Report of the Royal Commission on Life Insurance, Sessional Paper* 123a, 6 Edward VII, 1907, 132.

12. "The Royal Commission," *IF* 27, 7 (November 1906): 101; "Oronhyatekha," *IF* 28, 3 (March 1907): 42.

13. "Foresters Gather to Honor Chief," *Globe*, January 22, 1907, 10.

14. Canada, *Report of the Royal Commission on Life Insurance, Sessional Paper* 123a, 117.

15. Canada, *Report of the Royal Commission on Life Insurance, Sessional Paper* 123a, 122–31.

16. Canada, *Report of the Royal Commission on Life Insurance, Sessional Paper* 123a, 132–52.

17. Canada, *Report of the Royal Commission on Life Insurance, Sessional Paper* 123a, 195.

18. Canada, *Report of the Royal Commission on Life Insurance, Sessional Paper* 123a, 197–9.

19. *Frenzied Finance and the Foresters* (Ottawa: Crain Press, 1908?). Quote is on the first page.

20. *Hon. George E. Foster and the Insurance Commission: Statement of the Case in Parliament. Speeches of Mr. Foster, Mr. Borden and Mr. Lennox, with a Summary of the Charges and the Answers* (1908?)

21. Bliss, *Northern Enterprise*, 370–1; Lawrie Savage, "From Trial to Triumph: How Canada's Past Financial Crises Helped Shape a Superior Regulatory System," *School of Public Policy Papers*, University of Calgary 7, 15 (2014): 6–7, www.policyschool.ucalgary.ca/sites/default/files/research/savage-financeevol.pdf, accessed June 24, 2014.

22. Dustin Galer, "A Friend in Need or a Business Indeed?: Disabled Bodies and Fraternalism in Victorian Ontario," *Labour/Le Travail* 66 (2010): 23.

23. "'Oronhyatekha,'" *MT*, February 18, 1887, 960–61.

24. "Circulating their Deity," *MT*, July 26, 1895, 122.

25. "A Foresters Jaunt," *MT*, November 18, 1898, 672–3.

26. "Foresters and their Money," *MT*, September 28, 1906, 417. Similar articles appeared in other papers. See, for example the exchange of letters in "Very Cheap Life Assurance," *Pall Mall Gazette*, September 9, 1895, 5, September 16, 1895, 5, September 19, 1895, 5, September 23, 1895, 5, October 3, 1895, 5 and October 7, 1895, 5; "More Sawdust to the Blind the Public," *Economist*, Toronto, July 1904, 14–16 and "British Official Searchlights Turned on the I.O.F.," *Economist*, January 1905, 5–7. A more evenhanded report is "The Commission," *Office and Field*, September 27, 1906, 245–48, File Publications, Vol. 3, Royal Commission on Life Insurance Papers, RG 33, LAC.

27. Gayle M. Comeau-Vasilopoulos,"Oronhyatekha," *Dictionary of Canadian Biography* 13 (1901–10): 791–95; National Fraternal Congress, *Journal of Proceedings* 14 (1900): 28, 37–45; National Fraternal Congress, *Journal of Proceedings* 16 (1902): 428–30; J. Howard Hunter, "Sound Information," *Fraternity: A Compilation of Historical Facts and Addresses Pertaining to Fraternalism in General and the Fraternal System in Particular* (Rochester: Fraternal Monitor, 1910), 450; Abb Landis, *Life Insurance* (Nashville, 1914), 61; *IF* 21, 3 (September 15, 1900): inside cover.

28. M.J. Daunton, *State and Market in Victorian Britain: War, Welfare and Capitalism* (Rochester: Boydell Press, 2008), 295; Bliss, *Northern Enterprise*, 267; J.C. Herbert Emery, "Risky Business? Nonactuarial Pricing Practices and the Financial Viability of Fraternal Sickness Insurers," *Explorations in Economic History* 33 (1996): 195–226.

29. Supreme Chief Ranger's Report," *Reports of Officers* (1908?), 1–23, Envelope 16, MU 3927, F. Barlow Cumberland Papers, F 1132, AO; Elliott Stevenson to Union Trust, March 23, 1910, File 1906-10, B229409, E.E.A. Du Vernet Papers, F 2120, AO; "The Readjustment of Rates," *IF* 29, 5 (July 1908): 1; Warren Potter and Robert Oliver, *Fraternally Yours: A History of the Independent Order of Foresters* (London: Queen Anne Press, 1967), 84–86.

30. "The Commission," *Office and Field*, September 27, 1906, 245, File Publications, Vol. 3, Royal Commission on Life Insurance Papers, RG 33, LAC; Canada, *Royal Commission on Life Insurance*, Vol. 3, 2403, 2322, 2334, Vol. 1910, Department of Justice, RG 13, LAC.

31. "Independent Foresters," *Globe*, April 3, 1896, 10; "Dr. Oronhyatekha Funeral to be Held on Thursday," *Toronto Daily Star*, March 4, 1907, 1; "The Supreme Chief Ranger," *IF* 23, 12 (December 1902): 363; "The Supreme Chief Ranger," *IF* 25, 2 (February 1904): 26; "Good News," *IF* 26, 2 (February 1905): 21; "Foresters Gather to Honor Chief," *Globe*, January 22, 1907, 10; "Dr. Oronhyatekha Died in Georgia, Head of Independent Order of Foresters," *Toronto Daily Star*, March 4, 1907, 3.

EPILOGUE: LEGACY AND MEMORY

1. "Indians in Divorce Court," *Washington Post*, May 30, 1907, 2; "Oronhyatekha Alimony Case," *Herald*, New York, May 27, 1907, 5; "Notable Woman Called by Death," *Globe*, April 10, 1922, 1; "Oronhyatekha's Son," *Globe*, July 8, 1907, 1; "Dr. Acland Oronhyatekha," *Canadian Practitioner and Review* 32,

8 (1907): 508; "Buried on his Birthday," *IF* 27, 7 (August 1907): 106; Natalie Oronhyatekha to Superintendent of DIA, July 16, 1908, Estates — Acland Oronhyatekha — Mohawks of the Bay of Quinte — Tyendinaga District, File 482/37-2-2-360, M-2662, DIA, RG 10, LAC; File 3842, MS 887, Reel 714 and File 3502, MS 887, Reel 715, Hastings County Surrogate Court Estate Files, RG 22-340, AO; "Johnson-Oronhyatekha," *IF* 26, 3 (July 1906): 36.

2.　Six Nations Agency — Proposed Erection of the Oronhyatekha Memorial Hospital, 1912, File 402,265, Vol. 3169, C-11333, DIA, RG 10, LAC; DIA, *Annual Report 1913* (1913), H-122.

3.　"Two More from Six Nations put in Indian Hall of Fame," *Brantford Expositor*, August 22, 1966, 11.

4.　"Dr. Oronhyatekha — one of the first leaders of Foresters," YouTube (2014) www.youtube.com/watch?v=cozqLcneW8U, accessed August 16, 2014.

5.　Dr. Oronhyatekha file, Ontario Heritage Trust, Toronto.

6.　Dr. Oronhyatekha file, Heritage Toronto.

7.　Historic Sites and Monuments Board, Agenda Paper 2001-25 and 2001-25A (2001); Parks Canada, press release, "The Government of Canada Commemorates the National Historic Significance of Oronhyatekha and Christ Church, Her Majesty's Chapel Royal of the Mohawk," www.pc.gc.ca/APPS/CP-PR/release_e.asp?id=935&andor1=nr, accessed August 15, 2014; "An Oronhyatekha Memorial," *Toronto Daily Star*, November 30, 1907, 8.

8.　Clifford E. Rich, "Dr. Peter Martin, M.D. (Oronhyatekha)," *Canadian Masonic Research Association* 107 (1973): 12–22; David Harrison and Fred Lomax, "Oronhyatekha and the Independent Order of Foresters," *Knight Templar Magazine* (November 2013): 23–25, www.knightstemplar.org/KnightTemplar/articles/20131123.pdf, accessed August 23, 2014; Canadian Orange Historical Site, http://canadianorangehistoricalsite.com/index-29.php, accessed August 24, 2014; United Empire Loyalist Association of Canada, www.uelac.org/about.php, accessed August 16, 2014; Bay of Quinte Branch of UELAC Loyal Americans Hall of Honour Inductees, www.uelac.org/Honours-Recognition/Bay-of-Quinte-Br-Loyal-Americans-Hall.pdf. The commemorative statement can be found here: www.uelac.org/Honours-Recognition/bio/Hall-of-Honour-BofQ-Peter-Martin-2007.pdf.

9.　"Empire's First Skyscraper Renovate Temple Building," *Toronto Daily Star*, October 6, 1950, 4; "I.O.F. Plans New Building," *Toronto Daily Star*, July 19, 1950, 45; "Indian's Dream in Brass and Marble Consigned to Wreckers," *Toronto Daily Star*, August 21, 1969, 25; Lydia Dotto, "Toronto's Temple Building, Once Empire's Tallest, Comes Down," *Toronto Daily Star*, August

1, 1970, 25; Frank Rasky, "A Sanctuary for Toronto's past," *Globe and Mail*, November 6, 1981, BL1.

10. *History of the County of Middlesex, Canada, from the Earliest Time to the Present, Containing an Authentic Account of Many Important Matters Relating to the Settlement, Progress and General History of the County, and including a Department Devoted to the Preservation of Personal and Private Records, etc., Illustrated* (Toronto: Goodspeed, 1889), 229; Architectural Conservancy of Ontario, *Talbot Tour II* (London, 1988), 16–18; Architectural Conservancy of Ontario, Guide, 1990, Reel 3, London Room, London Public Library.

11. Donald Jones, "Canadian Indian doctor led Independent Order of Foresters," *Toronto Star*, October 18, 1980, G7; Canada, 1901 census, Toronto East, page 13, C-6498, SC, RG 31, LAC; City of Toronto, "Naming of Public Lanes in Cabbagetown" (2008), www.toronto.ca/legdocs/mmis/2008/te/bgrd/backgroundfile-11711.pdf, accessed August 14, 2014; Nicholaas Van Rijn, "Mohawk Honored By Tribute in Park," *Toronto Star*, November 13, 1995, A6; Jon Johnson, "The Great Indian Bus Tours: Mapping Toronto's Urban First Nations Oral Tradition," *The Nature of Empires and the Empires of Nature: Indigenous Peoples and the Great Lakes Environment*, ed. Karl S. Hele (Waterloo: Wilfrid Laurier University Press, 2003), 287. Some walking tours denote 211 Carlton as Dr. Oronhyatekha's residence, but city directories of the time record his address as 209 Carlton.

12. "Filed Will of Dr. Oronhyatekha," *Toronto Daily Star*, April 8, 1907, 11; "Dr. Oronhyatekha's Will," *Napanee Beaver*, March 15, 1907, 2; Estates — Acland Oronhyatekha — Mohawks of the Bay of Quinte — Tyendinaga District, File 482/37-2-2-360, M-2662, DIA, RG 10, LAC; Unlabelled newspaper clipping, Tyendinaga Scrapbook, T-11941, DIA, RG 10, LAC; Derek Baldwin, "Ceremony to honour local Mohawk's contributions," *Kingston Whig-Standard*, August 18, 2005, 6.

13. "Finest of All the Chrysanthemums," *Globe*, November 13, 1902, 12; "Forestry in Flower," *IF* 22, 12 (December 1901): 580; "The Most Beautiful Chrysanthemum Upon the Market," *IF* 32, 12 (December 1902): 368–70; *Peter Henderson and Co.'s Wholesale Catalogue of Seeds, Plants and Bulbs* (New York, 1904), 4; "Toronto," *Weekly Florists' Review* 15, 364 (1904): 6.

14. "New Variety of Musk Melon," *IF* 27, 6 (October 1906): 93.

15. Some Genealogy for the Cooks of Back Bay, Charlotte Co. N.B., CanadaGenWeb.org, www.rootsweb.ancestry.com/~nbpstgeo/stge7d.htm, accessed August 11, 2014; Maritime Museum of the Atlantic, "Oronhyatekha,"

Marine Heritage Database, http://novascotia.ca/museum/wrecks/wrecks/shipwrecks.asp?ID=3715, accessed August 11, 2014.

16. James B. Maracle, "'Heavens on Fire,' Oronhyatekha," *Mohawk Nation Drummer*, June 1998, 6; Viking 28 Association, "Oronhyatekha," http://viking28.com/index.php?option=com_content&view=article&id=89:oronhyatekha&catid=37:events&Itemid=64, accessed July 29, 2015.

17. Guy Vanderhaeghe, *The Last Crossing* (Toronto: McClelland and Stewart, 2002), 114–19, 219; email conversation between Hamilton and Vanderhaeghe, August 5, 2014.

18. David Else et al., *Lonely Planet Great Britain*, 10th ed. (China, 2013), 19. www.whitecap.ca/Detail/1552857999, accessed July 29, 2015.

19. Tanya Lloyd Kyi, *Canadian Boys who Rocked the World* (North Vancouver: Walrus Books, 2007), 10, 105–7.

20. Restless Precinct, http://restlessprecinct.ca/the-site, and Artists, http://restlessprecinct.ca/artists, accessed May 29, 2015; Email conversation between Hamilton, Reena Katz, and Alize Zorlutuna, October 17, 2014; Victoria Freeman, *Stand Up, Stand Out*, pamphlet, 2014.

21. See for example, the Foresters ad, *Toronto Daily Star*, November 6, 1936, 8. Foresters, Explore Our History, www.foresters.com/ca-en/about/pages/our-history.aspx#.U_kX42PLkXE, accessed August 23, 2014; Marianne Gerdes, *Shaping Our Future Together* (Don Mills: Foresters, 1997), 15, 20, 27.

22. J.N.D. Kelly, *St. Edmund Hall: Almost Seven Hundred Years* (Oxford: Oxford University Press, 1989), 83; St. Edmund Hall, History of the Hall, www.seh.ox.ac.uk/about-college/history-hall, accessed August 23, 2014.

23. Steve Brearton, "Leaders & Mavericks: Exceptional Political Alumni," *U of T Magazine* (Summer 2014), www.magazine.utoronto.ca/cover-story/political-leaders-who-went-to-u-of-t, accessed August 1, 2015; Susan Lawrence, "Curing Injustice," *U of T Magazine* (Spring 2002), www.magazine.utoronto.ca/feature/curing-injustice-u-of-t-social-justice-trailblazers, accessed August 1, 2015; University of Toronto, *National Report* (2002), www.nationalreport.utoronto.ca/friends.pdf, accessed August 21, 2014; *University of Toronto*, Great Minds, www.greatpast.utoronto.ca/GreatMinds/ShowBanner.asp?ID=76, accessed August 21, 2014; "Oronhyatekha," *U of T Medicine* (Spring 2014): 20, www.medicine.utoronto.ca/sites/default/files/UT_Medicine_Spring_2014_0_0.pdf, accessed August 21, 2014; *University of Toronto, 2015–2016 Welcome Guide* (2015), 2, www.md.utoronto.ca/Assets/FacMed+Digital+Assets/Undergraduate+Medicine+Education+MD+Program/Admissions$!2c+A

wards$!2c+$!26+Financial+Services+Office/2015-2016+Welcome+Guide.
pdf, accessed May 25, 2015.

24. Trudy Nicks, "'A Token of Remembrance:' The Oronhyatekha Historical
Rooms," Recollecting the Nineteenth-Century Museum conference, Ryerson
University, Toronto, May 15, 2015.

25. Quoted from Trudy Nicks, "Dr Oronhyatekha's History Lessons: Reading
Museum Collections as Texts," *Reading Beyond Words: Contexts for Native
History*, 2nd ed, eds. Jennifer S.H. Brown and Elizabeth Vibert (Toronto:
University of Toronto Press, 2009), 479.

26. Nicks shows how Dr. Oronhyatekha's collection can be (re)interpreted
in "The War of 1812 as Remembered in the Oronhyatekha Historical
Collection," *American Indian Art Magazine* (Summer 2012): 60–69 and "Dr.
Oronhyatekha's History Lessons," *Reading Beyond Words*, eds. Brown and
Vibert, 459–89.

27. Nicks, "Dr. Oronhyatekha's History Lessons," *Reading Beyond Words*, eds.
Brown and Vibert, 483–4.

BIBLIOGRAPHY

ARCHIVAL SOURCES

Archives and Research Collections Centre, Weldon Library, University of Western Ontario, London, Ontario
Leonard Family Papers.

Archives of Ontario, Toronto, Ontario
Benevolent Societies Corporation Files. RG 55-8.
Campbell, Alexander. Fonds. F 32.
Cumberland, F. Barlow. Fonds. F 1132.
Du Vernet, Ernest E.A. Fonds. F 2120.
Hastings County Surrogate Court Estate Files. RG 22-340.
McClurg, G. Mills. Correspondence. A.E. Williams/United Indian Bands of the
    Chippewas and the Mississaugas Papers. F 4337.
Millman, Thomas. Diary. F 4529.

Chancellor Robert R. Livingston Masonic Library of Grand Lodge, New York,
    New York
Peckham, William H. Papers. AR1997.1.

Diocese of Huron Archives, Huron University College, London, Ontario
Parish Register, 1829–1943, Her Majesty's Chapel of the Mohawks. PREG 912.

Foresters House, Toronto, Ontario
Independent Order of Foresters Archival Collection.
Independent Order of Foresters Museum Collection.

Greenslade Special Collections and Archives, Kenyon College, Gambier, Ohio
Allan Gale. Reference File.
Alpha Delta Phi. Papers.
Grade Books.
Humor at Kenyon. Reference File.
Kenyon Reveille.
Matriculation Book.
Oronhyatekha. Reference File.
Philomathesian Society. Records.

Heritage Toronto
Dr. Oronhyatekha file.

Library and Archives Canada, Ottawa, Ontario
Acland, Sir Henry Wentworth. Papers. R10912-0-6-E.
Canada. Department of Indian Affairs. RG 10.
Canada. Department of Interior. RG 15.
Canada. Department of Justice. RG 13.
Canada. Department of Transport. RG 42.
Canada. Ministry of Militia and Defence. RG 9.
Canada. Office of the Governor General of Canada. Papers. RG 7.
Canada. Royal Commission on Life Insurance. RG 33.
Canada. Statistics Canada. Census of Canada. 1852. 1861. 1871. 1881. 1901. RG 31.
Hall, Sydney Prior. Papers. R8195-0-X-E.
Lennox and Addington Historical Society. Papers. R14133-0-7-E.
Macdonald, John A. Papers. MG 26.
New England Company. Papers. R10819-0-8-E.

London Room, London Public Library, London, Ontario
Architectural Conservancy of Ontario. Guide. 1990. Microfilm #3.

Museum of the History of Science, Oxford, England
Acland, Sarah. Photograph Album.

Ontario Heritage Foundation
Dr. Oronhyatekha. File.

Private Collections
Martin, Dr. Peter. Diary. 1879–84.
Oronhyatekha family. Bible.

Queen's Own Rifles Museum and Archives, Casa Loma, Toronto
Nominal Roll. 1866.

Royal Ontario Museum, Toronto, Ontario
Boyle, David. Correspondence.
Independent Order of Foresters. Accession File. Department of World Cultures.

Stratford-Perth Archives, Stratford, Ontario
Oronhyatekha Clipping File.
Orr, R. Thomas. Scrapbook.

University of Toronto Archives
Oronhyatekha, Peter Martin. Alumni Record. A2003-0005.
Oronhyatekha, Peter Martin. File. A73-0026/352(94).
Wilson, Daniel. Papers. Langton Family Fonds. B65-0014/004.

Woodland Cultural Centre, Six Nations of the Grand River
Mohawk Ideals, Victorian Values. Exhibit Papers.

NEWSPAPERS AND PERIODICALS

Acta Victoriana. Toronto, Ontario.
Advertiser, The. Adelaide, Australia.
Argus, The. Melbourne, Australia.
Atlanta Constitution. Atlanta, Georgia.
Beaches Living Guide. Toronto, Ontario.
Belfast News-Letter. Belfast, Ireland.
Birmingham Daily Post. Birmingham, England.
Boston Daily Advertiser. Boston, Massachusetts.
Boston Daily Globe. Boston, Massachusetts.
Bristol Mercury. Bristol, England.

British Medical Journal. London, England.

Buffalo Express. Buffalo, New York.

Brantford Expositor. Brantford, Ontario.

Brisbane Courier. Brisbane, Australia.

British Medical Journal. London, England.

Caledonian Mercury. Edinburgh, Scotland.

Canada Medical Journal and Monthly Record of Medical and Surgical Science. Montreal, Quebec.

Canadian Architect and Builder. Toronto, Ontario.

Canadian Courier. Toronto, Ontario.

Canadian Craftsman and Masonic Record, The. Port Hope, Ontario.

Canadian Journal of Industry, Art and Science. Toronto, Ontario.

Canadian Journal of Medical Science. Toronto, Ontario.

Canadian Journal of Medicine and Surgery. Toronto, Ontario.

Canadian Magazine, The. Toronto, Ontario.

Canadian Miner. Toronto, Ontario.

Canadian Patent Office Record. Montreal, Quebec.

Canadian Practitioner and Review. Toronto, Ontario.

Canadian Presbyterian. Toronto, Ontario.

Chicago Tribune. Chicago, Illinois.

Christian Record.

Conservative Expositor. Brantford, Ontario.

Craftsman and British American Masonic Record, The. Hamilton, Ontario.

Craftsman and Canadian Masonic Record, The. Hamilton, Ontario.

Daily Leader. Toronto, Ontario.

Gazette. Montreal, Quebec.

Glasgow Herald. Glasgow, Scotland.

Globe. Toronto, Ontario.

Globe and Mail. Toronto, Ontario.

Good Templars' Watchword. England.

Grip. Toronto, Ontario.

Hartford Courant. Hartford, Connecticut.

Independent Forester, The. London and Toronto, Ontario.

Independent Forester and Forester's Herald, The. London and Toronto, Ontario.

Indian, The. Hagersville, Ontario.

International Good Templar. Toronto, Ontario, and Milwaukee, Wisconsin.

Journal of Education for Upper Canada. Toronto, Ontario.

Lancet, The. Boston, Massachusetts.

London Advertiser. London, Ontario.

London Review and Weekly Journal of Politics, Literature, Art and Society. London, England.

Los Angeles Times. Los Angeles, California.

Milwaukee Sentinel. Milwaukee, Wisconsin.

Mohawk Nation Drummer. Deseronto, Ontario.

Monetary Times: Trade Review and Insurance Chronicle. Toronto, Ontario.

Napanee Beaver. Napanee, Ontario.

New York Evangelist. New York, New York.

New York Sun. New York, New York.

New York Times. New York, New York.

Newcastle Courant. Newcastle, England.

Pall Mall Gazette. London, England.

Quiz: The Satirist. London, England.

Reynolds's Newspaper. London, England.

St. Edmund Hall Magazine. Oxford, England.

St. Thomas Journal. St. Thomas, Ontario.

Stratford Beacon-Herald. Stratford, Ontario.

Toronto Star. Toronto, Ontario.

Toronto World. Toronto, Ontario.

University of Toronto Medical Journal. Toronto, Ontario.

University of Toronto Monthly. Toronto, Ontario.

Vermont Chronicle. Bellows Falls, Vermont.

Volunteer Review and Military and Naval Gazette, The. Ottawa, Ontario.

Washington Post. Washington, D.C.

Weekly Florists' Review. Chicago, Illinois, and New York, New York.

West Australian, The. Perth, Australia.

Winnipeg Tribune. Winnipeg, Manitoba.

UNPUBLISHED PAPERS

Nicks, Trudy. "'A Token of Remembrance': The Oronhyatekha Historical Rooms." Presentation, Recollecting the Nineteenth-Century Museum conference. Ryerson University, Toronto, Ontario, May 15, 2015.

GOVERNMENT DOCUMENTS

Australia. *Report of the Royal Commission Appointed to Investigate and Report on Allegations Respecting the Acts of Certain Persons Connected with the Independent Order of Foresters, in Relation to Members of Parliament or Candidates for Parliament of the State of Victoria*. Melbourne: Robt S. Brain, 1904.

Canada. *An Act for the Gradual Enfranchisement of Indians, the Better Management of Indian Affairs, and to Extend the Provisions of the Act 31st Victoria, Chapter 42*. Statutes of Canada, 1869, c. 6. www.aadnc-aandc.gc.ca/DAM/DAM-INTER-HQ/STAGING/texte-text/a69c6_1100100010205_eng.pdf.

Canada. *Canada Gazette*.

Canada. *Sessional Papers*.

Canada. Department of Indian Affairs. *Annual Reports*.

Canada. Department of the Interior. *Annual Reports*.

Canada. House of Commons. *Debates*.

Canada. Parks Canada. "The Government of Canada Commemorates the National Historic Significance of Oronhyatekha and Christ Church, Her Majesty's Chapel Royal of the Mohawk." Press Release, August 21, 2005. www.pc.gc.ca/APPS/CP-NR/release_e.asp?id=935&andor1=nr.

Canada. Parks Canada. Historic Sites and Monuments Board. Agenda Paper 2001-25. 2001.

Canada. Parks Canada. Historic Sites and Monuments Board. Agenda Paper 2001-25A. 2001.

City of Toronto. *Naming of Public Lanes in Cabbagetown — Phase 1*. Staff Report, March 17, 2008. www.toronto.ca/legdocs/mmis/2008/te/bgrd/backgroundfile-11711.pdf.

Leslie, John, and Ron Maguire, eds. *The Historical Development of the Indian Act*. 2nd ed. Ottawa: Indian Affairs and Northern Development, 1983.

Province of Canada. *An Act to Encourage the Gradual Civilization of the Indian Tribes in this Province, and to Amend the Laws Respecting Indians*. Ch. 26. 20 Vict. 1857.

Province of Canada. *Sessional Papers*.

PUBLISHED PRIMARY SOURCES

Abstract of Report of the Proceedings of the Prohibitory Conference Held in Ottawa, Wednesday and Thursday, April 22nd and 23rd, 1874. [Ottawa?], [1874?].

Adam, G. Mercer. *Prominent Men of Canada: a Collection of Persons Distinguished in Professional and Political Life, and in the Commerce and Industry of Canada*. Toronto: Canadian Biographical Pub. Co., 1892.

Alpha Delta Phi. *Catalogue of the Alpha Delta Phi Society*. Utica, New York: Curtiss and Childs, 1870.

"Anthropologic Miscellanea." *American Anthropologist* 9, no. 1 (1907): 244.

Art Work on Toronto, Canada. Toronto: W.H. Carre and Company, 1898.

Bodley, J.E.C. *The Coronation of Edward the Seventh: a Chapter of European and Imperial History*. London, England: Methuen, 1903.

Bodine, William Budd. *The Kenyon Book*. 2nd ed. [Gambier, Ohio?], 1891.

Bowell, Mackenzie. *1868–69: Directory of the County of Hastings*. Belleville, Ontario: Intelligencer Office, 1869.

A Brief History of Public and High School Text-Books Authorized for the Province of Ontario 1846–1889. Toronto: Warwick and Sons, 1890.

Buffalo City Directory for the Year 1875. Buffalo, New York: Courier Company, 1875.

Busk, Henry William. *A Sketch of the Origin and the Recent History of the New England Company, by the Senior Member of the Company*. London, England: Spottiswoode, 1884.

Burt, Calvin C. *Egyptian Masonic History of the Original and Unabridged Ancient and Ninety-Six (96°) Degree Rite of Memphis: For the Instruction and Government of the Craft*. Utica, New York: White and Floyd, Printers, 1879.

By-laws and History of King Solomon's Lodge, A.F. & A.M., No. 22, G. R. C. Toronto, 1896.

Calendar of Queen's College and University Kingston, Canada, for the Year 1898–99. Kingston, Ontario: British Whig, 1898.

Canada Temperance Union. *Proceedings of the Second Session of the Canada Temperance Union held at Toronto, Ontario, September 7th, 8th, and 9th, 1869*. Napanee, Ontario: Henry Brothers, 1869.

Catalogue of the Theological Seminary of the Diocese of Ohio, and Kenyon College. 1857–58. Gambier, Ohio: Theological Seminary Press, 1858.

Catalogue of the Theological Seminary of the Diocese of Ohio, and Kenyon College. 1858–9. Gambier, Ohio: Cincinnati Gazette Company, 1859.

Catalogue of the Theological Seminary of the Diocese of Ohio, and Kenyon College, 1859–60. Gambier, Ohio: Cincinnati Gazette Company, 1860.

Chadwick, Edward Marion. *A Genealogy of the Brant Family from Ontarian Families*. Toronto: Rolph, Smith and Co., 1894.

Company for Propagation of the Gospel in New England and Parts Adjacent in America. Special Committee. *Mohawk Institution and Day Schools General Rules.* London, England: Taylor and Co., [1872?].

Cumberland, F. Barlow. *Catalogue and Notes of the Oronhyatekha Historical Collection.* Toronto: Independent Order of Foresters, 1904.

Dominion Alliance for the Total Suppression of the Liquor Traffic. *First Annual Meeting February 14, 15, 16, 1877.* Montreal: Wilson's Printing House, 1887.

Finch, Frances E., and Frank J. Sibley. *John B. Finch: His Life and Work.* New York: Funk and Wagnalls, 1888.

First Book of Lessons for Use in Schools. Montreal, Quebec: Armour and Ramsay, 1845.

Fitzgerald, William. *A Statement by the Superintendent of Insurance (Wm. Fitzgerald, M.A.) of Reasons why the Independent Order of Foresters should not have the Powers Granted them by Parliament.* Toronto: Monetary Times, 1895.

Fourth Book of Lessons for the Use of Schools. Edinburgh, Scotland: G. and J. Grierson, 1851.

Fraternity: A Compilation of Historical Facts and Addresses Pertaining to Fraternalism in General and the Fraternal System in Particular. Rochester, New York: Fraternal Monitor, 1910.

Frenzied Finance and the Foresters. Ottawa: Crain Press, [1908?].

General Catalogue of Kenyon College, Gambier, Ohio. Toledo, Ohio: Franklin Printing and Engraving, 1899.

The General Council of the Six Nations and Delegates from Different Bands in Western and Eastern Canada, June 10, 1870. Hamilton, Ontario: The Spectator, [1870?].

Grand Lodge of Ancient, Accepted and Free Masons of Canada. *Proceedings of the Grand Lodge of Ancient, Accepted and Free Masons of Canada, At a Special Communication, held at the Village of Trenton, on the 24th day of Sept., A. D. 1873, A. L. 5873. Also at Its Nineteenth Annual Communication, Held at Toronto, Ont, on the 8th & 9th days of July, A. D. 1874, A. L. 5874.* Hamilton, Ontario: Spectator Steam Printing Press, 1874.

Grand Lodge of Ancient, Free and Accepted Masons of Canada. *Proceedings of the Grand Lodge of Ancient Free and Accepted Masons of Canada, in the Province of Ontario, at Special Communications Held at Cayuga, 28th September, A. L. 5894, and at Napanee Mills, 16th May, A. L. 5895, also at the Fortieth Annual Communications Held at the City of Toronto on the 17th and 18th July, A. D. 1895, A. L. 5895.* Hamilton, Ontario: Spectator Printing Co., 1895.

———. *Proceedings.* [Hamilton, Ontario?], 1872.

Hale, Horatio. "Chief George H.M. Johnson, Onwanonsyshon, His Life and
Work among the Six Nations." *Magazine of American History* no. 13 (1885):
131–42.

*The History of the County of Brant, Ontario: Containing a History of the County its
Townships, Cities, Towns, Schools, Churches, etc; General and Local Statistics;
Portraits of Early Settlers and Prominent Men; History of the Six Nation
Indians and Captain Joseph Brant (Thayendanegea); History of the Dominion
of Canada, Miscellaneous Matters, etc., etc., etc.* Toronto: Warner, 1883.

*History of the County of Middlesex, Canada, from the Earliest Time to the Present,
Containing an Authentic Account of Many Important Matters relating to
the Settlement, Progress and General History of the County, and including a
Department Devoted to the Preservation of Personal and Private Records, etc.,
Illustrated.* Toronto, Ontario: Goodspeed, 1889.

*History, Statistics, Library, and Honorary Members of the Philomathesian Society
of Kenyon College.* Columbus, Ohio: Scott and Bascom's Press, 1853.

*Hon. George E. Foster and the Insurance Commission: Statement of the Case
in Parliament. Speeches of Mr. Foster, Mr. Borden and Mr. Lennox, with a
Summary of the Charges and the Answers.* N.p., [1908?].

Hopkins, J. Castell, ed. *Morang's Annual Register of Canada Affairs 1901.* Toronto,
Ontario: George N. Morang and Company, Limited, 1902.

Illustrated Toronto: the Queen City of Canada. Toronto, Ontario: Acme Publishing
and Engraving, 1890.

Imperial Grand Orange Council of the World. *The Imperial Grand Orange
Council, ..Dublin, 1903. Report of Proceedings.* N.p., [1903?].

Independent Order of Foresters. *Constitution and General Laws of the Supreme
Court of the Independent Order of Foresters also Laws Governing High Courts,
Subordinate Courts, Companion Courts, Juvenile Courts and Encampments of
Royal Foresters.* Toronto, Ontario: Hunter Rose Co., Limited, 1898.

———. *Constitution and General Laws of the Supreme Court of the Independent
Order of Foresters also Laws Governing High Courts, Subordinate Courts,
Companion Courts, Juvenile Courts and Encampments of Royal Foresters.*
Toronto, Ontario: Hunter Rose Co., Limited, 1902.

———. *Dedication Souvenir: pays $4.000 a Day for Benefits, has paid nearly
$6.000.000.00 in Benefits to Members and their Beneficiaries ... Temple
Building, Head office, Independent Order of Foresters, Toronto, Canada.*
Toronto, Ontario: Toronto Lith. Co., [1898?].

———. *Extra to the Independent Forester and Forester's Herald: K.O.T.M.,
Successful Termination of the Grand Review.* 1881.

———. *Fifty Years: Historical Souvenir of the Independent Order of Foresters.* Toronto, Ontario, 1924.

———. *The Ritual of the Independent Order of Foresters for Subordinate Courts.* Toronto: Hunter, Rose Co., Limited, 1899.

———. *Ritual of the Independent Order of Foresters for Subordinate Courts.* Toronto, Ontario: Hunter Rose Co., Limited, 1903.

———. *Ritual of the Independent Order of Foresters for Subordinate Courts.* Toronto, Ontario: Hunter Rose Co., Limited, 1905.

———. *Ritual of the Royal Foresters.* London, England: Advertiser Print. and Pub. Co., 1892.

———. *Souvenir: Independent Order of Foresters, 1903: Sketches and Cuts of Prominent Foresters with Enticing Pints with Regard to I.O.F.* Ottawa: Ottawa Print, [1903?].

Independent Order of Grand Templars. *Constitution of the Grand and Subordinate Temples of the Independent Order of Good Templars of Canada.* Hamilton, Ontario: Lawson and Co, 1866.

———. *Constitution of the Grand and Subordinate Temples, of the I.O.G. Templars, Canada.* Napanee, Ontario: Henry and Brother, 1874.

———. *Journal of Proceedings of the Sixteenth Annual Session of the R. W. Grand Lodge of North America, Held at St. Louis, MO, May 24, 25 and 26, 1870.* Cleveland, Ohio: Era Job Printing Establishment, 1860.

———. *Journal of Proceedings of the Twentieth Annual Session of the Right W. Grand Lodge Held at Boston, Mass., U. S., Portland, Maine, May 26, 27, 28, 29 and 30.* Napanee, Ontario: Canada Casket Steam Job Printing Establishment, 1874.

———. *Journal of Proceedings of the Twenty-Third Annual Session of the R.W.G. Lodge Held at Portland, Maine, May 22, 23, 24, 25 & 26, 1877.* Napanee, Ontario: Canada Casket Steam Printing and Publishing House, 1877.

———. *Journal of Proceedings of the Twenty-Fourth Annual Session of the R.W.G. Lodge Held at Minneapolis, Minn., May 28, 29, 30 and 31, 1878.* Napanee, Ontario: Canada Casket Steam Printing and Publishing House, 1878.

———. *Proceedings of the 30th Annual Session of the R.W. Grand Lodge I.O.G.T., Held at Washington, D.C., U.S.A, May 27th, 28th, 29th, and 30th, 1884.* Lincoln, Nebraska: Journal Company, State Printers, 1884.

Irwin, W. H., and Co. *City of London Annual, Alphabetical, General Miscellaneous and Subscribers' Classified Business Directory for 1876-'77 — to Which Is Added Directories of Strathroy, Park Hill, Lucan and Ailsa Craig.* London, Ontario: Advertiser Steam Presses, [1876?].

Kenyon College, Gambier, Ohio. From an Article, With Additions. Reprinted from Scribner's Monthly for March 1878. Columbus, Ohio: Cott and Hann, [1878?].

Kenyon College. Gambier, Ohio, 1844.

Kenyon College. Gambier, Ohio, c. 1880.

Kenyon College: Twentieth Anniversary of the Class of 1862. Rushville, Indiana: Republican Book and Job Office, 1882.

Ker, Robert, ed. *St. George's Parish Church, St. Catharines: Jubilee Celebration and Historic and Centenary Review.* St. Catharines, Ontario: Star Print, [1892?].

Keys, D.R. "Oronhyatekha, M.D." *University of Toronto Monthly* 7, no. 7 (May 1907): 167–69.

Knights of the Maccabees. *Constitutions and Laws of the Knights of the Maccabees of the World, Governing the Supreme Tent, Gt. Camps & Subordinate Tents.* London, England: Southam and Brierley, 1881.

Landis, Abb. *Life Insurance.* Nashville, Tennessee, 1914.

Lawless, Thomas. *The Canada Digest, I.O.G.T.* 2nd ed. Hamilton, Ontario: Thomas Lawless, 1872.

———. *The Canada Digest, I.O.G.T.* 3rd ed. Hamilton, Ontario: Thomas Lawless, 1875.

London Old Boys' Association. *London, Ontario, Canada, Semi Centennial, 1855–1905.* London, Ontario: London Printing and Lithographing Company, 1905.

———. *Official Souvenir Program, London Old Boys Reunion.* London, Ontario: A. Talbot and Co., 1900.

———. *Souvenir Programme, International London Old Boys at Home.* London, Ontario: A. Talbot and Co., 1903.

———. *Welcome Home, International London Old Boys' Reunion: Souvenir Programme.* London, Ontario: A. Talbot and Co., 1901.

Mackenzie, J.B. *The Six-Nations Indians in Canada.* Toronto, Ontario: Hunter, Rose, [1896?].

Malins, Joseph. *The Unlawful Exclusion of the African Race.* Birmingham, England: Grand Lodge Office, 1877.

Mavor, James. *My Windows on the Street of the World.* 2 vols. Toronto, Ontario: J.M. Dent and Sons, Limited, 1923.

McEvoy, Henry, ed. *The Province of Ontario Gazetteer and Directory.* Toronto, Ontario: Robertson and Cook, 1869.

A Memento of the Donors and Founders of the Theological Seminary of the Protestant Episcopal Church in the Diocese of Ohio, and Kenyon College; Being the Report of a Committee of the Board of Trustees, Presented September 27, 1860. Cincinnati, Ohio: Moore, Wilstach, Keys and Co., 1860.

Memorial Service, Hon. Dr. Oronhyatekha, J.P., Supreme Chief Ranger, Independent Order Foresters, Massey Hall, Toronto, Canada, Wednesday, March 6th, 1907, at 7:30 p.m., conducted by Rev. F. Wilkinson, Rector St. Peter's Church, Toronto. Toronto, Ontario: Hunter, Rose, [1907?].

Mills, B.H. *The Temperance Manual: Containing a History of the Various Temperance Orders.* Boston, Massachussets: Cyrus G. Cooke, 1864.

Minutes of the Fifteenth Session of the Synod of the Diocese of Huron, Held in London, on Wednesday, Thursday and Friday, June 5th, 6th and 7th, 1872. London, Ontario: Herald Printing Establishment, 1872.

Morgan, Henry J. The *Canadian Men and Women of the Time: a Handbook of Canadian Biography.* Toronto, Ontario: W. Briggs, 1898.

Mysteries of the Independent Order of Foresters Unveiled, or, Trapped at the altar of "L.B.&C." [Dublin, Ireland?], [1894?].

Napanee Pictorial Almanac and Lennox and Addington Book of Reference for 1873, Containing a Short Sketch of the Rise and Progress of the Town, an Alphabetically Arranged Directory of the Inhabitants, with much other Useful and Valuable Information for the People, also, Advertisements from Several of the Leading Businss (sic) Men of the Town and a Large Amount of very Interesting and Instructive Reading Matter. Prescott, Ontario: Beeman Bros., [1872?].

National Educational Association. *Journal of Proceedings and Addresses, Session of the Year 1891 Held at Toronto, Ontario, Canada.* New York: J.J. Little & Co., 1891.

National Fraternal Congress. *Journal of Proceedings.* Vols 1–21. 1886–1907.

National Sanitarium Association. *First Report of the Muskoka Sanatorium for Consumptives.* Toronto, Ontario, 1898.

———. *Second Annual Report of the National Sanitarium Association 1898–1899.* Toronto, Ontario, 1899.

———. *Third Annual Report of the Muskoka Sanatorium (Near Gravenhurst).* Toronto, Ontario, 1900.

———. *Fourth Annual Report of the National Sanitarium Association 1900–1901.* Toronto, Ontario, 1901.

———. *Fifth Annual Report of the National Sanitarium Association for 1901–1902.* [Toronto?], [1902?].

———. *Sixth Annual Report of the National Sanitarium Association for 1902–1903.* [Toronto?], [1903?].

———. *Seventh Annual Report of the National Sanatorium Association for 1903–1904.* [Toronto?], [1904?].

———. *Eighth Annual Report for the National Sanitarium Association for 1904–1905.* [Toronto?], [1905?].

———. *Ninth Annual Report of the National Sanitarium Association for 1905–1906.* [Toronto?], [1906?].

———. *Tenth Annual Report of the National Sanitarium Association for 1906–1907.* [Toronto?], [1907?].

Needham, Timothy. *The Negro Question and the I.O.G.T. Report of Conference Held in London, October 19, 20, and 21, 1876.* London, England: Kempster and Co., 1876.

New England Company. *History of the New England Company, from its Incorporation, from the Seventeenth Century, to the Present Time Including a Detailed Report of the Company's Proceedings for the Civilization and Conversion of Indians, Blacks, and Pagans in the Dominion of Canada, British Columbia, the West Indies, and S. Africa, during the Two Years 1869–70.* London, England: Taylor and Co., 1871.

———. *Report by a Committee of the Corporation commonly called the New England Company, of their Proceedings for the Civilization and Conversion of Indians, Blacks, and Pagans, in the British colonies in America and the West Indies, Since the Last Report in 1840.* London, England: J.P. Gibson, 1846.

———. *Report of the Proceedings of the Corporation Commonly Called the New England Company, for the Civilization and Conversion of Indians, Blacks, and Pagans, in the British Colonies in America. Since the Last Report in 1849, to the End of the Year 1858.* London, England: J.P. Gibson, 1859.

———. *Report of the Proceedings of the Corporation Commonly Called the New England Company, for the Civilization and Conversion of Indians, Blacks, and Pagans, in the British Colonies in America, for the Year 1859.* London, England: J.P. Gibson, 1860.

———. *Report of the Proceedings of the New England Company for the Civilization and Conversion of Indians, Blacks and Pagans in the Dominion of Canada, South Africa and the West Indies during the Two Years 1871–1872.* London, England: Taylor and Co., 1874.

Official Programme and Souvenir of the Royal Tour Showing the Progress of Their Royal Highnesses, the Duke and Duchess of Cornwall and York through Quebec and Ontario, 1901. Toronto, Ontario: Hunter, Rose, 1901.

Official Programme of Events Which Will Take Place in the City of Toronto During the Visit of Their Royal Highnesses the Duke and Duchess of Cornwall and York. Toronto, Ontario: Dominion Pub., [1901?].

O'Leary, A. *Delineation of Character as Determined by the Teachings of Phrenology, Physiology, and Physiognomy.* Boston, Massachussets: Bradley, Dayton and Co., 1860.

One Hundred Years of Temperance: A Memorial Volume of the Centennial Temperance Conference Held in Philadelphia, Pa., September, 1885. New York: National Temperance Society and Publication House, 1886.

The Ontario Medical Register. Hamilton, Ontario: C.E. Stewart and Co., 1872.

Oronhyatekha. "The Mohawk Language." *Canadian Journal of Industry, Science and Art* 10, no. 57 (May 1865): 182–94.

———. "The Mohawk Language." *Canadian Journal of Science, Literature, and History* 15, no. 1 (April 1876): 1–12.

Oronhyatekha, Dr. *History of the Independent Order of Foresters*. Toronto, Ontario: Hunter, Rose and Company, 1895.

———. "Indian Education." In *Journal of Proceedings and Addresses, National Education Association*, 234–38. New York: NEA, 1891.

Parker, Reverend T. F. *History of the Independent Order of Good Templars, from the Origin of the Order to the Session of the Right Worthy Grand Lodge of 1887*. New York: Phillips and Hunt, 1887.

———. *History of the Independent Order of Good Templars, from the Origin of the Order to the Session of the Right Worthy Grand Lodge of 1880. Together with an Exposition of the Order, by Past Right Worthy Grand Templar S. B. Chase*. New York: Phillips and Hunt, 1882.

Peirce, Isaac Newton, and Silvanus Phillips Thompson. *The History of the Independent Order of Good Templars*. Birmingham, England: Grand Lodge of England, 1873.

Periodical Accounts Relating to the Missions of the Church of the United Brethren established among the Heathen. Vol. 31. London, England: G. Norman and Son, 1880.

Peter Henderson and Co.'s Wholesale Catalogue of Seeds, Plants and Bulbs. New York, 1904.

Plowman, Thomas F. *In the Days of Victoria, Some Memories of Men and Things*. London, England: John Lane, The Bodley Head, 1918.

Pope, Joseph. *The Tour of Their Royal Highnesses the Duke and Duchess of Cornwall and York through the Dominion of Canada in the Year 1901*. Ottawa, Ontario: S.E. Dawson, 1903.

Province of Ontario Gazetteer and Directory, Including the City of Montreal, P.Q. 1895. Toronto, Ontario: Murray Printing Co., 1895.

Richardson and Punchard. *Directory of the City of Kingston with the Villages of Barriefield, Portsmouth and Cataraqui, and Towns of Gananoque and Napanee for 1873–4*. Napanee, Ontario: Henry and Bro's. Steam Book and Job Printers, 1873.

Ritual of the A. and A. Egyptian Rite of Memphis 96°. Also Constitution and By-Laws of the Sovereign Sanctuary, Valley of Canada. 1889.

Robertson, J. Ross. *The Cryptic Rite: Its Origin and Introduction on this Continent. History of the Degrees of Royal, Select, and Super-Excellent Master; The Work of the Rite in Canada with a History of the Various Grand Councils that have Existed from the Inception of the Rite in Canada till the Present Time.* Toronto, Ontario: Hunter, Rose and Co., 1888.

———. *The History of Freemasonry in Canada, from its Introduction in 1749, Compiled and Written from Official Records and from MSS Covering the Period 1749–1185, in the Possession of the Author.* Toronto, Ontario: George N. Morang and Company, Limited, 1900.

Rockwell, A.D. *Rambling Recollections: An Autobiography.* New York: Paul B. Hoeber, 1902.

Royal College of Physicians and Surgeons. *The Ontario Medical Register, 1870.* Hamilton, Ontario: C.E. Stewart and Co., n.d.

———. *The Ontario Medical Register, 1872.* Hamilton, Ontario: C.E. Stewart and Co., n.d.

———. *The Ontario Medical Register, 1874.* Toronto, Ontario: Monetary Times, n.d.

Russell, Alex Lord. *Illustrated Hand Book of Rifle Shooting, with an Appendix.* Toronto, Ontario: Hunter, Rose, 1869.

Sargant, Thomas. *The Freemason's Manual Containing the First, Second and Third Degrees of Freemasonry; Embellished with Symbolical Illustrations, Together with Installation, Consecration, and Dedication Ceremonies, Etc. Also, Rules and Regulations for Masonic Trials, Forms for Minutes, By-Laws, &c.* Toronto, Ontario: Masonic Publishing Co., 1880.

Second Book of Lessons for the Use of Schools. Montreal, Quebec: Campbell Bryson, 1849.

Sequel to the Second Book of Lessons, for the Use of Schools. Toronto, Ontario: Brewer, McPhail and Co. 1853.

Smily, Frederick. *The Medical Directory of Toronto and Suburbs.* Toronto, Ontario: Murray Printing Company, 1900.

Special Report by the Bureau of Education. Educational Exhibits and Conventions at the World's Industrial and Cotton Centennial Exhibition, New Orleans 1884–'85. Washington, D.C.: Government Printing Office, 1886.

Sutherland, James. *Sutherland's City of Hamilton and County of Wentworth Directory for 1868–69.* Hamilton, Ontario: A. Lawson and Co., [1868?].

Taylor, Conyngham Crawford. *Toronto "Called Back," from 1894 to 1847: Its Wonderful Growth and Progress, with the Development of its Manufacturing*

Industries and Reminiscences Extending over the Above Period. Toronto, Ontario: W. Briggs, 1894.

Third Book of Lessons for the Use of Schools. Montreal, Quebec: Armour and Ramsay, 1846.

The Toronto and Hamilton Society Blue Book: A Social Directory. Toronto, Ontario, 1902.

The Toronto City Directory 1901. Toronto, Ontario: Might and Co., 1901.

Transactions of the Buffalo Historical Society. Vol. 3. Buffalo, New York: Courier Co., 1885.

Turnbull, William W. *The Good Templars: A History of the Rise and Progress of the Independent Order of Good Templars.* 1901.

United Empire Loyalists Centennial Committee. *The Centennial of the Settlement of Upper Canada by the United Empire Loyalists, 1784–1884: the Celebrations at Adolphustown, Toronto and Niagara, with an Appendix, Containing a Copy of the U.E. List, preserved in the Crown Lands Department at Toronto.* Toronto, Ontario: Rose Publishing Co., 1885.

University of Toronto. *Annual Announcement of the Toronto School of Medicine in Affiliation with the University of Toronto. 22nd Session, from Oct. 1st., 1864, to April 1st, 1865.* Toronto, Ontario: Globe Steam Book and Job Press, 1864.

———. *Class and Prize Lists, 1864.* Toronto, Ontario: Henry Rowsell, 1864.

———. *Class and Prize Lists, 1866.* Toronto, Ontario: Henry Rowsell, 1866.

Wilson, Daniel. *The Huron-Iroquois of Canada: A Typical Race of American Aborigines.* [Ottawa?], 1884.

———. *The Lost Atlantis and Other Ethnographic Studies.* Edinburgh, Scotland: D. Douglas, 1892.

Youmans, Letitia. *Campaign Echoes: The Autobiography of Mrs. Letitia Youmans, the Pioneer of the White Ribbon Movement in Canada. Written by Request of the Provincial Woman's Christian Temperance Union of Ontario.* Toronto, Ontario: W. Briggs, [1893?].

BOOKS, ARTICLES, PAMPHLETS, AND THESES

Adams, Annmarie, and Stacie Burke. "'Not a Shack in the Woods': Architecture for Tuberculosis in Muskoka and Toronto." *Canadian Bulletin of Medical History* 23, no. 2 (2006): 429–55.

Anderson, Benedict R. *Imagined Communities: Reflections on the Origin and Spread of Nationalism.* Rev. Ed. London and New York: Verso, 2006.

Anglin, Gerald. "The Strangest Insurance Company in the World." *Maclean's* 64, no. 3 (1951): 10–11, 44.

Anstead, Christopher J. "Fraternalism in Victorian Ontario: Secret Societies and Cultural Hegemony." Ph.D. dissertation, University of Western Ontario, 1992.

Architectural Conservancy of Ontario. *Talbot Tour II.* London, Ontario, 1988.

Arthur, Eric Ross. *Toronto: No Mean City.* Toronto: University of Toronto Press, 1986.

Ash, Marinell. *Thinking with Both Hands: Sir Daniel Wilson in the Old World and the New.* Edited by Elizabeth Hulse. Toronto: University of Toronto Press, 1999.

Atlay, J.B. *Sir Henry Wentworth Acland, Bart., K.C.B., F.R.S. Regius Professor of Medicine in the University of Oxford: A Memoir.* London, England: Smith, Elder and Co., 1903.

Bator, Paul Adolphus. "The Health Reformers versus the Common Canadian: The Controversy of Compulsory Vaccination Against Smallpox in Toronto and Ontario, 1900–1920." *Ontario History* 75, no. 4 (1983): 348–73.

Beito, David T. *From Mutual Aid to the Welfare State: Fraternal Societies and Social Services, 1890–1967.* Chapel Hill: University of North Carolina Press, 2000.

Berger, Carl. *Science, God and Nature in Victorian Canada.* Toronto: University of Toronto Press, 1983.

Bliss, Michael. *Northern Enterprise: Five Centuries of Canadian Business.* Toronto: McClelland and Stewart, 1987.

Born, Pamela. "The Canon Is Cast: Plaster Casts in American Museum and University Collection." *Art Documentation: Bulletin of the Art Libraries Society of North America* 21, no. 2 (2002): 8–13.

Brown, R. Blake. *Arming and Disarming: A History of Gun Control in Canada.* Toronto: University of Toronto Press, 2012.

Buckner, Phillip. "Casting Daylight upon Magic: Deconstructing the Royal Tour of 1901 to Canada." In *The British World: Diaspora, Culture, and Identity.* Edited by Carl Bridge and Kent Fedorowich, 158–89. London, England: Frank Cass Publishers, 2003.

Carnes, Mark C. *Secret Ritual and Manhood in Victorian America.* New Haven, Connecticut: Yale University Press, 1989.

Chambers, Ernest J. *The Queen's Own Rifles of Canada: a History of a Splendid Regiment's Origin, Development and Services: Including a Story of Patriotic Duties Well Performed in Three Campaigns.* Toronto: E.L. Ruddy, 1901.

Comeau-Vasilopoulos, Gayle M. "Oronhyatekha." *Dictionary of Canadian Biography* 13 (1901–1910): 791–95.

Cooley, Thomas. *The Ivory Leg in the Ebony Cabinet: Madness, Race, and Gender in Victorian America.* Amherst: University of Massachusetts Press, 2001.

Craig, Barbara Lazenby. "State Medicine in Transition: Battling Smallpox in Ontario, 1882–1885." *Ontario History* 75, no. 4 (1983): 319–47.

Daunton, M.J. *State and Market in Victorian Britain: War, Welfare and Capitalism.* Rochester, New York: Boydell Press, 2008.

Dendy, William. *Lost Toronto: Images of the City's Past.* Toronto: McClelland and Stewart, 1993.

Duffin, Jacalyn. *Langstaff: A Nineteenth-Century Medical Life.* Toronto: University of Toronto Press, 1993.

Dunn, E.J. *Builders of Fraternalism in America.* Vol. 1. Chicago: Fraternal Book Concern, 1924.

Emery, George and J.C. Herbert Emery. *A Young Man's Benefit: The Independent Order of Odd Fellows and Sickness Insurance in the United States and Canada, 1860–1929.* Montreal and Kingston: McGill-Queen's University Press, 1999.

Emery, J.C. Herbert. "Risky Business? Nonactuarial Pricing Practices and the Financial Viability of Fraternal Sickness Insurers." *Explorations in Economic History* 33 (1996): 195–226.

Evans, Julie, Patricia Grimshaw, David Philips and Shurlee Swain. *Equal Subjects, Unequal Rights: Indigenous Peoples in British Settler Colonies, 1830–1910.* Manchester, England: Manchester University Press, 2003.

Fahey, David M. *Temperance and Racism: John Bull, Johnny Reb, and the Good Templars.* Lexington, KY: University Press of Kentucky, 1996.

———, and Jon S. Miller, eds. *Alcohol and Drugs in North America: A Historical Encyclopedia.* Santa Barbara, California: ABC-Clio, 2013.

Ferry, Darren. *United in Measures of Common Good: The Construction of Liberal Identities in Central Canada, 1830–1900.* Montreal and Kingston: McGill-Queen's University Press, 2008.

———. "'To the Interests and Conscience of the Great Mass of the Community': The Evolution of Temperance Societies in Nineteenth-Century Central Canada." *Journal of the Canadian Historical Association* 14 (2003): 137–63.

Files, Angela, and Ontario Genealogical Society, Brant County Branch. *Mohawk Chapel, Indian Baptisms, 1827–1840's.* Publication #187. Brantford, Ontario: Ontario Genealogical Society, n.d.

Freeman, Victoria. *Stand Up, Stand Out.* Toronto, Ontario: self published, 2014.

Friedland, Martin L. *The University of Toronto: A History.* Toronto: University of Toronto Press, 2002.

Galer, Dustin. "A Friend in Need or a Business Indeed?: Disabled Bodies and Fraternalism in Victorian Ontario." *Labour/Le Travail* 66 (2010): 9–36.

Gerdes, Marianne. *Shaping Our Future Together.* Don Mills, Ontario: Foresters, 1997.

Gidney, R.D. and W.P.J. Millar. *Professional Gentlemen: The Professions in Nineteenth-Century Ontario.* Toronto: University of Toronto Press, 1994.

Graham, Elizabeth. *The Mush Hole: Life and Two Indian Residential Schools.* Waterloo, Ontario: Heffle Publishing, 1997.

Graham, Robert J. "The Irish Readers Revisited: The Power of the Text(book)." *Canadian Journal of Education* 14, no. 4 (1989): 414–26.

Grand Lodge A. F. & A. M. of Canada in the Province of Ontario, Special Committee on Publications. *Beyond the Pillars: More Light on Freemasonry.* Hamilton, Ontario: Masonic Holdings, 1973.

Gray, Charlotte. *Flint and Feather: The Life and Times of E. Pauline Johnson, Tekahionwake.* Toronto: HarperFlamingo Canada, 2002.

Greene, Alma. *Tales of the Mohawks.* Toronto: J.M. Dent & Sons (Canada), 1975.

Greenslade, Thomas Boardman. *Kenyon College: Its Third Half Century.* Kennett Square, Pennsylvania: KNA Press Inc., 1975.

Hamilton, Michelle A. *Collections and Objections: Aboriginal Material Culture in Southern Ontario, 1791–1914.* Montreal and Kingston: McGill-Queen's University Press, 2010.

Harring, Sidney L. *White Man's Law: Native People in Nineteenth-Century Canadian Jurisprudence.* Toronto: University of Toronto Press, 1998.

Hattendorf, John B. *A Dusty Path.* Canton, Ohio: Consolidated Graphic Arts, 1964.

Heron, Craig. *Booze: A Distilled History.* Toronto: Between the Lines, 2003.

Herrington, Walter S. *History of the County of Lennox and Addington.* Toronto: Macmillan Company of Canada, Ltd., 1913.

———, and Roy S. Foley. *A History of the Grand Lodge A.F.& A.M. of Canada in the Province of Ontario, 1855–1955: The First One Hundred Years.* Toronto: McCallum Press Ltd., 1955.

Hill, Bruce Emerson. *The Grand River Navigation Company.* Brantford, Ontario: Brant Service Press, 1994.

Houston, Cecil J., and William J. Smyth. *The Sash Canada Wore: A Historical Geography of the Orange Order in Canada.* Toronto: University of Toronto Press, 1980.

Houston, Susan E., and Alison Prentice. *Schooling and Scholars in Nineteenth-Century Ontario.* Toronto: University of Toronto Press, 1988.

Hosley, William. *The Japan Idea: Art and Life in Victorian America.* Hartford, Connecticut: Wadsworth Atheneum, 1990.

Jamieson, Keith. "Oronhyatekha," *Rotunda* (Fall 2002), 32–37.

Jasen, Patricia. *Wild Things: Nature, Culture and Tourism in Ontario, 1790–1914.* Toronto: University of Toronto Press, 1995.

Johnson, E. Pauline. *Legends of Vancouver*. Toronto: McClelland, Goodchild and Stewart, 1911.

Johnson, Evelyn H.C. "The Martin Settlement." In *Some of the Papers Read During the Years 1908–1911 at Meetings of the Brant Historical Society*, 55–64. Brantford, Ontario: Courier, 1913.

Johnson, Jon. "The Great Indian Bus Tour: Mapping Toronto's Urban First Nations Oral Tradition." In *The Nature of Empires and the Empires of Nature: Indigenous Peoples and the Great Lakes Environment*, edited by Karl S. Hele, 279–97. Waterloo, Ontario: Wilfrid Laurier University Press, 2003.

Johnston, Charles M. *The Valley of the Six Nations: A Collection of Documents on the Indian Lands of the Grand River*. Toronto: Champlain Society, 1964.

Johnston, Darlene. *The Taking of Indian Lands in Canada: Consent or Coercion?* Saskatoon: University of Saskatchewan Native Law Centre, 1989.

Jones, Arthur Edward. *"8endake Ehen" or Old Huronia. Fifth Report of the Bureau of Archives for the Province of Ontario*. Toronto: L.K. Cameron, 1909.

Kealey, Gregory S. "The Orange Order in Toronto: Religious Riot and the Working Class." In *Essays in Canadian Working Class History*, edited by Gregory .S. Kealey and Peter Warrian, 13–34. Toronto: McClelland and Stewart, 1976.

Kelly, J.N.D. *St. Edmund Hall: Almost Seven Hundred Years*. Oxford, England: Oxford University Press, 1989.

King, Thomas. *The Inconvenient Indian: A Curious Account of Native People in North America*. Toronto: Doubleday Canada, 2012.

Knowles, Norman. *Inventing the Loyalists: The Ontario Loyalist Tradition and the Creation of Usable Pasts*. Toronto: University of Toronto Press, 1997.

Kyi, Tanya Lloyd. *Canadian Boys who Rocked the World*. North Vancouver, British Columbia: Walrus Books, 2007.

Law, Henry William, and Irene Law. *The Book of the Beresford Hopes*. London, England: H. Cranton, Ltd., 1925.

Leitch, Adelaide. *Floodtides of Fortune: the Story of Stratford and the Progress of the City through Two Centuries*. Stratford, Ontario: City of Stratford, 1980.

Lewis, Walter, and Lynne Turner. *By Bridge and Mill: A History of the Village of Frankford*. Kingston, Ontario: Lake Ontario Regional Library, 1979.

Macdonald, John A. *Troublous Times in Canada: A History of the Fenian Raids of 1866 and 1870*. Toronto: W.S. Johnston and Co., 1910.

McEwen, Catherine B., ed. *The Carty Chronicles of Landmarks and Londoners*. London, Ontario: London and Middlesex Historical Society, 2005.

McNab, David T. "George Martin," *Dictionary of Canadian Biography* 8 (1851–1860): 619–21.

Miller, J.R. *Shingwauk's Vision: a History of Native Residential Schools*. Toronto: University of Toronto Press, 1996.

Miller, Keith R. "Beyond Indian Leadership," *Tawow* 2, no. 2 (1971): 11–12.

Milloy, John S. "The Early Indian Acts: Developmental Strategy and Constitutional Change." In *As Long as the Sun Shines and the Water Flows: A Reader in Canadian Native Studies*, edited by Ian A.L. Getty and Antoine S. Lussier, 56–64. Vancouver: University of British Columbia Press, 1983.

Montgomery, Malcolm. "The Six Nations Indians and the Macdonald Franchise." *Ontario History* 57, no. 1 (1965): 13–25.

Monture, Ethel Brant. *Canadian Portraits: Brant, Crowfoot, Oronhyatekha*. Toronto and Vancouver: Clarke, Irwin and Company, 1960.

Müller, F. Max. *The Life and Letters of the Right Honourable Friedrich Max Müller*. 2 vols. London, England: Longmans, Green, 1902.

Nicks, Trudy. "The War of 1812 as Remembered in the Oronhyatekha Historical Collection." *American Indian Art Magazine* (Summer 2012): 60–69.

———. "Dr Oronhyatekha's History Lessons: Reading Museum Collections as Texts." In *Reading Beyond Words: Contexts for Native History*, 2nd ed., edited by Jennifer S.H. Brown and Elizabeth Vibert, 459–89. Toronto: University of Toronto Press, 2009.

Noel, Janet. *Canada Dry: Temperance Crusades Before Confederation*. Toronto: University of Toronto Press, 1995.

Parvin, Viola Elizabeth. *Authorization of Textbooks for the Schools of Ontario*. Toronto: University of Toronto Press, 1965.

Peck, Chauncey E. *The History of Wilbraham Massachusetts*. [Wilbraham, Massachusetts?], [1914?].

Pellatt, Lieutenant-Colonel Reg. *A Guide to Riflemen of the Queen's Own Rifles of Canada*. Toronto: Arthurs-Jones, 1924.

Pettit, Jennifer. "From Longhouse to Schoolhouse: the Mohawk Institute, 1834–1970." MA thesis, University of Western Ontario, 1993.

Potter, Warren, and Robert Oliver. *Fraternally Yours: A History of the Independent Order of Foresters*. London, England: Queen Anne Press, 1967.

Prentice, Alison. *The School Promoters: Education and Social Class in Mid-Nineteenth Century Upper Canada*. Toronto: McClelland and Stewart, 1977.

Prucha, Francis. *Indian Peace Medals in American History*. Lincoln, NE: University of Nebraska Press, 1971.

Queen's Own Rifles of Canada. *Book of Remembrance, 1866–1918*. N.p., 1932.

Reville, F. Douglas. *History of the County of Brant*. Brantford, Ontario: Hurley Printing Company, Limited, 1920.

Rich, Clifford E. "Dr. Peter Martin, M.D. (Oronhyatekha)." *Canadian Masonic Research Association* 107 (1973): 12–22.

Ritvo, Harriet. *The Platypus and the Mermaid and other Figments of the Classifying Imagination.* Cambridge, Massachusetts: Harvard University Press, 1997.

Rodwell, Warrick. *The Coronation Chair and Stone of Scone: History, Archaeology and Conservation.* Oxford, England: Oxbow Books, 2013.

Rogers, Edward S. and Donald B. Smith, eds. *Aboriginal Ontario: Historical Perspectives on the First Nations.* Toronto: Dundurn Press, 1994.

Sanders, William. "The History of the Richardson Lodge No. 136, G.R.C." *Proceedings of the Heritage Lodge 730* 33 (2010): 93–101.

Senior, Hereward. *The Last Invasion of Canada: The Fenian Raids, 1866–1870.* Toronto: Dundurn Press in collaboration with the Canadian War Museum, 1991.

———. *Orangeism: The Canadian Phase.* Toronto: McGraw-Hill Ryerson, 1972.

Shapiro, Linda, ed. *Yesterday's Toronto, 1870–1910.* Toronto: Coles Publishing Co., 1978.

Sheets-Pyenson, Susan. *Cathedrals of Science: The Development of Colonial Natural History Museums during the Late Nineteenth Century.* Kingston, McGill-Queen's University Press, 1988.

Sheppard, Osborne. *A Concise History of Freemasonry in Canada.* 3rd ed. Hamilton, Ontario: R. Duncan and Co., 1924.

Sherman, Reverend David. *History of the Wesleyan Academy, at Wilbraham, Mass. 1817–1890.* Boston: McDonald and Gill Company, 1893.

Sherwin, Allan. *Bridging Two Peoples: Chief Peter E. Jones, 1843–1909.* Waterloo, Ontario: Wilfrid Laurier University Press, 2012.

Shields, Norman. "The Grand General Indian Council of Ontario and Indian Status Legislation." In *Lines Drawn Upon the Water: First Nations and the Great Lakes Borders and Borderlands*, edited by Karl S. Hele, 205–18. Waterloo, Ontario: Wilfrid Laurier University Press, 2008.

Shields, Norman D. "Anishinabek Political Alliance in the Post-Confederation Period: The Grand General Indian Council of Ontario, 1870–1936." MA thesis, Queen's University, 2001.

Silverstein-Willmott, Cory. "Object Lessons: An Ojibway Artifact Unraveled; The Case of the Bag with the Snake Skin Strap." *Textile History* 34, no. 1 (2003): 74–81.

Smith, Donald B. "Macdonald's Relationship with Aboriginal Peoples." *Macdonald at 200: New Reflections and Legacies*, edited by Patrice Dutil and Roger Hall. Toronto: Dundurn Press, 2014.

Smythe, George Franklin. *Kenyon College: Its First Century.* New Haven, Connecticut: Yale University Press, 1924.

Spaulding, William B. "The Ontario Vaccine Farm, 1885–1916." *Canadian Bulletin of Medical History* 6, no. 1 (1989): 45–56.

Special Committee of the Supreme Council. *The History of the Supreme Council of the Ancient and Accepted Scottish Rite in Canada, 1868–1960.* Ottawa, 1961.

Spence, Ruth Elizabeth. *Prohibition in Canada.* Toronto: William Briggs, 1919.

St. Denis, Guy. *Tecumseh's Bones.* Montreal and Kingston: McGill-Queen's University Press, 2005.

Strong Boag, Veronica, and Carole Gerson. *Paddling Her Own Canoe: The Times and Texts of E. Pauline Johnson.* Toronto: University of Toronto Press, 2000.

Szasz, Margaret Connell, ed. *Between Indian and White Worlds: The Cultural Broker.* Norman, OK: University of Oklahoma Press, 1994.

Tomkins, George S. *A Common Countenance: Stability and Change in the Canadian Curriculum.* Vancouver: Pacific Educational Press, 2008.

University of Oxford. *Alumni Oxonienses, the Members of the University of Oxford, 1715–1886: Their Parentage, Birthplace, and the Year of Birth, with a Record of their Degrees. Being the Matriculation Register of the University, Alphabetically Arranged, Revised and Annotated.* Nendeln, Liechtenstein: Kraus Reprint, 1968.

University of Toronto. *The University of Toronto and Its Colleges, 1827–1906.* Toronto: University Library, 1906.

Vanderhaeghe, Guy. *The Last Crossing.* Toronto: McClelland and Stewart, 2002.

Vollick, Colin. "Oronhyatekha, the Independent Order of Foresters, and the Forester Island Orphanage." *Lennox and Addington Historical Society Papers and Records* 17 (1987): 55–75.

Vronsky, Peter. *Ridgeway: The American Fenian Invasion and the 1866 Battle that Made Canada.* Toronto: Allen Lane, 2011.

Walden, Keith. *Becoming Modern in Toronto: The Industrial Exhibition and the Shaping of a Late Victorian Culture.* Toronto: University of Toronto Press, 1997.

Wallace, W. Stewart. *A History of the University of Toronto 1827–1927.* Toronto: University of Toronto Press, 1927.

Wallach, Alan. "The American Cast Museum: An Episode in the History of the Institutional Definitions of Art." In *Exhibiting Contradiction: Essays on the American Art Museum in the United States,* 38–57. Amherst, MA: University of Massachusetts Press, 1998.

Wamsley, K.B. "Cultural Signification and National Ideologies: Rifle-Shooting in Late Nineteenth-Century Canada." *Social History* 20, no. 1 (1995): 63–72.

White, E.T. . London, Ontario: Chas. Chapman Co., 1922.

Zeller, Suzanne. *Inventing Canada: Early Victorian Science and the Idea of a Transcontinental Nation*. Montreal and Kingston: McGill-Queen's University Press, 2009.

ORAL AND EMAIL INTERVIEWS

Claus, Ella. Oral interview with Jamieson, Tyendinaga, Ontario. 1999.

Freeman, Victoria. Oral interview with Hamilton, Toronto, Ontario. September 19, 2014.

Horton, Michele. Phone interview with Hamilton. September 2, 2014.

Katz, Reena, and Alize Zorlutuna. Email communication. October 17, 2014.

Maracle, Eva. Oral interview with Jamieson, Tyendinaga, Ontario. 1998.

Vanderhaeghe, Guy. Email interview with Hamilton. August 5, 2014.

WEBSITES AND ONLINE PUBLICATIONS

Brearley, Donald. *Physicians: A Database of Short Character Sketches about Physicians from the Belleville Area (Roughly 45 Mile Radius) in Ontario Who Graduated before 1940*. Trenton, Ontario: Quinte Branch, Ontario Genealogical Society, 2016. www.rootsweb.ancestry.com/~canqbogs/pdf_files/Physicians_DrBrearley.pdf.

Brearton, Steve. "Leaders & Mavericks: Exceptional Political Alumni." *U of T Magazine*, (Summer 2014). www.magazine.utoronto.ca/cover-story/political-leaders-who-went-to-u-of-t.

CanadaGenWeb.org. *Some Genealogy for the Cooks of Back Bay, Charlotte Co. N.B.* www.rootsweb.ancestry.com/~nbpstgeo/stge7d.htm.

Canadian Orange Historical Site. canadianorangehistoricalsite.com/index-29.php.

"Dr. Oronhyatekha — One of the First Leaders of Foresters." Video (2014). www.youtube.com/watch?v=cozqLcneW8U.

Edwards, Brendan F.R. "Ethel Brant Monture: 'A One-Woman Crusade.'" *Historical Perspectives on Canadian Publishing*. Hamilton, Ontario: McMaster University Library, n.d. hpcanpub.mcmaster.ca/case-study/ethel-brant-monture-one-woman-crusade.

Foresters Financial. *Our Rich History of Helping Families*. Toronto: Foresters Financial, n.d. www.foresters.com/ca-en/about/pages/our-history.aspx#.U_kX42PLkXE.

Harrison, David, and Fred Lomax. "Oronhyatekha and the Independent Order of Foresters." *Knight Templar Magazine,* (November 2013), 23–25. www.knightstemplar.org/KnightTemplar/articles/20131123.pdf.

Lawrence, Susan. "Curing Injustice." *U of T Magazine,* (Spring 2002). www.magazine. utoronto.ca/feature/curing-injustice-u-of-t-social-justice-trailblazers.

Maritime Museum of the Atlantic. "*Oronhyatekha — 1940.*" *Marine Heritage Database.* novascotia.ca/museum/wrecks/wrecks/shipwrecks.asp?ID=3715.

Mitchell, Liam. "Oronhyatekha." *U of T Medicine,* (Spring 2014), 20. www.medicine. utoronto.ca/sites/default/files/UT_Medicine_Spring_2014_0_0.pdf.

Restless Precinct. *The Site.* restlessprecinct.ca/the-site.

RootsWeb. *The Haudenosaunee Project.* wc.rootsweb.ancestry.com/cgi-bin/igm. cgi?db= erikj.

United Empire Loyalists' Association of Canada. *About UELAC.* www.uelac.org/ about.php.

United Kingdom. Met Office. "Oxford." Historical Station Data. www.metoffice. gov.uk/climate/uk/stationdata/oxforddata.txt.

University of Toronto. *2015–2016 Welcome Guide.* (2015). www.md.utoronto.ca/ sites/default/files/2015-2016%2BWelcome%2BGuide.pdf.

———. "In Support of Research." *National Report 2002,* 20–42. www. nationalreport.utoronto.ca/friends.pdf.

———. "Oronhyatekha: First Canadian Aboriginal Medical Graduate." *University of Toronto Great Past.* www.greatpast.utoronto.ca/GreatMinds/ShowBanner. asp?ID=76.

A Vision of Britain Through Time. www.visionofbritain.org.uk/index.jsp.

Walrus Books Limited. *Canadian Boys Who Rocked the World,* catalogue copy. www.whitecap.ca/Detail/1552857999.

IMAGE CREDITS

Page No.	Credit
Page 20 (top and bottom).	*Canadian Courier* 1, no. 15 (March 9, 1907): front page and page 11, LAC.
Page 22 (top).	*IF* 24, no. 5 (July 1908): 11.
Page 22 (bottom).	*IF* 28, no. 3 (April 1907): 73.
Page 23 (top).	Courtesy of Canadian Museum of History, D-14724.
Page 23 (bottom).	Photo by Michelle A. Hamilton.
Page 24.	Courtesy of National Anthropological Archives, Smithsonian Institution.
Page 32.	*IF* 17, no. 1 (July 1896): 6.
Page 39.	Courtesy of National Anthropological Archives, Smithsonian Institution.
Page 40–42.	Courtesy of National Anthropological Archives, Smithsonian Institution.
Page 48.	Courtesy of Woodland Cultural Centre.
Page 53.	*Conservative Expositor*, Brantford, Ontario, April 18, 1854, 3.
Page 61.	Courtesy of Kenyon Military Academy Collection, GSCA, Kenyon College.

Page 63.   Courtesy of GSCA, Kenyon College, KSCA.FH1858034.

Page 65.   Courtesy of National Anthropological Archives, Smithsonian
                Institution.

Page 83.   Photo by Daniel Wilson; Courtesy of the Los Angeles County
                Museum of Natural History.

Page 88.   *Illustrated London News*, November 1861, 474. Courtesy of the
                Mary Evan Picture Library, London, England.

Page 96.   Courtesy of Bodleian Library, Oxford University, c176, folio 146.

Page 103.   Courtesy of Bodleian Library, Oxford University, c175, folio 366.

Page 110.   Courtesy of Deseronto Public Library.

Page 118.   Courtesy of Leonard Papers, Archives and Research Collections
                Centre, University of Western Ontario.

Page 121.   *Directory for the County of Hastings* (1869), 239.

Page 124.   Courtesy of the Lennox and Addington County Archives, N683.

Page 129.   William H. Peckham Papers, Chancellor Robert R. Livingston
                Masonic Library of Grand Lodge, New York, NY, AR1997.1.

Page 131.   *Canadian Illustrated News* 4, no. 5 (1871): 72–73.

Page 132.   *Canadian Illustrated News* 4, no. 7 (1871): 108.

Page 133.   Courtesy of Bodleian Library, Oxford University, c175, folio 138.

Page 134.   Courtesy of Bodleian Library, Oxford University, c175, folio 137.

Page 135.   Courtesy of National Anthropological Archives, Smithsonian
                Institution.

Page 154.   Provided by Amorin Mello and Nancy Stewart.

Page 163.   London Old Boys' Association, *Official Souvenir Programme*
                (1900), 48.

Page 176.   *Grip* 24, no. 22 (May 30, 1885): 4. Courtesy of the Archives and
                Research Collections Centre, University of Western Ontario.

Page 177.   *IGT* 13 (1900): iii.

Page 180.   Courtesy of Archives and Research Collections Centre,
                University of Western Ontario.

Page 188.   Courtesy of Bodleian Library, Oxford University, c150, folio 114.

Page 189.   *IF* 24, no. 8 (August 1903): 151.

Page 190.   National Medal Collection, LAC, 1986-79-6457.
(top).

Page 190.   Deseronto Public Library.
(bottom).

Page 194.	Courtesy of Lennox and Addington County Archives, 1998.146.4.
Page 195.	*IF* 21, no. 1 (July 1900): 32.
Page 196.	*IF* 22, no. 9 (September 1901): 441.
Page 198.	*IF* 22, no. 10 (October 1901): 485.
Page 210.	Courtesy of Deseronto Archives.
Page 211.	Courtesy of Woodland Cultural Centre.
Page 215.	Courtesy of Deseronto Archives.
Page 216.	Courtesy of Canadian Museum of History, 978.27.1.1 a-b, S94-16156.
Page 217.	Courtesy of Deseronto Archives.
Page 218 (top).	*Canadian Magazine*, June 1896, 135.
Page 218 (bottom).	*IF* 23, no. 8 (August 1902): 231.
Page 219–21.	Courtesy of Deseronto Archives.
Page 222.	*IF* 18, no. 1 (July 1897): 32.
Page 223 (top).	*IF* 15, no. 4 (October 1894): 100.
Page 223 (bottom).	*IF* 15, no. 4 (October 1894): 104.
Page 224 (top).	*IF* 15, no. 4 (October 1894): 107.
Page 224 (bottom).	*IF* 15, no. 4 (October 1894): 109.
Page 225.	*IF* 7, no. 1 (July 1896): 5.
Page 226.	Courtesy of Deseronto Archives.
Page 228 (top).	*IF* 16, no. 1 (July 1895): 4.
Page 228 (bottom).	*IF* 16, no. 1 (July 1895): 9. Courtesy of Special Collections, Vaughan Memorial Library, Acadia University.
Page 230 (top).	*IF* 19, no. 3 (September 15, 1898): 74. Courtesy of Special Collections, Vaughan Memorial Library, Acadia University.
Page 230 (bottom).	*IF* 19, no. 3 (September 15, 1898): 76. Courtesy of Special Collections, Vaughan Memorial Library, Acadia University.
Page 231.	*IF* 19, no. 3 (September 15, 1898): 77. Courtesy of Special Collections, Vaughan Memorial Library, Acadia University.

Page 233.   *IF* 19, no. 3 (September 15, 1898): 73. Courtesy of Special
              Collections, Vaughan Memorial Library, Acadia University.

Page 235.   *IF* 20, no. 2 (August 15, 1899): 40.

Page 240.   Cumberland, *Catalogue and Notes of the Oronhyatekha Historical
              Collection*, 16–17.

Page 248.   Courtesy of Deseronto Archives.

Page 265.   Courtesy of Deseronto Archives.

Page 266.   *IF* 19, no. 1 (July 15, 1898): 7. Courtesy of Special Collections,
              Vaughan Memorial Library, Acadia University.

Page 267.   Deseronto Public Library.

Page 270.   Photograph by Adrian Petry.

Page 274–75. Photograph by Adrian Petry.

Page 276.   Courtesy of Deseronto Archives.

Page 279.   Photograph by Manolo Lugo.

INDEX